Making Fascism in Sweden and the Netherlands

Making Fascism in Sweden and the Netherlands

Myth-Creation and Respectability, 1931–40

Nathaniël D. B. Kunkeler

BLOOMSBURY ACADEMIC
LONDON • NEW YORK • OXFORD • NEW DELHI • SYDNEY

BLOOMSBURY ACADEMIC
Bloomsbury Publishing Plc
50 Bedford Square, London, WC1B 3DP, UK
1385 Broadway, New York, NY 10018, USA
29 Earlsfort Terrace, Dublin 2, Ireland

BLOOMSBURY, BLOOMSBURY ACADEMIC and the Diana logo
are trademarks of Bloomsbury Publishing Plc

First published in Great Britain 2021
Paperback edition published in 2023

Copyright © Nathaniël D.B. Kunkeler, 2021

Nathaniël D.B. Kunkeler has asserted their right under the Copyright,
Designs and Patents Act, 1988, to be identified as Author of this work.

Cover image: Alles Voor Het Vaderland, Sluit U Aan Bu De W.A. (1943 All for the fatherland, Join to the
W.A.) Netherlands World War Two Propaganda to join the paramilitary division
of the Dutch Nazi Party, NSB © World History Archive / Alamy Stock Photo

All rights reserved. No part of this publication may be reproduced or transmitted
in any form or by any means, electronic or mechanical, including photocopying,
recording, or any information storage or retrieval system, without
prior permission in writing from the publishers.

Bloomsbury Publishing Plc does not have any control over, or responsibility for,
any third-party websites referred to or in this book. All internet addresses given
in this book were correct at the time of going to press. The author and publisher
regret any inconvenience caused if addresses have changed or sites have
ceased to exist, but can accept no responsibility for any such changes.

Every effort has been made to trace copyright holders and to obtain their
permissions for the use of copyright material. The publisher apologizes for
any errors or omissions and would be grateful if notified of any corrections
that should be incorporated in future reprints or editions of this book.

A catalogue record for this book is available from the British Library.

Library of Congress Cataloging-in-Publication Data
Names: Kunkeler, Nathaniël, author.
Title: Making fascism in Sweden and the Netherlands : myth-creation and
respectability, 1931–40 / Nathaniël Kunkeler.
Description: London ; New York : Bloomsbury Academic,
2021. | Includes bibliographical references and index. |
Identifiers: LCCN 2021011465 (print) | LCCN 2021011466 (ebook) | ISBN
9781350192331 (hardback) | ISBN 9781350192348
(ebook) | ISBN 9781350192355 (epub)
Subjects: LCSH: Fascism–Sweden–History–20th century. |
Fascism–Netherlands–History–20th century. | Sweden–Politics and
government–20th century. | Netherlands–Politics and government–20th
century. | Nationalsocialistiska Arbetarepartiet–History. |
Nationaal-Socialistische Beweging der Nederlanden–
History. | Fascism–Europe–History–20th century.
Classification: LCC D726.5 .K86 2021 (print) | LCC D726.5
(ebook) | DDC 324.2485/02–dc23
LC record available at https://lccn.loc.gov/2021011465
LC ebook record available at https://lccn.loc.gov/2021011466

ISBN:	HB:	978-1-3501-9233-1
	PB:	978-1-3501-9241-6
	ePDF:	978-1-3501-9234-8
	eBook:	978-1-3501-9235-5

Typeset by Integra Software Services Pvt. Ltd.

To find out more about our authors and books visit www.bloomsbury.com
and sign up for our newsletters.

For Lucian

Contents

List of Illustrations	viii
Acknowledgements	x
List of Abbreviations	xi
Introduction	1
1 Sweden and the Netherlands	29
2 Making the party: Party apparatuses and propaganda	49
3 Making the Leader: Party leaders and charisma	69
4 Making fascists: Uniforms and military subculture	95
5 Making fascism in Sweden: Spectacle and the 1935 *årsting*	123
6 Making fascism in the Netherlands: Spectacle and the 1935 *landdag*	143
Conclusion	163
Notes	179
Bibliography	232
Index	249

Illustrations

1 The NSAP-members who broke away from SNSP in 1933. Photographer unknown. National Archives of Sweden, Marieberg, SO Lindholm's collection (SE/RA/720834) — 51
2 The NSB General Council, 1933. Photographer unknown. Volk en Vaderland, 1933, no. 40. KB|National library of the Netherlands: C16 — 52
3 Sven Olov Lindholm, wearing the brown shirt of his party. Photographer unknown. National Archives of Sweden, Marieberg. Martin Ekström's archive (SE/RA/720615) — 70
4 Anton Adriaan Mussert, wearing the typical party black shirt and tie, 1932. Photographer: NSB Fotodienst. Rijksmuseum (NG-2007-35-141) — 73
5 'One for all – All for one'. The party salutes Lindholm at a meeting in 1938. Photographer unknown. Den Svenske Nationalsocialisten, 1938, no. 35. Kungliga Biblioteket (National Library of Sweden) — 81
6 'The NSB wants war!!!'. Artist: Maarten Meuldijk. Volk en Vaderland, 1935, no. 23. KB|National library of the Netherlands: C16 — 106
7 'Where we fight', DSN header with the small representation of a uniformed NSAP-member. Artist unknown. Den Svenske Nationalsocialisten, 1933, no. 26. Kungliga Biblioteket (National Library of Sweden) — 107
8 The NSB uniformed again. Mussert salutes five thousand marching WA-men in Amsterdam, November 1940. Photographer: NSB Fotodienst. Voor Volk en Vaderland, 2nd ed., edited by Cornelis Van Geelkerken, 1943 — 119
9 The NSAP marches from Stora Nygatan onto Slussen at the 1937 årsting. Photographer unknown. Den Svenske Nationalsocialisten, 1937, no. 38. Kungliga Biblioteket (National Library of Sweden) — 137
10 The NSAP marches along Kungsgatan at the 1938 convention, while onlookers watch from the bridge. Photographer unknown. National Archives of Sweden, Marieberg, SO Lindholm's collection (SE/RA/720834) — 139

11	The march leaders, Mussert walks second from the left, Van Geelkerken on the far-right. Photographer: NSB Fotodienst. Het Landdag Gedenkboek, 1935. IISG (International Institute for Social History): Bro N 188	149
12	The tent on the inside as the landdag is about to begin. Note the wide central aisle. Photographer: NSB Fotodienst. Het Landdag Gedenkboek, 1935. IISG (International Institute for Social History): Bro N 188	150

Acknowledgements

This book is based on my doctoral thesis, which I wrote at the University of Cambridge, under the supervision of Pedro Ramos Pinto and John Pollard. As such they both first of all deserve special thanks for their guidance, and many fruitful discussions during our supervisions. They have always been excellent at questioning my presumptions, and pointing me to what is less than obvious to the non-Dutch and non-Swedish historian. They were invariably content to let me pursue my research and writing under my own steam, but have nevertheless had an important hand in shaping the outcome, and as such this book owes a great deal to them. Further thanks is necessary for John, who has taught and helped me not just with this book but all my academic endeavours, and whose experience and insights have been precious in developing my own.

I am indebted to the immense service of the librarians, archivists and other staff at Cambridge University Library, Trinity College Library, the National Library of Sweden, the Dutch National Library, the National Archives of Sweden, the Dutch National Archive and NIOD in Amsterdam for their help in locating documents and literature for me, as well as supplying me with most of the images reproduced in this book. The staff at the Security Services archive in Arninge deserve special thanks, for efficiently supplying me with all the relevant dossiers pertaining to my research, making my life a great deal easier, and the staff of Cambridge University Library, who have helped provide the ideal space for pursuing and cogitating my research for a decade. My PhD research was itself made possible thanks to the generous financial aid of Trinity College, Cambridge, who provided me with the funding to cover all my expenses throughout, and has for years been the perfect monastic environment in which to study and produce knowledge.

I must also thank my friends and colleagues who have read the manuscript of this book, whole or in part, and have provided invaluable suggestions for improvement and correction, which include my PhD examiners, Aristotle Kallis and Chris Clark, as well as Anna Keyes and Helen Roche, who obligingly read the entire manuscript at very short notice. Needless to say, all errors and peculiarities that remain are my own.

Last but not least I thank my friends and family, and especially my partner, who has for many years supported and put up with my enthusiasm for this grim and unpleasant subject, and helped make the process of researching and writing this book not just manageable, but a pleasant experience.

Abbreviations

ARP	Anti-Revolutionaire Partij, Anti-Revolutionary Party
CHU	Christelijk-Historische Unie, Christian-Historical Union
DN	*Dagens Nyheter*, The Daily News
DSF	*Den Svenske Folksocialisten*, The Swedish People's Socialist
DSN	*Den Svenske Nationalsocialisten*, The Swedish National Socialist
FA	Frontavdelning, Front Department
HGS	Hervormd-Gereformeerde Staatspartij, Reformed-Reformed State Party
IF	Instruktioner för Frontavdelningar, Instructions for Front Departments
LO	Landsorganisationen, Trade Union Confederation
Nenasu	Nederlandsche Nationaal-Socialistische Uitgeverij, Dutch National Socialist Publisher
NIFO	Nederlandsch Indische Fascisten Organisatie, Dutch Indies Fascist Organization
NJS	Nationale Jeugdstorm, National Youth Storm
NRC	*Nieuwe Rotterdamsche Courant*, New Rotterdammer Newspaper
NSAP	Nationalsocialistiska Arbetarpartiet, National Socialist Workers' Party
NSB	Nationaal-Socialistische Beweging, National Socialist Movement
NSDAP	Nationalsozialistische Deutsche Arbeiterpartei, National Socialist German Workers' Party
NSNAP	Nationaal-Socialistische Nederlandsche Arbeiderpartij, National Socialist Dutch Workers' Party
NU	Nordisk Ungdom, Nordic Youth
PNF	Partito Nazionale Fascista, National Fascist Party
Porg	Partiorganisationen, Party Organisation
RKSP	Romeins-Katholieke Staatspartij, Roman-Catholic State Party
SA	Stormavdelning, Storm Department/Section
SDAP	Sociaal-Democratische Arbeiders Partij, Social-Democratic Workers' Party

SFKO	Sveriges Fascistiska Kamporganisation, Sweden's Fascist Combat Organisation
SGP	Staatkundig Gereformeerde Partij, State Reformed Party
SNSP	Svenska Nationalsocialistiska Partiet, Swedish National Socialist Party
SNU	Sveriges Nationella Ungdomsförbund, Sweden's National Youth League
SS	Schutzstaffel, Protection Staff
SSS	Svensksocialistisk Samling, Swedish Socialist Union
SSAP	Svenska Socialdemokratiska Arbetarpartiet, Swedish Social-Democratic Workers' Party
TF	Tjänsteföreskrifter, Service Regulations
VC	Vaderlandsche Club, Fatherland Club
VoVa	*Volk en Vaderland*, People and Fatherland
WA	Weerbaarheidsafdeeling, Defence Department/Section

Introduction

In Sven Olov Lindholm's short book on the rise and struggle of Swedish fascism, *Svensk Frihetskamp* (Swedish Freedom Struggle), published in 1943, there is a collection of photographs from the early days of the party. The collection clearly shows Lindholm's predisposition towards modern political meeting and rally culture – something to which he would adhere also in later years, attending marches and demonstrations in the 1960s – with photographs showing uniformed rallies and attentive crowds surrounding party speakers. The images of uniformed guards flanking elevated speakers, ranks of men carrying national and swastika flags, and youth marching to snare drums all seem familiar iterations of the fascist performance repertoire, many of them a kind of Nuremberg in miniature. The emulative character of these aesthetics seems obvious enough, perhaps an attempt to reproduce the spectacles of Riefenstahl and Speer, endlessly reproduced images of fascism that colour perceptions of the Nazi regime to the present day.

Yet, I was more interested in not the spectacle itself, but the signs of failure to produce it, the signs of inadequacy, the incongruities. One photograph of a meeting in the early thirties in Vänersborg shows a small crowd in winter coats, surrounding a speaker against the backdrop of a mansion. While most listeners are facing the speaker, with their backs to the camera, a couple of people are standing away from the rest, looking other ways, or having conversations among themselves, evidently not paying heed to the fascist meeting that was happening. While a little scrutiny reveals two large flags on either side of the speaker, barely visible, the viewer of the photograph is perhaps more likely to see what appears to be a small pig, grazing in the foreground. If the appeal and success of fascism depended on Riefenstahl-esque spectacle, it seems no wonder that these fascists never took Sweden by storm. In my research I became increasingly intrigued by what appeared to me as the farcical elements of fascist culture, something often noted by contemporary opponents of fascism, but rarely mentioned by scholars.

While this farcical quality was in some way perhaps to be expected from minuscule fascist groups with few resources or competencies, it was in reality strikingly ubiquitous. The conservative German opponent of the Nazis, Otto Michael Knab, gave an account of the Nazi takeover of a small Bavarian town in his 1934 *Kleinstadt unterm Hakenkreuz* (Small town under the swastika). While the book reproduces much of the image of Nazis as violent thugs, 'die grossenteils ungeschulte Horde' (the largely unschooled horde),[1] it is also notable for its humorous depiction of the Nazis. As the 'revolution' comes to the little town, the order is issued to raise the swastika banners all over town, but the brownshirts find themselves with too few banners. Unwilling to disregard the order, the local troops end up using a small square flag for the railway flagpole. 'And the little red cloth hastily climbed up, ten times higher than its own length. It must have been quite lonesome up there for the little emblem of the great revolution.'[2] This was more than the relatively banal and obvious insight that there was a large gap between the myth and reality of fascism, or how fascists saw themselves and how outsiders saw them. More importantly, repeating the performances that constructed that myth was not automatic, reflexive or trivial. And myth was not a static image or established narrative that was transferred or circulated; it was something at which one could succeed or fail, and thus something that was *done*.

In my research on the Dutch National Socialist Movement, more such incongruities struck me. The party leader himself, Anton Mussert, was emblematic: a short, stocky man with a background in civil engineering, typically dressed in a grey suit and hat, married to his aunt, he was a very far cry from the fascist ideal of masculinity. On early party photographs, the small suited man and his entourage make a strikingly bourgeois impression next to the black-uniformed paramilitary that surround them. Evidently, there were other projects at stake here, not least the appeal to respectability, with efforts to both live up to established expectations of fascism, but also construct an independent fascist image, creating distance between the national movement and regimes abroad. As a movement, without the support of a regime, but with foreign regimes as a reference point, fascists had a tall task harmonizing multiple, simultaneous projects, which often seemed at odds with each other.

†††

In the early 1930s, a new wave of rightist organizations hit Europe, in the shadow of the established Fascist regime in Italy and the rise of Hitler's Nationalsozialistische Deutsche Arbeiterpartei (National Socialist Workers' Party, NSDAP) in Germany. The small liberal democracies of the continent were no exception. In December 1931, the civil engineer Anton Mussert (1894–1946) founded the Nationaal-Socialistische Beweging (National Socialist Movement, NSB) in the Netherlands. Mid-January 1933, a young Swedish soldier, Sven Olov Lindholm (1903–98), broke away from the Swedish National Socialist Party, and founded a new fascist organization, Nationalsocialistiska Arbetarepartiet (National Socialist Workers' Party, NSAP). Sweden and the Netherlands were no strangers to fascists, which had already caused noise in the previous decade, but these movements caused more of a stir in public life than their predecessors. Lindholm's NSAP never managed to enter parliament, failing to collect more than 0.7 per cent of the national vote (1936), but quickly established itself as the largest and loudest of Sweden's fascist groups, with circa 12,000 members. Mussert's NSB on the other hand grew rapidly in its first years (up to about 50,000 members), and attained a highly unexpected 7.94 per cent of the vote in the 1935 provincial elections, breaking the mould for newly formed parties and focusing Dutch political debate on fascism for most of the 1930s. While some have seen these parties as a parenthesis in the political life of stable democratic regimes, no countries were immune to this new phenomenon in European politics. The appeal of their political myths was a crucial part of that.

Historical literature has dealt extensively with the themes of myth, spectacle and aesthetics in fascism, and this book shares some of that literature's concerns about the function and impact of fascist myths, but it is not interested in analysing or defining fascism through its mythology. The principal query is about the processes at work behind fascist myths, how myths were actually produced in practice, here termed *mythopoeia*, i.e. myth-making. While myths have often been explained as a form of propaganda, mythopoeia highlights limitations to political myth, revealing it as a pragmatic project that required resources, technologies, competencies and money, connecting arguably nebulous fantasy to matters of organization, finance and infrastructure. After all, as has long since been noted, ultimately the means of cultural production are unarguably material.[3] By drawing attention to the link between fascist myths and their production, other functions of myths within the party are revealed, as the role played by different sections of the party organizations and the cadres is foregrounded. Thus mythopoeia can explain the influences behind the shaping and changing of fascist myth over time, how it repeatedly mobilized fascist activists, and helped maintain party loyalty through long years of struggle. Consequently it also delineates the integral place of the mythopoeic process in the structure of fascist activism, while painting a diachronic picture of fascist myth.

The second concern of this book is to ground the analysis of fascist mythopoeia in the context of a cultural–political struggle over the semantic meaning of 'fascism' and 'national socialism'. In the words of David D. Roberts:

> The word 'fascism' was new in 1919, and no one knew what it meant; no one knew how whatever it denoted would develop. So even to say that 'they' – The Italians, the Fascists – 'invented' fascism is misleading. It was not something that could be invented. It simply emerged contingently from its contingent birth. It was through that contingent process that what came to be called fascism, first just in Italy, but then gradually more widely, came into the world.[4]

The point to emphasize here is that fascism from its inception was very much an empty signifier, and that through the production of myths about fascism, fascists were contributing to a public discourse about the meaning of this new political phenomenon of the interwar period.[5] Thus mythopoeia was a process in argument with liberals, conservatives and socialists especially, in which fascists actively tried to construct fascism for the public as a transcendently fantastical force. But non-fascist outsiders were not politically blank slates, without any prior notions of their own about fascism, particularly not in Sweden and the Netherlands which were in many ways entangled with Germany,[6] not least culturally and economically.[7] Fascists had to confront competing discourses about fascism's meaning, conflicting ideological hermeneutics that mediated the reception of fascist discourse and performance.[8] The themes of contested interpretations, competing discourses and challenges to what 'fascism' signified, make this book a cultural history about the political struggle for meaning in two different societies, connected by one of the crucial signifiers of interwar European politics.[9] The centrality of myth pushes analysis towards the assignment of meaning through narratives, 'an arena in which meaning takes form, in which individuals connect to the public and social world, and in which change therefore becomes possible.'[10] The research into myth is in the area of cultural history – the exploration of the generation of meaning and the structuring of the symbolic order[11] – while the focus on the process of myth-making, mythopoeia, draws attention to the practical and material dimensions of cultural production.

The Netherlands and Sweden provide the comparison to understand the significance of fascist mythopoeia in this context of public discourse about fascism. As two (supposedly) stable liberal democracies, both of which remained neutral during the First World War, they raise interesting questions about the operations of fascist movements and the dissemination of fascist myth within their borders. Swedish and Dutch fascists did not typically have a background of war experience, nor did the national political and legal cultures permit extensive violence, which did so much to shape the experience of Italian *squadristi* and the German SA. Carrying arms risked an effective ban of the party organization. Political uniforms were prohibited in 1933 – earlier than most countries[12] – and paramilitaries soon followed. In other words much of the organizational, experiential and aesthetic structures that shaped fascist myth-making in other countries was missing or limited here. At the same time public discourse about fascism was heavily influenced by the examples of the Italian and German dictatorships, which in the 1930s gained a largely negative image in the small democracies, which felt threatened by their German neighbour in particular (more so in the Netherlands than Sweden).

This was unpromising ground for fascist movements, yet nevertheless many movements did emerge throughout the interwar years, persistent in the face of repeated failures to break through. This provides an opportunity to answer questions about how fascist organizations retained a loyal following for decades, and sustained fanatical activism under discouraging conditions. It also elucidates the barely understood connection between fascism's international image as propagated by the fascist regimes and their enemies, and indigenous fascist movements' efforts to construct their own image of fascism, in a trying and ambivalent relationship with their counterparts in other countries. This was an 'era of fascism', in which much of the continent seemed to contemporaries to be turning fascist;[13] the situation of self-defined fascists in these democratic countries provides a fertile ground in which to study the cultural construction of fascism in Europe. How did established international ideas of fascism put pressure on smaller national movements to conform in their myth-making, while their own liberal democracies forced them to adhere to the norms of political respectability? Did their mythopoeic efforts shape the public perception of fascism at all, and how was it tied to the development of fascist subjectivities? And could Swedish and Dutch fascists really manage and afford the apparatus required to create a convincing mythic construction of fascism for themselves and their constituencies? How did their diminutive size, legal limitations and international context shape mythopoeic processes?

Respectability

Respectability denotes the quality of being deemed acceptable, adhering to broad social-political standards, being considered a legitimate option within the political field. Respectability is conformity to political and social standards. These standards are contextual. Respectability can mean very different things in different historical contexts, as we will see further on. What respectability – sometimes understood politically, sometimes socially, especially at the grassroots level – entails at times varied strikingly between the Netherlands and Sweden, while there were also obvious common features to the two mass democracies: shared political values that defined respectability which included non-violence; organization and discipline; and political professionalism. It also included strong social dimensions, but context sensitive ones: class, both in terms of bourgeois values, and support from the working classes was key to (national) socialist groups.[14] This is also reflected in Knab's work, and his contempt for the *Unanständigkeit* of the local Nazis. Others were very particular to the nation: loyalty to the monarchy was an important mark of respectability in Swedish bourgeois circles, but almost indispensable was the Netherlands' Orangism, the veneration for the royal House of Orange. While religion played a comparatively minor role in Sweden through the Lutheran Church,[15] Christianity was central to the political discourse of the Netherlands, which was dominated by confessional parties in government during the Interbellum. Gender was another ubiquitous, if frequently covert, aspect of respectability. The heavily gendered nature of fascism shone through strongly in its mythopoeia: masculinity was at the forefront of the myth of the fascist, while also crucial in its appeal to respectability with conservative gender values. George Mosse argued in *The Image of Man* that 'fascism merely expanded and embellished aspects of masculinity that had always been present', but was obsessively occupied with heroic expressions of manliness, expressed in physical combat and sacrifice – qualities often at odds with daily life and peaceful society.[16] Needless to say, this left very little space for women within these myths, and a dilemma for their role within the movements' mythopoeic projects.

Respectability, no less than myth, was something to be constructed, and indeed could be an integral element of fascist myth. As such it was not only constructed discursively, through emphasis on the legitimacy of the fascist cause, nationalist values, respect for law and order, or reference to national history. Rather, it was also performative, and as such was constructed through style, habit, behaviour, dress and props. As such, the standards of respectability could harmonize with fascist mythopoeia. But respectability also carried with it the imprint of convention, normality, politics-as-usual – bourgeois prose a far cry from the iambic pentameter in which fascist myth fancied to write itself. Adherence to hegemonic notions of legitimacy enshrined in respectability was thus not a strategic given in fascist mythopoeia. The overarching role of respectability in this book is thus to highlight the specific and variable social–political contexts, in the form of national standards of respectability, within which fascist mythopoeia worked, to bring out the organizational paradoxes and dilemmas this generated, and understand the strategic responses fascist parties formulated to solve them.

The comparative method is particularly valuable here, as the two broadly similar democracies help identify the common effects of democratic conditions on fascist movements, while the fascist movements in question were different enough in character, and trajectory, to pinpoint what was unique. Sweden and the Netherlands shared enough characteristics to set them apart from other European states in this regard: neutrality during the First World War, constitutional monarchy, lasting parliamentary democracy during the interwar period, cultural ties to Germany and so forth. But at the same time the fascist movements in question turned out quite differently, with Dutch fascists managing to acquire a significant following in the 1930s, and with very different political cultures. While fascism as a regime has been researched a great deal, there is tremendous analytical potential in studying fascist movements under trying and unpromising conditions, even (or especially) if they 'failed'. The Swedish National Socialist Workers' Party and the Dutch National Socialist Movement are – still under-researched – movements which can provide insights into the conditions of success and failure for fascism in Europe, the efficacy and limitations of fascist myth and organization, and the dynamics of mythopoeia within party culture and public discourse.

Fascism in Europe

The emergence of Mussolini and the *fascisti* in Italy in Milan in March 1919, and their rapid rise to power in 1922 through campaigns of violence and intimidation, as well as parliamentary politics, brought international attention to the notion of *fascismo*. The Fascists, their image rooted in *arditi* trench bravado and D'Annunzian theatrics, were doubtlessly a peculiar product of Italy's ambivalent role as victor in the First World War, and the country's own national circumstances including the *Biennio Rosso* (Two Red Years, 1919–20). But this did not prevent the world at large, as far afield as America and Asia, from taking notice of Mussolini's unusual new approach to politics, and perhaps especially state power and the suppression of socialism. Soon men and women everywhere across Europe and beyond saw something relatable in the Italian *fascisti* – something that, *mutatis mutandis*, could be applied in their own countries.

In the Netherlands, as in many other countries, the so-called March on Rome in October 1922 proved to be the decisive moment in persuading people that Fascism could be relevant and indeed desirable in their own country. At the end of 1922, a group of Catholic intellectuals around Emile Verviers (1888–1968) and the journal *Katholieke Staatkunde* (Catholic Political Science) hailed the Fascists as a new force to combat the dissolution threatening 'life in our time'.[17] The chief source of Verviers's ideas was the Integralism and anti-modernist crusade of Pope Pius X, not least his 1907 encyclical *Pascendi Dominici Gregis*.[18] Fascism however provided a new inspiration for Verviers and his ilk, perhaps because as Catholics they were already predisposed to look to Italy for inspiration, and less likely to think of politics as limited by national borders.[19] In Sweden one of the first politicians to take note of the Italian Fascists and Mussolini in particular was Elof Eriksson. Eriksson (1883–1965) was a leading figure of Bondeförbundet (Agrarian League), and key organizer of the famous Farmers' March in February 1914, which rallied behind the King's militarist position.[20] After losing his position as editor of the highly conservative *Södertälje Tidning* (Södertälje Newspaper) in 1925, Eriksson, who also had contact with German Nazi luminaries such as Julius Streicher and Erich Ludendorff, founded his own periodical, the long-running *Nationen* (The Nation). The highly anti-Semitic *Nationen* wrote strongly in favour of Fascist Italy, and supported various fascist groups throughout the interwar period.[21]

In 1919 Europe was a place where all countries, including old and new states, had to adjust to the realities of a war-torn continent and rapidly transforming political systems. Aside from the enormous costs of the war itself, there was also political fallout in the form of social upheaval and revolution, especially in central- and eastern Europe, although no country was unaffected. The First World War saw the end of several imperial dynasties that had ruled Europe for centuries. The epicentre was Russia. The Russian revolutions of 1917 saw the rise of the Bolsheviks to prominence, and the ensuing brutal civil war across Russia and its former imperial domains created a fearful new enemy of the Right. With the outbreak of the Finnish Civil War in January 1918 it became apparent that Bolshevik revolution might not be a purely Russian phenomenon, and counter-revolutionaries quickly portrayed it as a contagion.[22] Some countries like Germany and Hungary saw actual revolution, with native communists seizing power regionally or nationally, leading to bloody suppression by counter-revolutionary paramilitaries in the former, and a brief national soviet government in the latter, followed by a bloody counter-revolution in what became known as the White Terror. But there was no close correlation between the actual size of revolutionary threat and the fear of it, and the Right made the most of playing up these fears. Italian Fascists exaggerated the threat of revolution even as the power of the Left and the trade unions in Italy was declining.[23]

The neutral countries of Europe were inextricably entangled in the earth-shattering developments that were transforming the political makeup of the continent, even if they did not directly experience the violence of war, lost a generation of young men or had to deal with demobilized veterans, which some historians argued was responsible for the brutalization of interwar European politics.[24] It has become a cliché to describe the governments of north-western Europe as peaceful and stable democracies, even as peace-loving islands, mentally and culturally isolated from the rest of the continent.[25] Sweden and the Netherlands did not escape the socio-economic disruption of the war, and they reacted to the political developments in its wake as transnational phenomena that could occur at home.[26] In the Netherlands the leader of the Sociaal-Democratische Arbeiders Partij (Social Democratic Workers' Party, SDAP) Troelstra called for a proletarian revolution in 1918, but received little support, instead triggering the formation of rightist counter-revolutionary militias, albeit without the bloodshed seen in central Europe.[27] In Sweden the Social Democrats responded to the revolution in Germany that ended the Kaiser's reign and put a socialist government in place, with demonstrations in Stockholm that put pressure on the government to advance franchise reforms. Rightists, again fearing revolution, formed militias in Stockholm, also looking to the Finnish White *skyddskår* (protection corps) as a model. It was thus no surprise that the likes of Emile Verviers and Elof Eriksson saw something recognizable and useful in Mussolini's Fascists.

Attitudes to what this fascism actually entailed quickly developed from 1919 to 1925 however. Once the wave of revolution and civil war had died down, commentators became more sceptical of Mussolini's and other fascists' claims to be restoring or maintaining order, and fascism started to become associated with hooliganism, bullying and violence. But no sooner had the notion become established as a controversial new form of rightist politics, than a new breed of right-wing radicals emerged in Germany. Strongly rooted in the counter-revolutionary movement and paramilitary *Freikorps*, the National Socialists were taken over by Adolf Hitler who took inspiration from Mussolini and the Fascists in shaping the little Bavarian party into something more substantial.[28] It would take until 1929 before the Nazis started to take on the contours of a popular national party, but already in the first half of the twenties did National Socialism start to make itself felt outside of Germany as a Germanic form of fascism, contributing to the spread of anti-Semitism and race on the agenda of the European radical right. While commentators and adherents tried to distinguish between fascism and national socialism, they were evidently related, and regularly conflated with each other. Eventually, to some the terms were completely interchangeable, whereas to others they even were opposed.[29] They sprang forth from similar contexts, and influenced each other, according to the relative prominence of one over the other as times changed, with major turning points being Hitler's appointment as chancellor in January 1933, and the establishment of the Rome-Berlin Axis in October 1936.

Fascist groups that followed in the wake of Mussolini's 1922 March on Rome could hardly help but understand themselves as part of a European or even a global political development. Typically they positioned themselves in a camp alongside the new Right authoritarian regimes that emerged bit by bit in the interwar period; authoritarian states like in Portugal, Spain, Hungary etc. were often understood to be simply fascist regardless of the reality of their complicated relationship to that term. Simultaneously fascist movements liked to insist on their own national(ist) character. The embrace of various notions of a European or global fascism served to highlight the movements' part in an emergent new era. At the same time, what the self-styled fascists and national socialists of interwar Europe had in common, they also shared with other rightists, as there were no clear ideological dividing lines in the European Right. The two cases discussed here underline the messiness and contradictions of transnational fascism. While ostensibly sharing the same ideology, the Swedish NSAP/SSS abhorred the Dutch NSB for most of the 1930s for its rejection of anti-Semitism, while the NSB's attitude to the NSAP, after a visit to Sweden in 1937, was patronizing at best. Fascism, national socialism and other forms of right-wing politics were messily entangled, and there was no consistency in contemporary opinion as to where one ended and the other began, as ideas, aesthetics, programmes and political repertoires were freely transferred, changed, adopted and adapted as they circulated not just Europe but the world.[30]

Myth and interwar European mass politics

This transfer and circulation of an exciting new political repertoire were helped along by the rapid development of European mass democracy, and its underlying mass culture. One of the things that appeared particularly striking in association with fascist politics was doubtless the place of myth, though it is very important to note this was hardly unique to interwar fascism, or even the Right. Myths are here understood as moral narratives that are not strictly fictional, but ahistorical, with strong connotations of the fantastical,[31] or in a simpler sense 'an image which can inspire men', perhaps with 'some element of truth in it, but it is twisted into a vision that conforms to the desired ideal'.[32] Myths had been exploited politically before, but in the new era of mass politics brought on by technological modernity, acquired new forms and significance. Cultural pessimists of the preceding decades, commenting on the explosive growth of print journalism and new technologies of mass production, appeared to be proven right.[33] The 'masses' had acquired an ominous significance in European political culture already since the late nineteenth century, but it was the 1920s which really brought their political relevance to the fore.[34] 'The new politics drew the masses into rituals which connected to myths and symbols, which dramatized politics in spectacular ways.'[35]

From the perspective of the new political parties, Left or Right, mythic narratives could turn the inchoate masses into unified communities, create a sense of belonging and re-impose social order on a fractured society, through participation in ritual.[36] Myth occupied a peculiarly prominent place in the politics of interwar Europe. In this period socialist parties made currency out of the myth of the class struggle and ultimate redemption through the working classes. Marx's concept of Revolution was a mobilizing political myth, as was argued by the influential George Sorel, while he himself preferred the General Strike as a motivating myth that captured the essence of socialism.[37] After all, Sorel informs us, 'we do nothing great without the help of warmly coloured and sharply defined images which absorb the whole of our attention'.[38] Per Albin Hansson, the Swedish Social Democratic prime minister, also made a contribution with his myth of *folkhemmet* (the people's home). Rather than the postwar settlement leading to the firm establishment of rationalistic and moderate forms of democratic politics, interwar mass politics saw the rise of new political possibilities and profound uncertainties.[39] With new forms of politics on the Left and Right, myths seemed to underpin much of the appeal of emergent mass movements.[40] In the Netherlands, the cultural historian Johan Huizinga (1872–1945) observed this troubling development in general terms, and noted that by 1935 it was not limited to just the fascist dictatorships.

> So it has come to this in the civilized world. But do not believe that the degeneration of judgement is limited to the countries in which extreme nationalism has been victorious. Whoever looks around can repeatedly observe how, with developed persons, often youths, a certain indifference has come about to the reality of the figures that have entered their intellectual world. The categories of fiction and history... are no longer clearly separated. It is no longer of interest if the intellectual material can be verified. The rise of the idea *mythus* is the most important example of this. One accepts an illusion, in which the elements of wish and fantasy are consciously permitted...[41]

While not unique to fascism, 'the most self-consciously visual of all political forms',[42] fascists were the most open in their reliance on myth, and did so most visibly when they came to power in Italy and Germany.[43] Benito Mussolini openly proclaimed the value and use of myth in his own politics.[44] Adolf Hitler, echoing French crowd psychologist Gustave le Bon, affirmed the 'feminine' masses could be easily manipulated through simplistic narratives of good and evil, love and hate.[45] While fascists also offered more or less feasible political programmes to the public and appealed to constituencies' material interests and sense of respectability, they constructed a myth of not just the utopian fascist community, but of themselves. This was a myth that aimed to transcend daily politics, and represented fascism in fantastical terms, as a crusade against evil and chaos.

The fascist myth of fascism functioned as both identity and propaganda, as it mobilized members and attracted followers.[46] Fascist myth was highly performative in character, and expressed aesthetically: mass rallies, visually striking propaganda, fantastical sloganeering, and moving rituals. Fascist performances were a political theatre with a penchant for spectacle, a 'hothouse fusion of violence, myth, and aesthetics' – and served to construct a fascism that was dynamic, disciplined and impressive.[47] On this plane fascism was not a historically contingent political movement, but a history-making force destined to transform the eternal nation.[48] There was very little or nothing that was universal in self-styled fascists' party programmes across Europe, and as some attempts at international collaboration showed, like the 1934 Montreux conference, little basis for theoretical agreement.[49] But fascist myths were some of the most recognizable and shared elements among these right-wing movements and organizations, grounded in aesthetics and symbols that could happily transfer across borders.

Historiography of fascism

Scholars were left with the tricky task of defining fascism, a phenomenon that evoked lurid spectacles and horrendous violence, while emphasizing action over theory, and clearly could not be taken at face value. This task proved not altogether unappealing, as the veritable cottage industry that grew up around it shows.[50] While scholars in the eastern half of Cold War Europe had a solid Marxist framework with which to analyse fascism,[51] Western historians were more challenged trying to pin down the nature of this political force which clearly was of momentous importance for contemporary history, but lacked an obvious theoretical basis. The early historiography of fascism and scholars' attempts to define it has been covered extensively and many times before, so I will refrain from rehashing that material here. I will instead give a very brief overview of this literature insofar as it is relevant to this book's thesis, before focusing on the cultural dimensions of the problem and the current research trends.[52]

One early attempt at a definition came in 1963 from the conservative German historian Ernst Nolte, whose *Der Faschismus in seiner Epoche* (Fascism in Its Epoch, also published as *The Three Faces of Fascism*) showed fascism as being characteristic of the European interwar period, intellectually rooted in the nineteenth-century reaction against traditional politics, and Nietzsche's rejection of Judaeo-Christian *resentiment*. Nolte saw fascism as a *European* phenomenon, and highlighted three different variants (German Nazism, Italian Fascism and the French Action Française) to elucidate its character as a form of nationalist anti-Marxism.[53] This was effectively a variant of the genus-species model of fascism, which had started in fascist discourse already in the 1920s, but with a long life stretching into the twenty-first century. Nolte's proposal found no lasting traction however, as most scholars rejected his attempt to tether fascism to contemporary Marxism – especially in terms of terror methods and totalitarianism – and the following decades produced any number of alternative suggestions. More recently, among prominent contributions, Stanley Payne's *History of Fascism* which gave a veritable checklist of features fascism(s) possessed, with a strong place for anti-conservatism, anti-liberalism and anti-Marxism, while Robert O. Paxton's *The Anatomy of Fascism* used a diachronic model of different phases of fascism, with movement through to regime characteristics. Michael Mann's sociological approach produced a less than elegant definition of fascism as a form of para-militarism with a commitment to nation-statism, while even David D. Roberts has not been able to resist an attempt at definition in *Fascist Interactions*, in spite of trying to see fascism as 'an aggregate historical phenomenon' best understood as 'a unique, contingent sequence constituting a single, if obviously multifaceted, event'.[54]

It would be altogether unfair to suggest, as some have done, that the range of definitions and approaches to the problem over the past century has been unproductive and unhelpful. It can certainly be confusing, and the lay reader looking for a simple explanation of a widely used term is liable to be disappointed, but the various definitions and characterizations are reflective of different methodologies and approaches, many of which have in turn shed much light on the history of the European Right in this era. Yet it was not without reason that Gilbert Allardyce, in a much-noted 1979 article – 'What Fascism Is Not' – regretted the continued academic use of fascism as a concept, without the possibility of agreeing on a definition. The sheer variation of possible groups and personalities that could be included under the fascist umbrella tended to make definitions reductive, and the attempt to find the single aspect that unites them all a wild goose chase, if indeed there is a goose (not Allardyce's metaphor).[55]

At a relatively early stage in the postwar search for a definition the cultural turn encouraged scholars to effectively take fascist claims about fascism seriously, a not entirely uncontroversial proposal. The cultural approach to fascism, which analyses fascism 'from the inside out', grappling with the world view it constructed through discourse, performance and aesthetics, had been gaining ground since the 1960s. George L. Mosse's *Nazi Culture* (1966), presenting a collection of original Nazi texts with commentary, was one such work, which tried to answer the question of how fascism impinged on the consciousness of its subjects.[56] 'Fascism considered as a cultural movement means seeing fascism as it saw itself, to attempt to understand the movement on its own terms.'[57] With the 1970s cultural turn in political history, such approaches became more common. Aesthetics and spectacle have occupied a privileged position in the cultural analysis of fascism, often understood as part and parcel of its appeal. Ernst Nolte had described it as a 'spellbinding of the senses by pageantry and parades'[58]; Modris Eksteins saw Nazism as a 'beautiful lie' which through kitsch spectacle and excitement sought to displace ethical considerations.[59] Gerhard Paul's study of Nazi propaganda photography stated Nazism was ideologically void, instead best understood as a movement of propaganda, using aesthetic appeals to the emotions against the dry language and rational discourse of democracy.[60] Works on the Nuremberg *Parteitäge*, the spectacular choreography of Albert Speer, or the Nazi *Thingspiel*, have relied on similar narratives of a nihilistic fascism exploiting modern technology to aesthetically manipulate 'the masses'[61]; in Sweden Ingemar Karlsson and Arne Ruth described the Third Reich as turning society into a theatre, transforming citizens into a work of art, guising a spiritual vacuum and ethical monstrousness.[62]

By the 1990s Mosse assessed there had been growing awareness in the historiography of the role of aesthetics in fascism's appeal, but noted there was more work to be done on the function aesthetics played in self-representation and fascist subjectivity.[63] While 1990s historians like Jeffrey T. Schnapp, in *Staging Fascism* (1996), asserted that 'fascism often amounted to little more than a complex of ethical principles, credos, myths, and aversions, held together by opportunism and rhetorical-aesthetic glue', they recognized in the process that the aesthetic-symbolic dimension of fascism played a crucial role in its self-definition.[64] Simonetta Falasca-Zamponi's *Fascist Spectacle* (1997) similarly saw fascist aesthetics as building the Italian regime's power and asserting its authority, but at the same time creating its own story and identity.[65] For Mabel Berezin theatre in Mussolini's Italy was a way of forging a fascist community,[66] and went further in *Making the Fascist Self* (1997), reconstructing how the regime used mass rituals to create a fascist identity, with the public spectacles as a point of access for participants into the fascist community, merging the public and private self through emotional force.[67] In 1993, Emilio Gentile's *Il culto del littorio* (The cult of the fasces) revived the concept of political religion to underscore the religious-liturgical dimensions of fascist rituals, proposing that they bestowed a religious aura, exciting faith and devotion by imputing divine meaning to political phenomena.[68] While Gentile popularized political religion in the historiography, religion was only one of several registers in which fascists performed, while, his critics argue, the distinction between the concept's actual analytical value and enticing metaphorical suggestiveness remains unclear.[69]

Through the foregrounding of ritual, ceremonial or liturgical elements in fascism, which owed so much to the cultural turn's focus on rituals and symbols, as well as the 'discursive turn' of the 1980s,[70] historians were more prone to take political style and rhetoric seriously, and by extension the myths they conveyed. Alongside the spate of works on the cultural-aesthetic in fascism in the 1990s came Roger Griffin's *The Nature of Fascism* (1991), which foregrounded the matter of ideology again in the form of myth. His book argued for a heuristic ideal-type definition of fascism that would adequately capture what was new and unique about far-right movements, organizations and regimes of Europe between 1918 and 1945, and promote a fruitful analysis of fascist ideology in these terms. His minimalist definition of fascism as 'palingenetic ultra-nationalism' for short – an extreme nationalism driven by the myth of national rebirth – clearly captured the imagination of many students in the field, and eventually became a standard reference point in the historiography.[71] Griffin argued for the 'primacy of culture' in fascism, reconceptualizing ideology through myth (palingenesis), a focus on 'the underlying ideological matrix of fascist thought, policies and action, not on fascist "doctrine" itself'.[72] The 'New Consensus' Griffin asserted seems illusory and remains contested, and it is debatable to what extent Griffin's palingenetic orientation has actually led to useful new research contributions in the field, but either way his work is symptomatic of the entrenchment of cultural approaches to fascism.[73]

Some historians have regarded Griffin's cultural-ideological focus as generalizing, too synchronic and ahistorical, as well as too idealistic, arguing notions like 'palingenesis' lacked any sense of power or connection to real world activism. Michael Mann asked in *Fascists* (2004), '[h]ow can a "myth" generate "internal cohesion" or "driving force"? A myth cannot be an agent driving or integrating anything, since ideas are not free-floating. Without power organizations, ideas cannot actually *do* anything.'[74] But Mann, like other historians, has not been willing to disregard the cultural and mythic elements of fascism altogether in his research, and acknowledged that fascists' own beliefs need to be taken into account, no matter how irrational.[75] In the more recent historiography, Sven Reichardt has developed a 'praxeological' or cultural-pragmatic analysis of fascism, which focuses on the 'thinking within action', i.e. how cultural-ideological forms are revealed through fascist action and behaviour, rather than analysing ideas about the world. This is a way of not getting at the ideas themselves, but at the significant energy and fanaticism that fascism managed to mobilize, through their ideas.[76] Fascist culture, in the broadest sense of the word, is here tied to social practice, using concepts like Pierre Bourdieu's *habitus* and corporeal repertoire. Repeated actions, habits and practices had a creative dimension: fascist praxis was in this sense discursive, and generative of meaning, hence an element in the struggle for meaning.[77] In his book *Fascistischer Kampfbünde* (Fascist Combat Groups, 2009), Reichardt shows how violence was used socially to construct a fascist community, and culturally to create symbolic meaning for fascism as a revolutionary, disciplined, anti-bourgeois force.[78] Rejecting an identifiable essence or nature of fascism, Reichardt understands fascists dynamically in their immediate context, through their actions and performances and the meanings they generate.

Now the role of myth often occupies the centre stage of fascism, and as more than just propaganda. Griffin has proposed that myths could be used to understand fascist mentalities or subjectivities, and by extension their actions, moving beyond instrumental interests or programmatic ideological goals.[79] This has been practised in cultural approaches to fascism before, but without focusing explicitly on myth.[80] However, the insistence on palingenetic myth over any other, no matter how supposedly 'heuristic', has outlived its usefulness. The same is true of the academic construction of a 'generic' fascism. David D. Roberts is correct when he argues that the use of *a priori* frameworks such as heuristic definitions restricts our understanding of what fascists actually said or thought – myth and activism are far more multivalent and complex than that.[81] The use of definitions is unnecessary, if one recognizes that fascism, semiotically an empty signifier, was a historically contingent phenomenon which was and always remained a work-in-progress, open to interpretation and revision from all sides. Nietzsche's dictum, that whatever has a history cannot be defined, applies especially in this instance, where the focus is on tracing how contemporaries constructed fascism in the first place.[82]

Historiography of Swedish and Dutch fascism

The state of research on Swedish fascism can, until recently, be characterized as dire. The electoral failure of indigenous fascist movements in Sweden during a period most notable for the entrenchment of Social Democratic hegemony has given scholars little impetus to look into the Swedish fascists which have been commonly regarded as fundamentally alien to Swedish history.[83] Indeed, the bulk of scholarship dealing with Swedish fascism has focused specifically on anti-fascist opinion.[84] It was only in 1970 that Eric Wärenstam produced the first historical work on Swedish fascism, *Fascismen och Nazismen i Sverige, 1920–1945* (Fascism and Nazism in Sweden, 1920–1945), and since then new works have been few and far between.[85] And while Wärenstam laid the foundations for future scholarship, doing a great deal of impressive original research and source-collecting for the book, it is too short for any in-depth analysis. Wärenstam's description of the developments and failures of the most prominent figures on the fascist scene in Sweden was a crucial start for the historiography, and his plotting of the key developments still shapes how historians view the period today, but his understanding of fascist ideology was at times incoherent and vague, and he did little to elucidate the organization and inner workings of the fascist parties. Wärenstam had no interest in contemporary cultural approaches to fascism, so that his work, while comprehensive, gives no insight into what it meant to be a fascist in interwar Sweden.

The 1990s saw a new attempt by Heléne Lööw to write a history of Swedish fascism in her more extensive *Nazismen i Sverige, 1924–1979* (Nazism in Sweden, 1924–1979), following on her PhD thesis *Hakkorset och Vasakärven* (The Swastika and the Wasa Sheaf), but as the chronology suggests she considered interwar fascism mostly as the predecessor of neo-fascism, which was attracting attention at the time.[86] Lööw's thesis tackled matters of organization more thoroughly than did Wärenstam, but her work grouped together the multiple fascist parties she studied, and analysed them synchronically. It took until the twenty-first century for a call to be made for more serious academic research into historical Swedish fascism, with a 2002 article by Lena Berggren in the *Journal of Contemporary History*, 'Swedish Fascism – Why Bother?' (also published in *Historisk Tidskrift* as 'Swedish interwar fascism – An uninteresting marginal phenomenon or important research subject?').[87] Berggren, whose previous work focused on the intellectual history of anti-Semitism in Sweden, denied that fascism was alien to Swedish history, and questioned the idea that Swedish fascists were merely emulating the German Nazi party. Instead she emphasized how key fascist ideas about race, nation and society were prevalent in Sweden and did not depend on any German influence, and how Swedish fascists sought to maintain independence from German Nazism. Moreover, Berggren argued that past scholarship has been excessively moralizing, keen to denote fascist mavericks as outsiders in a country devoted to benevolent neutrality. With this starting point she hoped that the number of scholars working in the field would increase, and improve on 'the as yet embryonic fascist studies in Sweden'.[88]

As Berggren's angle suggests, she pursued the issue mainly through an intellectual history of fascism, as exemplified by one of her recent articles on Per Engdahl, a figurehead of Swedish fascism until the 1990s.[89] Klas Åmark's comprehensive 2011 work on Sweden's wartime relationship with Nazi Germany, *Att Bo Granne med Ondskan* (To Be Evil's Neighbour), investigates fascism in Sweden with unprecedented detail, and takes full account of both Lööw's and Berggren's research, but has a rather old-fashioned moralizing approach to the subject, and does not seek to understand the indigenous fascists in their own right.[90] Åmark's work is also symptomatic of a much stronger academic interest in Nazi Germany's influence on, and activities in, Sweden, rather than indigenous fascism.[91] Henrik Arnstad's *Älskade Fascism* (Beloved Fascism, 2013) is a work which understands fascism as a European ideology with a global reach, and relies heavily on Roger Griffin's palingenetic definition. While not presenting any original research, it broke the mould as one of the first Swedish books to look at fascism 'from the inside', although Arnstad devotes most of his attention to the radical right Sverigedemokraterna (Sweden Democrats).[92] Per Svensson's 2014 *Vasakärven och Järnröret* (The Wasa Sheaf and the Steel Pipe) is another example of this trend, investigating the origins of the Sweden Democrats in the interwar fascist milieu of Lund University, showing how new research is being stimulated by recent political developments in Swedish politics.[93] Such research tends towards a teleological analysis however, aiming firstly to explain contemporary political developments, and focusing heavily on the transfer of ideas and continuity of personnel over time.

More important to the concerns of this book is a 2009 monograph by Henrik Dammberg, *Nazismen i Skaraborgs Län, 1930–1945* (Nazism in Skaraborg Province, 1930–1945), which provides a detailed case study of fascist activism in one Swedish province. While Dammberg's conceptual understanding of fascism and inter-party differences is rather crude, his tracing of developments in party organization and campaigning tactics adds flesh to the bones of Swedish fascism research. His book looks at several fascist groups, particularly the NSAP and Svenska Nationalsocialistiska Partiet (Swedish National Socialist Party, SNSP), how they tried to win members and votes in the region, their electoral strategies, and the dissemination of propaganda, especially among school youth. His work also engages with incidents of violence and fascist terror.[94] While his work is local, the case study sheds some much-needed light on how fascist organization and activism worked in practice.

The first scholarly work to be focused on the NSAP specifically came from Viktor Lundberg in 2014, with *En Idé Större än Döden* (An Idea Greater than Death), which employs some of the insights of cultural theory, particularly poststructuralist discourse analysis, in analysing proletarian culture in Lindholm's party. Lundberg has based his analysis on much-needed original research in party and police archives, which have seen little use since the work of Wärenstam and Lööw in the seventies and nineties. While Lundberg's handling of Foucauldian and Althusserian concepts is sometimes clumsy, and often obscures the role of individual agency, *En Idé Större än Döden* nevertheless represents a hitherto rare, focused, scholarly engagement with Swedish fascism beyond the range of a research article.[95] It is one of the first to engage directly with fascist political culture in Sweden; his analysis also covers the role of myth in the NSAP, particularly that of 'workers' Sweden' (*arbetar-Sverige*), but he stays on the discursive level, and does not take into account other forms of cultural construction. More recently Johan Stenfeldt has also made a contribution with his monograph *Renegater* (Renegades, 2019), comparing the ideological development of Lindholm and Nils Flyg (1891–1943), the Swedish communist leader-turned fascist during the Second World War. While much more research on Swedish fascism remains to be done, the pace is clearly accelerating at present.

While Anglophone scholarship on fascism in the Netherlands remains scarce and generally poor in character, riddled with basic factual errors and out of touch with recent research, Dutch studies of fascism are rich in quantity and quality.[96] From its historical origins Dutch fascism spawned a large volume of literature, polemic and academic. The minor fascist groups of the 1920s did not manage to attract much of the attention that was then largely focused on Fascist Italy, but with the rise of the NSB in 1931, public and scholarly attention shifted towards the domestic scene. Of course, the spectacular growth of the NSDAP in neighbouring Germany helped foster a new-found interest in all things called national socialist, and this German connection would prove to be an irrevocable part of the literature on Dutch fascism. For instance P.A. Diepenhorst's *Het Nationaal-Socialisme* (National Socialism, 1935) understands national socialism as an essentially German ideology, and calls the Dutch and German national socialists 'children of one spirit'.[97]

After the Second World War, interest in the national experience of Nazi occupation was immediate. The collection of material for a special war archive, the Nationaal Instituut voor Oorlogsdocumentatie (NIOD, National Institute for War Documentation), started as early as 1944.[98] Directed by Louis de Jong (1914–2005), this collection became the foundation for an innumerable mass of writing on the Netherlands during the Second World War. de Jong's twenty-six volume on the Netherlands during the Second World War was published from 1969 to 1994, and remains a standard reference work for anyone studying the period. German historians have also contributed important work on this subject, not least Konrad Kwiet's 1968 *Reickskommissariat Niederlande* (The Dutch Reichskommissariat), a still useful analysis of the politics of the Nazification project in the Netherlands.[99] Works focusing on various aspects of the Occupation have been forthcoming constantly since the 1950s, as literature on fascism between 1940 and 1945 has gravitated around the Dutch experience of Nazi occupation.[100] As Dutch historian Jennifer Foray put it: 'To be sure, popular audiences and scholars alike remain highly captivated by – if not wholly obsessed with – the wartime years.'[101]

The foundations for a historiography of Dutch fascism in its own right were laid in the 1960s. G.A. Kooy's 1964 sociological study of the Winterswijk community and its high proportion of fascist voters, *Het Echec van een 'Volkse' Beweging* (The Failure of a 'Volkish' Movement), remains a standard work on the social makeup of the NSB.[102] The same year saw the publication of L.M.H. Joosten's *Katholieken en Fascisten in Nederland* (Catholics and Fascists in the Netherlands), perhaps the first serious study of the various minor fascist groups the Netherlands saw in the 1920s.[103] But it is A.A. de Jonge's *Crisis en Critiek der Democratie* (Crisis and Criticism of Democracy, 1968) which serves as the first comprehensive study of radical right currents in the period. Together with his *Het Nationaal-Socialisme in Nederland* from the same year, the two books give a solid overview of fascist organizations and ideology in the Netherlands.[104] However, as Konrad Kwiet pointed out in his 1970 article, 'Zur Geschichte der Mussert-Bewegung' (Towards a history of the Mussert movement), there was still need for a proper history of the largest and most notorious of fascist groups in the Netherlands, the NSB, as the literature was only concerned with the movement as a peripheral issue in the wider debate about occupation and collaboration.[105]

Since then a great deal of research concerning virtually all imaginable aspects of the NSB has been done, generally in tandem with the social-cultural turn, but initially without any engagement with NSB fascism 'from the inside out'. For a long time close discussion of NSB ideology or its particular political character remained rare, as they seemed to require some sort of empathetic engagement, an approach stigmatized by the war experience itself. In 1983 Ronald Havenaar contributed a very brief monograph on NSB ideology, *De NSB tussen Nationalisme en 'Volkse' Solidariteit* (The NSB between Nationalism and 'Volkish' Solidarity), but after that almost no studies were devoted to this area, nor did any works try to engage with it from a cultural angle for a long time.[106] Focus shifted instead predominantly to the organization of the NSB, social composition, the biographies of its members and their relationship with Nazi authorities.

It is only in the past decade that Dutch scholars have been keen to abandon a traditional approach to fascist ideology as a set of programmatic ideas and values, and have instead turned to culture to understand the NSB and their kind. Gerard Groeneveld's twin studies of NSB literature and musical culture, published in 2001 and 2007 respectively, are good examples of high-quality original research that has been done into Dutch fascist culture. Groeneveld's work is interesting for its subject of fascist discourse in published literature, which it analyses specifically with reference to the context of practical production. For instance he has gone to some length to reconstruct the process behind the publication of the Dutch translation of *Mein Kampf* (1939).[107] His work on NSB musical culture stands even closer to the subject of this thesis, connecting NSB music to its organization, examining the propagandistic aims of song, and the myths which poetic expression invoked, while also considering the reception of fascist music on the streets.[108]

With a more local perspective on the subject, Josje Damsma's and Erik Schumacher's *Hier Woont een NSB'er* (Here Lives an NSB-Member, 2010) is a stellar attempt to understand the NSB in Amsterdam as constituting a cultural community, with their own social rituals, pastimes and conventions, placing emphasis on the day-to-day life of its members.[109] The book also explores NSB relations with outsiders, and goes some way to confront the paradigm of NSB-members as social pariahs.[110] The authors paint a picture of the NSB's community, in which members could socialize with like-minded people, and find support when rejected by other communities (such as the church). This is in turn used to explain how cadres could be mobilized effectively; Damsma and Schumacher point to the social cohesion and 'cosiness' the party's organization generated.[111] This analysis is another contribution towards understanding the connection between fascist organizational forms, activism and culture, though the authors do not explore the significance of myth, while the analysis is strictly limited to 1940–5.

One recent addition to these new approaches to the NSB is René van Heijningen's 2015 *De Muur van Mussert* (Mussert's Wall).[112] The subject of his work is a ceremonial wall-like structure in Lunteren, built by the NSB in 1936, which fell into disuse during the German occupation, but stands to this day. Heijningen places the NSB rallies in the perspective of both 1930s political culture, and in comparison with Nazi Germany's Nuremberg rallies and Thingstätte, inspired by the likes of Griffin and Gentile. He gives some good insights into the political and personal decisions that lurked behind the organization of the rallies associated with the wall, and many of the practical issues that beset the meetings, while the theoretical side of his work is less strong however, using his cultural theoretical concepts more to justify his research rather than harnessing their analytical potential.

On the whole, work on the cultural dimensions of the NSB in the twenty-first century has been invaluable, and we know a great deal more about NSB subjectivities and myths than two decades ago. We also know thankfully much more about how the NSB's organization was implemented in practice, and how it related to party activism, although the picture here remains partial due to the selective or localized nature of research so far. As with the Swedish literature, there is however much more scope for the analysis of fascist myth-making, while the image of fascism, and the cultural production of fascism, has not been explored in performative terms, and tied to a wider political public discourse about fascism.

Transnational fascism

In the past five years or so historians of fascism have become increasingly keen to understand fascism in transnational terms. Simultaneously there appears to be the establishment of a new school of thought which recognizes that the use of definitions of fascism, heuristic, ideal-typical or otherwise, sits awkwardly within a transnational framework. The emphasis on transfer, and non-national context categories, highlights transformation, malleability, flux and open-endedness, which points to contingency rather than definition, process rather than stasis. Increasingly, historians feel like they are able to do away with definitions of fascism, and instead treat fascism itself as a transferrable and contingent sign, rather than a political category of analysis.

The study of transnational history goes back much further, but only first started to make an impact on fascism studies about a decade ago. Originally the 'transnational turn' was focused on the fascist regimes that have always been central to the field, looking particularly at Fascist Italy and Nazi Germany's foreign policy and international cooperation. Nation-states were still very much central in this analysis, but it also looked closer at how non-state actors facilitated fascist politics across borders within and between state structures.[113] Other studies examined the transnational history of fascist ideology itself, with a notable example being Michael Kellogg's *The Russian Roots of Nazism* (2005), which traced the movement and politics of White emigrés from Russia after the 1917 revolutions, and their intimate involvement with the German radical Right and the nascent Nazi movement.[114] Thus there was a strong awareness that fascists, in spite of their ultra-nationalism, not only could but *should* be studied in transnational terms. And while initial focus was on the regimes and their cooperation and rivalry, they opened up questions relevant to European fascism generally. At the time however there was still quite a significant lack of English-language monographs on key movements and organizations, which was essential to open up a field so heavily reliant on international cooperation among scholars looking beyond the nation-state. These studies would take at least another decade to manifest, though the histories of hitherto obscure but crucial fascist groups like the Romanian Legion of the Archangel Michael, or the Croatian Ustaša, now have up-to-date literature devoted to them.[115] Alongside the transnational turn in fascism studies, there was a simultaneous trend that can be characterized as an attempt at 'decentering' generic fascism. The point was well made by Roger Griffin in the *Fascism* journal, arguing in 2015 that the excessive focus on German and Italian regimes risked scholars constructing a historically spurious Nazi-Fascism to stand in for 'generic fascism'.[116]

Historians throughout the 2010s made an effort to look beyond these well-trodden case studies, and looked at fascist interactions with the regimes as not just a one way street of influence and coercion. An early contribution, noting the previous research on cross-border cooperation between fascist regimes, was Arnd Bauerkämper's 'Transnational Fascism', which made an effort to look at interactions between regimes and movements, and noted the persistent venues for exchange and transfer even where official institutional channels of cooperation proved inadequate.[117] Another notable hallmark of this approach was Aristotle Kallis and Antonió Costa Pinto's *Rethinking Fascism and Dictatorship in Europe* (2014). Not only did this edited volume look at how fascist politics, styles and ideas spread on their own throughout not just Europe but the world, it also included interactions with groups and regimes not always considered fascist, such as Franco's Spain, considering the selective borrowing from fascism without necessarily leading to 'full-blown fascism', whatever that might mean. Pinto's research on fascist corporatism also revealed how specific fascist ideas and policies found traction globally, especially in Latin America. Notions of 'hybridity' sought to nuance the categories of analysis with which fascism studies worked, while Kallis's 're-contextualization' served to underline that where people were influenced by fascism, they did not just do so reflexively. The conclusion called for the embrace of 'transnational dynamics' and 'complexity'.[118] The year 2016 saw David D. Roberts's theoretically highly developed contribution along these lines, *Fascist Interactions*, which attempted to give some theoretical structure to what he terms the 'restiveness' in current fascism studies. This restiveness was an unease with the preoccupation with definitions, and a desire to blur categories of fascism and other New Right phenomena, perhaps especially on the basis of a transnational approach. Roberts particularly advocated bringing out the sense of new possibilities, of experimentation in the new Right, and seeing fascism as a crucial part thereof. He speaks much of thus regaining a sense of the feel and texture of the new Right universe in Europe, the things that seemed at issue at the time, the possibilities that appeared to have opened. The history of fascism here is heavily premised on the contingent, and the ad hoc.[119]

It is in the last five years that the study of fascism in transnational terms has really taken off. After Roberts's summary of the current field and suggestions for future directions, came Bauerkämper and Rossinski-Liebe's edited volume *Fascism without Borders*, which neatly encapsulated the new priorities of the field.[120] Notably, some scholars have been picking up on calls to treat fascism itself as a malleable category that perhaps not only elided definition, but was best studied without definition[121] – i.e. as a category that was itself susceptible to the complexities and contingencies of transnational exchange and transfer. In a 2017 chapter, Kevin Passmore explicitly positioned the transnational approach *against* generic fascism: 'Whereas generic fascism theorists see discrete national movements as variations of a core, a transnational approach recognizes that protagonists used and transformed ideologies in quite different contexts for different purposes.'[122] The first review article on the transnational fascism literature by Ángel Alcalde was published in 2020, which noted that the trend had really taken hold. What some scholars will no doubt find difficult to accept is his assertion, with which the present author whole-heartedly agrees, that research on fascism no longer needs to be based on impossible ideal-types, preconceived definitions and 'generic' notions, which used to operate as the epistemological mould in the past.[123] Increasingly, it looks like a properly historical and transnational understanding of fascism, which acknowledges the contingency and open-endedness of its development, and what has been termed its *bricolage* character, are ultimately *antithetical* to any definition of fascism.

Although this book is a comparative study of two national case studies, it is rooted in the transnational approach to fascism that has taken hold. Historians of fascism can no longer afford to ignore that fascism was transnational in its origins, its evolution and its dissemination.[124] Thus, while this study is not transnational in its own right (it examines the two case studies comparatively, in isolation), it does aim to make a contribution to the transnational study of fascism by looking at how fascist elements – organizational, aesthetic, ideological, mythic – were transferred and re-contextualized, by analyzing them in the mythopoeic process. This is necessary; the foreign origin of some of the elements with which the NSAP and NSB constructed their fascism was a matter of political import in its own right, especially pertaining to the perception of their respectability and nationalist credentials, so that the manner of their transfer and (re-)deployment or re-contextualization ought to be understood as part and parcel of a transnational fascism. When analysing fascist mythopoeia in Sweden and the Netherlands, the open-ended and diachronic character of fascism as an empty signifier will also be apparent at national level, and is in fact essential to make the analysis possible. Theoretically, we may speak, perhaps a little awkwardly, of a mythic-semiotic constructivism, rooted in a transnational context.

Theory and methodology

This approach places political-cultural history within a social and at times microhistorical framework, in a way that is immediately relevant to the present purpose of analysing mythopoeia in the context of discourses about fascism. It brings out the aesthetic-emotional dimensions of fascism, questions of subjectivity and identity, and the mythic, while grounding them in pragmatic everyday concerns of resources, finances, competencies and political organization. It also favours the analysis of fascism as movements, rather than regimes.

Cultural pragmatism, by placing cultural expression in the realm of day-to-day action, underlines the contingency of fascism: constructed through mythopoeic performances, enacted by the party organization and the cadres through repeated actions. By bringing in cadres and organization into myth-making, the interplay of mid-level functionaries and activists, the aesthetic and spectacular can be analysed in practical terms, something which the cultural history of fascism has paid fairly little attention to.[125] Political spectacle, such as mass rallies or carefully choreographed rituals, required the close attentions of the party organization, as well as attention to matters of space and mise-en-scène. The aesthetics of fascism then can be seen as not just propaganda, or the locus of identity and representation, but the interface of practical organization and myth. At the same time it shows how fascists in the process practically engaged in a cultural struggle for the meaning of fascism, as the pragmatic requirements of fascist performances connect them to political activism. Beyond fascism, this can elucidate the importance of myth in the politics of interwar Europe, how it related to contemporary political organizations and infrastructure, and the viability of extremist activism under democratic conditions. As such it touches on some of the most significant questions of modern mass politics in the first half of the twentieth century, such as the connection between myth, modern technology and party organizations; the resistance of the democratic public sphere against new political-discursive techniques; and how extremist political actors participated in and exploited public discourse to further their ends.

From this cultural point of view fascist political performances were not just propagandistic or mobilizing, but mythopoeic. By means of understanding this mythopoeia as performative in nature and thus constructing the thing it signifies, one may see how this not only applies to organized political events, but also extends to unplanned incidents, behaviour, props and clothes. A street fight between a fascist and a communist – 'the everyday symbolic struggles on the street'[126] – could reify a narrative of fascism as a forceful bulwark against Bolshevism. The individual behaviour of a fascist member in a public space fed into public perceptions of what fascism was; the uniform a fascist wore itself contributed to the myth of fascism as a violent or disciplined force. These less organized, unscripted types of representation and behaviour formed a repertoire that was no less performative.[127] However, this repertoire of fascist expression could undermine the myth as well as reiterate it: unscripted performances carried risk, and in the interstices of mis-performance others significations of fascism 'leaked out', alternative narratives opened up for consumption by the public.[128] This dynamic points to the open-endedness of reception, and the irregular conveyance of myth: fascist performances had highly variable mythopoeic potential. Focusing on the process of the creation of meaning in mythopoeia, in the context of alternative narratives and discordant hermeneutics, allows for a dynamic analysis of fascist signification.[129]

Discourse did not float freely, but was bounded by human agency. Focus on myth and respectability through discourse risks being too synchronic; it is through attention to the practical aspects and contingencies of human social activity in performing, acting and reacting to discourse that agency is re-inserted. The concept of mythopoeia in particular stresses the active engagement of actors with discourse; even as fascist subjects themselves were produced by the same discourse, they and their opponents engaged in a constant re-evaluation and re-signification which destabilized meaning and brought about change.[130] Active engagement is emphasized specifically through the contingencies of performance, which accentuates the social dynamics of the production of meaning.¹³¹ Jeffrey C. Alexander employs a theory of performance in relation to ritual, which is particularly apt for understanding fascist mythopoeic performances such as rallies or marches. Centring on the pragmatics of social performance, Alexander sees performance as presenting an account to an audience, where '[s]uccessful performance depends on the ability to convince others that one's performance is true, with all the ambiguities that the notion of aesthetic truth implies'.¹³² Echoing the work of performativity theorist Erika Fischer-Lichte, it is argued the less contrived the performance is perceived to be, the more true seems the account it presents. This depends on practical skills and abilities of the actors, as well as access to the mundane material things that make the performance possible.¹³³ Elements like mise-en-scène, script, props, actors' abilities and the susceptibility of the audience all move to produce 'the emotional connection of audience with actor and text and thereby to create the conditions for projecting cultural meaning from performance to audience'.¹³⁴ It is a theory which relates the performance to its historical material and social organization and conditions, bringing out how those affect the communication of and identification with (mythic) narrative. It also leaves space for hermeneutics to intercede in the performance, as part of the social conditions that govern reception, as an antagonistic audience can discern the seams of the performance through their access to alternative discourses.¹³⁵

Alexander's theoretical framework is of limited use for understanding unscripted modes of mythopoeia, such as the mythopoeic potential that resided in day-to-day behaviour and lifestyle, clothing, composure, etc. Performativity theory as elaborated by queer theorist Judith Butler in the late 1980s and early 1990s offers a more solid basis from which to analyse mythic constructions of fascism beyond the organizational level.¹³⁶ To this end it is useful to first examine its theoretical roots, which will clarify how a reconfiguration of Butler's theory of gender is feasible in the very different context of fascism. Performativity theory, dating back to the mid-twentieth century, enjoyed a powerful resurgence in the late 1980s in cultural studies, when it started to replace the 'culture as text' approach. Performativity turned analysis upside down, discarding the method of 'reading' culture as a structured web of signs, and instead looking to performative (bodily) acts as being non-referential, i.e. not expressing any kind of pre-existing essence or stable identity.¹³⁷

The notion of performativity dates back to the 1950s, when English philosopher J. L. Austin gave a series of lecture at Oxford and Harvard on the topic of speech-acts, later published under the title *How to Do Things with Words* (1962). In brief his lectures developed the anti-positivist position that many utterances do not in fact possess any truth-value, focusing specifically on 'performative utterances'. Such utterances do not make a statement about the world, and, in appropriate circumstances, they amount to an action in the world. One of Austin's examples is the naming of a ship, where uttering the words 'I name this ship the *Queen Elizabeth*' actually performs the act of naming the ship. Alternatively: 'When I say, before the registrar or altar, &c., "I do", I am not reporting on a marriage: I am indulging in it.' This kind of utterance was dubbed for short 'a performative', generating a new theoretical field in the process.¹³⁸ While Austin made a great many other distinctions about types of performative and their conditions, here it only needs adding that performatives do not possess truth-value, but they may or may not be effective in performing the act they intend, which depends on conditions and circumstances. This failed or flawed functioning of the performative is not false, but *infelicitous*.[139] For the present purposes, the key point in the performative is that it is a productive act which, contrary to 'constative' utterances, is non-referential. It brings about a new situation or reality only with reference to itself. Crucially, performatives may need to be supported by external conditions, and may very well imply that what they bring about originates elsewhere (e.g. to establish legitimacy), but they are strictly constituted by the performative.

Austin's lectures were not widely noted at the time, but the idea of linguistic performativity had a lengthy afterlife, being elaborated and re-deployed at times to the point of unrecognizability. One such elaboration by Jacques Derrida had a strong influence on Judith Butler's theory. Derrida seized on Austin's discussion of non-serious performatives, such as 'hollow' speech acts performed on stage which do not possess performative force – 'the *etiolations* of language'[140] – and subverted the categorization of these infelicitous performatives. Where Austin characterized fictional speech as parasitic because it was citational, thus breaking down substantive speech, Derrida argued that all speech performatives were citational, and in fact their felicity *depended on* prior iterations, their *iterability*. 'If valid or original speech acts themselves involve an essential element of citation, this citationality cannot be marked off as that which invalidates fictional performatives as non-serious.'[141] Thus, even felicitous performatives are marked by that hollowness. Derrida's contention is important for the present study of fascism, not just because of his influence on later theorists of performativity that inform the analysis, but also for how it renders the understanding of fascism as a sign.

> This is the possibility on which I wish to insist: the possibility of extraction and of citational grafting which belongs to the structure of every mark, spoken or written, and which constitutes every mark as writing even before and outside every horizon of semiolinguistic communication; as writing, that is, as a possibility of functioning cut off, at a certain point, from its 'original' meaning and from its belonging to a saturable and constraining context. Every sign, linguistic or nonlinguistic, spoken or written (in the usual sense of this opposition), as a small or large unity, can be *cited*, put between quotation marks; thereby it can *break with every given context, and engender infinitely new contexts* [my italics] in an absolutely nonsaturable fashion.[142]

Fascism's referent – fascism as a performative utterance – 'is not outside it, or in any case preceding it or before it. It does not describe something which exists outside and before language. It produced or transforms a situation, it operates',[143] (as Derrida cites Austin) but it operates in a semiotic chain, citing prior iterations of fascism, re-contextualizing them and rendering new meaning. Fascism's citationality simultaneously underlines the historicity of the signifier, pointing to its dependency on previous iterations, and the possibility of a break with previous instances, the enactment of a new performance, new meaning.

So far it has been shown how performativity theory can elucidate the discursive construction of a sign such as fascism. While crucial, mythopoeia also and primarily focuses on not speech-as-action, but performance-as-action, action-as-habit, as-being. To this end the transposition of Butler's idea of gender performativity. Arguing, most famously in her 1990 *Gender Trouble*, that gender is performative, she relied on Austin's linguistic theory to show that gender is constituted through performative acts, gestures and speech, which frequently claims to have external reference points (e.g. sex), but is constituted by the performance itself. Echoing Derrida, Butler emphasized the importance of iterability, so that gender is found in social temporality, not substantiality.[144] Crucial then is the repeated performatives, a repetition of acts which constitute the gendered object. As in 'Signature Event Context', it is however the possibility of iteration that also makes possible the excising of the sign from its chain and placing it in new contexts, and constructing new meanings: 'the possibilities of gender transformation are to be found in the arbitrary relation between such acts, in the possibility of a different sort of repeating, in the breaking or subversive repetition of that style'.[145]

While her reliance on Austin (and Derrida) has been criticized as being overly concerned with discourse, and linguistic performativity, she clearly repurposes performativity to mean that acts, gestures and desires are performative.[146] Beyond scripted spectacles, mythopoeia continued with and within the individual fascist on the street, when identified as such, in the way they walked, talked, dressed or fought. 'Such acts, gestures, enactments, generally construed, are *performative* in the sense that the essence or identity that they otherwise purport to express are *fabrications* manufactured and sustained through corporeal signs and other discursive means.' Fascism in this sense has no ontological status apart from the acts that construct and constitute it.[147] Butler's idea of performativity as comprising the entire ontological status of gender can, *mutatis mutandis*, be transposed to the political identity and image of fascism, as a social-cultural phenomenon which is not a discreet entity. Such performative, constitutive acts do not just constitute identity, but also constitute it as a compelling illusion, *an object of belief*.[148] This is crucial to fascism's mobilizing potential. The discursive construction of fascism through mythopoeia, and the performativity of mythopoeia itself, points to fascist identity essentially as the enactment of a fantasy. Moreover, Butler's definition of performativity as being the requirement of a repeated performance to sustain the constitution of the thing itself is particularly useful here. 'This repetition is at once a re-enactment and re-experiencing of a set of meanings already socially established; and it is the mundane and ritualized form of their legitimation.' The identity is then made up through 'the stylized repetition of acts'.[149] Performativity points not only to how mythopoeia constructs 'fascism' outside of organized spectacle or textual discourse, inscribed onto the 'surface' of the fascist body, but also the connection between mythopoeia and fascist identity as the enactment of fantasy. Lastly, this conception allows one to avoid the mistake of assuming that 'fascism' is something that can be properly embodied, that a 'fascist' is someone whose performance has any referent beyond themselves. Properly understood, the performativity of fascism means that whether outsiders perceived self-identified fascists as they represented themselves has nothing to do with the 'truth' of their representation, but the credibility of their performance.[150]

While cultural pragmatic approaches to fascism, if not always explicitly recognized as such, have been relatively common in the past decade, performative analyses of fascism remain scarce; if not so much in studies of Italian and German fascism, certainly among the minor movements.[151] But fascists at the movement 'stage', without the support of the state, or even any big investors, are particularly good subjects for the study of how daily activist behaviour, and the modern political party such as it emerged after the First World War, could make themselves count (or not) in public discourse.

Sources and methods

The Swedish NSAP and Dutch NSB have both left ample archival material which details the functioning and development of their respective party apparatuses. These sources of the day-to-day administration of the parties are essential in providing the pragmatic basis for their cultural practices, and give the requisite insight into the resources and organization at their disposal to perform fascism. Meetings, rallies, marches and other elements of the fascist repertoire were extensively discussed and analysed by functionaries, in internal correspondence, circulars, minutes, reports and similar administrative material, which gives a handle on the practical aspects of mythopoeia. The NSAP in particular was also extensively monitored by the secret police, so that the police archives provide extensive descriptive material of party activities, the internal mood and plans for the future, as well as volumes of confiscated party material, both published and confidential. Often this internal material gives flashes of insight into the precise intentions behind the parties' outward presentations to the public, and their internal aims. But much of the resulting mythopoeia, the performances on the ground, is supported best by the newspaper material. The weekly party newspapers represent a large bulk of continuous fascist discourse that was constantly involved in the mythopoeic process. This newspaper discourse was itself a performative, discursively constructing fascism, but also supported embodied performativity by guiding readers in their interpretation of the performances, for instance through highly ideological and verbose reports on rallies. Where available, non-fascist newspapers, local and national, are used to provide a contrasting perspective on these events, and show how the mythopoeic endeavour was actually received, and highlight its inevitable flaws and seams. Together these various sources, official and informal, public and confidential, allow the reconstruction and comparison of local fascist mythopoeic practices, and their corresponding reception.

The NSAP and NSB's activities consisted of a repertoire of meetings, rallies, marches, conventions and other forms of propaganda which all relied heavily on a mythic construction of fascism. Doubtlessly inspired by their foreign neighbours, but with a great deal of modification and innovation, the Swedish and Dutch parties did not simply propagate an ideology, but *constructed* fascism as a political phenomenon on the national stage. Fascism, already an empty signifier at this stage in history, was not *represented* by these groups, but constructed – and that construction was *mythic* in character. Nor, then, was this just a matter of propaganda, but also of identity, mobilization and morale. This was construction that conformed to a collectively and individually held fantasy, was made up less of programmatic statements and reasoned argument, and more of images, sounds, feelings, aesthetic impressions and moral narratives that gave meaning to these. Fascism did not, strictly speaking, exist beyond the repertoire of political performances and discourses that generated these impressions. It is the practical process of the mythic-performative construction of fascism, denoted as *mythopoeia*, which is at the centre of this book, and around which all analysis revolves.

The first, but not the most important, of my aims in the following chapters is to show what myths the Swedish and Dutch self-styled fascists created. These myths were several, varied and malleable: they changed over time, and the exercise to excize them from their historical context and deploy them here as discrete units risks being misleading. Undoubtedly their description here is itself an act of construction which puts flesh and bones on something often quite ephemeral. That means that the selection of myths for analysis is to some extent arbitrary; in my choices I have attempted to provide a varied, comprehensive and representative sample which demonstrates the different applications, methods and requirements of fascist myths at all levels of the party organization.

What the myths were is entirely secondary to the primary aim of analysing *how* they were created, how myth was *done*. So I will explore the various stages of organization, activism and planning that were involved in mythopoeia, with emphasis on the practical and mundane, the performance rather than the discourse, the phenomenological over the theory. As historians we are incorrigibly dependent on text as a gateway to the elusive supposed historical reality, so that naturally textual sources must be extensively deployed to reconstruct action, but they are here then regarded principally as an access point. The main interest here is in how performances, meetings, rallies, marches or rank-and-file behaviour and presentation were used mythopoeically.

Analysing myth as a process, as something made, and particularly as something made collectively, is not a uni-dimensional exercise. It requires looking not just at the methods of production, but also the means of production to borrow a Marxist phrase. We need to know what resources fascists had at their disposal in making myths: manpower, money, organizational structures, space, props, infrastructure, etc. Likewise, I want to show how circumstances influenced how mythopoeia was done, with respectability as the guiding light. Circumstances changed in many respects for the NSB and NSAP over the thirties, particularly in terms of electoral success, the national mood vis-à-vis fascism and the Italian and German regimes, the economy in the wake of the Great Depression, and perhaps most importantly the legality of certain modes of political expression. Essentially such circumstances amounted to what politics were respectable or otherwise viable, what myths were feasible, what function they fulfilled and how they were constructed.

None of these aspects of the analysis can be studied in isolation. Circumstances and context, means and resources, and methods of myth-making and indeed the character of the myths *an sich* always interacted with each other, leading at the top of the parties to the formulation of specific mythopoeic strategies. As will become evident, mythopoeic strategies were aimed both at outsiders (propaganda), and at the party membership, and sometimes they would conflict, a conflict typically situated in the conundrum of respectability. The picture I paint in these chapters is in many regards a messy one, as myths intersected, changed, and overlapped in contradictory ways; the comparison of Sweden and the Netherlands however should show there were specific dynamics to the way a mythic fascism could be made, and how different strategies panned out. At the end of the analysis then, there should be a clearer idea of how and why certain fascist myths were constructed, both at a national-political level and at the everyday grassroots level.

†††

The analysis of this book unfolds in a more or less hierarchical fashion. The first chapter will provide some important national context to the history of the NSAP/SSS and NSB, as many readers are unlikely to be familiar with the interwar history of Sweden and the Netherlands. There I offer a short overview of the emergence of mass democracy in both countries, particularly in the context of the First World War, before giving separate accounts of the Dutch and Swedish interbellum.

Chapter 2 provides in some ways the foundations for the analysis, and looks at the party apparatuses of the NSB and NSAP/SSS. Fascist mythopoeia requires organization, and the party organization is at the heart of this process, providing a natural starting point. This 'filing cabinet level' of investigation also serves as an introduction to the two fascist parties, and allows us to understand how the mythopoeic practices of the following chapters were organized and managed. This chapter analyses the party apparatuses of the NSB and NSAP, as they emerged in 1931–3, and their development throughout the 1930s. It shows that the apparatus was at the heart of mythopoeia, as it determined how events were organized, the rank-and-file disciplined, and was the tool of the party Leader to impose his vision of fascism. Central to this point is the organization of propaganda within the parties, taking into account the administration of the propaganda department, the distribution of party literature, the role of the party newspapers in the construction of fascism, and the crucial organization of public meetings to spread the gospel of fascism. It is demonstrated how the party apparatuses controlled the mythopoeic process, and were fundamental to the construction of fascism.

Chapter 3 looks at the top of the parties, at the Leaders, the most obvious single supposed embodiment of fascism. While this is in a sense the 'top level' of the investigation, it is not simply a top-down perspective. It starts with a short biography of Mussert and Lindholm, essential information on their careers and personalities, so that it can be understood what kind of role they played within their parties, and to what extent the persons in reality contrasted with the myths that were constructed around them. Once their personalities and style of life and work are established, it is shown what authority they possessed within the party, and how they functioned as leaders. The chapter is then devoted to analysing the various mythic constructions of Mussert and Lindholm as Leaders who were made over time, and how they were received by both a sometimes fanatical and devoted rank-and-file hungry for a Leader of mythic proportions, and a more sceptical public and political opponents, which the party machinery sought to appease by more respectable constructions of the leaders. Special attention is paid to the rituals and ceremonies which helped Mussert and Lindholm perform their part – bringing in the crucial performative element into the analysis.

Having analysed the parties as organizations and the key individuals who led them, Chapter 4 moves on to the members who actually composed the movements, the rank-and-file on the streets. This grassroots level shows the manifold and diffuse constructions of fascism, and builds the analysis around the party uniform, and the militaristic myths that attended it. Political uniforms were (and are) ubiquitous in the popular image of fascism, black and brown shirts being as much of an instant identifier of fascists as were symbols like the swastika. Consequently the wearing of a uniform was crucial in the construction of the members as fascists, alongside a number of other mythopoeic props that are also considered (badges, boots, flags and banners, etc.). The uniform functions as the interface for the discussion of a host of related issues that impacted deeply on fascist myth and its relationship to respectability in Sweden and the Netherlands. It was central to a militaristic subculture, which constructed fascism as a kind of army on a crusade to vanquish its enemies, engaged in a sacred struggle against evil. It was also essential in projecting fascism as powerful and capable of combat, which at the same time conflicted heavily with appeals to respectability, as outsiders ended up viewing fascists as violent thugs or a dangerous paramilitary that could start a civil war – a view that was reinforced by legal restrictions on wearing uniforms in public in these countries.

Chapters 5 and 6 draw on the insights and information from the previous three, and will reconsider the themes they introduced, while moving on to a new topic: the party conventions of the NSB and NSAP. Chapter 5 is dedicated to the Swedish 1935 *årsting*, while Chapter 6 investigates the Dutch *landdag* the same year. The usually annual party conventions were a mass meeting of the cadres with their Leader, and designed to be a spectacular manifestation of fascism, thus moving analysis to the holistic construction of a myth of fascism, as opposed to a myth of fascists, parties or Leaders. These rallies were extensively recorded for the benefit of both members and the public, and represent the pinnacle of fascist mythopoeia. Like the uniform, or the figure of the Leader, the rally was another core part of fascism's image in Europe. Aiming to gather together as many of the entire movement in one place, and orchestrate a spectacle of fascist power and unity, they required considerable organization and resources. I emphasize the numerous practical requirements of putting on a performance which constructed fascism in the fantastical register that was intended. The chapters do two things: introduce new themes (spectacle, immersion, aesthetics) and reconsider those of the former chapters in more detail and in a wider context, through a micro-historical analysis. The historical subjects are the two party conventions organized by the NSAP and NSB in 1935, for both of which ample documentation has survived. The latter part of Chapter 6 is devoted precisely to how the spectacles were conveyed to non-fascists, and its efficacy in constructing the desired mythic image of fascism. Press reports from various sources are considered, and contrasted what members' own impressions of the events, to conclude to what extent fascists were successful in projecting their mythic constructions to the public.

1

Sweden and the Netherlands

In retrospect, success for fascism never seemed likely in the states of Sweden and the Netherlands. Compared to countries where fascism gained a significant foothold – Italy, Germany, Austria, Hungary, Romania, et al. – the two minor states of north-western Europe both appear as pictures of stability, peace and democracy. This chapter will sketch out the two countries' political structures and developments that explain this stability, while also providing important qualifications and adjustments to this picture. This starts with the basis of Swedish and Dutch democratic parliamentary government, before moving on to compare their specific historical developments during the First World War, and the interwar period which covers the emergence of fascism in the two countries.

Democracy

In 1918, Sweden and the Netherlands, with small populations of *c*. 6 and 7 million respectively, were small states that tended to stay on the sidelines of European politics. Both had once been great powers in the early modern period, peaking in the sixteenth century, but now found themselves with little power to influence continental developments. Little was left of Sweden's Baltic empire, other than perhaps a domineering disposition towards fellow Scandinavian states, such as Norway which attained independence from Sweden in 1905, or Finland, which still possessed an influential Swedish minority, but had been under Russian rule since 1809, gaining its independence in 1917–18. The Kingdom of the Netherlands bore little resemblance to the United Provinces or the Dutch Republic anymore, possessing a somewhat larger cohering territory in Europe but without the military or naval power. Aside from its Carribean colonies, it did however also control a very important colony in the Dutch Indies (Indonesia), which it maintained until 1949.

Sweden's interwar parliamentary democracy was one which developed gradually over the course of several decades, its history often described as peaceful to the point of tedium.[1] It was the result of a series of compromises between liberals aiming to reduce the power of the executive, and conservative forces keen to maintain traditional, royalist, power structures for as long as feasible.[2] Representation through the four estates in parliament, *riksdagen*, was abolished in 1867, replaced by a bi-cameral parliament that lasted until 1970. While the liberal constitution seriously restricted the power of the monarchy, the king played an active role and held the power to choose the government until the end of the First World War, and retained a political counselling function throughout the interwar period. The franchise was limited to men of income or property, the latter giving a natural advantage to farmers.

The modern state of the Netherlands emerged in the first half of the nineteenth century, with the break-away of Belgium in 1830, leaving the Netherlands with the Catholic provinces of North-Brabant and Limburg. The kingdom's constitution was revised in 1848, when William II of the House of Orange saw the way the wind was blowing and conceded a liberal democratic state.[3] The Dutch parliament, the States General (*Staten-Generaal*), was divided into a lower house, the Second Chamber, fixed at one hundred seats in 1888, and an upper house, the Senate or First Chamber, representing the Provinces with fifty seats. As in Sweden, suffrage was initially limited to men of some wealth, with the liberals working in both countries to expand the franchise over the decades, gradually eliminating checks and limitations, and reducing the role of the monarchy.

In both countries the rise of socialism in the last quarter of the nineteenth century played a significant role in attaining this goal. The Netherlands had already seen syndicalists and other revolutionary socialists emerge in the 1870s, with F. Domela Nieuwenhuis as the first socialist in parliament 1888–91, but the most important development was the formation of the SDAP in 1894 by the parliamentarians, heavily inspired by the Marxist sister party in Germany.[4] In Sweden, socialism likewise came from a German direction. The Swede August Palm, a member of the First International, was banished from Germany in 1877 under Bismarck's *Sozialistengesetze*, and returned to his native Malmö, a growing industrial and commercial city where he started advocating revolution.[5] While the conservatives in parliament reacted with growing anti-socialist repression throughout the 1880s, 1889 saw the founding of *Sveriges socialdemokratiska arbetareparti* (Sweden's Social Democratic Worker's Party, SSAP).

With the socialists' voter base primarily among the poorer working class, they naturally shared the liberals' interest in expanding the franchise. While orthodox Marxists abhorred an alliance with the liberals, reform-minded socialists won out and helped pave a path towards universal suffrage by the end of the First World War. The achievement had detrimental consequences for the liberal parties in both cases, first in the Netherlands already before the First World War, in Sweden in the 1920s, as it undercut most of their power base.

In the Swedish parliament, change was driven by the liberal Folkpartiet (People's Party), which headed most governments until the 1930s. However, its strength was predicated on its support among the middle classes, and the voting reforms it drove through reduced its majority. In 1904 the various conservative groupings in parliament were loosely organized in Almänna valmansförbundet (General Electoral League), commonly referred to simply as Högern (The Right), which actively resisted democratization, not fully accepting representative parliamentary democracy until the early 1930s. While the People's Party had secured 40.2 per cent of the vote in the 1911 elections against the Right's 31.2 per cent, from this moment on the former would be in more or less continuous decline until 1948. The Right had lost a significant amount of its parliamentary support through the voting reforms of 1907 which introduced proportional representation, pushed through by Right leader Arvid Lindman

(1862–1936) in the hope of securing conservative positions in parliament in the face of a rapidly growing socialist movement. The two general elections of 1914 saw the establishment of the Social Democrats as Sweden's largest party, a position it has maintained until the present day.[6]

It is worth elaborating a little further on the parliamentary divisions in the Netherlands here. The Dutch Right was defined by the confessional parties. Most of the politically organized Calvinists of the country had little sympathy for the liberal state, nor did the recently enfranchised Catholic minority, concentrated in the south, symbolically divided from the rest of the country by the Maas river. Throughout the late nineteenth century this led to a confessional organization against the liberals, and later against the socialists, that would last until the Second World War, and which found its primary expression in pillarization (*verzuiling*). The primary issue over which Calvinists and Catholics united against the liberals was the school struggle, specifically the allocation of state funding for schools. Originally funding was designated exclusively for secular state schools, which promoted 'Christian virtues', but not necessarily Calvinist or Catholic doctrine. Throughout the second half of the century the confessional parties worked to equalize funding for their own religious schools, with 1878 marking a point of no return as schools were made more expensive with raised teacher salaries among other things, which non-state schools had to fund themselves.[7]

The school struggle led to the founding of the Anti-Revolutionaire Partij (Anti-Revolutionary Party, ARP) by Abraham Kuyper (1837–1920) in 1879, the first centrally organized political party, uniting the Calvinists. The Christelijk-Historische Unie (Christian-Historical Union) was formed in 1908, which appealed to liberal Calvinists, and tended to resist the aggressive segregation of the Protestants from the state that Kuyper promoted.[8] The Catholics were united under what would eventually become the Roman Catholic State Party. Together they formed what the indomitable Kuyper dubbed the 'Antithesis' (against paganism), which would achieve its goal in the school struggle in 1917 in the Pacification laws, and make up a Christian conservative majority in parliament for the entirety of the interwar period.

The formation of confessional parties and the victory for publicly funded religious schools (and one university, Amsterdam's Calvinist *Vrije Universiteit*) served to sharply enhance pillarization, the political and social segregation of the Netherlands around a few distinct 'pillars': the Catholics, the Protestants and the socialists. Each had their own parties, schools, clubs, newspapers, unions and so forth, and tended to primarily work for and employ people of their own group. Politically, this served on the one hand to stabilize the parliamentary system, while on the other it created a focal point for anti-establishment opposition that threatened democratic legitimacy in the 1920s and 1930s.[9]

The First World War

Sweden and the Netherlands remained neutral throughout the First World War, and managed to avoid most of the violence of the conflict. Coalition emergency governments were formed which maintained the neutrality line in spite of strong pressures, internal and external, to join a side, and national sovereignty was maintained. Without soldiers united by the experience of combat, and the social dislocation following demilitarization, nor a context of large-scale leftist rebellion, these democracies lacked some of the strongest drives for the formation of fascist movements.[10] But Sweden and the Netherlands did not escape the socio-economic disruption of the war,[11] and while they did not produce a class of ex-service men that could provide a ready organizational basis for fascism, there were several political groups that could be sympathetic to a new breed of rightist politics. As the example of the 1918 Finnish Civil War demonstrated, it was possible for a country with virtually no prior combat experience, and a long tradition of strong civic institutions, to rapidly descend into violent factionalism and murderous brutality.[12]

The Netherlands found itself in a particularly exposed position, with the German invasion of Belgium happening close enough for curious Dutch citizens to witness the fighting from the border. The 1913 cabinet of the independent liberal P.W.A. Cort van der Linden (1846–1935) – the last liberal prime minister until 2010 – remained in power until September 1918, although it was always a minority government supported by the CHU and only at times the ARP. Already in 1905 Queen Wilhelmina, by no means content to be simply a ceremonial figurehead, had concluded that in any conflict the country ought to remain strictly neutral between the Great Powers.[13] The Dutch refusal to block supplies from reaching Germany soon incurred the anger of Britain however, leading to a temporary blockade of the country. While the Allies and the Netherlands eventually arrived at a compromise, the Netherlands could not avoid shortages and rationing by the end of the war.[14] While Dutch cabinets throughout the previous decades had pursued classic liberal economic policies, the war saw sudden and heavy intervention in the economy to maintain production and welfare, not to everyone's satisfaction.[15] At the same time hundreds of thousands of Belgian refugees entered the country fleeing the conflict.

Internally the country was divided. The old interpretation that the neutral Netherlands was socially and culturally isolated from the rest of Europe to the point of indifference no longer rings true. Broadly the mood was one of fear and insecurity, although the military mobilization to secure the borders stimulated a small degree of war enthusiasm as well, with a handful enlisting in foreign armies.[16] While the necessity of neutrality was rarely contested, there was a powerful undercurrent of shame and resentment of Dutch powerlessness, its military weakness, and inability to live up to its former status as a great imperial power. News of (German) massacres and atrocities gave a powerful boost to pacifism, but there was also a great deal of admiration for the power of the German military machine, and even defence of Germany's invasion of Belgium and Luxembourg (including from Kuyper).[17]

Sweden, although its sympathies were even more one-sidedly with Germany, also retained a strictly neutral government. The so-called 'courtyard government' of Hjalmar Hammarskjöld (1862–1953) established in February 1914, independent but conservative and royalist, remained in power, and a parliamentary pact of unity maintained support among the parties. Hammarskjöld was derided by his opponents for his inflexible and formalistic approach to neutrality which also landed Sweden in trouble with the Allies, causing shortages there as in the Netherlands when Britain blocked supply deliveries. Hammarskjöld was accused of despotic government, and in 1917 he was forced to resign, leaving government in the hands of the moderate conservative Carl Swartz (1858–1926).

Many conservatives, including King Gustav V, were highly pro-German in their politics, while Germany itself agitated for an alliance with Sweden, including via the tabloid *Aftonbladet* (Evening Paper), in which it had bought majority shares. The Left was generally on the side of the Allies, though pro-German attitudes were also present among the Social Democrats.[18] Circa seventy Swedes volunteered to fight in the German imperial army, including several future fascists.[19]

Thus, while the two states managed to remain neutral throughout the war, their governments were often under fire, the countries politically divided. Both the Netherlands and Sweden suffered economically from the war, especially due to the loss of trade with Germany, and the Netherlands had enormous debts by 1919.[20] Sweden got into conflict with Britain over its exports of iron ore and foodstuffs to Germany; in 1917 Hammarskjöld's government had to introduce rationing.[21] As bread prices on the black market rocketed, riots broke out, which were suppressed by the police and military. The revolutionary atmosphere in neighbouring Russia proved infectious, and a break-away faction from the SSAP, led by Zeth Höglund, made calls for a soviet republic in Sweden. In the Netherlands Cort van der Linden had created a myriad of crisis committees to arrange rationing, which maintained a semblance of order while criticism of the government grew. At the end of the war the Dutch army was in a state of unrest to the point of open rebellion, encouraging the government to speed up demobilization. In light of socialist uprisings in Germany, the Dutch cabinet considered making concessions to the socialists at home.[22] By mid-November 1918 this encouraged SDAP leader Pieter Troelstra to take the opportunity to call for revolution. Troelstra discussed the formation of workers' and soldiers' soviets to replace the government, but found there was insufficient support and the momentum petered out, an episode commonly dubbed 'Troelstra's mistake'.[23]

In Sweden, after the 1917 elections saw the loss of further seats for the Conservatives, the King failed to negotiate a coalition government, and was ultimately forced to appoint Liberal leader Nils Edén as prime minister of a Liberal–Social Democratic government, who forced through the constitutionalization of the monarchy. In the wake of the Russian Revolution and the November Revolution a year later in Germany, the Conservatives supported electoral reforms, intimidated by the revolutionary atmosphere, which included Social Democratic demonstrations in the wake of the German upheaval.[24] The plan to push through women's suffrage was included in the government's proposal, but was limited to a right to vote in municipal elections. Women were emancipated from male guardianship in 1920, while full suffrage was only granted in 1921.[25] In the Netherlands universal suffrage and a compulsory vote were introduced in 1918, with proportional representation for the Second Chamber. The contentious school question was also settled in 1917.[26] As in Sweden, one of the immediate consequences was the decline of the Liberal Party, and the growth of the SDAP into the second largest party in parliament. However, Troelstra's mistake gave the confessional Right an excuse to avoid collaboration with the Left, while the Catholic party had grown to be the largest party in parliament, and the fundament for all interwar governments. The bishops had in any case prohibited cooperating with socialists bar in a situation of 'extreme necessity'.[27]

An important footnote to Swedish neutrality and the rapid but peaceful democratic reform process is the civil war in Finland that broke out in January 1918. Following the 1917 February Revolution in Russia, the movement for Finnish independence had gained new life, further encouraged by the Bolsheviks' support. However, the Russian Provisional Government dissolved the Finnish parliament that had given the Social Democrats a majority, and called for new elections, which gave a slim majority to the Right. With the waves of strikes that had started in the summer, and the Social Democrats embittered by the Right's parliamentary tactics, the Finnish political situation became increasingly polarized. The November Revolution that set off the Russian Civil War took the initiative out of the hands of the Social Democrats' parliamentary wing, and handed it to the revolutionary factions. At the same time the massive growth of White protection corps around the country against this background encouraged the formation of more paramilitary Red guards, making armed confrontation increasingly likely. By the end of January 1918 tensions broke out into civil war, as General Gustav Mannerheim was ordered to quash the Red rebellion.[28] On 20 February 1918 the Swedish government declared its neutrality in the Finnish Civil War that had broken out at the end of the previous month, to the dismay of the Swedish Right. While hopes for intervention on the side of the White government in Vasa were dashed, circa 1000 volunteers were permitted to cross the border and serve in General Mannerheim's White Army.[29] At the same time the government covertly supported White Finland with armaments and other resources.[30] The volunteers included a high number of Swedish officers, which created the backbone of the Finnish army, but also an all-Swedish volunteer unit, the so-called Swedish Brigade (*svenska brigaden*).[31] While much of the bourgeois (*borgerlig*) press in Sweden reported with some enthusiasm and even pride on the volunteer unit, socialist papers were unsurprisingly less keen on the soldiers seen to embody the hopes and goals of the Right. Upon their return to Sweden in May 1918, many workers from the Swedish Brigade found that they had been anathematized by the trade unions, who condemned the cold-blooded killing of the 'members of brother organizations'.[32]

Few, if any, Dutch men managed to find their way into the rightist militaries that roamed central-eastern Europe in this period, but many did serve in the civil militias that were spawned in response to Troelstra's call for revolution.[33] These paramilitary groups were formed on local initiative in 1918 in the major cities, to defend against 'revolutionary turmoil'. They were soon put under state control, but were distinctly right-wing, and included the Reformed Cornelis van Geelkerken (1901–76), later co-founder of the NSB.[34] Like van Geelkerken, many militia men came from an ultra conservative religious background, and combined nationalist sentiment with a powerful fear of atheist socialism.

The two countries managed to avoid the extreme ends of disorder and violence at the end of the war, and in both cases Liberal parties managed to push through electoral reforms, which would characterize the politics of the interwar period. However, to portray the Netherlands and Sweden as 'islands of peace' during the war or after misses the significant degree of political polarization that had taken place and which in fact in some cases actually drove democratic reform. Hopes for and fears of revolution emerged there in response to events in Russia, Germany and Finland, either pushing conservatives on the defensive as in Sweden, or on the offensive as in the Netherlands. It also brought out the potential for violent political conflict in these smaller neutral states, even if it either petered out or found its outlet in foreign wars. While neutrality made the experience of the First World War vastly different for these countries in comparison to the direct participants, the Swedes and Dutch were nevertheless inextricably entangled with developments on the European continent. The war demonstrated this amply, and it would remain a fact of the interwar period for both countries, even if they did at times understand themselves or take an interest in promoting their states as peaceful, modern and democratic havens of tranquility.

The Dutch interbellum

With the end of the First World War a new era of mass democracy began. The voting reforms of 1917 in the Netherlands had produced a representational parliamentary system with compulsory voting based on a franchise including men and women regardless of property. There was no threshold for entry in the Second Chamber. This resulted quickly enough in the entry of a host of small narrow interest parties into politics during this period, many of which only ever briefly held one seat in parliament. However, some of these, such as the Calvinist splinter parties, would be able to put significant pressure on their larger counterparts.[35] Concurrently with the entry of the mass of the population into political engagement was the maturity of media and especially newspaper culture.

Some of the most important trendsetting newspapers of the Netherlands were already decades old, including the liberal *Nieuwe Rotterdamsche Courant* (New Rotterdam Newspaper, NRC) since 1843, the Catholic *Maasbode* since 1868, Abraham Kuyper's Calvinist *De Standaard* (The Standard (of the Word of God)) since 1870 and the socialist *Het Volk* (The People) since 1900. In the interwar period many of these papers grew to tens of thousands of subscribers, making this a time dominated by the national daily, as 38 per cent of all papers in the Netherlands had national coverage, while 96 per cent of all households subscribed to a daily paper.[36] This newspaper culture was also crucial to pillarization, as it not only formed a united picture of the news across the nation, transcending regional divisions, but also divided the nation by confession and ideology.[37]

Not only a time of maturity for older forms of media and communication, the era also witnessed new forms of political propaganda, in the Netherlands as in the rest of Europe. For the first time the country saw political mass meetings and marches, bringing politics to the streets in new ways and a new scale. While the national socialists would be best known for their political spectacles and rallies in the 1930s, the SDAP was already in the 1920s engaged in similar forms of ritualized mass political meetings.[38] Similarly the Catholics, no strangers to ritual, took to public processions and elaborately choreographed rallies in colourful uniforms to spread the word. Most eye-catching was perhaps Jacques van Ginneken's Grail Movement (*De Graal*), which also deployed technology such as film cameras to capture the performances of the young Catholic girls' organization.[39] The spread of film and photography, the relatively easy access to mass printing, and the new mass basis of democracy and national politics defined the face and form of Dutch politics in this period.

Meanwhile the Dutch economy was slowly recovering from the damage of the war, and remained very stable throughout the decade. Women generally remained outside of the labour market, something that would not change significantly until the 1970s, while labour unrest was at a minimum. Pillarization is generally held responsible for this stability, establishing and maintaining powerful social norms and labour discipline within each community. The economy retained its traditional 'open' character, which with low tariffs and low wages made the Netherlands something of an entrepreneurial haven.[40] The Dutch Indies provided a significant boost to national wealth, although it is important to note that the Netherlands' economic reliance on the great colony was actually gradually and significantly reduced over these years.[41]

While pillarization was an important factor in social and economic stability, in parliament the picture was more fraught. The war, which saw the erection of a several miles long electric fence along the southern border, separated the Catholic provinces of Limburg and North-Brabant from Belgium, which resulted in closer integration with the rest of the Netherlands. This undermined the widely held view of the Netherlands as a Protestant nation, key proponents of which included Queen Wilhelmina, who played an important role in the cabinet formations of the 1920s.[42] The new mass politics now heavily reinforced the RKSP's position as the largest party of the Netherlands,[43] consistently gaining around 30 per cent of the vote throughout the period.[44] September 1918 saw the first cabinet ever to be led by a Catholic prime minister, Charles Ruijs de Beerenbrouck (1873–1936), who would remain a commanding presence in the lower house for much of the interbellum. The RSKP was the basis for all governments in the 1920s and 1930s, which would without exception be of the Right.

The SDAP nevertheless became a significant force in Dutch politics in this period, as the new franchise made it easily the second largest party in parliament, with about a quarter of the electorate behind it. Since Troelstra's attempted revolution in 1918 the SDAP was held in suspicion by the Right, excluding it from government until 1939, with the Calvinist parties in particular having little sympathy for the socialists' policies. The persistent exclusion of such a large party created considerable headaches in the numerous cabinet formations of the period however, especially since the SDAP and RKSP actually saw eye-to-eye on many issues. The Catholic doctrine of cooperation only in times of 'utter necessity' already foresaw that the situation would become untenable.[45]

While the RKSP tried to maintain internal unity over the parliamentary alliances, the Protestants were already divided, further complicating the matter. Since the early twentieth century the CHU had split itself off from the ARP in protest against its sharp segregation of the Protestants in the nation, preferring cooperation with the Liberals and maintaining a vision of a Protestant Netherlands. At the same time many Calvinists were unhappy with ARP and CHU cooperation with the Catholics after the school struggle. Further splinter parties were formed from both of them, in the form of the orthodox Calvinist Staatkundig Gereformeerde Partij (State Reformed Party,

SGP) and the unitary *Hervormde-Gereformeerde Staatspartij* (Reformed-Reformed State Party, HGS) which entered parliament in 1922 and 1925, respectively.[46] Pillarization was clear-cut in the case of the Catholic and socialist pillars, but the Calvinists make for a muddled picture. Aside from theological differences in the Dutch Protestant churches since the nineteenth century, parliamentary alliances highlight the considerable political disagreements among Calvinists which brought Kuyper's Antithesis to breaking point. The symbolic endpoint came in 1925, when the SGP and HGS managed to force through an amendment to withdraw Dutch representation (*gezantschap*) at the Vatican, forcing the Catholic-led cabinet to resign.[47]

With the definitive end of liberal rule in the States General and the end of the school struggle with the Pacification of 1917, the parliamentary arithmetic of cabinet formations had become fraught indeed. From 1918 to 1929, parliament saw cabinets continuously being dissolved and reformed, often requiring royal intervention. The last cabinet of the decade was an extra-parliamentary one on orders of Wilhemina, led by CHU leader Dirk Jan de Geer (1870-1960), which was intended as an intermezzo government, but simply maintained the status quo from 1926 to 1929, containing predominantly Calvinist, Catholic and liberal ministers.[48] The end of the school struggle had brought out the old enmities between Catholic and Protestant politicians, while the Calvinists were divided amongst themselves over the phenomenon of pillarization, a term first coined in the 1930s. Cooperation with socialists remained anathema for the Right, even though the reformist Social Democrats were a natural ally for Catholic politicians influenced by the social elements of the papal encyclical *Rerum Novarum*, and later *Quadregesimo Anno*.[49] The liberals were too weak, and themselves divided, to help create a majority government. The power of the Right had been evident in their reforms of the liberal state system, but after that they had become once more sharply divided by their obvious differences.[50]

This was a key part of what some Dutch historians have termed the 'small crisis of democracy', marked by a fractious parliament and unstable governments, and still pervasive scepticism towards the new mass democracy.[51] In the second half of the interwar period, while national government stabilized somewhat, it also saw the emergence of anti-democratic movements, not least the NSB, as well as certain authoritarian tendencies in ARP Prime Minister Hendrik Colijn (1869-1944). These were all at least partially symptomatic of the drawn out economic depression in the Netherlands, which kept unemployment in the hundreds of thousands throughout most of the 1930s, aggravated by the retention of the gold standard until the very end.

The Netherlands was hit by the Great Depression in 1931, when Britain left the gold standard and Germany, the Netherlands' largest trading partner, introduced foreign exchange controls. The country's open economy had already caused trouble for the agricultural sector, not unlike in Sweden, with the import of cheap grain from the United States, but the economy at large remained stable until that point.[52] Unemployment remained low compared to other European countries for a while, but then peaked severely much later, in 1936 at about 630,000, or 23.5 per cent.[53] The exchange rate of the guilder remained very high, depressing exports, since the Dutch Central Bank possessed large gold reserves, and could maintain the value without effort. Maintaining the gold standard and the government's consequent deflationary measures aggravated the sluggish economy in the 1930s, but to Colijn the gold standard was not just an economic imperative, but a moral one. In September 1936 his cabinet finally devalued the guilder, the last country in Europe to relinquish the gold standard, mere hours after Switzerland, as the Gold Bloc collapsed.[54]

Needless to say Colijn's regime came under heavy fire for its management of the crisis, but he managed to remain in power from 1933 to 1939. While the NSB as well as the communists made the most of this crisis of capitalism and popular discontent to propagate their politics, colonial army veteran Colijn – successor to the titanic Kuyper – quite successfully forged an image as a powerful, masculine, statesman, unafraid to take tough measures.[55] There is also evidence he briefly considered taking an authoritarian direction, inspired by examples such as Mussolini, including changes to the constitution to allow authorities to curtail civil rights more easily.[56] A symbolic moment came in January 1933 with a mutiny at the large Dutch battleship *Zeven Provinciën* (Seven Provinces), when the predominantly Indonesian crew protested reduced salaries and the arrest of strikers.[57] Colijn's government threatened the mutineers with bombing the ship if they did not surrender, something that was actually realized when the bomb that was intended as a warning signal accidentally hit the vessel, earning the prime minister the lasting nick-name 'Torpedo-Colijn'. In the Netherlands itself the event had a polarizing effect, as communists supported the mutiny (which did not have any actual Marxist inspiration), in turn leading liberals and the Right to fear a more general crisis of authority and the state.[58] Colijn's unapologetic stance and position as a natural leader of the hard Right made him popular among many voters outside of the Calvinist pillar, while some groups even made extensive, if ludicrous, plans to install him as head of a fascist state.[59]

While Dutch interwar government under Colijn in particular had a rather equivocal attitude towards parliamentary democracy, and approved of authoritarian measures against socialists, it had a distinctly ambivalent attitude towards fascism. The German Nazis' struggle with the churches made a bad impression on most of the Dutch Right, while anti-Semitism was a political taboo, naturally avoided by any respectable Dutch politician.[60] Dutch Jews, a community of over 100,000, *c.* 1.5 per cent of the population, were well-integrated into Dutch society, generally urban and socially diverse. While anti-Semitic attitudes definitely existed among the Gentile population, it was essentially unrespectable (*onfatsoenlijk*), and clashed with the Dutch self-image as a historically tolerant nation.[61] Indeed the ARP, also in response to the NSB's anti-Semitism in the later 1930s, marked protection of the Jews from injustice as an urgent demand of a Christian politics.[62] Conversely it must be noted that a few years later the Dutch administration was strikingly obedient and efficient in collaboration with the Nazi authorities during the Occupation. Bureaucrats and police forces registered, rounded up and deported the Dutch Jews to certain death with limited resistance from the general population (the 1941 February Strike being a notable exception as a protest against Nazi Jewish policy)[63] ultimately murdering over 70 per cent of the national Jewish community, also with extensive help from NSB collaborators.[64]

There existed clear venues for a violent and repressive radical Right politics, and some kind of fascism, during the 1930s in particular. The abiding authority of

Prime Minister Colijn, a former colonial army lieutenant who had served in General Joannes Van Heutsz's vicious scorched earth pacification of Aceh at the turn of the century,[65] shows there was popular support for authoritarian measures centred on the maintenance of the empire. Ethan Mark has argued, most recently in his study of the several Dutch interwar monuments to Van Heutsz, that the global crisis of empire that threatened the Dutch East Indies translated into significant support for fascism, especially at the imperial frontline among opponents of the so-called 'ethical politics' which aimed to gradually grant Indonesia independence. The 1920s saw small nationalist organizations in Indonesia formed after Mussolini's example, such as the Verbond Nederland en Indië (Netherlands and Indies Union) in 1923. More influential was the Vaderlandsche Club (Fatherland Club, VC) in 1929, opposing the Governor-General's moderate rule of the colonies, as well as Indonesian nationalism and communism. The month the NSB was formed, December 1931, also saw the formation of the Nederlandsch Indische Fascisten Organisatie (Dutch Indies Fascist Organization, NIFO), which gained a considerable boost after the *Zeven Provinciën* incident, particularly from VC members.[66] The NSB enjoyed greater support in the Indies than any other party, for whom the NSB promised a bulwark against the threat of anti-colonialism to their privileges. This was particularly true of the Indo-European community, which constituted *c.* 70 per cent of NSB membership in Indonesia – like NIFO, the NSB considered itself a non-racist organization. This changed in the second half of the decade however, as the *volkse* party faction gained more influence, and turned against the Indo-Europeans (undermining its Indonesian support base in the process), excluding them from the party in 1938. Regardless Mussert was insistent throughout the decade that the heart of the fascist struggle was in the Netherlands, not its colonies, which played a supporting role.

Smaller fascist groups had already emerged in the early 1920s. The first were the group of Catholic intellectuals around the *Katholieke Staatkunde* periodical edited by Emile Verviers, which was initially a rather conservative paper in the anti-modernist tradition of Pius X, but which started to take a new political direction after the March on Rome.[67] The group never grew beyond the periodical, not least because it incurred the displeasure of the bishops.[68] The decade did see the rapid emergence and dissolution of a number of other fascist parties: particularly the Verbond van Actualisten (League of Actualists) in 1923, led by Sinclair de Rochemont, and briefly supported by Verviers, but it disappeared in 1925 when it was cut off from the funds supplied by the millionaire Alfred Haighton.[69] Figures like Sinclair and Haighton would continue to quarrel through a number of other fascist parties throughout the decade, but attracted fairly little attention, and achieved less.

The key moment for the rise of fascism in the Netherlands unexpectedly turned out to be the 'Belgian Treaty', first mentioned in 1925, which occasioned a nationalist outcry, and created the necessary pressure for radical Right organization, particularly beyond a confessional politics. The treaty would allow Belgian access to the Moerdijk canal via Antwerp, and, supported by France, the right to pass through the canal with battle ships if necessary. Nationalists decried this 'Belgian Versailles', impinging on Dutch sovereignty; at their head was a nationalist civil engineer, the young Utrecht Chief of Water Management, Anton Mussert. The treaty was abandoned under the pressure, and momentarily brought Mussert into the political limelight, which would eventually lead him to successfully found his own party, the NSB, in 1931.[70]

The NSB railed against divisive social-confessional structures, and pleaded for an organic national unity, attracting that remnant of Dutch society which fell outside the pillars, typically including many former liberals. Unlike the fascist parties of the 1920s, or the new rivals including the faction-prone and radically Germanophile Nationaal-Socialistische Nederlandsche Arbeiders Partij (Dutch National Socialist Workers' Party, NSNAP) parties (they were distinctly prone to splitting), the NSB enjoyed a meteoric rise in the first half of the 1930s. The provincial elections for the Senate gave the NSB a very impressive 7.94 per cent of the vote, a result not equaled by any newcomer party on the Dutch political scene until the twenty-first century. The general elections of 1937 however demonstrated that the NSB's momentum had already petered out, almost halving the vote it had attained two years prior. All the same the NSB contributed to the sense of a crisis for Dutch democracy, and appeared a serious threat to national government from 1933 to 1937, with the growth of the national socialists continually under discussion by the government from 1934 onwards.[71] It must be borne in mind that unlike in Sweden, the NSB was a real threat to the governing parties, quickly surpassing the Protestant Right in terms of membership numbers, while partially occupying the same space on the Right, especially where Protestants opposed pillarization.

But while the Swedish government, led by the Social Democrats, could afford to largely ignore the little fascist groups, Dutch Right governments took firm action in the form of various repressive counter measures, not exclusively aimed at the NSB, but certainly fueled by its growth. Political uniforms in public were banned in 1933. Paramilitary organizations such as the NSB's Weerafdeling (Defence Department, WA) followed in 1936 though the law was technically not passed until 1939. Parliament enacted legislation banning members of revolutionary organizations from being part of civil militias, the army and then the civil service.[72] While Mussert initially managed to convince Colijn not to put the NSB on the proscribed list, the latter soon changed his mind. In May 1934 Mussert himself was forced out of his job as Chief Engineer. Attitudes towards the NSB were also heavily influenced by actions of the Nazi state over the border in Germany, not least Hitler's attitudes towards the Protestant and Catholic churches of Germany, which caused boundless irritation in the Netherlands.[73] Early in 1934 the Catholic pillar shored up its stance against fascism, when the episcopacy issued a pastoral letter warning against the dangers of fascist parties, and the year after threatened to withhold the sacraments from whoever offered significant support to the NSB. The pastoral letter, *Salvation in the Lord*, issued on 2 February 1934, speaks volumes on contemporary perceptions of Mussert and the NSB, as well as how perceptions of German nazism informed views of indigenous fascists:

> It is difficult to discern in how far various fascist or national socialist currents accept the 'total state' […] but sooner or later they will certainly end up under this influence of the deification of the state or nation. The great intellectual currents of global developments usually influence each other in irresistible ways … […] A certain moderation on the part of the leadership is … not the slightest security for

the future development of a movement. [...] Moreover, it is more than likely that every fascism and national socialism in the Netherlands will in the long run be controlled by a group of people, who largely do not share our world view.[74]

Relations between the Netherlands and Nazi Germany were tense for the entire decade; Hitler's government regularly complained about criticism of the Nazi state and pushed the Dutch government to restrain the Left especially. Ironically, while Germany's actions and interference reflected negatively on the NSB, German attitudes towards the party were also highly negative, particularly about Mussert who was perceived as bourgeois and Jew-friendly.[75] The invasion of the Netherlands on 10 May 1940 finally transformed German Nazi tactics towards the country from intimidation to outright coercion, while it ultimately enthroned the NSB as key collaborator.

The Swedish interbellum

In reaction to events on the European mainland, Sweden too entered a new era of mass democracy with the end of the First World War. With the appointment of the Liberal Nils Edén as prime minister and the constitutionalization of the monarchy, voting reforms were pushed ahead. After a committee had modified the government proposal with a number of conservative checks (voting age raised from twenty-one to twenty-three, exclusion of those who had not paid municipal tax in three years, proportional representation in the First Chamber, etc.), the constitution was changed with support of a large parliamentary majority in December 1918. Women were emancipated from male guardianship in 1920, while formal equality was finally assumed only in 1921, partially due to consciousness of lagging behind other Nordic countries.[76]

Unlike in the Netherlands, the new mass democracy did not go hand in hand with a strong newspaper culture or other nationally shared forms of mass communication. Access to radio was still very limited until about 1937, and newspapers were read less, with very few papers seeing national distribution. The largest paper by far was the liberal independent *Dagens Nyheter* (The Daily News), with several hundred thousand readers in the interwar period. A close rival was *Svenska Dagbladet* (The Swedish Daily) as well as *Stockholms-Tidningen* (The Stockholm Newspaper) papers which saw rapid growth in the early twentieth century thanks to new modern printing presses. One innovation to change the Swedish news landscape in this era was the tabloid, which gained a particularly strong foothold in the capital, with the hard Right *Aftonbladet* at the forefront, printing some 160,000 copies daily.[77] It is a striking contrast with the Netherlands that all of these papers were independent, and that most of the party political press had a far smaller spread and narrower distribution, reflecting a politically far less polarized and less segregated population, but also significantly more regionalized.

Economically the 1920s were notable for the depression in the aftermath of war, with high levels of unemployment, reduced exports and declining prices. Swedish industry quickly recovered after 1922, though the agricultural sector did not. Sweden was the first European state to return to the gold standard.[78] Industries were quickly modernized as the state took over old companies relying on outdated technologies, while Left and Right governments both promoted ties between the state and the industrial business world, taking a close interest in economic planning and scientific management, but mistrustful of big business and excessive capital concentration. This time was even regarded as the industrial equivalent of Sweden's early modern Golden Age.[79] The Swedish Lantsorganisationen (Trade Union Confederation, lit. The Country Organization, LO), closely tied to the SSAP, aimed principally for peaceful coexistence with capitalism, and promoted compromise and cooperation with employers.[80] The latter half of the decade witnessed the rapid growth of industry and rises in workers' living standards, while farmers' lagged behind.[81] By 1930 trade and industry employed 50 per cent of the population, the agricultural and forest industries employed only 38 per cent, down from 50 per cent in 1900, and 44 per cent in 1920.[82] It is also important to note that in sharp distinction to the Netherlands, which saw exceptionally high levels of labour discipline in spite of low wages, Sweden's interbellum was marked by large labour conflicts. Already in 1909 LO had organized a general strike in Sweden in response to the Sveriges Arbetsgivareförening (Sweden's Employers' Association, SAF) lockout, in a year-long battle that ultimately defeated the trade unions in 1910. But LO had recovered both members and confidence in the interwar period, and Sweden continued to see industrial unrest until the Second World War, partially due to communist agitation.[83]

The Swedish political landscape was reorganized in the following decade, reflecting the decline of the Liberal Party and the rise of the Social Democrats. The previous opposition between conservatism and liberal progressivism gave way to a conflict between socialism and bourgeois conservatism. The Right maintained 24–29 per cent of the popular vote, while the Social Democrats continued to gain support, c. 30–41 per cent. The period 1920–33 was a period of brief minority governments, as cooperation between Socialists and Liberals broke down, while Folkpartiet split into two parties (the Liberal Party and the Free-Minded National Association) over the 1923 Prohibition Referendum.[84] The year 1921 also brought the creation of the conservative nationalist Agrarian League, and the Swedish Communist Party, which soon split into *Sillénkommunisterna*, loyal to Moscow, and the independent *Kilbomskommunister*, led by Nils Flyg.[85] Carl Gustaf Ekman's (1872–1945) *frisinnade* (free-minded) Liberals managed to play an influential role during this period, tipping the parliamentary scales in its favour. For instance it was Ekman who ensured the socialist government of Hjalmar Branting's successor, Per Albin Hansson (1885–1946), could push through military spending cuts in 1925, albeit in moderated form.[86]

Military spending was already a source of national controversy before the war, and one of the defining issues between Left and Right. Sweden saw extensive debate about military security, underpinned by long-running fears of the neighbouring Russian Empire, sustained by the close cultural ties which Sweden held with Finland.[87] The 1911 Socialist-Liberal government of Karl Staaff (1860–1915) opposed extensive military spending, much to the dismay of the king and nationalist circles. In 1912 *Ett Varningsord* (A Word of Warning) was published by the famous explorer Sven Hedin, a highly Russophobic tract which was distributed in over one million copies. That year conservative groups campaigned to privately fund an F-class battle ship for the

Swedish navy, with remarkable popular success. Debate came to a head during the so-called Courtyard Crisis (*borggårdskrisen*) in February 1914, when 30,000 farmers marched on the capital to express support for increased defence spending and Gustaf V, who headed the opposition to Staaff with the encouragement of Queen Victoria. In a speech written by Sven Hedin, Gustaf V directly opposed government policy, and referred to the army and navy as 'my army' and 'my navy', triggering a constitutional crisis and the government's resignation. Hence the 1925 cuts, which forcibly retired numerous soldiers and officers, caused consternation among the Right, and indirectly led to the formation of the Swedish Fascist Party.

The 1928 general election brought the Left-Right conflict to a head, in a contest commonly nicknamed the 'Cossack Election' after the Right's fear-mongering strategy. The SSAP and communist party formed an electoral alliance under the name of the Workers' Party, prompting the Right to stoke fears of Bolshevism. The Right party's youth organization, Sveriges Nationella Ungdomsförbund (Sweden's National Youth League, SNU), a rather more radically anti-democratic organization than the mother party, was particularly vociferous in equating Swedish socialists with barbaric, Asiatic Bolsheviks bringing death and ruin. An entirely representative example of SNU propaganda warned against the decay of society and end of the family, illustrated with racist stereotypes of Bolsheviks at a slave auction for white Swedish women. The election resulted in a conservative government under Arvid Lindman.[88] Some historians have also explained this by suggesting Scandinavia was too heavily composed of lower middle-class traders and small farmers to be particularly comfortable with Marxists categories of capitalist exploiters and proletarians.[89] The years after the 1928 election saw a moderating shift on the part of the Social Democrats towards a more inclusive rhetoric, epitomized by Per Albin Hansson's notion of *folkhemmet* (The People's Home).[90]

While the 1920s were still a time of parliamentary uncertainty, with several shifts between the Left and Right as Sweden adapted to the new democratic system, the 1930s saw the formation of a strong and lasting Social Democratic regime. Sweden did not escape the Great Depression, but it was comparatively mild, and after the SSAP's poor results in 1928, decisively handed the initiative to the Socialists. Sweden was one of the first countries to leave the gold standard. The social democrats secured 41.7 per cent of the vote in the general elections of 1932, negotiated a deal with the Agrarian League, allowing Per Albin Hansson to form a majority government by compromising with a key player of the Right.[91] This was the famous *kohandeln* (horse trading), which formed the basis of government for most of the decade, and allowed firm government intervention in the Swedish economy. Whether SSAP economic policies and *kohandeln* indeed brought Sweden out of the Depression remains up for debate, but it did wonders for the Social Democrats' reputation and popularity.[92] Under the Minister of Finance's explicitly Keynesian economic programme unemployment was virtually eradicated, the economy prospered once more – not least the metal industry, which benefited from rearmament in Germany – while agriculture experienced the advantages of the Agrarian League's protectionist policies and mechanization.[93]

During this period the SSAP vote increased from 37 per cent in 1928 to 45.9 per cent in 1936, peaked at 53.8 per cent in 1940 (and thereafter remained firmly at about

40 per cent until the 1990s). Membership of the Social Democrats more than doubled in the 1930s, from 227,000 in 1930 to over 487,000 in 1940.[94] The SSAP was already a reformist rather than a revolutionary party by the end of the First World War. The 1920 party congress still had distinct Marxist overtones, and during the 1920s there were still communist elements in the party that opposed Branting's and Hansson's moderate party line. These were primarily led by Zeth Höglund (1884–1956), who had split off from the SSAP to form the aforementioned Swedish Communist Party which itself immediately split in two. Höglund rejoined the Social Democrats in 1926, but remained a convinced communist.[95] But over the interwar period the SSAP shed more and more of its Marxist thinking and rhetoric, and particularly after the Cossack elections aimed to appeal to all Swedes regardless of social status, with the promise to create a prosperous and fair society inclusive of private businesses, which looked after all vulnerable Swedes. The alliance with the Agrarian League was one product of this strategy, even if the League itself was divided and ambivalent about its socialist allies.

To negotiate the alliance the Social Democrats had reached out to Axel Pehrsson-Bramstorp (1883–1954) over the head of the party leader Olof Olsson i Kullenbergstorp (1859–1934), who died shortly after. The Agrarian League typically held around 14 per cent of the vote. While the League was generally of a conservative bent, and possessed many nationalist, and even fascist, elements, Pehrsson-Bramstorp hedged his bets against the bourgeois Right, and traded support for far-reaching social protections for some moderation of those measures and extensive market protections for farmers and the timber industry. Tensions and disagreements remained however, especially over the military defence budget, which led Hansson's government to resign in June 1936, shortly before the general elections. Pehrsson-Bramstorp's replacement League cabinet proved extremely short-lived. Many of the ministers proved resoundingly unqualified for their posts, while parliament was not in attendance during the summer, so very little was accomplished. The Social Democrats' election campaign as an opposition party turned out highly successful, and in September Hansson formed a new government, again with the League as a junior partner, relegating the Pehrsson-Bramstorp cabinet to history as the 'holiday government'.[96]

The League was uncertain whether to join the second Hansson cabinet, but ultimately agreed to secure continued control over the agriculture portfolio, in return for supporting the Social Democrats' plans for building the welfare state. Apart from majority support in *riksdagen*, the welfare plans were buoyed by a rapidly recovering economy, as noted partially helped along by Nazi Germany's rearmament.[97] The interwar period in Sweden was thus characterized by the steady growth of the Social Democrats, with shifts in government in the 1920s, but in the 1930s showing a decisive trend of a sharply declining Right under a vigorous Social Democratic regime. In contrast to Colijn in the Netherlands, any authoritarian tendencies were discouraged in the Right, which ousted its youth movement when it overtly turned to fascism in the early 1930s.

Fascism in Sweden did not in any way buck this trend. That being said, there were several disturbing political patterns and tendencies in Swedish interwar politics which make for a darker picture – the country was by no means 'immune' to fascism.[98] Some degree of anti-Semitism was ubiquitous among nationalists (*nationella*), by no means just fascists, even if the Swedish Jewish population was very small.[99] Overt racism was to be found on both the Left and Right, while eugenics was supported by various Swedish governments. A state eugenics institute, Rasbiologiska institutet (Institute for Racial Biology) was founded in 1922 in Uppsala, first led by Herman Lundborg (1868–1943). He and several of the institute's most influential scientists had extensive ties to Germany, and came to play an important role in contributing to and supporting Nazi German biopolitics in the next decade.[100] In 1933 the Swedish government enacted coercive sterilization laws which affected tens of thousands of (primarily women, working-class) victims, in the service of the Social Democrats' social eugenics agenda, which also specifically targeted the Roma population.[101] At the end of the 1930s Swedish university students – not least in Lund – protested against Jewish refugees from Germany entering the country, encouraged by fascist campaigns like those of the NSAP/SSS.[102] There existed a highly established indigenous right-wing intellectual tradition, with figures like the political scientist Rudolf Kjellén, who coined the term 'geopolitics', informing later Nazi ideas in Germany.[103] Overtly fascist and other radical Right organizations had sympathizers in high places, not least academia and the military where reactionary and Germanophile attitudes abounded,[104] which could hand the radical Right undue influence.[105]

Fascist groups emerged in the early 1920s, and failed to make significant gains with the electorate, never succeeding to emulate the rapid rise of the Dutch NSB. In Sweden the first fascist group was thus a limited affair, in the form of the Svenska Nationalsocialistiska Frihetsförbundet (Swedish National Socialist Freedom League, SNFF) founded in 1924 by the Furugård brothers, Birger, Sigurd, and Gunnar. Their party was directly inspired by a meeting with Hitler's NSDAP the year before, but in spite of an ambitious party organization they never managed to grow beyond their home place in Deje, Värmland.[106] It was in the second half of the decade that the first serious and lasting groups were formed. In 1926, after the government's cuts to military spending the previous year, another fascist group was founded by a handful of soldiers and officers stationed in Stockholm. Sveriges Fascistiska Kamporganisation (Sweden's Fascist Combat Organization, SFKO) was led by war volunteer Konrad Hallgren who had served in the German army, *furir* (squad leader) Sven Olov Lindholm, and Lieutenant Sven Hedengren. They were backed by Elof Eriksson, who lent the support of *Nationen*. This black-shirted group was predominantly concerned with anti-parliamentary and military politics, and the threat of firstly communism (Hedengren himself monitored communist groups for the army), and secondly the Jews. The SFKO may have had as many as 7000 members. It was also an example of how minor fascist groups nevertheless acquired important and somewhat dubious connections in influential strata of Swedish society. In the late 1920s a paramilitary organization was founded in Stockholm, recruiting and arming civilians with the express aim of assisting police in the case of an attempted socialist revolution. It was formally commanded by General Bror Munck, an in-law relative of Gustav V. While the organization never ended up actually organizing any training sessions or similar, it was provided with side arms and machine guns, via a group of army officers and SFKO members, including Sven Hedengren. Hedengren himself had been trying to organize SKFO after the Finnish White protection corps of the civil war.[107] The guns in question came from Germany, where they were sourced by Horst von Pflugk-Harttung, a former *Freikorps* officer under Waldemar Pabst, residing in Sweden after the murder of Rosa Luxemburg and Karl Liebknecht. When SFKO fell apart, Konrad Hallgren informed the police of the illegal arms, leading to an inquiry into the Munck Corps, and ultimately a law against private paramilitaries in 1931.

SFKO soon broke with Elof Eriksson, partially because Hallgren thought Eriksson focused too much on anti-Semitism. Over the years Lindholm, mostly in charge of propaganda and the party newspaper, *Spöknippet* (Fasces), came to take a leading role within SFKO, while his friend Hedengren was increasingly occupied with military service. In 1929 Lindholm and Hallgren were invited to the Nuremberg Party Rally where they met leading German Nazis. The trip was arranged via Max Pferdekämper, a veteran Nazi and close associate of Heinrich Himmler, who worked to bring the new Nordic fascist organizations within the NSDAP sphere of influence (it is unlikely the Swedes were fully aware of this). Pferdekämper would go on to become a long-term friend of Lindholm, well into the 1950s at least.[108] At that year's party congress it was announced that SFKO's organization would be modified to more closely resemble that of the NSDAP, and the name was changed to Nationalsocialistiska Folkpartiet (National Socialist People's Party). The following year the first attempt was made to merge Sweden's far-right movements into Nysvenska Nationalsocialistiska Partiet (New-Swedish National Socialist Party) which around the New Year of 1930/31 became Sveriges Nationalsocialistiska Parti (SNSP) based in Gothenburg.[109] Birger Furugård (1887–1961) became national leader (*riksledare*), while his deputy, Lindholm, took care of organization, as well as editing the party newspaper, *Nationalsocialisten* (The National Socialist).[110]

Things looked promising at first for the newly unified party, but ideological disagreements were immediately evident, while Furugård was easily influenced by emerging factions.[111] The main division in the SNSP was between the Left and Right, the former associated with Lindholm, the latter with Furugård and the party officers who advised him. No doubt there were some personal differences as well between the hard-working Lindholm and the alcoholic Furugård.[112] After two years of mounting tension, a split was triggered by the poor election result of 1932. In spite of vigorous campaigning in West Sweden, especially in Värmland, the work did not pay off: SNSP gained 15,170 votes, 0.6 per cent of the total. If there was a silver lining for the SNSP, it was in the fact that nearly half of these votes came from Gothenburg, 5.7 per cent of the city's votes, indicating at least some local voting base. Lindholm confronted Furugård in January 1933 about the party's poor leadership, shambolic economy, the corrupt and conspiratorial behaviour of what he termed 'the bourgeois junta' (*borgarjuntan*) and the party's Germanophilia (*tyskeriet*), but according to Lindholm Furugård refused to acknowledge his mistakes.[113] After failed attempts at reconciliation the following days, the disagreement came to a head when Lindholm and Furugård deposed each other on January 14, somehow attracting the attention of the police and press,[114] which forced the schism out into the open.¹¹⁵ The following day the founding of the NSAP was a fact. Like the SNSP it was a hierarchical, brown-shirted party, centred on an ideology of vicious anti-Semitism and biological racism that saw in Sweden the purest example of the Aryan race. Unlike the SNSP, it was considerably more explicit in its appeal to workers as the core of the future Swedish fascist community.

Within the next two years, the NSAP established itself as the largest fascist party in Sweden. Party formations across the country were encouraged to pick sides, and while it is unclear how many immediately joined the NSAP, eventually the vast majority turned away from Furugård's SNSP. This process was consummated when Furugård gave up on politics in 1936, and dissolved his party. Before then the SNSP had already split even further, most crucially when Furugård broke with his own Party Officers after an attempt to depose him in October 1933.¹¹⁶ Furugård and the SNSP headquarters moved to Karlstad, while the 'rebels' joined the recently founded Nationalsocialistiska Blocket (National Socialist Bloc), an alliance doomed to failure under its dismally uncharismatic leader, Finnish civil war veteran Colonel Martin Ekström (1887–1954).¹¹⁷

However, while the NSAP managed to hold centre stage in fascist politics, it remained a very small stage indeed. Lindholm's party peaked in the mid-1930s, with over 10,000 members, but no electoral success in sight.¹¹⁸ At the beginning of what would be four decades of Social Democratic hegemony, Swedish public opinion remained largely indifferent to fascism, and the NSAP failed to significantly increase its electoral support. In the 1936 general elections, the NSAP secured c. 17,000 votes (of 20,000 for fascist parties), which amounted to a dismal 0.7 per cent of the total. An attempted makeover of the party in October 1918, which changed the name to Svensksocialistisk Samling (Swedish Socialist Union, SSS) and traded the swastika for the royal Vasa dynasty's heraldic wheat sheaf, did not improve the party's fortunes.¹¹⁹

The NSAP's and other fascist groups' lack of public support, and the absence of a credible far-Left treat, meant the Swedish establishment did not act as firmly as it did in the Netherlands. Nevertheless similar laws against political uniforms and paramilitaries were passed, but their application in both cases was comparatively lax, the former especially, which left enforcement to the discretion of local police forces. Like the Dutch, the Swedes' attitude to fascism was significantly shaped by the actions of Nazi Germany, and to a lesser extent Fascist Italy. Pro-democracy movements were organized, and a strong distaste for fascism spurred the Left to action against native organizations even if they did not pose a substantial threat, e.g. leading LO to expel fascists from its organizations.¹²⁰ On the other hand the reaction from the Right was much more sympathetic, especially compared to the Dutch confessional response. There was little overt ecclesiastical opposition, while many influential figures in business, the aristocracy and especially the military had warm feelings towards Nazi Germany with which Sweden maintained its close economic and cultural ties. Thus, while fascist sympathies were perhaps more widespread and influential in Sweden than voter- or member figures would suggest, this did not translate to more immediate political influence for the NSAP/SSS specifically. The party struggled to stay afloat during the war, with many of its functionaries called in for military service, while others such as Sven Hedengren volunteered in the Finno-Soviet wars of 1939–44. The German invasion of Norway and Denmark, condemned by Lindholm, did not help the party's prospects. It did not contest the 1940 elections, and by the 1944 SSS had dropped down to 0.1 per cent of the vote. Nevertheless it continued after the war, until finally Lindholm threw in the towel in 1950, and dissolved the party, terming it 'an honest effort'.

2

Making the party: Party apparatuses and propaganda

Reproducing fascist fantasies through discourse and performances that bore the hallmarks of authenticity required not just fascist will, but the means of symbolic production.[1] It required an extensive propaganda apparatus which commanded the numbers, competence, organization and finances, to ensure the performative discipline of its members, orchestrate political theatre on a grand scale and interpose a mythic hermeneutics between audience and performance. Converting the public and mobilizing the cadres required practical and material resources. To this, organization was crucial.

Dutch and Swedish scholarship have hitherto largely disregarded in-depth analysis of the respective party apparatuses of the NSAP and the NSB.[2] While the sources are available, the countless forms, regulations, reports and other administrative documents that filled the party filing cabinets are still rarely used to their full extent. Some historians have simply assumed that the apparatuses were carbon-copies of the NSDAP (itself hardly a static organization). For the Dutch NSB some of the work has been done, including some impressive studies of regional and local organizations, but never as an end in its own right, and not in any greater detail.[3] For the Swedish NSAP, this work has barely been done at all.[4] But the inner workings of the party apparatus can be highly informative, and give a direct insight into some of the chief concerns of the party.

This chapter explores the party apparatuses of the NSAP and the NSB, detailing the organization; outlining the chain of command to see who bore responsibility for the execution and implementation of propaganda; the tools of propaganda available to each party to construct and disseminate their myths; and the role of the rank-and-file, who were the fundament of all mythopoeic efforts in their smallest details. The overall purpose is to give a heuristic overview which can serve as the basis for the analysis of specific mythopoeic performances. Once the division of responsibility and the means of implementation are sketched out, the discussion goes on to describe the organizational structures that were in place in both movements to actually orchestrate their political performances and discourses, and connect them, culminating in the public meeting. The public meeting was at the performative forefront of fascist mythopoeia, as the party newspaper was at its discursive front.

This comparative description naturally relies heavily on the regulations, rules and directives of the parties, but also entails an analysis of the qualitative differences between the two organizations, and highlights their flaws and the obstacles they faced. Here it will quickly become apparent that while the NSAP and NSB relied on the same organizational model, and closely shared a party structure, in practice they worked remarkably differently, as the workings of the apparatuses were highly contingent on their national context and political fortunes.

Character of the party organizations

The NSB and the NSAP both started out as strictly hierarchical organizations, with a centralized command structure, with more or less dictatorial powers assigned to the *Algemeen Leider* (General Leader) Anton Mussert and *Partiledaren* (Party Leader) Sven Olov Lindholm. Whereas the fascist movements of the 1920s in Sweden and the Netherlands tended (theoretically) to be ruled by oligarchical councils,[5] the new movements of the 1930s took a leaf from the book of the later NSDAP.[6] These parties tended to be known as the Mussert-Movement or Lindholm-Movement. Power flowed directly from the headquarters in Utrecht and Gothenburg (later Stockholm), with limited autonomy for local party formations. The pyramidal hierarchy was in both cases based on a flow of responsibility from the Leadership, consisting of a Headquarters of Departmental leaders, to the District Leaders, Circle Leaders, Group Leaders, down to Block Leaders. In both cases the District Leaders (*gewestelijk leider* and *distriktsledare*), based on the German *Gauleiter*, were often part of the Leadership (NSB) or closely cooperated with it (NSAP). This structure, as the Swedish police observed, was carefully copied from the NSDAP – the NSAP kept diagrams of the German party structure at their headquarters.[7] The NSB organization, designed by Mussert, was less elaborate from its inception, and used the fifteen-member Group as its smallest unit.[8] The most important level for political organization and collective action in the NSB was the Circle (*kring*, theoretically 1000–4000 members), for which most of the regulatory material was written, while in the NSAP principal organizational action devolved to the Local Group (*ortsgrupp*, seventy-five or more), rather than the Circle (*krets*).

At the head of the Swedish NSAP hierarchy stood the Party Leadership (*partiledningen*), a body with significant authority, with the Party Leader as *primus inter pares*. The body assembled at least once a week.[9] NSAP leadership at times resembled a hybrid between the collegial structure of the 1920s and the *Führerprinzip*.[10] The Leadership, consisting of over a dozen members with ever-shifting roles and responsibilities, changed far too frequently in its precise constitution to detail in full, and in most cases there is little biographical information available on the individuals who held office. But a few figures are worth mentioning.

The person closest to Lindholm was the Deputy Leader. Initially this position was held by Gunnar Svalander, a key figure in the party 1933–6, who initially held the position of Party Secretary, and later that of the highly influential Party Organizer.[11] Svalander was in the first years crucial in overseeing the organization and party projects such as the annual conventions. Eventually he rebelled against Lindholm after the electoral disappointment of 1936, and was replaced as Deputy by Per Dahlberg.[12] Dahlberg, the intellectual of the movement, with a degree in political science and

Figure 1 The NSAP-members who broke away from SNSP in 1933. Oscar Landahl, sitting in front row, on the far-right; Per Dahlberg, second row, on far-left; Lindholm, second row, third from the right; Gunnar Svalander, back row, third from the left. Photographer unknown. National Archives of Sweden, Marieberg, SO Lindholm's collection (SE/RA/720834).

economics, was the party's chief ideologist, and worked closely with the *partiledare*.[13] Perhaps politically the most astute of the chief functionaries, he was considered something of a moderating force in the party, and appears to have been one of the main movers behind the 'New Direction' (*nyorientering*) towards respectability at the end of 1938. He worked as a party speaker, wrote numerous articles for the party papers and held a number of other influential positions in the NSAP throughout the decade. These included editor of the weekly party newspaper, publisher and editor of the monthly theory journal *Nationell Socialism*, leader for the Political Commission (Polkom), Press Chief, Party Organizer and head of the members' training and education service. He quit in 1940, after being called in for military service. Another ubiquitous figure was Oscar Landahl, a popular party speaker, but most importantly Party Chief of Propaganda in 1933–5. He was also the party's electoral candidate for Gothenburg. As chief of propaganda he was replaced in 1935 by Erik Fahl, another speaker and sometime Political Secretary with growing influence in the party. Eventually he would become permanently employed as organizer for Western Sweden in 1939.[14] Fahl's replacement as propaganda chief was Björn Dahlström, a lawyer by training, and son of the famous socialist writer Kata Dahlström (1858–1923), but already in 1939 replaced by Bertil Siven. Herbert Hultberg was a loyal colleague of Lindholm, who worked as

Party Secretary from 1936, and organized the daily business of Headquarters. Bertil Brisman was a political advisor for Lindholm, and Polkom Secretary with a particular interest in cultural politics and briefly Party Organizer in 1936, and a party speaker.[15]

In the Dutch NSB there was no real alternative to Mussert's increasingly charismatic leadership, who worked closely together with the loyal party co-founder Cornelis Van Geelkerken, who acted as Deputy Leader and General Secretary.[16] (Van Geelkerken was also briefly in charge of Department II (Finance), General Leader of Propaganda in 1936, and leader of the evanescent youth movement, the Nationale Jeugdstorm (National Youth Storm, NJS).) Aside from Van Geelkerken, Mussert relied extensively on his secretary Christina Wilhelm van Bilderbeek, the first female member of the party, who would remain in her highly influential position until the end of the Second World War. While she possessed no formal authority within the party, she was necessarily well-informed of everything that happened in the administration, and keen to protect Mussert from seemingly dubious people. After the war it turned out she had made herself extremely unpopular with virtually all male functionaries in the NSB, including Van Geelkerken, something explained not least by the highly sexist complaints against a woman holding such an important function.[17]

Mussert did not seem to have relied extensively on other HQ members, and individual Department leaders did not appear to have yielded much influence outside of their spheres. Instead, influence in the party was significantly tied to Mussert's favour, and whoever he had most use for at the time, although several historians have suggested the Leader was often the one being used – (as suggested by his secretary and his wife Maria Witlam). Count Maximilianus Marchant et d'Ansembourg, District Leader for Limburg and North-Brabant, and a key member of the party Church Council for Catholics, always wielded a great deal of authority, and was NSB representative in the Dutch Senate from 1935. The Calvinist Blood and Soil theorist E.J. Roskam

Figure 2 The NSB General Council, 1933. From left to right, standing: H. Reydon; J.F. Overwijn; F.E. Farwerck; H. van Duyl; K.H. Tusenius; F.W. van Bilderbeek; J. Boddé; C.W. van Bilderbeek. From left to right, sitting: F.A. Smit Kleine; S.A. van Lunteren; C. Van Geelkerken; A.A. Mussert; J. Hogewind; T. Bakker; J.W.C. Danner. Photographer unknown. *Volk en Vaderland*, 1933, no. 40. KB|National library of the Netherlands: C16.

was another member of the Church Council (for the Reformed), and director of the National Press office. J. Hogewind – a former colonial army officer – was Commander of the paramilitary WA until its disbandment in 1936,[18] and F.W. van Bilderbeek played an important role as Head of Finance and Administration. Finally there was Martinus Meinouds Rost van Tonningen, a former League of Nations diplomat from Austria, and personal friend of Heinrich Himmler, who joined the party in 1936 and was immediately assigned as editor of the party's new daily newspaper *Het Nationale Dagblad* (The National Daily). He played an important role as a radical Germanophile ideologist, but largely during the Occupation, and with limited success on account of his tremendous unpopularity in the party.[19] These different leadership organizations were also reflective of Mussert's and Lindholm's competencies and responsibilities in the party. While Mussert could invariably be found in his office in Utrecht, centrally located in the emerging Dutch conurbation (*Randstad*),[20] Lindholm was occupied as the chief party speaker for months at a time during his propaganda tours, which took him as far afield as Lapland and Norrbotten.[21] Mussert by contrast sometimes only spoke at propaganda meetings two or three times per month, in cities no more distant than Hilversum or Dordrecht.[22]

The structures of the organizations did not remain static, and were improved regularly, especially after elections which tended to foreground problems in the apparatus. It was particularly the geographical administration of the party branches which they had inherited from the NSDAP which required adjustment. In 1935, after the Dutch May elections, the leadership structure of the essential Circles was changed in the NSB, with the Circle Leader being integrated into a troika with a Head of Propaganda and a Head of Staff, so that the Circle Leader would no longer be swamped by administrative issues.[23] After the disastrous 1937 elections, the handful of *gewesten* were abolished to instead be replaced by twenty-four *distrikten*, undercutting the power of District Leaders, and allowing more precise management from Headquarters. With roughly two *distrikten* per province, it allowed a closer connection between locality and Headquarters, also addressing complaints about a lack of immediate contact with the centre.[24] The headquarters were constantly expanding: new headquarters were created in Amsterdam, Hilversum (1936) and The Hague (1937), as new functions were created, or the dozen departments redistributed to match up geographically with their responsibilities.[25] The party expanded rapidly in Indonesia from December 1933 onwards, but with an administration peculiar to itself; in 1934 a Central Secretariat was established in Bandung to centralize administration, member registration and propaganda in the Dutch East Indies.[26] With Mussert's visit in 1935, the Indonesian NSB's organization was brought in line with that of the metropole, after which it also saw a large increase in funds from members' donations. Unlike the party in the Netherlands, the colonial branch did not contest the government, rather overtly supporting the harshly repressive colonial authorities. Doubtless this left a great deal of money to fund the metropolitan party: Mussert claimed that by 1937 fully one third of all funds came from Indonesia, representing 5 per cent of the membership.[27]

In Sweden, the NSAP reformed the District system several times. *Distriktschefer* (North, East, South-East, South, and West) were instituted gradually across the country as more branches were established; these were then given a make-over in

1936 when they were re-named *landsinspektörer*,[28] and reduced in number (the party gave up on the North, as growth there was frustrated).[29] They were renamed *ländermän* in 1938,[30] until the system was finally abolished in 1939, to instead focus on *kretschefer*, the Circle Leaders, as the connecting point between centre and locality.[31] The reasons for these changes will be explored further below. The NSAP's centre of gravity also shifted over time, quite unlike the NSB in Utrecht. Headquarters were initially placed in Gothenburg, where Birger Furugård's SNSP was first located. But as the party started to expand in Stockholm in 1934–5, the organization moved east, with more and more of the organization established in the capital, until Headquarters was moved there in 1937. The Gothenburg branch crumbled only a year later, especially as underperformance in the elections meant it lost much of its funding.

Centrally propaganda was organized by the parties' respective propaganda departments. In the NSAP, *propagandaavdelningen* was headed by the Party Chief of Propaganda, and coordinated by the Party Organizer. The department was subdivided into a Meeting Department, Writing Department and News Centre.[32] In November 1938, with the appointment of Björn Dahlström, the organization was expanded to include a functionary for the technical side, and a propaganda council was formed to coordinate propaganda better.[33] The NSB Propaganda Department (Department III) was led by a Propaganda Leader, aided by the Propaganda Council. The department was responsible for five areas: the speakers' service, external propaganda, written propaganda (in conjunction with the Press Department), film and photo propaganda, and the negligible Labour Front.[34] While little archival material remains to elucidate how the internal workings of these departments played out in practice, the resulting decisions were implemented by Circle functionaries. In the Netherlands, Circles maintained their own Propaganda Department with a corresponding Propaganda Leader, immediately subordinate to the Circle Leader, who received instructions from the central department, and worked together with the Circle Leader to implement the directives.[35]

The NSB propaganda functionaries also had, unlike the NSAP, a considerable information-gathering organization at their disposal. A Documentation Service existed from the party's inception. Via the Central Bureau of Documentation, the rank-and-file were to send local news reports concerning the party to Utrecht, including evidence of corruption and similar information against opponents, and generally keep HQ informed of anything relevant to its propaganda efforts.[36] The Bureau in turn compiled and organized the information it received, added its own analysis of daily media and current affairs, and provided a digest for party speakers,[37] as well as a library that could be consulted by propaganda functionaries.[38]

In Sweden directives tended to be issued by District until 1939; District Leaders had more autonomy from the Propaganda Department, and could direct regional propaganda on their own initiative.[39] Correspondence shows that in Sweden local functionaries frequently needed to be privately admonished in writing, so that the organization was less bureaucratic in character.[40] The difficulty of directing the geographically isolated Swedish groups was circumvented to some extent by the monthly *Porg* (*partiorganisation*) paper, the compulsory and 'confidential organ for the NSAP's functionaries'. In theory a supplement to the *Tjänsteföreskrifter* (Service

Regulations, TF) written by Lindholm;[41] in practice it helped the central departments direct functionaries nationally, although as *Porg* itself noted, not all functionaries executed its orders down to the smallest detail,[42] nor, quite bizarrely, did all functionaries subscribe for that matter.[43]

Propaganda apparatuses

Next to the party leaders and propaganda departments, the party newspaper was always the most important propaganda organ. In fact, the NSB's *Volk en Vaderland* (People and Fatherland, VoVa) and the NSAP's *Den Svenske Nationalsocialisten* (The Swedish National Socialist, DSN) were at the heart of the mythopoeic apparatus of their respective organizations, fulfilling a major mobilizing, organizing and propaganda function.[44] VoVa and DSN not only were the face of the movement,[45] but also explicated party ideology, organized the rank-and-file, issued directives and notified the members of news and changes. They were also the first and foremost propaganda to be distributed on the streets, earning money for the party. The newspapers were the glue that held the entire propaganda effort together, the movements' 'most powerful weapon', serving to make members and sympathizers more militant, and making the indifferent susceptible to the ideas of the party (Mussert),[46] 'the very spine of our freedom struggle' (Lindholm).[47] In theory subscription to the papers was compulsory for all members,[48] though in practice a sizeable minority only bought the paper occasionally.[49] Until the party acquired its own printing press in August 1938, DSN was printed by Simonsons tryckeri in Gothenburg.[50] In 1980 Lindholm claimed the income generated by DSN was actually sufficient to balance out the costs,[51] but a postwar enquiry into SSS finances shows that at least by 1939 the National Socialist Press joint stock company was under serious strain and making a loss.[52] The stock company was set up in 1937 as a means of financing a printing press and in the hope of turning DSN into a daily, but never succeeded.[53] According to Lindholm's diary, DSN finances were abysmal when it was first published, while 'us "employees" lived at subsistence level'. However, it seems that hard work and donations from members and sympathizers ultimately did bear fruit, and between 1935 and 1938 DSN was published on a bi-weekly basis (Wednesday and Saturday), something VoVa never did.[54] On the other hand the Mussert-run publisher Nenasu (Netherlands National Socialist Publisher) actually published a daily newspaper besides VoVa, *Het Nationale Dagblad*, edited by Rost van Tonningen, though this was a consistently loss-making endeavour.[55] VoVa, always dense with advertisements, like all NSB publications, made a reasonable profit – a VoVa financial report for the first quarter of 1936 shows it earned Nenasu 11,400 guilders.[56] By a rough estimate up to a quarter of VoVa's columns were taken up by advertisements, compared to less than 5 per cent of DSN's. Nenasu was owned by Mussert himself, and evidence suggests he channelled some of the profits into his own pockets.[57] DSN generally sold 10,000–20,000 of each issue,[58] VoVa around 80,000 on average.

Lindholm was the editor-in-chief of DSN until 1935 (which earned him a prison sentence when one author wrote an illegal article) while Mussert's only legal connection to the paper was as owner of the publishing house. The editorial office of both papers saw a relatively high turnover. Mussert wrote leading articles for the paper on a regular basis, and Lindholm's diary shows he was occupied daily with writing articles for DSN, even when he was on tour.[59] Leading articles from the Leader helped establish a party line, and reinforced loyalty to the Leader through the construction of his charisma. VoVa's and DSN's centralizing effects were exploited to mobilize the cadres, especially in the latter case where the paper frequently functioned as a substitute for circulars.[60] Initially VoVa had a similar sort of messaging board function, but around 1935 all internal information was strictly limited to circulars. Before then, reports on meetings, information about upcoming ones, requests for materials and expertise, notifications of promotions and changes in the party were spread liberally across the pages, providing members with indispensable information about their party, and, unintentionally, outsiders with a window into the party's organization.

As one of the principal means of disseminating the movements' myths among the public, and supporting the organization financially, distribution of the newspapers occupied the parties constantly. Local branches bought copies of the paper from the publisher, and sold them at a slight profit, to invest in further propaganda and the expansion of the local formation.[61] Apart from subscriptions, copies were distributed via various outlets such as kiosks like *Pressbyrån* (The Press Bureau) in Sweden, or tobacconists like the NSB-supported *De Driehoek* (The Triangle) in the Netherlands.[62] Copies sometimes had to be sold covertly under the counter, especially in Sweden when the NSAP was in conflict with LO.[63]

As was common for newspapers in Sweden at the time, the NSAP relied on the railway network for distribution – the papers would be delivered at a central collection point early in the morning in Gothenburg or Stockholm, from where they would be transported all over the country to the local kiosks, and for delivery at local branches. Little remains in the archive of guidelines developed for the further sale of DSN by party colporteurs, which made up the majority of DSN sales. For VoVa on the other hand continuously updated rules and regulations exist, instructing in painstaking detail how the paper was to be sold and advertised. VoVa representatives were responsible at the Circle level, being a compulsory part of the Circle Propaganda Department, appointed after negotiation with the Circle and Group leaders.[64] By comparison the organization for DSN was far more basic. In 1938 it still did not even have a register of subscribers, to the frustration of local branches in particular, who were responsible for collecting subscriptions.[65] Nationally the DSN editorial office worked together with the Propaganda Department and Political Secretary to coordinate propaganda.[66] Group Propaganda leaders were in charge of colportage locally, and Block leaders were assigned the responsibility of organizing house visits. Colportage was regarded as the duty of any party member, the most basic form of activism which any militant ought to manage. However, unlike the NSB, the NSAP also employed outsiders as colporteurs, including boys as young as twelve, suggesting this universal duty may not have been fulfilled as reliably as desired.[67]

The VoVa and DSN distributors, colporteurs, were the most visible and regular manifestation of the party to the public. Every day, party members took up posts in public spaces or patrolled neighbourhoods, advertising the paper to passers-by. Colporteurs were the most obvious fascists the public encountered on the streets, and thus functioned as immediate participants in the parties' mythopoeic efforts. They were, in Mussert's words, 'the lancers of the Movement', itself a phrase redolent of myth, of heroic soldiers of war in a tradition going back to early modern times.[68] The fantastic description was not entirely inappropriate, as they were indeed not only the members the public would most commonly encounter, but also those most likely to be involved in violent incidents, especially in the Netherlands. VoVa colporteurs were frequently also members of the WA.[69] Newspapers regularly carried reports of fights breaking out between colporteurs and communists, fights which could occasionally escalate into veritable riots.[70] Particularly after the ban on political uniforms, it was precisely the selling of the party newspaper which identified one as a fascist. For instance in 1935 a French anarchist shot two NSB members, one identifiable as a VoVa colporteur.[71] Consequently colporteurs often required protection, which, until the ban on paramilitary formations (15 June 1934 in Sweden, in effect 1 August that year; 1939 in the Netherlands though Mussert preemptively dissolved the WA in 1936), was provided by the paramilitary SA/A-groups in the NSAP and WA in the NSB, magnifying the fascist presence on the streets.

With the party newspaper in hand, perhaps flanked by a paramilitary guard, the party member had to performatively enact the fascist myth which the paper constructed discursively. Fascist colporteurs did not just sell a paper, but also their image. In the NSB the emphasis here was foremost not on a soldier myth, but on respectability. The guidelines for colportage emphasized that:

> Colportage is not allowed on Sundays and Christian holidays, and never in the immediate vicinity of churches. Everything which is in conflict with good taste, must be avoided, such as provocative behaviour and colportage directly next to rival colporteurs. It must in particular be ensured that the public is not needlessly irritated by pushy or cumbersome behaviour.[72]

House visits in particular required 'trim' or 'decent' (*nette*) people, capable of 'very correct behaviour'.[73] It appears that it took the NSAP rather longer to develop detailed guidelines for colportage, as the first such instructions date from 1938. The 'Instruction for *frontavdelningar*' (Front Departments, FA – the militant part of the party, successor to the SA and A-groups) states that:

> The Front Man does not need to be a saint or ascetic, but he may not be pulled along by the indecent swirl of pleasure and entertainment, with which Jewish profiteers want to ruin our people. [...] Colporteurs must observe such behaviour that he attracts the interest of the public, but *without* in any way whatsoever being 'ostentatious', and provocative even less so.[74]

Notably both parties permitted female members to participate in colportage, one of the few active propaganda duties women were allowed.[75] In the NSAP the emphasis was on a different kind of respectability, and more on that most ubiquitous of fascist ideals, discipline. The militants were 'political soldiers' in the great war for the conquest of Sweden, who would make a good impression through their 'un-criminal discipline', 'which affects Swedish people beneficially, and counteracts the lie that we would be foreign mercenaries of some sort'.[76] The NSAP 'strove to have an *elite* of competent and reliable members, who are not just knowledgeable regarding the ideas but also dedicated to their leader'.[77]

Party meetings

On the foundation of ideologically educated, physically trained and disciplined cadres, the central administration would construct its myths through spectacular political performances that would pique the interest of the public, win over new members and, of course, voters. There was a veritable 'National Socialist meeting culture' as one Swedish police report put it, and even the young, understaffed NSAP arranged 546 public meetings in 1933 alone.[78] Given the importance and frequency of meetings in the fascist mythopoeic repertoire, the party apparatuses naturally developed standardized procedures for their organization.

The first step for any public meeting was hiring a room, building or public space, of appropriate size to house the event. Generally this seems to have gone without too much ado, although there were occasions when the responsible organizers failed to arrange a room in time or acquire permission, out of ignorance or miscommunication,[79] or due to the party's reputation.[80] In the NSAP the former appears to have been common enough that *Porg* urged functionaries in 1937 to 'answer letters regarding the organization of meetings immediately, and not wait until the last minute, or even just ignore them altogether'.[81] The NSB placed particular emphasis on the hiring of spaces of an appropriate size, ideally slightly too small for the expected audience to enhance the impression of strong public interest.[82] Notably the division of responsibilities for the organization of meetings was more formalized in the NSB, being divided up between the Chief of the Meetings Service, Circle Propagandist and Circle Leader.[83] The TF merely noted that meetings should usually be instigated by the Party Leadership or Circle leaders, but in practice any member could organize a public meeting for the party.[84]

Once the functionary responsible had made the necessary arrangements for the meeting, the cadres were put in charge of advertising for the meeting. Sometimes the help of the paramilitaries was called in; in Sweden the party youth group Nordisk Ungdom (Nordic Youth, NU) could also help. Meetings were advertised to members in VoVa or DSN; sometimes advertisements were placed in local newspapers.[85] The rank-and-file sold tickets to the meetings where necessary, and leafleted the local area, ideally daily, well before the meeting was due.[86] Lindholm's diary records that he often participated in leafleting for his own meetings, especially when the local party group had neglected to prepare adequately.[87] Leaflets were handed out to passers-by, delivered door-to-door or pasted on walls and other more or less appropriate surfaces, sometimes by a team overnight.[88] One circular noted the NSB had received a complaint from the Dutch Railway Service that leaflets had been pasted onto trains, and admonished members never to cause offence through the distribution of propaganda.[89] The Swedish police archives are littered with complaints about and investigations into illegal pasting (*klistring*). This was a persistent problem throughout the 1930s, but never resolved – invariably the local leaders or the Leader of Propaganda would deny ordering such methods, or any knowledge of who might be responsible.⁹⁰ Party leaders did forbid 'irresponsible pasting' as harmful to the movement, but there is no evidence any actual action was ever taken to put a stop to it.⁹¹ In fact, one 1935 letter from Lindholm orders a functionary to withhold information from the police, 'because it's the *police's job* to find out who has been leafleting'.⁹² Both parties recognized the necessity of an appropriately decorated space. After all:

> a meeting of NSB-members is something different from a meeting of democrats. Our meetings should witness of the new spirit of the Nat. Soc. Movement … the interested or even merely curious visitor, as well as the opponent …. should from the moment of entering the building … continuously be in contact with that new spirit … To that end each person with a task to fulfil in preparation for, during, or after the meeting, should fulfil it with all the militancy, dedication and care, which characterize a good NSB-member.⁹³

The mise-en-scène was far more regulated and uniform in the Netherlands compared to Sweden. NSB instructions directed the Chief of the Meetings Service to decorate the speaker's chair and table on the podium with a red–black cloth. Banners with appropriate slogans were hung up, with a special recommendation for a banner with the Leading Principle at the back of the room. Excessive and brightly coloured decorations were to be avoided at all costs: '[o]ur gatherings are not a carnival. The decorations serve to give expression to a cheerful, but otherwise serious, and more or less rigidly steadfast atmosphere'.⁹⁴ The podium was decorated in a way that was simultaneously tasteful, simple and impressive. In the middle of the background hung a large NSB flag, in front of the flag a bust or portrait of the Queen. On either side of the NSB flag, national flags and smaller party flags were placed. Against the lectern, decorated with an orange-white-blue or black-red cloth, was a portrait of the *Algemeen Leider*. Tables for the press were placed to the side of the podium. Party standards with a guard were situated on the sides of the podium foreground. In characteristically sexist fashion, it was left to women members to check whether decorations were in order.⁹⁵ The NSAP's TF simply noted that '[t]he meeting hall should, as well as can be, be decorated with flags, National Socialist motivational slogans, and the like'.⁹⁶ The rest seems to have been left to local initiative. Standard bearers, usually members of the SA, were conventional, but otherwise much of the staging was ad hoc.⁹⁷ It was especially during the numerous outdoor meetings that things like a podium had to be improvised: in his memoirs, Lindholm mentioned using oil barrels, snow heaps, a road side ditch, soap boxes and memorably 'a boat in the water off the beach, like Jesus'.⁹⁸ The difference of *Inszenierung* between the NSB and NSAP can perhaps be attributed to the material availability of props and people for setting up the meetings – NSB meetings were typically organized in the vicinity of a party office (*kringhuis*) in urban areas, whereas the NSAP was scattered far and wide across Sweden, and propaganda teams often had to rely on whatever could fit in a car, if one was available at all.

But the most crucial aspect of any meeting was of course the speaker. The remains of the original NSAP/SSS archive contain a particularly large proportion of correspondence about the arrangement of speakers for various meetings across the country, which created a considerable workload for Headquarters. As the southern District Leader put it to the Party Organizer, then Gunnar Svalander, '[t]he external work is after all incredibly important, for without new people there will be stagnation, and to get new people we require speakers, and we do not exactly have an overflow of those'.[99] With meetings as one of the foremost mythopoeic tools, speakers were in very high demand, but acquiring actually competent ones in specific places at specific times placed a great burden on the party apparatus. The relatively few trained and certified speakers had to be notified, travel (usually by train) and accommodation arranged, speeches prepared and advertisements placed in the papers.[100] Costs and reimbursement had to be negotiated, which could particularly be a problem with some of the poorer branches, especially when rooms had to be hired as well.[101] The demand for speakers meant some of the most popular ones had to attend dozens of meetings across the country over the course of a few months – not least the most popular party speaker, Lindholm – something which inevitably led to overworked speakers.[102] *Porg* warned that this undermined the training of new speakers, who were not given due opportunity to practise at meetings, indicating a remarkable inability of the central administration to impose specific speakers on local branches. 'It has come to the point where a few of the party's speakers are going to wear themselves out, while new speakers never get the opportunity to properly get started. [...] Is it not still the case in some places, that *if the desired speaker cannot be acquired, you neglect to organize meetings altogether?*'[103]

The provision of party speakers was far better regulated in the NSB, through the Central Bureau of Propaganda, which maintained a database of all certified NSB speakers across the country. NSB formations could only hire certified speakers, and the speaker's status determined whether they were allowed to answer audience questions after the speech. Rather than arranging reimbursements between the speaker and local formations, speakers could claim standard maximum sums from Department III.[104] Money for the reimbursements was levied from the local formations, which paid a fixed fee for speakers at all public meetings, depending on their rank, determined by their past experience and the size of the meetings they could speak at. (Circles could also, with special permission, get trainee speakers for 2 guilders, from the Regional training schools where available.) This arrangement solved the problem of evenly distributing costs for party formations, which were generally wealthier in the centre and west of the country, where most of the speakers lived, and poorer in the north, east and south, which would otherwise not be able to afford to reimburse the travel costs.[105] It must also have been an incentive to local formations to hire less experienced speakers to save money, circumventing the NSAP's problem of overworked popular talent, and ensuring the most capable speakers remained available for the largest meetings. Another NSB arrangement which made the organization of speakers much easier was the Gewestelijken Vervoerdienst (Regional Transport Service), which made cars available to speakers when they otherwise would not be able to reach the meeting in time, get a train back home on the same day or simply be able to save money on transport for the party.[106]

The structure of the actual meetings was quite similar in both parties. Meeting programmes and reports for both have survived in considerable numbers, allowing for a certain degree of generalization. Meetings were the principal tool for expanding the party membership – they spread awareness of the movement, and provided information, but they also imposed a mythic image of fascism on the audience. With an audience that ideally consisted of a mixture of both party members and outsiders, they served simultaneously to mobilize the cadres, and acquire new members.[107] Party publications were always sold immediately before and after the meeting, frequently by women members.[108] The opportunity was also used to collect donations, to support the local formation or to finance an upcoming event or campaign.[109] A successful meeting would yield new members at the end of it. In areas in which the parties did not yet have any formations, public meetings were essential to establish a presence. Meetings were a means of 'conquering new territory'.[110] Hence it was crucial that people who had been attracted to these meetings were given the correct idea of the movement, i.e. one in line with the party's mythic construction. In accordance with the centralized character of the organization, a general party line was established for how this was meant to be conveyed, so that all meetings would have a similar character – again, more so in the NSB than the NSAP.

In an NSB meeting, as the audience entered the room, guards and standard bearers were already at their stations – carrying of political flags in a public meeting was illegal, but holding them *in situ* was not. The meeting was led by the local leader, who opened the meeting with a brief introduction of a few minutes – this was not intended to be a speech in its own right, though that did happen on occasion. Then the main speech would commence, lasting approximately one hour, followed by a brief break during which audience members had the opportunity to buy propaganda material and apply for membership.[111] Afterwards there could also be an opportunity to answer questions from the audience, if the speaker had the authority. The end of the meeting was invariably announced with the singing of the national anthem, the *Wilhelmus*.[112]

NSAP regulations left more to local initiative. They were held as late in the day as possible, ideally the evening, to ensure the largest possible audience. Sundays were avoided for this reason, though exceptions were permissible, especially in the countryside where meetings were adjusted to the farmers' work schedules. They were typically organized by the local Chief of Propaganda, who like his NSB equivalent divided responsibilities between the staff. Here too the paramilitary was used to guard the meeting, and take note of any known communists in the audience. After paramilitaries were outlawed, protection of the meeting was left to the police authorities. To open the meeting, a procession of standard bearers entered the meeting place to marching music, then took up their stations in front of the podium, followed by music – the reverse procedure would be used to mark the end of the meeting. Apart from the main speaker, someone had to be present to provide an introduction and an afterword. For larger indoor meetings, it was also desirable to have multiple speakers if possible. Here too, it was cautioned that the introduction was not to be a speech in its own right. The conclusion was to be limited to purely informative announcements, about membership, papers, contributions, the next meeting and so forth. Music was a standard part of NSAP meetings, and songs were often sung on several occasions throughout the evening if a positive reception was expected. Members were spread out accordingly in the room to be able to lead songs effectively, as well as any exclamations of approval for the speaker.[113] A typical meeting with one main speaker had three songs scheduled, invariably party songs, often written by Lindholm.[114] Once the meeting was formally concluded, an unscheduled period was left to discuss questions with the audience, sell propaganda material and recruit new members, provided no fights broke out.[115]

Challenges and differences

The two organizational structures were self-evidently inspired by the same source (the NSDAP) but when compared notable practical differences emerge. Broadly speaking the NSAP was a weaker organization relying on autonomous local formations, while the NSB was heavily centralized and tightly regulated.

The centralized party organization of the NSB mapped closely to the urban infrastructure of the Dutch conurbation, with its headquarters in the capital of Utrecht province, approximately 50–60 km away from Amsterdam, Rotterdam and 's-Gravenhage in Holland, which all had strong concentrations of NSB members,[116] and disproportionate numbers of NSB voters – over 10 per cent.[117] This west-centre concentration left peripheral NSB Districts isolated, including comparatively large ones like Drenthe or Limburg and North-Brabant. But this was also an opportunity for Mussert to further concentrate the party's financial power in Utrecht, turning it into a monetary redistribution hub for the chief propaganda activity of meeting organization, and taking national control of speaker access. Through a combination of the dense Dutch railway network and its own transport service, NSB propagandists could be sent all across the country from the urban centre, or the cadres could be brought together in one place for a rally.[118] But travel was expensive; for instance in 1936, the Headquarters administration alone incurred costs of 21,515.04 guilders for travel and car maintenance, out of 124,185.68 guilders total.[119] The hierarchical organization managed to effectively coordinate propaganda efforts at Circle level, no doubt facilitated by the NSB's urban concentrations, meaning Mussert could feasibly orchestrate nation-wide efforts through the District Leaders, as was evident from the electoral campaigns of 1935, 1937 and 1939. As is evident from the surviving rules and regulations for Circle propaganda, the centre closely directed the mythopoeic apparatus in the localities, and had the necessary financial and organizational leverage to ensure their discipline. The Department of Organization and Personnel deemed it desirable to centralize NSB power even further, recommending in the wake of the 1935 elections that the party should aim to 'completely annul Circle autonomy', though this was never achieved in practice.[120]

Such control over the minor party branches was unthinkable in the NSAP, which relied heavily on the initiative of District Leaders, especially in Gothenburg and Stockholm, from whom many of the surviving propaganda directives originate,[121] and where much of the membership was concentrated. Beyond the cities, those functionaries did not have much insight even at the Circle level – far too comprehensive an organizational unit for the Swedish countryside – and instead effective organization devolved to the largely autonomous Local Groups (*ortsgrupp*) or Departments (*avdelning*). These smaller formations of a few dozen or a hundred members were scattered across the country, with little ability to coordinate campaigns, and with only limited oversight from the Party Leadership which lacked the necessary control agents. If the surviving correspondence from NSAP Headquarters is representative of party communications, it is glaringly obvious that the party throughout the 1930s did not possess the necessary organization to exert control at a national level, and would not have been able to expand without significant restructuring. In 1986 Lindholm himself described it as a 'paper tiger'.[122] As the organization of meetings showed, communication was frequently directly between the Party Leadership in Gothenburg or Stockholm, and *ortsgrupp* or *avdelning* leaders. From time to time formations would go altogether silent, stop paying membership fees, request propaganda material or send the monthly reports which were one of the few means the centre had to control the periphery.[123] To illustrate, one letter from Party Secretary Hultberg to a Värmland Circle leader mentioned that the Botilsäter formation

> seems to be gone altogether. Since the formation was formed we have not heard anything from them. No message, no report: the formation leader does not answer letters. He is a farmer and of course that sort has a lot to do at the moment, but do note that the formation was formed already 3.2.37, so one feels he should have had the opportunity to let us hear from him at least once.[124]

The distance from Stockholm to Botilsäter is approximately 370 km, and approximately 70 km from Karlstad, home of the Värmland Circle Leader in question. Such distances, never even remotely an issue in the Netherlands, made controlling local rogue formations very difficult, and checking up on them unfeasibly cumbersome and expensive, even more so in light of the NSAP's poor finances.[125] Conversely, matching the exploits of the NSB to mobilize an absolute majority of the party membership to attend a party convention was inconceivable. Not only were train travel costs for such a large-scale operation excessive, but the Swedish railway network was not nearly as extensive as its Dutch equivalent. Nevertheless, the NSAP did successfully manage to coordinate travel to the annual party convention (*årsting*) by means of busses instead, ensuring that rural members who had never seen Gothenburg or Stockholm before could attend the great event.[126] Not everyone could afford the bus, but some members simply walked the hundreds of miles if necessary. The infrastructural and organizational obstacles the NSAP faced were severe, but not insurmountable.

Comparing Mussert's and Lindholm's respective functions within their parties, it is apparent that it was not only geography which explains the NSAP's deeply flawed centralization. Lindholm and Mussert fulfilled very different functions within their organizations, which goes some way towards explaining the organizational strength and centralization of the NSB vis-à-vis the NSAP. The peripatetic Lindholm was frequently occupied with a wide variety of party work, ranging from the editing of DSN, writing articles, organizing meetings, giving speeches and writing poetry, to the most basic tasks normally left to cadres: advertising meetings, leafleting towns and recruiting new members. His annual propaganda tours took him away from the headquarters for entire seasons, forcing him to rely on the rest of the Party Leadership. Mussert on the other hand was invariably found in Utrecht. Rules and regulations, meeting minutes, circulars and correspondence show Mussert to have been directly involved in the construction of the basic party organization in 1932–3, and its expansion for the rest of the decade. Organization and direction defined Mussert's day-to-day tasks. As noted earlier, Mussert acted as speaker only a handful of times per month at the beginning of the NSB's organization. At the same time, Lindholm could be speaking at several meetings per day. This was also at least partially due to personal aptitude, a contrast between the civil engineer Mussert and the health-obsessed military man Lindholm, who later confessed to having had no real understanding of his party's finances.[127] Nevertheless, Lindholm was always the (more or less) undisputed leader of the NSAP/SSS, and of the surviving rules and regulations like TF, it is evident they were written by Lindholm, as he wrote in his diary. That this was not left to another member of the Leadership, like the Party Organizer, is interesting, and suggests Lindholm tried to retain as much control over the basic party apparatus as possible in his absence, even if perhaps others were more qualified to take charge of party organization. It also hints a little at Lindholm's 'despotic nature' for which his detractors attacked him.[128] Power was not only much more centralized in the NSB, but also naturally more focused in Mussert's own hands. While Mussert did see internal opposition during the 1930s, especially after the 1937 elections, he retained a far steadier hold on the party leadership, prevented serious break-away movements from forming, and managed to secure his leadership even during the turbulent years of the Nazi Occupation.

Although Mussert had a strong hold over the party administration, and Utrecht could regulate the activities of the localities in considerable detail, this was not without its drawbacks. The expansive party bureaucracy was perceived by some members as stultifying, not least as the still new apparatus did not always work efficiently. In July 1934, W. van der Goes van Naters – a high-ranking functionary who would rebel against Mussert in 1937 – wrote a litany (co-signed by three other functionaries) to Van Geelkerken to complain about the departments of Organization and Propaganda. 'Firstly the Dep. Organization floods the entire N.S.B. with circulars, correcting circulars, additional circulars, circulars which contradict each other on vital points. And through this paper waterfall, local authorities are confused and halted in their own work.'[129] To his mind the fascist battle was supposed to be *against* officialdom and organizational bungling. If anything the propaganda department was even worse:

> instead of being a centre of zeal, which pushes and encourages the *entire* Movement, one notices little else from it but bookmarks of different formats and with different imprints: a petite bourgeois patchwork shop goings-on [*klein burgerlyk lapjes winkel gedoe*], which for outsiders is only ridiculous, and distracts the attention of N.S.B.-members away from the greater goal and task, towards rubbish irrelevancies.[130]

The problem of (incompetent) over-administration was reflected time and time again in what was termed the *kankergeest*, the 'grumbling spirit'.[131] Complaints of grumbling among the rank-and-file were common enough to warrant mention in party rules – for instance one of the official 'duties of the *Weerman*' (WA paramilitary member) was 'silence' – '[n]othing has a more paralysing effect or corrodes the good spirit more than grumbling and gossip'.¹³² Already in a 1934 report to Mussert, John Boddé – inspector of the southern Netherlands – pointed to grumbling as the chief flaw of the Brabant circle. Bergen op Zoom was particularly dysfunctional: 'Bergen op Zoom and grumbling are synonymous.'¹³³ Members were often reluctant to be so closely directed by Utrecht, and there was recurring trouble with internal cliques, which could seriously hamper party activism.¹³⁴ A related problem was gossip in the branches, of which there are numerous mentions in the archive.¹³⁵ Already in June 1933, one distressed member wrote, in a letter addressed 'to my Leader', to complain that over-organization had dampened enthusiasm for the Movement.

> In the past I once complained about the considerable disorder at Headquarters, though I then added, that I thought it was such a nice place. I enjoyed the enthusiastic stories, about colportage, etc. Every time I had been in Utrecht, I also felt a more enthusiastic NSB-member. There was élan, zeal, though no work got done. Now, work gets done, but there is no enthusiasm, like there used to be. [Now] a visit to Headquarters has the same effect on me as a visit to a tourist bureau. I've received an answer to the questions I asked. […] Currently we are being 'administered' from Utrecht, while we wish to be led by Utrecht, and spurred on.¹³⁶

In 1936 a letter to the leader of the Department of Training raised concerns that 'the idea – the organism [of National Socialism] – DOES NOT PERISH due to organization'. After all, it was argued, 80–90 per cent of people left the movement 'on account of organization and other reasons – because everyone, once became a member with and through enthusiasm'.¹³⁷

Nothing seems further from the assessments typically heard of the NSAP's unpaid cadres. As one police report put it:

> One will not be able to find greater self-sacrifice from the members in any other political party, members who without any compensation whatsoever, dedicate themselves fully to party activity. This can to a large extent be explained by that the party's main cadres are composed of youths, who with glowing enthusiasm use most of their spare time to advance the party.¹³⁸

Indeed Lindholm seems to have been very able to awaken the enthusiasm of Swedish youth. Unlike the NSB's diminutive youth movement, the NSAP's *Nordisk Ungdom* (NU, Nordic Youth), it's 'most important special organization', amounted to a significant portion of the fascist cadres, and they actively participated in party activities as militants.¹³⁹ But youthful enthusiasm combined with considerable *de facto* local autonomy meant that the cadres could also be a real headache to the Party Leadership. In 1935, one local leader complained to the Party Organizer Svalander that '[i]t is difficult to get "the boys" to work independently, but they have to if we are going to be able to keep the whole thing going. […] Whenever I get home from a [propaganda] tour they have only done the things that are absolutely necessary, and they do not understand how to act on their own.'[140] As Henrik Dammberg observed, some local branches consisted exclusively of school boys and girls.[141] Inexperience and incompetence were not the only trouble with young members. Active insubordination was far more common in the NSAP than it was in the Dutch party, and there are instances where local branches actively refused orders from Headquarters. For instance Branch 225 in Arvika in 1937 simply refused to organize a meeting requested by the Chief of Propaganda, Erik Fahl.[142] Several letters from the Leadership complain of a lack of discipline.[143] 'There are still some formations which think they can act whichever way they like. If they mercifully deign to answer [letters], everything has to be prepared for them like a laid table.'[144] Another common problem was illegal activities such as unlawful leafleting, though NSAP members were also prone to more violent forms of law-breaking. One 1937 police memorandum noted that NU deliberately provoked fights at meetings, to the chagrin of some of the older members present who demanded that the NU be banned from the annual party convention. Others on the other hand argued the NU should be allowed to participate 'to make sure something happens', arguing the party would be noticed and discussed more that way.[145] (NU-members were also more likely to flagrantly violate the law against political uniforms,[146] and the NU organ *Makt* (Might) actively encouraged regular violations to undermine the law.)[147]

Nevertheless, the NSAP's at times anarchic militants could be highly effective. This appears from a party analysis of the Gothenburg city elections in 1934, in which the administration noted approvingly that in terms of street propaganda 'we have been fully able to rival our opponents, and even surpass them', an impressive feat for such a small and new party.[148] But the unruliness of the cadres showed through. During a speech by the Minister of Finance at a Social Democratic meeting, some members had dropped a large placard attached to ten balloons, decorated with a large swastika and the letters NSAP, from a window in the roof, which slowly descended into the meeting place to the astonishment of onlookers. The party leadership noted that 'we must remember that our opponents tend to portray and regard us as childish pranksters. It might be unnecessary to pander to this perception'.[149]

†††

The two party organizations and their antithetical problems as portrayed here were reinforced by the political and social contexts in which they emerged. The bureaucratic, 'stuffy', NSB organization, firmly putting the reins in the hands of Mussert and Utrecht, was well-suited to the legally restrictive conservatism of the Netherlands. It would have been unthinkable in the Dutch organization to let members get away with breaking the law against political uniforms, which did not permit any liberal interpretations of its prohibitions. Throughout the 1930s, Dutch authorities increasingly treated the NSB as a revolutionary organization; the party leadership was constantly on its guard against anything that could get the movement banned altogether. Nor were violent and independent militants commensurate with the NSB's attempts to win over parts of the Dutch populace with profoundly conservative notions of law and order, particularly liberal conservatives, Calvinists and Roman Catholics, who were among the principal targets of party propaganda. These groups were far more likely to be impressed by the myth of an orderly, disciplined and ultimately respectable army, rather than the fiery enthusiasm of revolutionary youth.

The attitude of the Swedish authorities was far more permissive, perhaps not least because the NSAP never was a serious threat to the established political system in the way the NSB was in the mid-1930s. The law against political uniforms could still permit the wearing of uniform-like dress, and the various successors to the SA could just about pass as civilian formations. At the same time Lindholm's focus on workers and farmers and his unveiled contempt for *borgerligheten* (bourgeois establishment) made it much less urgent for the NSAP to construct an image of the party as a respectable force in a bourgeois sense, instead foregrounding the myth of a revolutionary army. While violence was rhetorically condemned by the Party Leadership, it also alluded to the necessity of illegal means of gaining power, possibly not wishing to dampen the useful enthusiasm of its more radical activists.[150] Unlike the NSB, the NSAP did not enjoy nearly the same amount of press coverage, while during the mid-1930s it still had to share the spotlight with rival fascist parties, which tended to construct fascism as far more conservative. Consequently the violence of the undisciplined cadres should also be seen in the context of the NSAP's urgent need for the attention of the Swedish press.

In spite of their great differences in practice, the apparatuses underline one fundamental issue: adopting the German NSDAP party structure wholesale was inherently problematic and complicated, and required considerable modification to the original design over time. This chapter has shown that describing its organization as a German 'carbon-copy' is far too simplistic, and does not actually give any sense of how the party apparatus operated in reality. It has also brought out a number of problems that existed within the NSB apparatus, while the comparison has foregrounded the problems and development of the organizations. Particularly the basic issue of geography and public infrastructure stands out – ostensibly similar parties with similar organizations faced completely different situations on account of the very large differences between the Dutch and Swedish landscape and population distribution. This was largely to the advantage of the NSB, but it also was the basis for completely different styles of administration, which brought its own problems in the Dutch case. The Swedish fascists managed to some extent to overcome many of the obstacles they faced, and in spite of their small size managed to display impressive zeal and activism. As the next chapters will show, while the party apparatus was the fundament for party activity, and by extension the fascist mythopoeic project, the resources behind it did not stand in a deterministic relation to the results.

3

Making the Leader: Party leaders and charisma

The centrality of the figure of the leader to fascism was already well-established by the time the NSB and NSAP were formed. The Dutch and Swedish public were largely familiar with the importance of *il Duce* in Italy or the *Führer* of Germany, and a range of smaller native fascist leaders had cropped up in the previous decade. By 1933 there was little doubt that a single authoritative leader figure was essential to a fascist movement. The 'Leader principle' or *Führerprinzip* has since been firmly integrated into academic discussions of fascism as well, regularly used as an identifying feature of fascism.[1] Particular attention has been paid to the notion of the charismatic leader.[2] Largely based on the examples of Hitler and Mussolini, ideas abound of fascism as a political movement closely connected to a Leader with almost supernatural qualities.[3]

Neither Lindholm nor Mussert fit such models of fascism very comfortably, but much the same has been said about the reality of Hitler's personality.[4] Ian Kershaw has pointed out that the myth of the heroic Hitler was at crass variance with reality (as has Richard Bosworth regarding Mussolini),[5] but noted that at the same time the Hitler myth played a crucial integratory function in the Third Reich.[6] Biographical studies of the Swedish and Dutch leaders have been extremely limited. There has been no monograph about Lindholm until as late as 2019, with Johan Stenfeldt's comparative ideological study of Lindholm and Nils Flyg, the communist leader-turned pro-German during the Second World War.[7] The most recent, and only, full-length scholarly biography of Mussert was published in 1984.[8] In terms of charisma, Lindholm and Mussert have not struck very impressive figures. Scholarship on Swedish fascism has largely ignored Lindholm as a personality,[9] and even a recent article by Victor Lundberg on Lindholm and his ideas makes no real reference to Lindholm as a leader.[10] This is particularly curious in the presence of substantial archival material on and from Lindholm personally. Mussert on the other hand has traditionally been used as a negative example, a tedious technocrat, thoroughly bourgeois,[11] 'a spiritual and moral vacuum'.[12] The short, middle-class, civil engineer married to his aunt, Maria Witlam, was too easy to mock. While recent work by Tessel Pollmann has sought to correct the liberal bourgeois interpretation of Mussert somewhat, there are still no academic studies of him as a charismatic Leader.[13] Attempts to understand the cultural construction of Mussert as Leader have also been sparse, including Gerard Groeneveld's brief discussion of NSB literature about Mussert.[14] These images of the leaders of the NSAP and NSB are, as will become apparent, understandable insofar as they reflected the reality of their personalities. Both Lindholm and Mussert were initially reluctant to embrace a leader role in the style of Hitler or Mussolini, and instead focused on developing the myth of the party. As authoritative leaders in parties that wholeheartedly subscribed to hierarchical leadership, they had a crucial role to play at the heart of the organizational apparatus, and consequently in the parties' mythopoeic endeavours.

There was a demand from the rank-and-file for something like a charismatic Leader, and if their personalities were not up to scratch, the appropriate Leader could be constructed. Arguably the historiography has been too focused on the reality of Mussert and Lindholm, and not enough on their myths, which played a very real and effective role in sustaining their respective movements. Charisma then is not to be treated as an inherent personal quality – a dubious analytical exercise anyway – but as something artificially constructed around the person, i.e. a myth.[15] The charismatic leaders were created through a mythopoeic process – one to a significant extent driven from below.[16] Again, this was something that was influenced directly by the movements' resources and means. This process was not simple or flawless, but it was effective. Lindholm and Mussert *became* the party, and to a greater or lesser extent embodied its myth. Mythopoeia could entirely reconstruct them as individuals, at least as far as the faithful were concerned. The mythopoeia of the Leader was directly tied up with the devotion of the membership, and the desire for a leadership cult, and succeeded in creating a lasting charismatic bond.

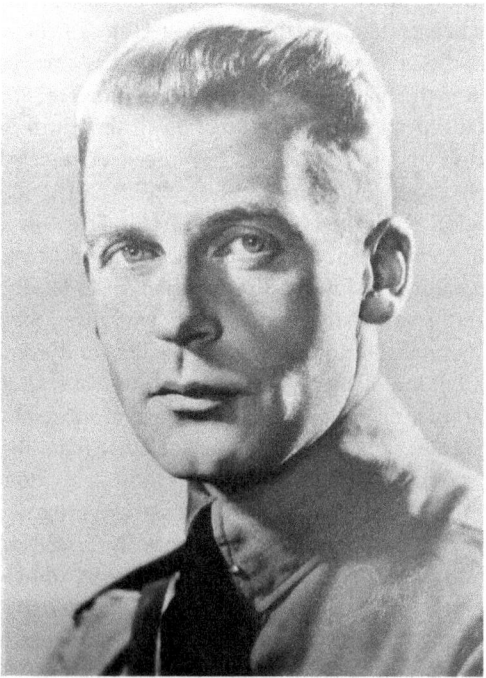

Figure 3 Sven Olov Lindholm, wearing the brown shirt of his party. Photographer unknown. National Archives of Sweden, Marieberg. Martin Ekström's archive (SE/RA/720615).

The popular demand for a charismatic fascist Leader conflicted with the respectability that both leaders at different times sought to exhibit. If fascist members themselves were inspired by external (foreign) sources in their desire for a Leader, non-fascist outsiders too were aware of what models inspired the NSB and NSAP. Neither Swedish nor Dutch mainstream democratic media had a rosy view of fascist dictators, so that the myth of the Leader played directly into hostile representations of fascism as tyranny. At the same time the impressive propaganda imagery that was promulgated from Italy and Germany to the international press provided a neat measuring stick with which to beat Lindholm and Mussert as inadequate would-be Führers. Members' desires and public opinion were two contradicting driving forces in NSB and NSAP mythopoeia, which was always an ongoing process, rather than a synchronic achievement. From 1933 to 1938, the Leaders were in constant flux, buffeted by opinion and political necessity in a dialectical trial and error process of mythopoeic construction.

Life and character of Sven Olov Lindholm

Sven Olov Knutsson Lindholm was born on 8 February 1903, in Jönköping, the son of Sigrid Johansson and Knut Axel Lindholm. Lindholm grew up in a semi-rural household, and was raised to love his *hembygd* (homeland), and by extension the fatherland – 'but it was mostly nature, which was the root of that love'.[17] His merchant father and his friends who frequently visited were typically *nationella*, bourgeois nationalist and conservative supporters of the Right, which was reflected in how Lindholm was raised.[18] This would prove formative, although largely in a negative way, as Lindholm rejected right-wing classism. After leaving school at the age of sixteen, Lindholm joined the Royal Artillery Regiment in 1920, going through NCO-training. He remained there until 1927, at which point the regiment was decommissioned, and Lindholm moved to the Svea Artillery Regiment in Stockholm.[19] During this period he became a leading functionary of SFKO, founded in 1926. In 1929 he attended the NSDAP Nuremberg rally as a guest, and had the opportunity to briefly speak to several of the party leadership, including Hitler. More importantly for his ideological development were his December 1932 conversations with Gregor Strasser,[20] whom Lindholm admired throughout his life, and mentioned as a key influence in his memoirs.[21] (Though it should be noted that at least some of the admiration for Strasserism was retrospective, and dates to Lindholm's postwar reflections on national socialism's development.) Overworked, he resigned from military service in 1930 to commit himself fully to the party, which at this point was merged with Birger Furugård's SNSP.[22] Throughout the 1930s Lindholm would continue doing occasional military service, but mostly earned a living with party work. It was also during this period that he met Kersti Andersson, whom he married in 1939 after proposing to her at the annual party convention. However, Kersti died from leukaemia in 1941, at the age of twenty-three.[23] During the war Lindholm was promoted to sergeant in the artillery, but was forced to retire in 1942 after it became public that he was in charge of military defence against a potential Nazi coup. He continued his work as party leader until 1950, when the SSS was disbanded.

Lindholm lived a long life after that, finding work in a typeface factory, Monotype.[24] He re-married to Vera Schimanski (1928–), a German postwar émigré, who shared his fascist ideology. However, over time Lindholm's ideology radically changed, and he came to renounce fascism altogether. Eventually Lindholm and Vera divorced in 1960–2 for their political differences.[25] The remaining decades of his life Lindholm engaged in anti-nuclear and anti-war activism, and studied the emerging literature on fascism, corresponding with a number of Swedish historians in the 1970s and 1980s. He also wrote his memoirs, *Soldatliv och Politik* (Soldier Life and Politics), and edited his diary, both dedicated to his daughter. He died in 1998, at his home in Rönninge.

In his memoirs Lindholm recalled the household literature as being formative for his ideas: Johan Runeberg, Viktor Rydberg, Esaias Tegnér, Verner von Heidenstam, Bertel Gripenberg – Romantic Swedish classics of the nineteenth century, and reputed contemporary nationalist poets.[26] Lindholm was an avid reader throughout his life, with a clear thematic pattern: military life, Swedish history, Romanticism and Nordic culture. Viktor Lundberg has argued that, quite in line with these interests, Lindholm was heavily influenced by Ernst Jünger as well.[27] However, Lindholm, who otherwise reliably made note of his reading material in his diary and other writings, never mentioned reading any of Jünger's works, so that Lundberg's claim must be regarded with scepticism. Lindholm's lifestyle was shaped in obvious ways by the military, but also by the ideology of Are Waerland (1876–1955) – a Finno-Swedish amateur philosopher and dietician with a racialist bent – which was reflected in his lifestyle.[28]

Together with health and military life, Lindholm's ideology was characterized by a corresponding obsession with youth. The idealization of youth was of course perfectly common among fascists at the time, as well as the Swedish health- and sport movement (*frisksportrörelsen*) in labour ideology, which was peaking at this time.[29] Next to the Swedish landscape, it was youth which most inspired Lindholm to write poetry, and his speeches and articles consistently emphasized Swedish youth as the key to political success. The documents produced by the organization of the annual propaganda tours give the most insight into Lindholm's day-to-day life. His diary shows a pattern of rising early, working hard throughout the day and into the night, interspersed with outdoors exercise, and lake-bathing, regularly subjecting the body to cold temperatures. His diet typically consisted of rye bread and raw vegetables, and *kruska* (a type of porridge) for breakfast, what Waerland termed *lakto-vegetabilisk råkost*. His daily regimen was one he also inflicted on his colleagues during the summer, with a preference for lakeside camping. In his own words: 'Save us, old soldiers, from all desire for comfort, and for all extravagances. In all things we only desire *order*.'[30] His somewhat ascetic lifestyle became almost proverbial within the party. If that was a point of admiration for the cadres, his 'Waerlandism' was not. His rejection of alcohol was not well-received,[31] and one can only imagine how his *kruska* cooking classes were received by party members.[32]

Figure 4 Anton Adriaan Mussert, wearing the typical party black shirt and tie, 1932. Photographer: NSB Fotodienst. Rijksmuseum (NG-2007-35-141).

Life and character of Anton Mussert

Less is known about the early life of Anton Adriaan Mussert, but he could hardly have been more different from Lindholm. He was born on 11 May 1894 in Werkendam, in North-Brabant. His father, Joannes Leonardus, was Catholic, but converted to Protestantism when he married Frederika Witlam. Joannes Leonardus was a liberal conservative school teacher who seems to have had a lasting influence on Anton,[33] in spite of his premature death.[34] The historian Jan Meyers argued that this was a fiercely patriotic Orangist household, something which marked Mussert as a conservative bourgeois liberal.[35] As such he fell largely outside the confessional pillars of Dutch society, and his Christianity seemed largely negative in character. But as will be shown later, he would come to develop his religion to be more in tune with the serious Christian political culture of the Netherlands. Unlike Lindholm, Mussert had no taste for literature, or music for that matter, and seemed almost culturally illiterate. His main interests were in history, with a similar national-romantic education to Lindholm, and engineering. His interests in engineering and organization defined his character for life, and even in prison after the Occupation he wrote and proposed new ideas on the subject. Generally he was unsociable; not unpleasant, but humourless and pedantic, and with few friends. He attempted to join the navy, but was rejected as constitutionally inadequate, on account of his diminutive stature. Instead he went to a

Technical College to acquire a master's degree as civil engineer, and he would brandish the title it earned him (*ingenieur, ir.*) for years to come. During the First World War Mussert got some taste of military life, when he managed to join the reserve army.[36] However, he had to go home again for a prolonged illness, during which time he was taken care of by his aunt, Maria Witlam, a 38-year-old nurse. In 1917 they married, with royal dispensation for the incestuous union, and much to the dismay of his family, especially Anton's mother who fiercely opposed the marriage to her sister.[37]

After the war he made a career as civil engineer in water management in Utrecht, attaining the prestigious office of Head Engineer at the impressive age of thirty-one through a mixture of talent and careerist cunning.[38] He spent his spare time reading about history, engineering and politics, with weekly visits to the Jewish Jitta family to play Bridge.[39] A member of the liberal conservative Vrijheidsbond (Freedom Union, after 1937 the Liberal State Party) like his father, his work brought him into nationalist politics when the 1925 Belgian Treaty unexpectedly united water management with nationalist controversy. The treaty concerned Belgian access to the Moerdijk canal via Antwerp, and under the treaty, supported by France, the right to pass through the canals with war ships if necessary.[40] Mussert became a leading figure in the national protest against the treaty, which was successfully abandoned under the pressure. Inspired by his political success, Mussert became increasingly interested in politics, leading him to eventually found his own party in 1931, together with his colleague in the treaty protest, Cornelis Van Geelkerken (1901–76).

In 1934, the law against civil servants in revolutionary organizations forced Mussert into a career of full-time politics, his fame or notoriety growing with the NSB. May 1940 became a turning point as the German Occupation and the establishment of a Reichskommissariat offered the prospect of real political power. But with collaboration – albeit of a very difficult and conflicted sort, with open hostility between the NSB and the SS – Mussert quickly became one of the most hated figures of the Netherlands. After the war he was put on trial; his time in prison was spent writing letters, proposing new engineering projects and a justification of his political actions.[41] He was executed on 7 May 1946.[42]

Beyond a short war-time diary and his prison notes, little has been written by Mussert to elucidate his thinking, or the development of his personal ideology. Like Lindholm, Mussert denied he ever read *Mein Kampf*, and it seems his conversion to fascism came with reports and propaganda from the rising NSDAP in Germany, and an admiration for Mussolini that was common in the Netherlands of the late 1920s and early 1930s, as it was elsewhere in Europe.[43] Historian Ronald Havenaar denied Mussert had any kind of ideology at all, pointing to the theoretical poverty of his thought, instead seeing him above all as an organizer.[44] There was doubtlessly no originality in Mussert's programmatic statements, and a great deal was copied directly from Germany and Italy, but this must be qualified. Beyond clearly stated ideological positions, Mussert's thoughts were strongly grounded in patriotic histories of the Netherlands and the Dutch Republic. His liberal-romantic patriotism was in many ways conventionally bourgeois, but also made for a consistent and unique fascist ideology.[45] Together with his passion for engineering, it gave Mussert a very distinct ideological profile.

†††

Lindholm and Mussert were not just the human face of the leadership vis-à-vis the rank-and-file, but the face of the party to the public. As public-facing figures the personalities of the leaders were most immediately on display, rather than by virtue of their office, reflexively bestowing their particular traits on the party. The NSAP's myth of a revolutionary socialist *arbetareparti* owed a lot to Lindholm himself. The simplicity of his speech, his common habits, as well as his personal background as a low-ranking army officer in the Swedish artillery promoted the party image.[46] By contrast it was Mussert's background as a leader in the 1925–7 protest against the Belgian Treaty which established his patriotic credentials (his ideas about the treaty and for diplomacy with Belgium were published in the liberal NRC, and later as a book),[47] while it was his prestigious job as Head Engineer that gave the NSB such respectable appeal.[48] Lindholm's and Mussert's functions in the party leadership were not entirely separable from themselves as persons. Thus, while the party leaders were themselves situated at various points *within* the apparatus's mythopoeia of the party, there was also an implicit equivalence between them and the party myth.

Techniques of construction

But it was not enough for Lindholm and Mussert to simply function as public leaders in their respective organizations. The formal roles which the parties bestowed on them, and the rather un-exciting reality of their personalities, were insufficient for *fascist* Leaders. In other words, the party membership, rank-and-file, functionaries and the leadership had a pre-established idea of what a leader was meant to be like in such an organization. Neither of the leaders had read *Mein Kampf*, at least in full,[49] and did not necessarily share the notion of a 'genius' Leader,[50] but they were doubtlessly influenced by the propaganda material and reports coming out of Germany, and to a lesser extent Italy. In the third ever issue of DSN, Per Dahlberg wrote, in a statement on the principles of National Socialism, that 'a leader cannot be conjured forth through advertisement or empty declamations, [rather] he works through *the power of his personality*'.[51] There was an understanding that fascist leaders had to be more than just competent, as implied by the extraordinary authority the party leaders enjoyed. There were other important figures in the NSB and NSAP which could make claims to leadership on the basis of competence, or who were equally good at commanding a crowd as their superiors. Mussert was perhaps a decent speaker – opinions were certainly divided[52] – but the Deputy Leader and General Secretary Cornelis Van Geelkerken was generally held to be more engaging, handsome and taller.[53] Regional leaders could command their own loyalties: southern District Leader d'Ansembourg for instance received requests for signed portraits of him from devoted members.[54] In Sweden, Lindholm had acquired a great deal of experience as speaker and propaganda organizer in SFKO and SNSP,[55] but Per Dahlberg rivalled those qualities, while NU leader Arne Clementsson (1915–?) seems to have been an excellent speaker, and even something like a charismatic leader in his own right.[56] Consequently, since neither

Lindholm nor Mussert occupied the position as Leader naturally, at least not very securely, it was necessary to construct them as Leaders.

One of the first and most direct ways of doing this was through dress and demeanour, which relied on handy signs to mark the leader as *the* Leader. They took on the roles of military commanders in speeches and articles, which was complemented through the wearing of uniforms, which underlined the hierarchical and unquestionable nature of the relationship of the leader to his followers. Mussert favoured a simple tailored, black or grey military jacket with a white shirt and black tie, which, while denoting him as an officer over his troops, set him above the dress regulations of the party, denoting his special rank. Lindholm by contrast favoured the brown shirt SA-uniform of his party. His image of the Leader was that of the *primus inter pares*, and relied on close identification with his followers. In the style of military commanders, the party leaders led marching columns through cities during rallies,[57] or subjected party branches to solemn reviews as if army regiments, letting the members march past as they theatrically saluted the columns from a platform.[58] Both leaders used standards as explicit symbols of their authority.[59] It was a simple, but evocative visual language which easily marked the men not as conventional party leaders or administrators, but something special, which allowed them to more effectively perform the role of natural Leader, and was seamlessly integrated with the militaristic myth of the party army. In parties where part of the attraction was to be a missionary fascist soldier, military imagery could convincingly make a Leader for the cadres.

In practice most members did not often see their party leaders in the flesh however, especially not in countryside NSAP branches, which did not get a visit from Lindholm more than once every few years. To maintain the idea of the natural and unquestionable Leader, repetition was required in some form. This was managed particularly through print media, and the regular replication of images and text. Both DSN and VoVa produced standardized portraits of the Leader, which were featured on the front page of the papers whenever relevant, usually to emphasize the leaders addressing the members directly, their names printed in large capital letters. Generally depictions of the Leader were more common in VoVa than DSN – Catholic daily *De Tijd* wrote Mussert should solicit for a job as advertising doll.[60] To celebrate Mussert's return from the Dutch East Indies in 1935, NSB artist Meuldijk produced an idealized portrait of the Leader, emphasizing his most celebrated facial features – 'the Napoleonic figure with that imposing head, in which the mouth accentuates the force of will like a deep trench'[61] – which was regularly reprinted in VoVa. It is of note that it tended to be the same portrait that was used over and over again, familiarizing members with a single image of their Leader, which over the years acquired an iconic status. These portraits of the Leader had a special status unlike others, and had to be treated with due reverence – for instance NSAP members were not allowed to in any way commercialize Lindholm's image,[62] nor use his picture or name in propaganda without special permission.[63] Beyond portraiture, party publications also used techniques of design and placement to give special prominence or significance to the words of the leader, emphasizing his special relationship to the party. Any editorial by Mussert was placed on the front page of VoVa, usually taking up the entire page, and with his name prominently displayed in capital letters. From time to time quotations from the Leader were printed in a banner at the bottom of the page of the paper, where it would also place quotations from patriotic historical figures like William the Silent.[64] DSN seemed to have eschewed quite such blatant methods of highlighting Lindholm's significance, but did give enormous prominence to his speeches, especially after the annual party convention, the *årsting*. Simply summarizing his speeches was not enough. In 1934, being only a six-to-eight page paper, DSN printed every word of Lindholm's *årsting* speech, spreading it through several issues over more than a month, taking up almost a quarter of the paper.[65] Party publications, being the one piece of media to which party members (and the public for that matter) were exposed on a regular basis, were not simply a mouthpiece of the Leader, but were specifically designed to construct him as a Leader, a figure of unparalleled authority.

The myth of the fascist Leader required Lindholm and Mussert to not just be authoritative, but popular. Leaving aside whether or not they indeed were, efforts were certainly made to portray them as such. The propaganda apparatuses were highly observant of attendance figures at meetings featuring the party leader, quick to point out applause and cries of agreement, and generally emphasize the loyalty of members to their Leader. The NSAP employed claques to express support for Lindholm, though it is unclear to what extent.[66] At the first *årsting*, DSN pointed out the 'especially strong tributes' that were made to Lindholm, and printed in the front page header that Lindholm had been 'acclaimed with ovations' at the rally.[67] Whenever Lindholm appeared on stage, he was immediately met with 'endless jubilation', and cries of 'hell Lindholm'.[68] If the reader who had never met Lindholm was in any doubt as to the enthusiasm that Lindholm could generate in his audience, DSN could paint a vivid and exclamatory picture of the supposedly electrifying character of his speeches:

> Like threatening thunder the rumbling of the applause filled the enormous circus tent! The Leader had spoken and the followers had been forged together into one single unit, ready for battle! While Lindholm had been speaking, all doubts had disappeared; problems, which one had been pondering for weeks, were solved; the lines were now clear; the goals for the fight stood out plain and firm before one's eyes and the will to continued struggle had become even more hard as iron than ever before![69]

Whether there was a word of truth to these descriptions of Lindholm's effect on his audience is uncertain, but the mantric insistence on the enthusiasm of the crowds in every meeting report did help construct Lindholm as a charismatic leader.[70] Some of the formulaic expressions employed by DSN found their way into branch reports of meetings with Lindholm.[71] The rhetoric of VoVa was a little less fervent in its assessment of Mussert's speeches, opting instead to simply describe a meeting as 'an evening of fervent zeal'.[72] At the march to the RAI meeting hall for the April 1935 party congress in Amsterdam, Mussert marched at the head of the party troops, while people pushed and shoved on the pavements and hung from their house windows 'to see Mussert'.[73] Appearing in the hall to speak, the audience burst out in ovations, as the Leader benevolently regarded his audience. 'Then Mussert made the well-known gesture', VoVa wrote, 'as if cutting the ripe wheat with a single stroke – the loud ovations ceased'.⁷⁴ When the *Algemeen Leider* spoke at a meeting for the first time after a prolonged illness, his appearance was immediately met with 'thundering shouts of *hou-zee*', as he made his way up to the podium.⁷⁵ While commentators have been sceptical about the rhetorical talent of the Swedish and Dutch fascist leaders, and Dutch historians have been keen to deny any charismatic qualities to Mussert in particular, VoVa and DSN present a very different image of the leaders.⁷⁶ In party media, the leader came across as a natural leader, one who led not just through his competence, but due to his innate commanding stature, his inexplicable but unquestioned authority, and the charismatic bond with his followers which was expressed in their wild and tremendous enthusiasm.⁷⁷ There was no particular need for this discursive construction to directly correspond to the reality of Lindholm's and Mussert's persons, because these repeated statements of Leader qualities were fundamentally performative in nature; that is, they created what they ostensibly described – no doubt imperfectly, but certainly not ineffectively. Thus, the creation of the Leader was largely a top-down mythopoeic process enacted through the party apparatus.

Grassroots pressure and devotion

While the parties' propaganda apparatuses constructed the leaders as charismatic fascist Leaders, neither Mussert nor Lindholm seemed very comfortable performing these roles, at least initially. Both seemed aware enough of their own lack of any superhuman talents, and little of the propaganda work had yet been done to render their leading positions in the organization indisputable. Around 1932–3, the two leaders seem to have mostly been preoccupied with securing the organizational foundations of the party and attracting a membership, with little notion of any extraordinary demands of themselves. But soon they found that while they may not have required any particular adulation from their members, many of the members who came to the new movements desired a Leader to venerate.

A June 1933 letter from one member to Mussert linked the nature of the NSB as a fascist movement to Mussert's role as leader – if Mussert was not prepared to take on the role of a true Leader of his followers, '*can we be sure that the N.S.B. intends to be a fascist organization*'.⁷⁸ It was rumoured that Mussert opposed a cult of personality (*persoonsvereering*), and had prohibited the '*heil Mussert*' salute, instead idiosyncratically opting for the maritime greeting *hou-zee* (hold sea). As Mussert's rather technical title of *Algemeen Leider* (General Leader) suggests, the 'AL' saw himself as not a predestined Leader, but as a leader elected for his competence. At the first party congress in Utrecht, January 1933, he acknowledged that '[t]he fascist worldview places the life-affirming force of the personality against the dead weight of majorities. It desires strong authority; it desires personal leadership. In our own organization we will of course have to set an example.'⁷⁹ But the nature of that leadership was immediately underlined as elective; Mussert promised that if a better, more competent leader emerged, he would withdraw immediately.⁸⁰ VoVa reported that the congress subsequently declared him General Leader with great enthusiasm. His anxious devotee pointed out:

But the masses want a cult of personality, the masses want a symbol: can '*begeisterung*' really emerge from the daily administration of for instance 3 people, a triumvirate? [...] And so you too must be a symbol for our Movement, and the people must not know you, they must not know you as an ordinary mortal, they must only see and hear you on the stage, or at the head of the troops.[81]

Mussert's response to the letter has not survived, but it is evident that in spite of any discomfort he may have felt, the leadership did acknowledge the existence of a grassroots demand for Mussert to be a charismatic Leader. That fascist loyalty to the *Algemeen Leider* was quickly taking on forms beyond the merely conventional is suggested by one letter from a party functionary in December 1933. He and his wife had decided to name their new-born child Anton Adriaan: 'we see in you the example of a good Patriot and an upright fascist, and also hope that this will be a guide to him for the rest of his life.'[82]

Lindholm only seemed to demand from his members something like the loyalty of soldiers to their officer, but the socialistic myth of the party emphasized the fundamental equality of the leader with his followers, and made 'voluntary discipline' the basis of party hierarchy. In his 1980–1 interview, Lindholm noted his own discomfort with anything like a cult of personality in 1935: 'I wasn't particularly fond of that, but unfortunately I had to accept it. Because the fact is that it made a strong impression, on both followers and spectators – they wanted things like that.'[83] While the evidence outside of party publications is relatively sparse here, Lindholm's assessment decades later does seem to correspond to the strong desire some branches expressed to have the *partiledare* speak to them.[84] In fact party correspondence shows the leadership deliberately used Lindholm's visits as a reward mechanism.[85] There was also the dreadful poetry members sent in to DSN: 'They had no ideals to acclaim, / they had no Lindholm, they, – like us.'[86] Adulation apparently came automatically from the members, much in the same way as in the Netherlands, in a way that suggests prior expectations of the fascist leader. Whatever the extent of the rank-and-file's demand for a leader cult, it was an opportunity the party leadership did not leave aside. The fascist leader had a crucial mobilizing function in the party organization. To encourage and sustain devotion to the leader could only enhance that function, but this required more than just the discursive construction of popularity.

One of the means of satisfying grassroots demand for a leader cult was through idolizing imagery, poetry, songs and the like, and making these directly available to the membership. It has been noted how portraits of the Leader were frequently put on the front page of party publications, newspapers, brochures and so forth, which could quickly give them an iconic quality. Odes in the form of poetry were another form which attempted to develop a cultic appreciation of the Leader in the NSB. In July 1935 VoVa featured the first poem in dedication to Mussert on the front page, in acclaim of his flight to and from the Dutch Indies[87] – *De Tijd* commented sarcastically on the VoVa poem celebrating 'the immaterial fact, that someone who visits the Indies, also returns'[88] – after which they featured in the paper a couple of times per year for the rest of the decade. 'The drums of Mussert' glorified the Leader's call to arms, while 'The word of the leader' envisioned Mussert as 'a hero'.[89] The Swedish

DSN by contrast was remarkably void of such poetic celebrations of the *partiledare*. The paper did however feature Lindholm's own poetry, which was another way in which members could engage with him, the party organ becoming a platform for his image as a sensitive Swede, baring his soul, communicating the mysteries of nature and struggle.[90] To permit members to engage even closer with Lindholm's poetic products, a gramophone recording was made of his party anthem *Friheten leve!* (Freedom lives), a popular song frequently sung at party meetings.[91] Members could purchase one of the thousand records, for 2.50 kronor, directly from the party supply service or certain stores.[92] Beyond this endeavour, there appear to have been surprisingly few attempts in the NSAP to further members' interactions with the Leader through merchandise. Postcards with a portrait of Lindholm in SA uniform and one of his poems were sold, allowing members to possess a representation of the Leader, but not much more.[93] In the Netherlands, commercialization of the Leader's image was much more common.[94] After all, the NSB did not have the same socialistic ethos as the NSAP, while Mussert clearly had a more refined instinct for business.[95] Portraits of Mussert in various sizes were advertised to the members, so they could display their loyalty to the Leader in their own homes.[96] In 1934 a 'film booklet' was made. 'By quickly passing the pages through one's fingers, a living picture is formed of the General Leader.' This was 'of great propagandistic value', according to the propaganda department.[97] When Mussert returned from his successful trip to the East Indies by airplane, a commemorative plate was gifted to him, of which subsequently 600 copies were made available to the more devoted members.[98] Moreover, every party convention was used as an opportunity to sell high-quality, illustrated commemorative books, which prominently displayed numerous pictures of the Leader, as advertised in circulars and VoVa, for prices as low as 0.75 guilders.[99] For most of these examples of merchandise it is unfortunately impossible to know what kind of investment they entailed for the party, how much it profited from the sales, or indeed how popular they were – though the continued annual production of the commemorative books suggests they were well-received. Regardless, they demonstrate a willingness of the party leadership to commercialize Mussert's image, and disseminate his image in various forms into the households of thousands of members, simultaneously satisfying and encouraging the cadres' devotional desires. It also highlights the difference in financial capacity between the NSB and the NSAP, the latter lacking much of the resources and competence that would have made this particular method of developing the leader cult possible.

Owing to this lack of resources, the mythopoeia of the charismatic Leader was less refined in Sweden, and relied more on the physical presence of Lindholm, which suited his itinerant leadership style.[100] In the mythopoeic development of the NSAP cult, personal presence was used to emphasize the special, unbreakable bond between the Leader and his 'never failing troops of swastika-warriors, unwaveringly devoted to their leader', rather than on Lindholm as a person.[101] Members had to not just be loyal to the ideas, but absolutely dedicated to their leader as a condition for party membership.[102] It was the *årsting*, held every year except 1936, which formed the centrepiece of the NSAP's ceremonial devotion to Lindholm. 'Out in the countryside, the fighters look towards Stockholm filled with expectations this Pentecost. After another year of struggle, loyalty, and sacrifice, they will now get the opportunity to come together with comrades from the entire country and meet their Leader.'[103] During the event which went on for two days, members would attend multiple speeches from the leadership, and attend outdoor rallies complete with marches through the city. While ostensibly an occasion for collective decision-making and an opportunity for the rank-and-file to enter into dialogue with the leadership, in practice the event was an opportunity to mobilize the membership and rubber-stamp the leadership's decisions. For Lindholm personally it was a moment to be in contact with his followers, and accept their adulations, the moment when the 'fighting battalions march in the capital and gather around their young chieftain'.[104] On the first day of the convention, the 'leader day', the Party Leadership conferred with party functionaries from branches across the country, but on the second day the Party Leader would speak to the rank-and-file (usually around 2000 members). In 1934 'Lindholm had tried to avoid personal acclamation from the members, but it was the only thing at the convention that failed – completely spontaneously the bubbling shouts of *hail* came to him, from the depths of a thousand hearts.'[105] By 1935 a ritual was developed for the *årsting*. Once all members were gathered, the band played a song such as *Friheten Leve!*, and the Leader ascended the podium to ovations and shouts of *hell Lindholm*. 'An outsider cannot understand the heartfelt contact that exists in a moment such as this between Leader and followers, but we know that this natural, voluntary solidarity, founded on the kinship of souls, only exists among us', DSN insisted.[106] After a lengthy speech assessing the continued party struggle, Lindholm made an appeal for onward struggle. With the close of the

Figure 5 'One for all – All for one'. The party salutes Lindholm at a meeting in 1938. Photographer unknown. *Den Svenske Nationalsocialisten*, 1938, no. 35. Kungliga Biblioteket (National Library of Sweden).

speech, Lindholm shouted out to his followers: 'One for all!', to which the audience responded with a resounding: 'All for one!' (*En för alla – Alla för en*).[107]

The choreography was simplistic, even trivial, but the event amounted to a covenant between the Leader and his followers. Annually renewed, it was a mythopoeic ritual sanctifying the charismatic bond between Lindholm and the NSAP with a solemn vow to mutual devotion, one that filled a genuine need amongst the cadres. However, it is important to note that the *årsting* never managed to gather more than perhaps one-fifth of the total party membership. Thus, in the end the actual mythopoeic potential of ritual relying on the personal presence of Lindholm was directly limited, even if the mythopoeic potential was magnified through reproduction and dissemination in print.

The Dutch *landdagen* had a similar character to those of the NSAP, but appear from VoVa's reports to have been more varied from year to year, as were the *Hagespraken* in Lunteren held every year from 1936 to 1940. At the start of the 1934 regional party congress (*landdag*), Mussert suddenly entered unannounced, strode up to the podium to the sound of snare drums, accompanied by a uniformed guard, and mounted the elevated platform to ovations and shouts of *hou-zee*; a conventional choreography that doubtlessly constructed Mussert as a fascist Leader, but did not do anything out of the ordinary, and maintained the hierarchical separation of Leader and followers, seeking to impress the audience more than anything else.[108] With minor variations, it was a ritual uniformly repeated through the 1930s, its components echoing those of not just the NSAP, but fascist groups all over Europe.

Rather more intriguing is the evidence that various NSB departments were by the mid-1930s working on ceremonies to develop the emergent cult of the leader with religious overtones, specifically designed to move the audience, and give the Leader mythical status. Two documents survive, one (1935) from the Council for Ecclesiastical Matters by the Catholic John Boddé, and another (1936) from the shadowy Council for *Volksche* Culture, by the Reformed E.J. Roskam (also a member of the ecclesiastical council). It is unclear whether the suggestions were ever fully implemented, but as will be made clear further on, at least elements were incorporated into mythopoeic ritual. Council Secretary Boddé suggested that for a one hour meeting, after a short speech, the present members would sing the 1626 hymn *Wilt heden nu treden* (We gather together), and subsequently proceed to gather around the Leader (presumably in a semi-circle). Boddé insisted that the ceremony 'does not become a veneration of the Leader, no deification. Rather, we gather around our Leader, we swear loyalty, and the Leader accepts that, and places himself *precisely because of that* with us before the face of our Creator.'[109] The initial two lines of the first verse would emphasize 'the beautiful symbolism': 'We gather together before God the Lord, / Him above all we praise with our hearts.'[110] Metaphorically facing God, Mussert would have stood before his loyal devotees, guiding them onwards in subservience to the Lord. 'Then we will experience a moment with which one can go on [fighting] for a year, and which one will never forget. Surely we must try to touch people in the deepest parts of their being.'[111] In his letter to Mussert, Roskam suggested a prayer ceremony to follow the main speech. In Mussert's speech to the audience/congregation, he would emphasize the charismatic bond with his followers: 'Our Movement is too large for us to maintain personal contact, even though we would like to. But even though that is not possible, that does not mean that there is no mystic bond which links us together and binds us.'¹¹² The speech continued to affirm it was a bond forged by God Himself in the struggle for an honest cause. In silence the audience then listened to a trumpet playing *Nader mijn God tot U* (Closer to you, my God), before Mussert commenced a prayer to the 'God of the Netherlands', after which he announced the singing of *Wilt heden nu treden*, optionally replacing the final verse (which historically had anti-Catholic implications) with an appeal to the Trinity.¹¹³ In this ceremony, the construction of the Leader as a priestly figure was taken even further, interceding with God for the Movement. It is uncertain whether these specific forms on paper were ever fully implemented, but they are a clear indication of the direction in which party institutions were taking the Leader myth by the middle of the decade, using ritual means to progress mythopoeia, and were doing so in cooperation with the party leader.

Regardless of the personal qualities of Mussert and Lindholm, the mythopoeia of the Leader through these more or less 'cultish' methods met a deeply felt need among some members, and successfully created a thoroughly loyal core of militant devotees, if not necessarily a large one. There are a number of key moments through which this can be assessed, if in a limited way. When Lindholm spent time in prison from 17 March to 17 May 1935, he received numerous letters of support from his followers, and the first buttercups of the season from female members. Throughout April, Lindholm was literally inundated with flowers, which he had to eventually move out of his cell because of the overwhelming scent.¹¹⁴ He wrote happily to his mother of the floral contributions from his devotees.¹¹⁵ For his release in May, hundreds of party members had travelled to the prison to greet him – one NU-boy handed over yet another bouquet – and welcome him back to the struggle.¹¹⁶ Many NSAP members clearly felt a strong sense of loyalty to Lindholm personally, and a need to demonstrate their commitment in some material way. Such opportunities did not often present themselves, but were used when they did. A cultic devotion to Lindholm as Leader persisted among a small core of members, who even through great setbacks, the difficult war years and perhaps even harder postwar years until 1950, remained loyal to him.

The greater survival of the NSB party archive makes an assessment of devotion to Mussert a little easier, as some of the correspondence gives an insight into the rank-and-file's personal feelings about their Leader. On the occasion of the third *landdag* in Amsterdam, 1935, some felt the need to 'personally express [their] feelings of honest veneration' for Mussert.¹¹⁷ One member wrote the day after the *landdag* to thank her Leader for 'the glowing words which you spoke to us', which spurred her on to place her 'entire being in the service of the NSB, and as a woman to help you as much as possible with the great work for the good of our Fatherland'.¹¹⁸ Another family wrote enthusiastically of their experience of the entire event, '[h]owever, the climax for us all was seeing the figure of the General Leader, far in the distance, heavily lit and standing tall above his thousands of loyal followers, as if on the forecastle of his admiral's ship!'¹¹⁹ The most important sign of loyalty to Mussert came after the electoral failure of May 1937, which was followed by an attempt to oust Mussert in the autumn by Goes van der Naters, and other leading functionaries in Department X (*Vorming*, Education) including J. Hogewind. Mussert loyalists were summoned to the Goudsberg in Lunteren on 9 October for an impromptu meeting, ('MUSSERT calls for his faithful', as the summons put it),[120] and at least some 15,000 members turned up (35,000–40,000 according to VoVa) at their own expense to profess loyalty to their *Leider*.[121] The meeting was finished with the song *Voor Anton Mussert zijn wij in het gevecht* (We are in this fight for Anton Mussert),[122] and a recording of Luther's *Ein feste Burg ist unser Gott* (A mighty fortress is our God).[123] Hundreds more sent in professions of loyalty before and after.[124] One party branch sent in the signatures of all the members who could not make it to Lunteren but wished to 'hereby profess their unshakeable loyalty to the *Leider*'. 'Loyal until *death*!', a handwritten note added dramatically.[125] Devotion to Mussert personally had clearly been generated over the years, and when put to the test it turned out to be a useful tool, and was in and of itself sufficient to mobilize the NSB on a large scale. In spite of numerous challenges to his leadership, especially during the German Occupation, even as the membership was decimated, Mussert always managed to maintain his position, being able to reliably fall back on his mythic status as predestined Leader of the Movement.[126]

Challenges to and evolution of the myths

While the various mythopoeic methods constructed Lindholm and Mussert as 'generic' fascist Leaders in some sense, there were important differences, with significant implications for the quality and nature of their leadership and the fascist myth. But crucially the development of the myth of the Leader was a process: it was never in any sense complete, was in no sense all-encompassing, and changed substantially over time. The devotion of party loyalists and the need for mobilization were not the only factors driving mythopoeia, as the party organizations also had to contend with respectable opinion, and a vindictive press's attitudes to fascist leader cults. These prohibited any kind of straightforward apotheosis of the Leader, not least because political opponents interrupted mythopoeia with their own, less flattering narratives.

The myth of Lindholm was perhaps the least fantastical, and largely static compared to Mussert's, but multi-faceted and subtle. It derived more from Lindholm's actual person – a young, tall, blond soldier with a love for the Swedish landscape – and relied on a more egalitarian notion of leadership. Maybe Lindholm was as wary of a cult of personality as he claimed in the 1980s, but his supposed modesty as a fascist Leader was exploited all the more for that. As shown above, NSAP mythopoeia focused particularly on his relationship to his followers rather than his own charismatic qualities. While Lindholm's leadership was hardly democratic in the conventional sense of the word, he held his position with the approval of the loyal membership. As a 1938 circular put it: 'Our opponents' propaganda often has an animus against the Nordic leader principle. They confuse our leader with oriental idols and small-German *gauführer*. Our leader is a Swedish *folkledare* [people's leader] and nothing more. The first among comrades.'[127] The humble leader was *primus inter pares*, in accordance with the Nordic chieftain tradition. The young chieftain deserved his position as a leader who was always at the front of his troops, leading them into battle, doing the brunt of the work, taking responsibility for the party. Carrying over his habits and activities from his time as an SNSP propaganda functionary, Lindholm was established as the Leader 'on the frontline'.¹²⁸ DSN portrayed a vivid picture of him: constantly at meetings, touring the entire country to evangelize in the remotest villages, from Scania to Haparanda, doing his duty like all the other activists, with a small unwaged team, sleeping in tents, living hand to mouth through the sale of newspapers, propaganda and donations. Every year, during the summer months in particular, but also in the depths of winter, the paper kept the readers up to date on Lindholm's latest meetings, successes and sacrifices, setting an example to the cadres, an apostle spreading the gospel. Illustrated with Lindholm's own photographs, it showed members how their leader lived out in the field, rising early to bathe in the lakes, going to bed late at night after a hard day of often dangerous activism, or braving arctic weather conditions to spread his message to Finnish lumberjack communities in the far north.¹²⁹ Lindholm was the perfect fascist activist, above all an example to his followers. In the words of one District functionary, 'in the last instance our struggle is a matter of will, and it is the will to life which pushes us to sacrifices of almost any magnitude, and in this, as in all other cases, Lindholm is our example.'¹³⁰ The principle of the leader as an example to his followers was institutionalized in the party directives for activists (1938), which emphasized that members were loyal to their leader because they were first and foremost loyal to the ideas, which the leader embodied.¹³¹

It was in this that Lindholm's myth culminated: he was the NSAP incarnate; he embodied fascism. The semantic slip from example to personification was made deliberately by Lindholm himself with the inception of the party. In his article 'To the National Socialists of Sweden' in the first issue of DSN, he justified the breakaway from SNSP with the notions of example and personification: 'One must demand from the *leadership* of this nat. soc. party that they are not just men who are honest, competent, and thoroughly familiar with their political task, but also that they through their personal example *represent* the ideas. Of a *leader* himself, finally, one demands that he *personifies* the ideas also in his life and in his actions.'¹³² In the wake of the 1937 party congress, DSN proclaimed in its headline: 'NSAP and Lindholm are one'.¹³³ A narrative of the party's origins as a moral and idealist break with corruption and compromise – represented by the SNSP – was closely tied to the construction of Lindholm as the ideal fascist embodiment of the party. This myth was annually reified with the 15 January celebration of the founding of the NSAP, an opportunity to develop a narrative with Lindholm as the moral hero purging Swedish fascism of its 'bourgeois corruption', destined to lead his followers to victory through the struggle and sacrifice he embodied.¹³⁴

> The man who had led them [Furugård], had failed them – it now depended on those who felt their responsibility before the people, whether everything was going to collapse, whether the sacrifices made up to this point would be in vain. They knew that they needed to act, and on that dark January day the revolution came. Lindholm raised his hand to strike. Lindholm raised his hand for renewed struggle. Around Lindholm they gathered, the oldest and most honest fighters of Swedish National Socialism.¹³⁵

As the idealistic and moral manifestation of fascism, Lindholm was increasingly associated with an above all uncompromising fascism. In the latter half of the decade, the party apparatus increasingly emphasized Lindholm's ethos as the salvation of Sweden. A police informant noted in March 1937 that Party Organizer Bertil Brisman 'depicted Lindholm as the man "who will save [*frälsa*] the Swedish people from their oppressors"'.[136] In one 1935 letter a former member of Lindholm's propaganda team wrote that life felt meaningless without active participation in the struggle, and fighting alongside Lindholm, who made life worth living. '*Lindholm* the leader will lead the people out of hardship and sorrow.'[137] Over the years a myth of Lindholm was constructed, that of a humble fascist Leader, pure and saintly in life, capable of saving the nation through his example, followed by a willing army with which he had a special, personal bond. Within a short span of time, this appears to have convinced at least some, and underpinned the devotion of the cadres, and mobilized them to unusually self-sacrificing forms of activism. As will be shown later, the corresponding mythopoeic efforts were sharply reduced in intensity around 1938, and came under fire from various directions, but for most of the 1930s it was an important factor in the cohesion and mobilization of the NSAP.

During the first years in the Netherlands, the NSB mainly tried to shape Mussert's image in line with his social status, his past as a nationalist campaigner, and as civil engineer. Rather than mythicizing his capacities, emphasis was on his technical competence derived from a highly successful career, and hard organizational work, which made him above all a *responsible* leader. The General Leader was *ir. Mussert* [*ingenieur*],[138] a respectable politician who abhorred violence,[139] who engaged in performative acts of loyalty to the House of Orange – e.g. the public sending of telegrams to Queen Wilhelmina at party rallies.[140] That Mussert's image and reputation provided a solid foundation for mythopoeia is evident from some of the initial press reports. In reaction to the first party convention, one paper wrote:

> Nothing but good is known about his past as engineer of water management. His love for his country and people is above suspicion. Indeed he has not started with bombast in a theoretical void, rather he has prepared the first appearance to the outside world methodically like a conscientious civil servant. Everything must really have been completely and neatly in order.[141]

The paper also favourably compared the NSB's engineered organization to the preposterous indiscipline of previous fascist parties; the liberal conservative paper *Algemeen Handelsblad* agreed.[142] In the first years the party made the most of this: quite uniquely in European fascism, this became a myth of the Leader as civil engineer. Mussert was portrayed as a responsible civil servant with a dedication to both state water management and the party, who fulfilled his duty in both capacities until forced to resign from his office by the 1934 law against civil servants in revolutionary organizations (Mussert argued the law itself was right in principle, but that the NSB was not a revolutionary organization).[143] That moment marked the decline of this particular construction of Mussert's myth, but it never went away entirely. While the myth would undergo radical alterations in the following years, as late as 1944 it was still brought up, with the publication of the Nenasu biography *Mussert als ingenieur* (Mussert as engineer).[144] But the heyday of this myth was the first few years of the NSB, when it could count on sympathy from the conservative press. In February 1933 VoVa proudly quoted the local Utrecht newspaper in its description of the leader, this 'young chief engineer of water management (*Rijkswaterstaat*), who builds roads in the day and spends his free time building up a movement, for which he has great expectations, is a born leader and organizer'.[145] In the NSB myth, engineers were ideally suited to be fascists: born organizers, and leaders of the people. And Mussert was the perfect engineer, demonstrated through his every action. At a rally in Amsterdam: 'The arrival of the leader is announced; with thundering calls of *houzee* Mussert goes to the podium in the middle of the hall. In everything Mussert shows himself the engineer: the straight line is the shortest path between two points.'[146]

In line with the respectability and supposed leader qualities that came with the skills of a civil engineer, Mussert was also constructed as a strongman to rival the prime minister, and a moral guardian of society. In the years 1932–4 Mussert was presented as an alternative to the Anti-Revolutionary Hendricus Colijn, who Mussert argued only weakened state authority through his compromises with the SDAP.[147] Through his editorials the *Algemeen Leider* consistently came out in defence of state authority and the, if necessary, violent suppression of unrest and disorder, as well as Christian morality in the face of cultural decadence.[148] In his October 1933 Utrecht convention speech, Mussert shunned terror, rejected racism, and stated that Dutch National Socialism considered the Queen to be the personification of power in the country, and 'fully recognizes the Christian character of the nation'.[149] The bourgeois undertones of Mussert's respectability were palpable, to the point where it became a source of complaint in the party: many members were prone to use 'un-fascist' modes of address for the Leader, referring to him as 'Mr Mussert' and the like, much to the chagrin of other members.[150] Mussert's respectability was banal, but was a crucial part of the mythopoeia of the Leader, and retrospectively turned out to be a stepping stone towards a less mundane myth.

As the NSB entered a damaging political contest with the Catholics and Calvinists in 1934–5, suffering the opprobrium of ecclesiastical censure, the party organization and Mussert increasingly emphasized the positive Christian dimensions of their ideology. In Mussert's own rhetoric, faith in God, while always an aspect of the 'leading principle', was pushed to the fore as the decade progressed (contrary to the claims of Tessel Pollmann who argued the reverse).[151] As seen previously, it was precisely after 1934 that the party leadership developed mythopoeic ceremonies with heavy-handed Christian overtones, presenting Mussert as an ecumenical alternative to Colijn, RKSP leader Piet Aalberse, or CHU leader Dirk Jan de Geer. At the 1937 *Hagespraak*, Mussert castigated the three main confessional parties for their perverted sense of decency and respectability [*fatsoen*].[152] In 1939 Mussert, in a speech about the decline of agriculture, invoked God to attack the government as sanctimonious, founded on the atheistic principles of the French Revolution. 'Whoever considers all this, for him it is no wonder that there is a rumbling over our fatherland. This is a miracle: that the Almighty endures it any longer, this state order which tramples and despises the laws of its Creator.'[153] From 1935 onwards there was a noticeable increase in Mussert's references to God, and his rhetoric became increasingly biblical.[154] He portrayed the fascist mission as the conscientious salvation of the people in duty to God, portraying the NSB as a martyrs' organization in God's service: 'At the end of every human life it does not matter one bit if the farewell happens in a prison or a stately bed ... it only matters, if you have done your duty, in accordance with your honour and conscience, to God and man.'[155] The mythopoeic qualities of his airborne journey to and from the East Indies in the summer of 1935 were exploited to depict the leader not as a daring, heroic man[156] – although this was discussed by the General Council[157] – but as one protected by Providence.[158]

The image of bourgeois respectability was pushed to the background, if not eliminated, to instead turn Mussert into a Leader with a holy mission, a priestly figure. In January 1937, an article by the Head of Department X described his experience of meeting Mussert in 1927: a charismatic man had emerged in defence of his people, 'touched by the hand of destiny'.[159] Where Lindholm always emphasized the long-term struggle and need for sacrifice in the face of constant (electoral and financial) adversity, Mussert, buoyed by the meteoric success of the NSB in its first three years, relied on themes of destiny and imminent salvation. A new age was dawning on Europe, and Mussert was the first in the Netherlands to realize it. As he put it at the second *Hagespraak* in 1937, also in the Dutch people a divine spark had taken hold, which spoke of resurrection, and the victory of good over evil.[160] 'We stand in the middle of the period in which history is made'.[161] The NSB followed a path, on which it had found the love of God, and it wished to keep pursuing the way in which God would stay with them. In the current darkness there was a burning fire, 'that a Movement has emerged in our people ... which has shown its indestructability, and gradually makes itself ready to fulfil its calling that history has ordained'.[162] No longer just a thoroughly respectable Christian gentleman, Mussert was constructed as a biblical prophet, echoing the voice of the Lord, calling to the people to heed the coming of a divinely ordained era. 'A new era is coming: that era is Mussert. Irresistible. He is the voice of the coming Netherlands.'[163] At the December 1936 commemoration of the founding of the NSB, Mussert declared that 'God's judgement is being executed over all that has shown itself sinful, both in the individual and in the people' – a new era is coming in the history of nations.[164] Commanding the flags to be lowered, and his audience to rise and stand still in silence, Mussert recited a prayer:

> We do not ask, that we will be spared suffering, sorrows, and ardour in the
> coming years;
> We do not ask, that it may go well for us;
> We do not ask, that our wishes and our desires are fulfilled,
> because not our will be done.
> But we ask on this evening, at the beginning of a new battle period this one thing:
> that God give us the insight, the courage, the determination, the honesty, the
> good faith, which are necessary to be a good tool in His hand, serving for
> the resurrection of this people, which we love, so that the Fatherland, so that
> the *Imperium* will not be lost, but will be maintained and the way up will be

steadfastly walked according to His will.
We now sing together: *Wilt heden nu treden*.[165]

Christian credentials were indispensable for a respectable politician in the interwar Netherlands, and a religious outlook had been, albeit in the background, part of Mussert's image since 1933. But as the years went on, initial success, as well as hostility from the authorities, drove a mythopoeia which transformed the respectable bourgeois leader, the down to earth civil servant, into a charismatic prophet–priest figure. Additionally, people in the Ecclesiastical Council argued that 'increasingly calling on God's aid at our meetings has found resonance and finds this more and more amongst the best and most serious of our *Volksgenooten*', even as Germanic-pagan ideas were also gaining ground in the party.[166] In some respects respectability had been jettisoned in the mythopoeic process, but in this myth the NSB had found a handy marriage between the demands of respectability for Christian virtue, and the expectation of, and desire for a charismatic, fascist Leader.

Outsider perspectives and challenges

The mythopoeia around the leaders of the NSB and NSAP was thus managed with mainly the party membership in mind, building on the grassroots demand for a devotional object. The uninitiated tended to be much less impressed by the fantastic representations of the Leader. A 1937 report by the Anti-Revolutionary *De Rotterdammer*, on a Senate speech by a CHU speaker, is illustrative of how opponents perceived and portrayed Mussert's Christian myth:

> [Mussert's National Socialism] does try to hide its true nature with pretty words. Sometimes they are also virtuous words, which however immediately betray that they are merely the words and concepts, handled by those, who do not know their Christian meaning ... It is an horrendous abuse, an abhorrent method for misleading the simple. Nevertheless [sic] ... Mussert's National Socialism is equally pagan and objectionable in its principle foundations as the German [equivalent], which he imitates. Unchristian, unhistorical, and revolutionary, concluded Prof. Anema. And rightly so.[167]

One ARP preacher, Bik, took things a little bit further: 'the brainless Mussert – that great St Nicholas figure ... every show of friendship from him I regard as a kiss from Satan – the N.S.B. is Satanism in disguise'.[168] Mussert's ever more virtuous Christian image and the increasingly liturgical rituals did not necessarily impress an antagonistic press, which was keen to highlight the pseudo-pagan elements in a party that was already tarnished with the Nazi German brush. Mythopoeia did not take place in a vacuum, and opponents exploited fractures in the party's performance of (Christian) respectability to undermine Mussert's myth. Although it was naturally impossible to make the Mussert myth flawlessly convincing, the party apparatus did counter the hostile feedback and wholeheartedly engaged in a public struggle to define Mussert as a symbol of fascism. The above quotation from *De Rotterdammer* was found in a press summary compiled by the NSB's Central Documentation Bureau, which monitored press reports from all over the country, with the aim of informing party propagandists such as speakers, and providing them with the tools to offer a rebuttal, and interject the NSB's own narrative in a struggle to reify party myths in public discourse. VoVa was constantly engaged in a battle with hostile media,[169] recounting and denying unfavourable reports from the 'lie-press'.[170] The NSAP was engaged in a virtually identical battle with the 'deceitful Jewish *systempressen*' (the System Press),[171] but by contrast made few overt efforts to construct Lindholm as a respectable figure – certainly not in any Christian sense as Lindholm and the party showed limited sympathy for the Lutheran Church and Christianity in general.[172] But, like Mussert, Lindholm's myth was still vulnerable to comparison with foreign dictators, opening it up to accusations of an unrespectable, un-Swedish lack of patriotism or dangerous dictatorial tendencies. Lindholm was compared to 'small-German *gauführer*' and the like, or just mockingly 'the Führer',[173] while a Czech socialist Prague-based paper, *Neuer Vorwärts*, described Lindholm as 'truly Goebbelesque'.[174]

Both party leaders were the target of damaging comparisons to the leaders of Nazi Germany, which were made not just to make them look dangerous, but also ridiculous. Positing Hitler as a charismatic and impressive original, the Swedish and Dutch leaders were juxtaposed to present a pathetic picture.[175] In 1933 the liberal NRC described the NSB leader as 'Mr Mussert playing as Hitler'[176]; the same year the socialist paper *Het Volk* printed photographs comparing Mussert and Hitler saluting their followers from their cars, captioned 'Like the master, so the servant!',[177] and *De Maasbode* called Mussert a Hitler caricature.[178] In 1937, before the general election, NRC noted sardonically that if the Netherlands was to be a dictatorship it would need a dictator 'of great stature': 'many NSB-members are already coming to their senses'.[179] A 1934 biography of Mussert stated that '[h]e remained the leader of an assignment; what he was *not*: a prophet who was going to make the crowd ecstatic'.[180] Similarly, the Swedish priest Per Gyberg described Lindholm as a man devoid of rhetorical talent, monotonous, lacking in imagination and clumsy in his performance – an anti-demagogue, one could not but help compare unfavourably to his German counterparts.[181] *Göteborgs-Posten* compared Lindholm favourably to Birger Furugård ('a buffoon'), but also depicted the row with other Swedish fascist leaders as childish; in Sweden the sheer plurality of competing 'little Führers' was a common way to denigrate them.[182]

Beyond the respectable press, some commentators were also happy to point out just how short Lindholm and Mussert fell from the mythic constructions produced by the party, opting for *ad hominem* approaches that portrayed them as grotesque simpletons. 'How is it possible', wrote one columnist, 'that thousands of Netherlanders "work themselves up into the hysterical worship of a completely ordinary bourgeois"'.[183] *De Tijd* wrote that 'mister Mussert is a completely ordinary, well-off gentleman', with an unfortunate predilection for black trousers 'which are not the most flattering on his small figure'.[184] An exaggerated emphasis on the charismatic qualities of the Leader tended to be countered by a close examination of their actual personal qualities. While it appears the Dutch press was generally very reluctant to pry into Mussert's private life during the interwar years, one propaganda leaflet of unknown origin, most likely from 1937, took the opportunity to point out that '[o]n 19 September 1917, at the city hall at de Steeg, ANTON ADRIAAN MUSSERT, 23 years old, unemployed, married Maria Witlam, the sister of his mother, a nurse, twice as old as him. ... Mothers of sons, imagine something like that. Your son with your sister!!'[185] Lindholm's private life did not offer quite the same opportunities for portraying him as a perverted hypocrite. Nevertheless the left-wing press was keen to undermine his image as the natural, tall, fit, healthy and handsome soldier, caricaturing him as strange and ungainly, an unkempt 'nazi wastrel' and gangster boss cravenly vying for German approval.

The inherently flawed nature of mythopoeia, particularly when focused on actual, physically present human beings, did not only cause problems with outsiders; in the interstices of the mythopoeic process scepticism grew among the members, especially higher functionaries. By 1940 the Swedish police had picked up on signs that some of the members were unhappy with some of Lindholm's decisions in the SSS, showing that he was far from unquestionable.[186] In 1937 there were already some rumblings that Lindholm was 'running out' as leader, was becoming arrogant and pompous.[187] One functionary, in a somewhat treasonous letter to Hermann Göring, described Lindholm as an undiplomatic and unsuitable leader 'in most people's opinion', even suggesting perhaps Birger Furugård should be made leader again.[188] Mussert also had his sceptics in the NSB, something that is particularly evident from some of the party's disciplinary dossiers; for instance his pro-Italian stance on the invasion of Abyssinia attracted criticism from some of the members, though others considered it wrong to say so.[189] In spite of the mythopoeic attempts to construct Lindholm and Mussert as undisputed and natural leaders, they had to contend with potential alternatives to their leadership. In both cases this was made painfully evident to them in the wake of electoral failure, which provided a natural opportunity to question myths, and consider alternatives. The 1937 autumn rebellion of Department X and former WA-commander J. Hogewind highlights how those who stood closest to the Leader were also the most liable to exploit mythopoeic flaws. The NSB rebellion may have failed, but nevertheless thousands of members left the party after the electoral disaster in May that year, an important reminder that Mussert's myth as prophetic and predestined Leader was to some extent contingent on success, and by no means subscribed to by the entire membership.

Lindholm's myth was far more stable. Rather than a prophet predicting imminent and total victory, the ascetic frontline soldier-chieftain promised a long and hard struggle demanding the utmost discipline as per his own example. Consequently, the opening for scepticism and outright rebellion did not immediately come from the lack of electoral success – never as dramatic as the NSB's loss of half its vote in 1937 – but from his and the Party Leadership's decision to alter and even reverse the mythopoeia the party apparatus had worked on for years. After years of constructing Lindholm as the moral and uncompromising revolutionary Leader of Swedish fascism, the *nyorientering* (New Direction) created a new, respectable Lindholm, a suited nationalist politician open for compromise with other parties. This was a gradual process. Although the official announcement of the *nyorientering* came at the end of October 1938, for the past year and half at least, members could spot that change was afoot. A secret police informant noted that there had been a rebellion against Lindholm in Gothenburg in 1937, perhaps also out of resentment that headquarters was moving to Stockholm, and its leaders were purged at that year's party congress.[190] During this time, not only was some of the anti-Semitic rhetoric toned down, but the pictures of Lindholm were increasingly not of the Leader in uniform, but neat and kempt in a suit and tie. When he announced the changes at a meeting in Stockholm, attendees noted he was behaving very oddly:

> Lindholm finished his speech by letting out a fourfold 'long live' the N.S.A.P.!? Now there were some members who cheered, and others who 'hailed', and some who kept silent. Was Lindholm drunk or had he become bourgeois? It had never happened before in the history of the N.S.A.P., that an ordinary member had 'long-lived' [the party], and now the leader himself did it. What was the meaning of this? [...] The meeting was finished with a very strange – not to mention oppressive – atmosphere.[191]

The change in image and behaviour was striking, and members immediately picked up on the shift towards respectability, something which could only be profoundly damaging of the charismatic bond that was integral to the Lindholm myth. In January 1939, the party organ even published a remarkable deconstruction and denial of Lindholm's myth. A transcript of a speech by the leader himself stated that 'already in the beginning of our community of struggle I warned that you should not regard me as some kind of super human or wizard, but I have promised to fight honourably and place myself foremost in line for our sacred cause'.[192] Lindholm, previously a living symbol of fascism, now found that there were other symbols to rival him, symbols which retained their mythic charge. When part of the NSAP/SSS broke away to form *Solkorset* (The Sun Cross), under the leadership of the SA branch leaders Nils Björkman and John E. Runefelt, they portrayed it as an act of loyalty to the swastika, and the ideas it represented. In abandoning the old myth of the radical and uncompromising Leader under the swastika banner, and compromising with Jewish capital (it was rumoured), Lindholm had betrayed the cadres and the NSAP's ethos intrinsic to the Leader myth: a frontline fighter, one of and equal to his own. 'We National Socialists are loyal to our leader, as long as he is loyal to us. One for all – all for one.'[193]

†††

In 1932–3, neither Lindholm nor Mussert fit the then established mould of the charismatic fascist Leader. Both had years of political experience of one kind or another, and were used to more conventional relations to their colleagues and followers. With the establishment of their own fascist parties, they quickly found themselves under pressure from the party's lower echelons to perform the part of the fascist leader. With the active support of their colleagues at the top, the party apparatus started the mythopoeic process straight away. While this initial period was more or less the same in both movements, the following stages diverged significantly. The NSAP quickly established Lindholm as a young Nordic chieftain, fighting for his followers as the first among equals and the living embodiment of the fascist idea. This remarkably insular myth saw little change or variation from 1933 to c. 1938, nor did it need to. Relatively unconcerned with any external notions of respectability and not expecting major electoral success or growth in the near-future, it could afford to strengthen Lindholm's bonds with his followers and, at least at first, ceaselessly mobilize the cadres on a path of continuous sacrifice. It must however be added that the scarce resources of the NSAP limited the efficacy of this strategy: establishing loyalty through personal contact was difficult with Sweden's geography, even as financial necessity dictated such a cost-free method.

In the NSB on the other hand, 1932–4 saw an attempt to establish *ir.* Mussert as a respectable nationalist politician, a responsible and even technocratic alternative to the corrupt and failing parliamentary government, but firstly found that this failed to satisfy the devotional demands from the cadres, and secondly that the pointed measures taken by the authorities, secular and spiritual, undermined that narrative. In the second half of the decade, spurred on by the electoral success of 1935, the party organization set to work to recreate Mussert as a priestly figure who had foreseen the future, and heeding God's call, was leading his people to national resurrection. It was a fantastic myth, and seemed to put an end to internal complaints about the banal and bourgeois leader, while simultaneously offsetting concerns about the growth of pseudo-pagan discourse and symbolism in the party around the same time. Mythopoeia was by no means linear. While different stages can be discerned, the phases were intertwined, and various myths co-existed at the same time, with different intensities and trajectories – especially in Mussert's case. Neither leader hit upon any kind of 'winning formula' that would stabilize or focus mythopoeia.

The Dutch general elections of 1937 demonstrated the inherent problems. The party leadership's response to the more fanatic parts of the membership may have had great mobilizing potential, but to many outsiders it was evidently perceived as sanctimonious at best, and dangerous cultic behaviour at worst, Satanic worship even. However, internally the Mussert myth was of considerable value in maintaining party cohesion at this difficult time. The 1937 challenge to Mussert's authority was seen off quickly and without endangering the party organization, as the Leader exploited the cult of the leader to mobilize his loyalists to counter the rebellion. In the period of 1937–40 mythopoeia remained in the same register, with no real changes made until the hectic days of the Occupation. Even in the latter period Mussert managed to maintain a loyal following, which desperately placed its trust in him as their saviour until the final collapse in May 1945.[194]

One may speculate that Lindholm may never have faced a rebellion of any sort had the NSAP leadership not radically altered the mythopoeic course in 1937–8. Doubtless there were already some murmurs of dissatisfaction before then. The cadres could not be permanently mobilized, and the lack of notable progress in the elections reflected badly on the party's first and foremost activist, leading to dangerous levels of frustration. Where Mussert saw off a revolt by exploiting the charismatic bonds that his myth had forged, the NSAP leadership wilfully cut them by reversing much of the mythopoeia in a turn to political respectability, hoping to catch more votes and members. The subsequent *Solkors* break-away put the spotlight on alternative objects of devotion to the mythic Lindholm. The rebellion the following year of the young and radical Arne Clementsson and the NU underlined the willingness of others to perform the myth of charismatic Leader.[195] While Lindholm survived the internal turmoil, some level of scepticism and unrest persisted for years to come, while the SSS continued to haemorrhage followers even as it sought to establish an alliance with other radical Right organizations.

Respectability did not seem to be of any real concern to the NSAP for most of the 1930s, but as the years went on the Leader himself, active as a fascist politician since 1926, started to feel the frustration of being perpetually on the fringe. Contrary to Mussert, who after little more than a year experienced a form of spectacular political success, and subsequently settled into a, more or less, comfortable if limiting niche between fantastic myth and respectability, the NSAP had effectively painted Lindholm into a corner. The radical and uncompromising embodiment of the idea was going nowhere fast, but turning away from this myth could not be anything but profoundly damaging to Lindholm's authority and the prestige of the party. The tendency of the Leader myth to supplant the party itself that has been observed in Germany and Italy was not present in the NSAP or NSB.[196] In different ways, and with varying if ultimately similar results, both Lindholm and Mussert were caught up in a mythopoeic dialectic that could fully satisfy neither their cadres nor the respectable electorate at the same time.

4

Making fascists: Uniforms and military subculture

The fascist uniform was a cultural nexus of peculiar importance in the struggle to assert the meaning and nature of fascism. No other prop in the political performances of the NSB and NSAP carried the same weight of signification, was so heavily inscribed with symbolism. The association between uniforms and fascism was well-established by the early 1930s. Both parties drew on this, in self-conscious homage to the precedents of Mussolini's blackshirts and the brown-shirted German storm troopers. The shirt of the appropriate colour was the most recognizable part of these uniforms, but not the only one. Various other articles of clothing, accessories and insignia completed the uniform, each part echoing the whole. At their full potential, the uniforms were worn collectively in larger groups, a full ensemble worn with insignia, in a march or similar ritual occasion with flags, music and other symbols, which underlined a militaristic discipline. Therefore, while the uniform is the focus of this chapter, it must also deal with the wider culture of symbols and behaviour of the rank-and-file that was inextricably linked to the garments, and which made up what can be termed a fascist military subculture.

While the ubiquity of uniforms in fascist political culture has been widely acknowledged and discussed, especially in the German historiography, analysis has rarely been in great depth. Many historians have dismissed uniforms and the associated signs, symbols and paraphernalia as too superficial to be worth discussing.[1] For instance, Gerhard Paul's otherwise-insightful study of visual Nazi propaganda before 1933, *Aufstand der Bilder* (Revolt of the Pictures, 1990), only has little over one page on uniforms.[2] A more detailed and holistic analysis of fascist uniforms has been made by Sven Reichardt in *Faschistischer Kampfbünde* (Fascist Combat Leagues), looking into the German SA and Italian *squadristi*. Reichardt's research reveals some of the practical issues behind the images of uniformed troops that Gerhard Paul studied, and connects this to the emotional effect they sought to produce. Rather than just using a propaganda angle on uniforms, Reichardt also comments on the social cohesion and political identity that uniforms facilitated.[3] But mostly uniforms have been studied as one small part of a larger spectacle, rather than as a nexus of fascist culture and myth, to which other symbols and behaviours can even be viewed as epiphenomenal.[4]

Scholars have also placed the uniform in a wider political and social context, noting the tactical uses of uniforms in fascist paramilitaries, the impact of uniformed men on the street[5] or analysing it as a symptom of the mass politics of the modern era.[6] Surprisingly, for such an obviously cultural phenomenon it has rarely been studied in terms of cultural production. Historians with a cultural approach to fascism, such as George L. Mosse, Emilio Gentile or Roger Griffin, have tended to overlook the uniform. But there are exceptions, of sorts, one of which is Klaus Theweleit's rather dated and problematic psychoanalytical study of *Freikorps* literature, *Männerphantasien* (Male Fantasies, 1983), which explores the fascist relationship to the body and sexuality.[7] Again it is not the uniform specifically which is highlighted here, but the interface of military culture and pseudo-sexual fantasy is relevant. Theweleit's analysis, while rather ahistorical, does understand the militaristic objects and behaviour of the soldiers as *producing* reality, and the manifestation of a fantasy, which makes it highly applicable to the mythopoeic project discussed here. Theweleit, then, attempted in a sense to reconstruct the mythical content of the fascist imagination.[8]

> Here even the most improbable actions were redolent with significance. The simplest salute became a symbol of submission to an authority that bound both parties in mutually fruitful association. The slow march, tempo one hundred fourteen, became the physical and spiritual expression of discipline to the brink of death. [...] In the first instance, what the troop-machine produces is itself – itself as a totality that places the individual soldier in a new set of relations to other bodies; itself as a combination of innumerable identically polished components.[9]

Theweleit brought out the significative richness of the actions and signs associated with military life. But, while the psychological dimension of fascist uniforms is unavoidable, this chapter frames the fantastic and performative dimensions of the uniform in cultural terms: their primary role is constructing fascism. Secondly, unlike any previous analyses, this chapter puts the uniform centre stage, with everything understood only in relation to the uniform, as a means of foregrounding the importance of this mythopoeic prop in the cultural understanding of fascism.

The Swedish and Dutch governments were well aware of the power political uniforms could possess, and in 1933, with an eye on developments in central and southern Europe, passed legislation prohibiting the wearing of political uniforms in public.[10] Compared to their Dutch equivalent, the Swedish regulations were vague and not very comprehensive, prohibiting 'the wearing of a uniform or similar dress, which serves to highlight the wearer's political orientation'.[11] The legislation was technically a warrant for local authorities (made into law in 1947),[12] leaving it up to them to wrestle with questions as to which and how many garments constituted a uniform, and whether or not they indeed indicated a specific political orientation.[13] In the Netherlands, Article 435a – partially inspired by Sweden[14] – stated: 'He who publicly wears, or carries, garments, or conspicuous marks of distinction, which are expression of a particular political orientation, will be punished with incarceration of a maximum of twelve days or a pecuniary fine of at most one hundred and fifty guilders'.[15] This law had been proposed already in 1932, initiated by Right concerns about communism,[16] but was only implemented when street violence became more frequent with the growth of the NSB.[17] The Dutch law too had its ambiguities, particularly whether certain marks or insignia were indeed conspicuous (*opzichtig*), and whether certain uniforms, garments or similar could really be regarded as being the expression of a political orientation.[18]

Thus the bans on uniforms, while they were in many ways effective, could not fully seal off this particular mythopoeic wellspring. Apart from flouting the law, fascists found subtle ways of circumventing it, leading to repeated public debate about the efficacy of the law and the threat of fascism, keeping the issue alive throughout the decade. The laws only applied to uniforms worn in public, making the distinction between private and public crucial to party meetings, and retaining a well-defined legal place for the uniform in the movement.

Evocative in the extreme, and indelibly tied to the performativity of its wearer, the uniform was an unstable signifier. The evocations of the fascist uniform were equivocal, and prey to infelicitous associations. The inherent militarism, paradoxically at once denied and encouraged by the party apparatus, imbued the clothing with the threat, or promise, of violence. The unity it symbolized strengthened the feeling of comradeship, while marking fascists as outsiders.[19] The allusion to the German brownshirts and Italian blackshirts made native fascists part of something much bigger than a national movement, even when their own organization remained small, but undermined their patriotic credentials.[20] Fascist political uniforms proved to be powerful mythopoeic objects, and were strong amplifiers of fascist performances and spectacles, but dangerously double-edged. As a lynchpin in much of the public discourse about fascism in its most militaristic guise, the uniform functioned as a defining battle site in the cultural shaping of the national understanding about fascism and its role in national political life. This made it an obvious target for unsympathetic interpretations, but as party commitment to this symbol showed the key role it played in the fascist symbolic order guaranteed its place in the fascist mythologies.

Appearances, practicalities and regulations

In its most basic form, the uniform of the NSAP and the NSB consisted of a shirt – a brown one in the former, a black one in the latter. In the NSAP, standard models were available from the party supply service, though they could be purchased elsewhere as long as they followed the required model. The Swedish police has left precise notes on the NSAP shirts from the 1935 raid of the Gothenburg headquarters, which describe a military-style shirt, highly reminiscent of German SA-shirts, 'made of a brown khaki fabric, provided with epaulettes'.[21] None of the NSB regulations prescribe a certain model or even style of shirt. Apart from the shirt, the only part of the fascist uniform that was considered absolutely essential was the party insignia: in the NSAP a swastika, worn on the left lapel,[22] for NSB-members a triangular emblem, featuring a rampant gold lion against a black and red background. 'Wear your insignia!' VoVa reminded readers in every issue.[23] A small enamel pin was a cheap and easy way of readily identifying oneself and others as fascists. Shirt and insignia were only the minimum requirement however, and a full uniform was desirable.

In Sweden the brown shirt was ideally worn with shoulder boards indicating district and branch, a blue armband, featuring a yellow swastika, as well as a brown tie, a brown visor cap and a claw belt on the waist with a shoulder strap (*koppel*). Trousers were ideally breeches in brown, grey or a similar colour, with leather boots, but not shoes.²⁴ Dutch uniform regulations were not as extensive. If a 1935 proposal by WA-leader J. Hogewind was actually implemented, as seems likely, the rank-and-file simply needed a black shirt with a black tie, decorated with a thin red-white-blue stripe; the insignia; and dark trousers, with a black belt. A suit jacket over the shirt was permitted. For functionaries of the rank of Circle Leader or higher, uniforms were more elaborate, and included breeches, boots and a visor cap.²⁵ The Swedish *stormavdelning* uniform closely resembled that of the ordinary members; a black tie instead of a brown tie on the shirt, collar tabs, special insignia and a brown coat for winter.²⁶ Members of the *Weerafdeeling* on the other hand stood out strongly from their NSB counterparts, wearing the black shirt with an all-black uniform consisting of a jacket, breeches, riding boots or shoes with leather gaiters, a waist belt and shoulder strap, a visor cap and assorted insignia indicating rank.²⁷ It is notable that the NSAP in Sweden eschewed jackets, and made a far less formal impression than the NSB with its black and grey uniforms, which evoked a mixture of militarism and cleanliness, instead of the egalitarian simplicity of the plain brown shirts.

To create something of a uniform impression, the thousands of party members had to be actually supplied with their uniforms and associated paraphernalia. After an initial stage when the NSAP leadership itself supplied materials via Party Treasurer Karl Kristern,²⁸ Lennart Fornander was in charge of the supply service (*partiintendentur*), which stocked all garments and insignia required, where they could be bought by members individually or via branch leaders.²⁹ Uniforms could be acquired from independent suppliers,³⁰ but members had to request the correct dimensions and other details from the supply service; the NSAP was keen to ensure members' uniforms were identical.³¹ Shirts cost 6 kronor, party insignia 1.50 and a waist belt no less than 4.25 kronor. A full uniform for an SA-member, boots not included, cost in total as much as 17.75 kronor, and had to be acquired piece by piece by many members, who were often unemployed, or underage.³² The uniform of a regular member did not cost much less. The desirable leather boots were not supplied by the party's supply service, and were a considerable expense for members – one letter to a Karlskrona member looking for leather boots at a reasonable price received the reply that boots regionally cost about 33 kronor ready-made,³³ and 45 kronor custom-made.³⁴ It is not surprising that hiking boots with leg wraps or similar were an acceptable alternative. It might also offer a clue as to why the proud owners of actual leather riding boots tended to wear them even after the law against political uniforms got them in trouble with the authorities.³⁵

Dutch party members were looking at similar prices, but the NSB supply service (Department VII, Dienst Materiaal) headed by A.J. Hartman did not supply full uniforms, only insignia and accessories.³⁶ Instead shirts had to be bought from independent suppliers, who happily advertised their black shirts in VoVa, for prices of 2–3 guilders, roughly equivalent to the cost of the NSAP's shirts.³⁷ This made any major party occasion that called for uniforms an excellent advertising opportunity.³⁸ However, a full uniform for a member of the WA cost far more than that of his SA equivalent. At a Headquarters meeting in 1935, concerns were raised that while 80 per cent of members were workers, the uniform cost 17–18 guilders, which most could not afford.³⁹ WA-members had to pay for their own uniform, which they could pay off piece by piece via their WA company (*Vendel*) administrator.⁴⁰ It must have been an egregious expense, given that the uniform could not be worn in public after 1933.

In the 1935 police interrogation of Lindholm, he noted a strong decline in the members' demand for uniforms after the 1933 ban.⁴¹ One can imagine a similar trend in the NSB, though the party administration could not have had any direct insight into purchases outside of the WA. The laws against political uniforms had created a sharp division between the appearance of the party internally, and the party in public. Generally, instructions give the impression that the NSB leadership responded to the ban by an even greater insistence that members should wear the uniform any time when legally possible, and one can imagine members were more than happy to if they had already bought one.⁴² The NSAP's internal organizational paper *Porg* reminded functionaries that the order to wear the uniform 'is still valid and *now even more so*, when wearing it in public is forbidden'.⁴³ For the 1935 NSB party convention in The Hague, only uniformed WA-members could participate in the ceremonial march,⁴⁴ while a directive for the 1934 NSAP party convention ordered all participants to immediately acquire a uniform if they did not have one already.⁴⁵ For most of this period then, the black or brown shirt was commonly worn only at internal party events, but not at public rallies and the like or individually on the street. Legally, the only way an outsider in the Netherlands would encounter a fascist in uniform was if they were invited, as a sympathizer or otherwise, to a closed party meeting. In the Netherlands the legal journal *Recht* (Right) published an article in 1936 about fascist meetings which were found to have been public in character, and therefore uniformed members in breach of Article 435a. The article was recommended reading for members.⁴⁶ When members had to travel to a meeting or function which required the uniform, public spaces were traversed fully covered up. For the 1935 convention in Amsterdam, WA-members were ordered to travel to the venue in full uniform, but with no visible parts exposed.⁴⁷ For other occasions the NSB supply service had made 'blackshirt protectors' available for 40 cents: a kind of collar, buttoned around the neck, with an attached scarf of some sort, which could be unfolded to cover up the black shirt with one of six colours. 'Especially the effect of the upcoming *Landdag* march through the streets of Amsterdam will be elevated, if these colourful protectors are worn a lot, and the procession will be given a gay appearance,' a circular explained optimistically.⁴⁸

In spite of prohibitions and exhortations, there were disagreements between the leadership and the rank-and-file as to when uniforms should be worn. It is evident from Swedish police observations that many members did not wear a uniform even to internal meetings.⁴⁹ The fact that the NSB and NSAP several years after the ban still urged members to wear their uniform at all times possible indicates a disciplinary problem. This problem came to the fore in the case of party insignia, where the scope for wearing them was more extensive, yet many members still neglected to wear it. *Porg* complained at the end of 1935 that there were still too many members who 'could not stretch out their hand [in salute], [and] don't wear the party insignia'.⁵⁰ In a 1936 NSB disciplinary case in Hilversum, one member outright stated that 'I personally do not attach the slightest value to the pin and the black shirt'.⁵¹ The uniform and attendant insignia were by no means valued equally by all members, and the acquisition and even wearing of uniforms whole, or in part, had its obstacles. Yet for all those troubles, and more, the uniform remained a staple of fascist mythopoeia.

Militarism and respectability

Not just aesthetic clothing or practical outfits, the fascists' uniforms were rich in associations and symbolism, already before they arrived on the national stage. The fascist political uniform was not left to speak for itself, but was consciously imbued with a party-particular ideological symbolism, most overtly through its discursive construction in party publications. 'Symbols', in Jeffrey Schnapp's words, 'were a privileged site of self-definition for fascism'.[52] In the words of the NSAP party directives, TF: '[t]he National Socialists' service clothes are a symbolic expression of the struggle we wage. For us it is not some kind of military uniform, but a working shirt which makes us all equal in our duties for the same goal.'[53] In 1938, an order from Mussert regarding symbols in the NSB explained:

> The Movement has started its struggle for the resurrection of our People with as external signs: the black shirt and the fascist salute, the black-red flag, and the insignia. The black shirt is our official dress, adopted in honour of Mussolini and his blackshirts, who have given the signal for the resurrection of Europe, accepted as an expression of our comradely cohesion in the struggle for People and Fatherland. [...] None of us would ever think of taking away these external signs of our struggle.[54]

Community and equality in struggle were themes both the NSB and the NSAP emphasized, and both consciously referenced foreign fascist movements in their choice of colour. A united community of militants, in which all class differences were obliterated in the service of a common cause: the Fatherland; part of a new political age that was sweeping across Europe.

But, in spite of Mussert's assertions to the contrary, the external signs were not static in either party, not least on account of the awkward dynamic between militarism and respectability. The uniform constantly evoked militarism, but the parties, especially the NSB, were keen to temper the associations with violence.[55] One illustrative example is NU-leader Arne Clementsson's 1937 article on the meaning of soldiers. 'When someone in Sweden in these days of decline mentions the word *soldier*, everyone recoils and see in their mind's eye the militarized dictatorships on the march, threateningly prepared to crush the last outpost of culture – the democratic North.'[56] Clementsson shows the NSAP was self-conscious about the problematic associations of a uniform. He argued for a distinction between the *military* and the *soldierly*, fascism embodying the latter. Likewise, VoVa wrote that 'National Socialist self-control' (*tucht*) was 'disciplinary, not military'.[57] The often-precarious legal situation of the movements shaped discourse in this regard, moderating the military connotations lest they became a legal stick for political enemies.[58] We may regard Lindholm's decision in 1937–8 to change the uniform to a dark blue shirt with a grey tie in the same vein. The idea to change the shirt was first discussed in 1937. A letter from the eastern District Leader to Lindholm approved of the idea to 'change the uniform to give it a more marked Swedish character': 'A clear difference [from Germany] in uniform should more strongly mark our will to independent national life.'[59] The dark blue colour of the shirt, with the splash of grey, was reminiscent of the Carolingian army under the Swedish 'soldier-king' Charles XII, a figure much admired in Swedish right-wing circles generally.[60] Here the uniform was given recognizably patriotic connotations, something helped along by the decision to swap out the swastika for *vasakärven*, the coat of arms of the Vasa dynasty. Thus symbols, signs and colours guided the spectator towards a more respectable reading of fascist appearances.

In symbolically enacting the party in particular, and fascism in general, it was crucial that the uniform-wearer adequately perform the myth of a respectable, patriotic fascist. Hence the NSAP and NSB were keen to inscribe certain behaviours onto the uniform. The wearer was not to merely carry the symbolic uniform around like a metaphorical sandwich board, but symbiotically bring out its fantastic qualities, just as the uniform constructed the individual as a fascist. The first blueprint document for NSB membership already noted the importance of combining the wearing of the uniform with suitable behaviour.[61] The party leaderships and the propaganda departments understood, in Judith Butler's words, that 'the body is not a self-identical or merely factic materiality; it is a materiality that bears meaning, if nothing else, and the manner of this bearing is fundamentally dramatic.'[62] Wearing the uniform, the insignia, and using the NSB salute was compulsory, and in doing so the member should always 'carry himself with pride and dignity.'[63] As Hogewind put it, 'Each NSB-member will consider, that when dressed in uniform, he (she) bears witness to the NSB, and that he (she) then, even more than otherwise would be the case, must be an example of decency, punctuality, politeness and comradeship.'[64] The NSAP's 1937 TF instructed that '[e]ach member should wear his brownshirt with pride and when wearing it strive more than ever towards good comportment.'[65]

To make sure members lived up to the fascist myth in public, physical and ideological training was required. The active member was 'obliged in all cases, when commanded, to wear the black shirt, the uniform, the insignia and to use the N.S.B. salute. He will always know to carry himself with pride and dignity.'[66] While NSAP discourse was less focused on respectability, in practice the Swedish party had no less stringent moral standards for the cadres. The minimum age was seventeen, and members were required to be Swedish citizens, and not be 'descendant from Jews or "coloured" racial elements', while they also, with a markedly different emphasis from the NSB, 'had to be known for decency and not have behaved in an un-solidary fashion towards colleagues during legitimate social wage conflicts.'[67] The NSAP's origins in the split from the SNSP fed into its myth of fascism, and the devotion it required:

> The National Socialist Workers Party was founded precisely through a moral revolution, which purged careerism and corruption from the ranks. And now it is up to us, to not just get as many followers as possible, but the most important thing is for us to get decent comrades, such as can work for the victory of the mission, for the good of their national brothers [*folkbröder*] and not for their own.[68]

It was recognized that not every new member could be a consummate fascist, but they were theoretically expected to dedicate themselves wholeheartedly to becoming the uncompromisingly disciplined political soldiers of fascist myth.[69] To instil the necessary discipline, members were trained by means of special schools, study circles, quasi-military training camps, and subjected to intellectual, technical and physical training. In the NSAP, members were encouraged to join the militant part of the organization (SA and its successors), and participate in activities such as sports, gymnastics, orienteering and musical practice.[70] Physical training was encouraged, and Lindholm trained NSAP and NU groups personally, frequently with gymnastics and hours-long marches in the woods.[71]

After the uniform bans, the individual member in public was still required to enact a myth of fascism through their behaviour – a myriad of individuals performatively constituting fascism through their endlessly repeated acts as fascists, a collective corporeal repertoire.[72] 'Those who cannot abandon pleasures for work in the service of the party are not worthy of the name National Socialist. Through his idealistic will to sacrifice and fearless energy, good bearing, and faultless behaviour the A-group man will instil respect for the ideas and the NSAP.'[73]

> National Socialism is not just a political opinion but a world view, which first and foremost aims to change people and give them new goals. This view must also impress its character on its carrier, not just in matters of judgment, but also in the way of life and bearing. It conflicts with our world view to engage in the habits of bourgeois society. National Socialists should not participate in the degenerate pleasures of modern society, or be known as restaurant visitors and the like.[74]

The importance of good behaviour was underlined even further when members were in uniform. The shirt naturally enhanced the association of the individual member with the party, so that the party's reputation was at stake, but the garment did more than that. As the eye-catching uniform minimized or even erased the individual character, the members no longer merely constituted themselves as fascists, as NSB or NSAP members – rather they came to embody the party itself, fascism, externalizing the fantasy. The powerful symbolic quality of the uniform transformed the performative, from a set of repeated acts constituting individual political identity, into a mythopoeic performance. Uniformed members became living parts of the myth, creating it in their presence and actions.

Thus it was through trained and disciplined bodies in space – on the street, in the meeting room – that the uniform made the myth. Evocative and inscribed with symbolism, when worn the uniform bestowed its qualities on the body, which through repeated performative acts constituted the fascist myth, i.e. constructed a Swedish or Dutch fascism.[75] The uniform, as a performative aid to corporeal signification, more effectively than any other prop inscribed the fantasy of the fascist onto the body.[76] The black- or brown shirt uniform was of course not the only signifier to be laden with significance from the outset of the 1930s: the stretched arm salute and the swastika (avoided like the plague by the NSB) were similarly powerful signifiers of fascism.[77] Together they amounted to a corporeal repertoire, a set of signs and acts by which members produced themselves as fascists: salutes, slogans, marching steps, even a firm gaze and a straight back could be part of this. This was made quite explicit in Swedish fascist discourse in particular, which spoke of a new 'style' which the NSAP brought to Swedish life. As in the aforementioned Clementsson article, 'Soldier is composure, style' – the NU-member was to be the personification of a straight-backed attitude.[78] By contrast to be a bourgeois was characterized as less a matter of class or ideology, but style.[79] Similarly, the NSB emphasized the contrast between its disciplined troops, and the disorganized and rowdy left-wing opponents they faced on the street, a difference that foregrounded the connection between the meaning of fascism, and the corporeal signification of fascists, produced in acts and composure.[80]

Props and public space

Having established the workings of the mythopoeic uniform, it becomes evident that the function it fulfilled in its mythopoeic capacity differed depending on whether it was directed inward or outward, particularly after the law established a radical distinction between private and public wear. In public, the mythopoeic effect was enhanced by acting in concert. In 1933, the symbolism of classless unity and struggle was strengthened by a plurality of uniformed actors – 'here there is no difference of social class, the ideas unite and the brownshirt unites them'[81] – while utilizing common techniques of demonstrating strength and numbers.[82] The uniform itself, by definition, possessed that peculiar quality of being empowered through multiplicity, so that it really came into its own on occasions of mass meeting.

To this end, other props were also available. The uniform proper was not the only object with a strong mythopoeic charge, even if it was the most powerful one. Rather, as Article 435a recognized, there were certain props which could be interpreted as an extension of the uniform, and in the Netherlands were legally treated the same way.

> To the outside, uniform dress on its own, chosen as a sign of a particular political orientation, also when further organization is disregarded, has an impressive effect on the public. This effect is then also intended foremost by those who introduce the uniform [into public life]. One wants one's followers to be clearly recognisable and make an impression through their numbers. Meanwhile it is usually not left at this alone, and one starts also acting in concert, in organized formations.[83]

These mythopoeic props as extensions of or supplements to the uniform were one of the differences between the two countries, as they were more commonly allowed in Sweden during the 1930s.[84] For instance, armbands and insignia also served to identify party members, or highlight group hierarchy. But it was typically flags which added the greatest symbolic charge to a gathering. With their large size and bright colours, party or national flags served to tie a group together visually, emphasizing the unity of idealism as well as sheer numbers. NSAP meetings were invariably decorated with the party's bright yellow swastika flag, even more so after 1936 when the leadership directed formations to only use swastika flags in meetings.[85] Group numbers, props, performative acts like the salute, collective behaviour and so forth, came together to complete, enhance and dramatize a mythopoeia first and foremost instigated by the uniform, but which could also function without it. '[B]y marching through the street with firm and disciplined force, with a fearless gaze and song, with style. These youths come with music and radiant swastika flags, in their hands they hold flaming torches, and they march with composure and determined will.'[86]

Thus props could also be used to further public mythopoeic demonstrations after the uniform bans, and exercised a similar function in the fascist symbolic universe. The NSAP managed to stand out during the party convention marches of May 1934, marching through Stockholm in long columns of 1700 participants. The procession carried sixty flags (blue-yellow-red swastika flags and Swedish national flags), marked the march through song and hail-chants, and hoped to impress the audience with an exhibition of discipline. 'The swearing, spitting, and fists of the reds, the blatant communist attempts at provocation, nothing worked; they marched calmly in their ranks, sang battle songs and raised resounding shouts of hail.'[87] The Dutch NSB on such occasions made heavy use of the national flag in its dynastic orange-white-blue version, de-emphasizing party identity in favour of patriotic symbolism and respectable loyalty to the House of Orange. In some cases the red-black party flag was even prohibited, and the black shirt replaced with merely dark clothes.[88] The impressive appearance of flags in a procession, and the intrinsically respectable nature of the national flag, made it an appealing mythopoeic prop for the NSB. Correspondence shows that before major marches through cities Mussert requested permission to carry exclusively Dutch flags in the procession.[89] This happened sufficiently often that the national flag became a recognizably fascist feature, not just at political demonstrations but also festivities such as the Queen's birthday or Princess Juliana's wedding in 1936.[90] This was much to the dismay of the conservative Right.[91] When in 1937 the government settled on the red-white-blue tricolour as the official Dutch flag, the NSB protested that the *oranje-blanje-bleu* version represented the historical unity of the people and the confessions, and loyalty to the House of Orange. This further underlined its associations with Orangist patriotism,[92] again to the irritation of the Calvinist Right in particular.[93]

The NSAP and the NSB tried to deal with the uniform ban through legal circumventions, and other mythopoeic props and acts that were still publicly available. It was an organized attempt to propagandize the mythopoeic faculties which existed in the uniformed internal meetings, and bring them to the public. It is evident that the NSB always paid particular attention to respectability as a core part of its myth, while by contrast the NSAP at the same time insisted on its use of party flags, even to the exclusion of national flags. Of course this practice came to an abrupt end towards the end of 1938 when Lindholm's *nyorientering* abolished the swastika, and self-consciously turned to more traditional Swedish symbols, i.e. more in line with NSB practice up to that point, while the latter shifted towards the use of *less* traditional and patriotic symbolism, introducing symbols like the wolf's hook (see below).[94]

Fetishism and private use

If public demonstrations served to proselytize, internal party meetings and rallies above all aimed to mobilize. Here the uniform served a different function. Shorn of both legal restrictions and immediate public scrutiny, the mythopoeic dynamic was altered.

Internally, the uniform served to reify the myth of the party as a fantastic army, 'the militant, spiritual army', as Mussert put it,[95] 'a political army, which believes in the calling of the NSB. You are the soldiers of that army.'[96] In the NSB the army myth became only stronger with time, as the oath written in 1936 highlights. As new members swore to wear the shirt and insignia with honour and dignity, the Circle Leader emphasized:

> We too are an army, and such an army, as can be compared to that of the various Crusades ... we too *act*, without asking, without complaint [...] because we know, that the Leader goes in the vanguard of the battle for a mighty ideal! – We too are zealous. Animated by the example of our Leader, by seeing our Standard.[97]

Conversely, in Sweden NSAP members were trained to 'become a soldier in the future army of the socialist people's community',[98] 'a youth army with fanatic faith and a will as hard as iron'.[99] In wearing a uniform at the meeting, the member became a soldier of a mighty, transcendent force, tied together by bonds of comradeship. 'Your place is in the freedom army, / you have soon forged yourself a sword', declaimed one DSN poem – 'Your Sweden calls you: / Your place is in the freedom army, / join, become a fighter, a man'.[100] The NSAP was particularly sensitive to the *kampanda* (spirit of struggle) and comradeship that permeated large uniformed meetings. As Porg explained, '[w]ith the uniform a renewed *kampanda* always follows, which elevates the impression of the meeting and has a good effect on new comrades.'[101] There was nothing quite like a uniformed gathering of party comrades to strengthen the bonds of 'comradeship and the will to victory'.[102] This myth was discursively relentlessly reified through military metaphors, which in publications as well as internal documents imagined the parties as armies which 'conquered' and 'attacked', waged 'war', 'a struggle for freedom' and 'bloody battles'.[103] 'Our struggle is revolutionary and fought honourably. You are needed at the front.'[104] Visual depictions of the party often relied on military references, constructing the party as a fantastical military army.

This potent symbolic construction of the fascist army went hand in hand with the fetishization of the uniform, and was often indistinguishable from it. While outwardly the NSB and NSAP repeatedly underscored the non-violent nature of this uniformed army, the latent quality of the uniform as a metaphor of violence was implicitly encouraged.[105] 'They conveyed the sensual image of a uniformed nationalism, of dynamic youthfulness, male dominance and uncompromising violence,' happily encouraging members to surrender themselves to the militaristic power fantasies that were overtly and covertly propagated.[106] While Mussert claimed the uniforms were merely handsome and practical, both parties turned the uniform into a fetish.[107]

Figure 6 'The NSB wants war!!!' Artist: Maarten Meuldijk. *Volk en Vaderland*, 1935, no. 23. KB|National library of the Netherlands: C16.

Party discourse and imagery invariably constructed the uniformed member as a, above all, powerful and masculine figure, disciplined, martial and implicitly violent. It was a construction which systematically excluded women from the myth, for whom the fascist symbolic universe seemed to have no place. On one of the extremely rare occasions that VoVa printed a photograph of uniformed women, the emphasis was on their neatness and orderliness, by contrast with the dissolute women of the SDAP. In this regard both the fascist movements were predictably conservative, denying the connotations of power and violence in the depiction of uniformed women, if they were depicted at all.[108]

The NSAP's depictions of the party member were perfectly uniformed, overemphasizing the masculinity of the fascist, but did not appear to have access to any artists of the same (still not very impressive) calibre as the NSB, instead using somewhat more abstract depictions most of the time. The result was eerie, but highly appropriate: an idealized figure unrecognizable as an individual – the perfect fascist, nothing but a uniform. These smaller images were recycled over and over again as column headings and the like, repeatedly imprinting on the young membership the importance of the uniform.

VoVa never missed a chance to describe a fully uniformed WA company, 'dashing file after file, the faces taut with the storm strap around the chin. There they go, martial in the black uniform with the wide waist belt and shoulder strap: masculine youth.'[109] DSN was similarly delighted with the SA: 'They wear blue tabs on the collar, it is Stockholm's SA under its leader [Sten] Hermann – firmly paced boys, used to "liberate the streets" for themselves. […] [then] it is Gothenburg's brisk SA with its group leader Linder at the front. They are recognized by their yellow collar tabs, and their bold countenance – people that are scared of no one.'[110] Visual representations of the WA had to unfailingly show them as a completely uniformed troop; when the NSB prepared a film about the WA, Hogewind required thirty of only 'the most decorative *weermannen*' in full uniform.[111] With no exceptions, artistic depictions of the idealized fascist figure were of male figures, tall and often visibly muscular, with strong jawlines and steely eyes; the uniform tightly fitted, shoulder strap straining across the chest,

Figure 7 'Where we fight', DSN header with the small representation of a uniformed NSAP-member. Artist unknown. *Den Svenske Nationalsocialisten*, 1933, no. 26. Kungliga Biblioteket (National Library of Sweden).

lace-up or riding boots impossibly tight on the calves. This imagery cultivated a power fantasy that was intrinsic to the fascist myth created by the uniform; the association of the uniform with power was a strong one. In 1936, the head of Department I wrote to Mussert, to urge a simplification of the uniforms' '±102 distinctions', adding somewhat concerned, 'that there exists in our Movement a certain urge for distinctions; with this [I am] expressing the hope, that this is not in order to, through the distinction, indulge a certain lust for power'.[112]

While depictions of the complete uniform were favoured, specific parts of the uniform had a particular attraction to some members. There was evidently a desire to wear these as part of a uniform beyond what regulations strictly dictated. District Leader d'Ansembourg wrote to Van Geelkerken that 'I have been asked whether non-members of the WA are permitted to wear waist belts with a shoulder strap, and if this is e.g. prescribed for certain functionaries. The wearing of a black shirt with black or dark grey trousers requires at least a black belt, and that is why many instead wear a WA belt with shoulder strap. [...] Is there any objection to this?'[113] (There was not.)[114] It is notable that members bothered to inquire about and purchase such accessories, given the cost of leatherwear. Under Sweden's less strict uniform regulations, the secret police observed that members took the opportunity to at least wear certain parts of the uniform, especially breeches and riding boots.[115] The boots were sufficiently iconic by the mid-1930s that the liberal independent DN described Nazis as 'some gentlemen in boots'.[116] Though not uncommon in VoVa, DSN was particularly obsessed with the description of the 'compulsory nazi-boots', as *Göteborgs-Posten* called them,[117] rarely failing to take the opportunity to describe the rhythmic beat of marching heels on the pavement, an aural and visual signifier of violent force and numbers, mused over in painstaking detail. Boots were invariably marching, always resounding, always rhythmic, firmly paced, forceful, redolent of order and discipline.[118] Even in part, the paraphernalia of the mythopoeic uniform proved intensely evocative, 'the sensual embodiment of the political idea'.[119] In spite of the obvious symbolic qualities of the uniform, party discourse intriguingly went very far in highlighting the physical dimensions of the uniform, evoking the sensory impressions, the sounds, sights and feelings of uniforms.

Notably, when a new uniform was made for NU in conjunction with the 1938 *nyorientering*, the new model was ironically if anything more militaristic: 'army coat and breeches entirely like the army's latest model and in the same colour', including the indispensable riding boots and shoulder strap.[120] The appeal of the shoulder strap in particular, a glossy strap of leather across the chest which catches the eye in so many photographs of uniformed fascists, lay perhaps in an implicit promise of violence. For the 1934 *årsting*, SA-guards were instructed that the military accessory, '[the] *shoulder strap* attached at the waist belt with *karabiners* was "also useful"' for self-defence.[121] The instructions did not specify how, though it does not require much imagination. Notably these instructions were only issued orally according to Party Organizer Svalander.[122] The shoulder strap was also one of the parts of the uniform Lindholm felt had to be disposed of with the New Direction, as a means of reconstructing the party myth in a more respectable, and perhaps less fetishistic direction.[123] The response of many members was extremely negative, and some refused to compromise on this matter, probably why the new NU uniform remained so militaristic in style.

In both movements the uniform was imbued with a special aura, and became an object of reverence in its own right, regarded with pride and adoration. The myriad close descriptions of the uniform in fascist discourse delineated it as a sacred object in the fascist symbolic order. While laws largely succeeded in keeping them off the street, they can only have served to reinforce the mythopoeic power of the uniform within the parties, distancing it from the secular world, associating it even stronger with the close-knit militarized community, an elite group with a holy mission. In an informal ceremony on the night before Article 435a came into effect, uniformed NSB-members gathered on a square in Utrecht, in the rain with Mussert, 'commander of the growing army'. After a short speech, and singing of the *Wilhelmus*, the dozens of assorted members ritually removed their black shirts at the stroke of midnight, raising them in the air in a show of defiance to onlookers, and the promise to one day wear them again on that same street.[124] (The NSAP did not turn the uniform ban into such a ceremony, instead opting to push the limits of the law for as long as possible.)[125] In another rather remarkable illustration of the peculiar position of the shirt in the NSAP's culture, the fifth *årsting* in Stockholm featured a little exhibition, curated by then-NU leader Gösta Hallberg-Cuula (1912–42). (Hallberg-Cuula himself was something of a legendary figure in the party – a romantic fascist soldier with an eye patch, who was killed in battle as a volunteer in the Finno-Soviet wars of 1941–4.[126] His grave became a pilgrimage site for Swedish neo-Nazis.)[127] The exhibition put the black, brown, and blue shirts of the SFKO and NSAP and other uniform paraphernalia on display, while Hallberg-Cuula himself was dressed in the old SFKO black shirt.[128] Under the guidance of Sven Hedengren and various party members in the police and military, foreign guests from Scandinavia as well as a *Völkischer Beobachter* representative were shown the enshrined items.[129]

The movement uniform possessed a powerful and sacred symbolic charge, which elevated the party member from their individuality, and made them into a privileged part of the holy mission, imbued with the righteous strength this fetish bestowed. The mythopoeic force of the uniform harmonized with its fetishistic attractions, an aesthetic armour that promised violent power to the wearer, while turning them into a living embodiment of an army – the party, led by a divinely ordained Leader, part of an irresistible force of destiny: fascism. Bertil Brisman invoked this myth by quoting the nationalist Finno-Swedish poet Örnulf Tigerstedt, his description of Caesar's armies evoking the Swedish SA, a new type of man, a new world view, a new era.[130] As a concrete symbol in which the individual could literally immerse themselves, there was no possible connection to the myth more immediate than the uniform.[131] In uniform, in a symbiotic process of 'performing fascism', the individual was annihilated, sensuously dissolved in the fantasy of political myth. The poem 'Like one man', published in VoVa before the fifth NSB *landdag*, is worth citing here by way of illustration.

> At the Congress I will be
> As thousands who with me came
> In that foaming current of the wave: small,
> Without ranks and without names;
> One single voice in the 'hold sea!'
> Which will be shouted across the streets,
> Just One man in Mussert's army,
> One of the unknown soldiers.
> In my black shirt amidst the black
> Of the others entirely lost,
> Yet I will hear the beating of my heart
> Even in the heartbeat of the masses.
> And in might I will be One,
> In endurance, in desire,
> Be One in courage and in power,
> And With these I will conquer![132]

Public reactions

For all the mobilizing force the uniform possessed, and crucial as it was in the mythopoeic process, it was a double-edged sword. The fascist symbolic order which defined the uniform was not invulnerable to contradiction, and while its actors could follow a script, they were not liberated from arbitrary divergence. Uniquely marking the wearer as a fascist, the uniform amplified the consequences of infelicitous performances, shattering the authenticity of the performance and disenchanting the audience.[133] The uniform could be said to have been over-inscribed with symbolism, over-burdened with signification, in a way that was easily exploited by political opponents.

Most immediately and of greatest public concern was the threat of violence and disorder that seemed to be caused by the uniforms. Both parties were under suspicion of trying to instigate a civil war, particularly in regions where communists were also strong. Mindful of the political unrest that had led up to the establishment of the Italian Fascist and German Nazi regimes, state authorities including the secret police (both the Dutch Centrale Inlichtingendienst, [Central Intelligence Service, CI] and

Sweden's secret police) kept an eye out for any disturbing activities such as military training and weaponization. When uniforms were banned in 1933, DSN portrayed the legislation as a slanderous accusation that the NSAP was hostile to the state (*statsfientlig*).[134] But the fascist uniform was also a simple concern of law and order, and in 1933 rival parties were keen to point to the provocative effect uniforms had on those of differing political opinions, i.e. the Left.[135] Rows about the provocative effect of uniformed fascists persisted throughout the 1930s. A Swedish police report of 1933 monitoring the national socialist organizations tells of the frequent disorders wherever the NSAP had meetings, especially at the Stockholm Auditorium concert hall. While these rarely got out of hand, they required a considerable police presence.[136] In the Swedish countryside, matters were worse. Communists would regularly disturb fascist meetings, which often ended with physical fighting and property damage.[137] Lindholm himself recounted numerous incidents of serious physical violence, peaking at a meeting in Sandviken in 1935: the square was filled with an angry crowd of circa three thousand. 'I could not speak over the roaring [of the crowd] and had to duck to avoid the rocks being thrown. Have never before experienced such madness, could speak for at most 5 minutes.' Police aborted the meeting, the crowd tried to overturn the party car and the windows were smashed.[138]

Uniforms were by no means the sole cause of unrest, which was after all usually due to profound ideological differences, and banning uniforms did not put an end to such disorders. However they were a central part of arguments about the inherently disorderly nature of fascism. While some groups appreciated the anti-communist stance, and saw socialists as the primary offenders during any unrest, conservatives were suspicious of fascist claims to be serving law and order.[139] Uniformed and sometimes armed resistance – even to communism – was an intolerable usurpation of state authority, especially in the eyes of the Dutch confessional Right. Apart from citing concerns about public disorder and the provocative character of uniforms, RKSP minister Josef Van Schaik warned that 'such a, more or less military, power-development of political orientations alongside legal authority – even if it is, initially perhaps *bona fide*, dressed in the form of assistance to the authorities – cannot be tolerated in an ordered state'.[140] In the Netherlands, where for the period 1933–7 the NSB seemed like a genuine threat to the established political system, Mussert did surprisingly little to alleviate fears of civil unrest and violence, opting for a rhetorical carrot-and-stick approach. In response to the various laws passed against the NSB and similar organizations, particularly the law against political uniforms, he stated that 'every attempt to block the legal path of a new spiritual current within a people, for which the historical time has come, is in essence an attempt at civil war', words quoted in large font by VoVa, something which cannot have put conservatives or legislators at ease.[141]

In conjunction with the use of trained paramilitary formations, the uniformed party armies – even if banned in public – were under constant scrutiny for organized criminal intentions, particularly a coup d'état. The considerable number of files that are stored in the Swedish secret police archive is itself evidence of the scrutiny under which the NSAP was placed, as are the surviving CI documents showing even small NSB meetings were monitored by state agents. The Swedish secret police kept a file on 'illegal activities' specifically, investigating rumours of a coup d'état.[142]

Fascists were also included in military investigations into the spread of extremist propaganda among military personnel, although, as Heléne Lööw has shown, fascists were typically not considered very seriously compared to communists.[143] The security services' close eye on paramilitary formations was underpinned not least by the memory of the Finnish Civil War in 1918, which broke out to a significant extent on account of the escalating formations of armed militias on both sides, and mutual anticipations of violence.[144] Sweden had already had a controversy about paramilitary formations in 1931 when the Munck Corps was discovered to have illegally imported firearms from Germany, a small group tenuously connected to the SFKO via Sven Hedengren.[145] Sven Hedengren (himself under scrutiny from the secret police) was interrogated about the Munck Corps and its arms supply.[146] Lindholm himself viewed the corps sympathetically, although he considered it too bourgeois in character.[147] The corps was disbanded and Parliament passed a law against private armies.[148] Thus the connection between fierce anti-communism, fascism and armed paramilitaries had already been made in the public mind. When DN reported on fascists in Sweden, it was almost exclusively in the context of violence and disorder. The left-wing press regularly portrayed the NSAP as a criminal organization, plotting to overthrow the state with armed violence, while the police turned a blind eye – the inconclusive 1935 investigation into the supposed continued existence of the SA particularly enraged socialists, especially when prosecutors failed to act on a number of illegal weapons that had been found.[149] The police itself was particularly concerned with the high proportion of military men in the party, even more so when in the latter half of the decade the NSAP organized them internally as the Brown (later Blue) Army and Navy. Sometimes these would march alongside the standard bearers to help out in case of fights, at other times they just lent a splash of military colour to the picture.[150]

In the Netherlands, while Mussert dissolved the WA at the beginning of 1936 in anticipation of a law against paramilitary formations, suspicions that the party kept training members in secret persisted.[151] *De Tribune* reported that 'the WA is dissolved in appearance only. The uniform had been put away, [but] "with a ball of camphor"', quoting Hogewind (now head of Indian Affairs) at a party convention in Batavia (Jakarta).[152] Conservative newspapers remained concerned about the displays of military-style discipline in NSB marches, the association of fascism with the paramilitary uniform strongly impressed on their minds.[153] 1934 *De Tijd* reported rumours that the NSB was secretly introducing cells into the civil militias.[154] The natural association of the uniform with paramilitaries, a link heavily encouraged by fascist discourse, cast a permanent shadow of suspicion on the NSB and NSAP, and was welcome ammunition for the Left, which readily used it to portray fascism as a form of organized crime. Already in 1933, the liberal progressive NRC warned that even unarmed uniformed formations could in the future quickly develop into something more sinister – 'weapons are easy to acquire'.[155] Accurate or not, in public discourse political uniforms became a sign of disorder, and the laws against uniforms and paramilitaries tainted it doubly with the association of illegality, an association that stuck even when worn legally at party meetings. One article from *De Tijd*, based on a report by the Anti-Revolutionary *Rotterdammer*, speaks volumes with its title: 'The forbidden N.S.B.: Impermissible defence squads after foreign model', recounting rumours that the NSB was preparing an illegal paramilitary group like the *squadristi* or German SA.[156] Even as the parties themselves emphasized their anti-communist credentials, and portrayed their uniformed formations as a bulwark of law and order, the symbolic uniform was easy prey to hostile perspectives which reinterpreted it as a threat to the peace or the state.

One of the concerns behind both the Swedish and Dutch legislation was recent developments in central Europe, particularly Germany of course. While the main fear was for a brownshirt or communist takeover of the streets, the argument hinted at a more insidious accusation, that of foreign associations. This was the greatest obstacle to the NSAP, which already in so many regards resembled the German NSDAP, and whose brown shirts were suspiciously similar to those of the German SA. In 1938 this was even criticized by the German Ministry for Propaganda, which stated in a report to Heinrich Himmler that Lindholm had committed the error of copying NSDAP paraphernalia too closely.[157]

The NSB's black shirts did not expose it to quite the same kind of criticism, particularly as Fascist Italy was regarded as much less threatening than the Netherlands' eastern neighbour, but the wearing of political uniforms on the street was still regarded as something distinctly un-Dutch, 'a more or less ridiculous urge to imitate foreign methods'.[158] Both SDAP newspaper *Het Volk* and the liberal conservative *Algemeen Handelsblad* thought the 1933 *landdag* constituted an awful lot of 'visual militaristic messing about', which seemed '"awfully un-Dutch" for such a patriotic-acting group'.[159] Thus the wearing of uniforms, while partially a reminder that the fascists were part of something much greater than merely the national movement – 'the great current of the new age'[160] – that part of something greater was to many outsiders threatening. Black- or brown shirted fascists looked like potential foreign infiltration, a constant reminder of their ideological cousins dangerously close to home.[161]

The hostile press happily integrated the predilection for uniforms into their narratives of a criminal, dangerous and foreign threat. Actual fascist law-breaking contributed to this. This was particularly evident in Sweden, where NSAP members were often ready to push the limits of local authorities' willingness to use their warranty, and the party hierarchy often lacked the means of enforcing discipline. As usual newspapers jumped on any occasion to point out fascists flouting the law – the communist *Ny Dag* reported the case of a colporteur selling DSN in uniform, defending himself in court with the claim that he had no choice, as these were the only clothes he owned.[162] DN reported several times on *Lindholmsnazister* being arrested for flouting the law, usually with a sense of humour about the proceedings.[163] The party propaganda teams, Lindholm told during his 1980–1 interview, were frequently taken to the police station immediately after meetings, to be photographed and judged as to whether they had worn political uniforms.[164] Frequently these encounters did not end with any charges, as local police found it difficult to prove that visor caps, or boots and the like could constitute a uniform, when individual garments were commonly worn by local inhabitants. Only once, in August 1933, were Lindholm and his team actually fined for wearing political uniforms in Skene, Västergötland.[165] So throughout the decade the police would be constantly frustrated by NSAP members making a very particular impression with their garments, without being able to charge them. One police memorandum reported in late 1937:

> It would however certainly not do any harm if the nazis left their boots at home when they held their outdoors meetings, since it is probably the uniform-like clothes which really gall the southerners in particular. If the nazis were dressed 'like normal' people, then the troublemakers wouldn't know which ones were nazis or not when they left the meetings, and would have no one to harass as is always the case at the moment.¹⁶⁶

Both organizations struggled to control the party militants when it came to violent action, which predictably backfired with the press. In the NSAP it was particularly the youth movement which caused trouble. Under Clementsson's leadership the daughter organization encouraged illicit acts of daring and provocative behaviour, culminating in the break-in at a communist party office in Gothenburg, at the instigation of the young leader.¹⁶⁷ *Ny Dag* dismissed the act as 'ridiculous, the way in which our puberty-nazis realize their fantasies about the desirability to "live a life of danger"'.¹⁶⁸ Lindholm later used the occasion as an excuse to fire Clementsson. The NSB was by contrast nothing if not a respectable army, emphasizing cooperation with the authorities, and always full of praise for the police which it claimed to support wherever possible, particularly by letting the WA lend a hand in law enforcement.¹⁶⁹ However, as G.J.A. Broek's research has shown, it was often precisely this category of militants which refused to submit to Mussert's respectable party line, even long after the dissolution of the WA in 1936.¹⁷⁰ To some members the legal path smacked of 'liberal decency', arguing the party should not avoid conflict with the law, fearing the party army was being filled up with

> decent, well-meaning Fatherlanders, but who are scared to death that someone will smash their windows, who would find it terrible if a shoemaker addressed them as 'comrade', people who might sometimes put on a black shirt, [but only] after first having confirmed over telephone that their friends and acquaintances are also doing it. [...] Soldiers of faith [*heilsoldaten*] an IJmuider church paper called us, and that is what we need to be, *soldiers* of faith, who fight for the salvation of our People and Fatherland.¹⁷¹

In the first years of the NSB seemed more prone to permit deliberate acts of daring that fit in with the myth of a heroic army. For instance, Hogewind permitted a colportage march into the red neighbourhoods of Amsterdam, with a group of fully uniformed WA-men, simply to disprove the notion that this would be impossible without being assaulted by the reds.¹⁷² The same month the NSB sent a 150-strong band of colporteurs and WA-men, with reinforcements from Hilversum, to the overwhelmingly socialist community of Bussum in North-Holland. The trip provoked a riot, requiring a large police force to restore order. VoVa proudly reported the discipline and dignity of the heroic soldiers on the front page.¹⁷³ One year later, by contrast, these sorts of expeditions to red neighbourhoods were absolutely prohibited as damaging to the NSB, even though some groups would continue to ignore the leadership in this regard.[174]

Uniformed indiscipline, an incongruence antithetical to fascist myth, occurred in both parties, and made easy targets for hostile constructions of fascism. In spite of the exhortations of rules, directives and functionaries, no member fully conformed to the fantasy of the perfect, uniformed, disciplined fascist. Fascists had a script to follow, but sometimes forgot, sometimes wilfully ignored its injunctions. Not every member was a dedicated fanatic, not all lost themselves in the fantastical mythopoeic process. Nor was every organized collective performance a success: the uniformed fascist spectacle came with a pre-established reputation in Sweden and the Netherlands, one that required significant numbers and resources to live up to. Not only were opponents – Socialist, Catholic, Calvinist, Liberal – unwilling to accept the fascist myth at face value, if at all, but they were ready to interject their own constructions of fascism in the interstices of mythopoeia, interstices opened up by infelicitous performances.

The NSB's first public performance, the first *landdag* in Utrecht, 7 January 1933, had a dubious impact. While surviving HQ correspondence shows that the event was an important factor in the initial upsurge in members to the young movement, much of the media observed the diminutive uniformed rally with scorn.[175] One fascist wrote in March to express his admiration for the bravery of men performing in uniform with hostile crowds, but also noted that the uniforms might be perceived to be ridiculous and theatrical, literally 'monkey suits' (*apepakkies*).[176] Social Democratic *Het Volk* sardonically described it as 'decent fascism', 'but in essence no less crude'. It was the parade which attracted most of the paper's derision. 'There were, carefully counted, thirty small uniformed men, and the circumstance, that they were being inspected by "leader" Mussert with the necessary preparations, did not take away the fact that the entire fascist "army" consisted of thirty men.'[177] Noting that they wore black shirts like the Italian fascists, *Het Volk* concluded that 'this group too is inspired by hideous murder-fascism, with its crude, bombastic performances and its deplorably low intellectual standards'.[178] Numbers definitely mattered in a uniformed demonstration, and their want could seriously undermine the mythopoeic effect of such performances. The group being measured against the standard of foreign 'fascist armies', their 'heroic' discipline placed in a more mundane national context, the impression made through a different hermeneutic lens was primarily ridiculous, not fantastic.

The NSAP that same year probably experienced much the same thing, at their first convention of a few hundred attendees, but rather than the written scorn of the newspapers they were mostly met with silence, as DSN complained.[179] After the 1934 party congress, the local *Göteborgs-Posten* was one of the few papers that reported extensively on the event, drily noting the haphazard adherence to the law against political uniforms, with the presence of boots, barely concealed brown shirts and brown visor caps. While the militaristic discipline of the NSAP march was noted, the overall impression was chaotic, mostly due to the shouting and taunts of counter-demonstrators, and the sometimes violent police intervention.[180] DSN's instructions for the 1935 *årsting* implored members to remove uniforms in public, reminding them in large font that 'the carrying of nat.-soc. *uniform paraphernalia is absolutely forbidden*', underlining that breaking the law would harm the party as a whole.[181]

The thug was one of the most common and harmful constructions of fascism that the NSAP and the NSB faced,[182] the portrayal of fascism as simultaneously a form of organized and undisciplined violence, threatening and chaotic. The NSB's Disciplinary Council, partially set up to resolve internal disputes, functioned chiefly to protect the party's image and settle cases for the benefit of the party in case of disciplinary infractions.[183] While many of the surviving carbon copies of the case files deal with various forms of internal insubordination, there are also numerous instances of members flouting behavioural prescriptions, while wearing insignia, particularly while drunk.[184] Naturally this contributed to the image of fascists as undisciplined and immoral boors, and did not just undermine mythopoeic efforts, but straight up reinforced negative stereotypes. The habit of some members to arm themselves for fights, at meetings and in public, was most conducive to breaking up the myth of fascism as a respectable and disciplined force. One 1934 letter, from the NSAP southern District Leader Nils Wenchert to a local functionary, even implied that while weapons were not considered part of the uniform, the leadership did not object to them. 'You'll have to get truncheons yourself individually, because they don't belong to the equipment.'[185] Lindholm also recounts that members of the propaganda teams regularly brought truncheons to meetings, and recounts several instances in his diary of groups attacking communists with truncheons, though this seems to have more or less stopped after the law against paramilitaries was passed.[186]

Armed members seem to have been more of a problem for the NSB, in spite, or perhaps because, of stricter laws against carrying arms of any sort.[187] NSB-members were on numerous occasions in 1933 found to illegally carry truncheons, knuckledusters, blackjacks and even firearms, leading to several trials which particularly *Het Volk* reported, denouncing them as 'armed Mussert-fascists'.[188] By far the most embarrassing incident involved Mussert himself in May 1937, when, during a visit to the communist-dominated neighbourhood Blauwe Zand in Amsterdam, he and his chauffeur fended off a hostile crowd with a whip, and his chauffeur with a pistol (a Mausser revolver or semi-automatic). The heavily publicized incident went to trial, and while Mussert was never convicted, the case allowed the gleeful reconstruction of the quasi-uniformed Mussert carrying a less-than-respectable whip in the street, flanked by a thuggish gun-toting chauffeur, picking fights in leftist neighbourhoods. The investigation allowed newspapers to repeat and elaborate the story for several days, shortly before the general elections. VoVa tried to depict the incident as an assassination attempt on Mussert, but papers like *De Tijd* chose to focus on the less heroic aspects of the confrontation. '[O]ne thing is for sure, and that is that Mussert carried a whip, when he was visiting party members by car in the known communist neighbourhood, while his chauffeur carried a revolver,' the paper wrote in an article entitled 'The Hero of the "Blue Sand"' (*Blauwe Zand*).[189]

The mythopoeic potential of the uniform was powerful, but a significant minefield. Moments of indiscipline, collective or individual, made for infelicitous performances that were easily integrated into alternative constructions of the fascist movements. The uniform made fascist movements into militaristic armies, a myth that members carried with them even when the uniform was left at home or covered up. The deliberately cultivated connotations of discipline, organization, power and militarism leaked easily beyond the boundaries of respectability, within which party discourse attempted to frame and secure them. Discipline was not trivially enforced in practice; the tight bond between uniform and behaviour did not come automatically, but had to be trained and regulated. The corporeal repertoire of salutes, steps and straight backs was far easier to inculcate than respectable behaviour, which was open to individual judgement. In practice it was easily thwarted. Members were simultaneously encouraged to wear the uniform with honour and devotion, and forbidden from showing it off outside of private, party events – arguably an invitation to insubordination, especially for younger members. Neither the NSB nor the NSAP possessed anything like the resources or opportunities to train their cadres into an actually militarily disciplined and smoothly functioning army, where each member stuck rigidly to a fascist moral discipline, always dignified, powerful, masculine, yet respectable. In an organization of thousands or tens of thousands, individual misbehaviour was inevitable – as it was in all parties – and reports of infractions and crimes were quickly carried across the country. But mythopoeia did not end at the performative stage. The fascist press continued to engage in a battle for the significance of these performances, countering hostile outsiders' portrayals of fascist misdemeanour, juxtaposing the image of a thuggish, criminal, foreign, or revolutionary fascism with their myth of a respectable, dignified and patriotic fascism.

Grassroots attachments and military subculture

If uniforms were a keystone of unsympathetic interpretations of fascism, and an unreliable tool from a disciplinary perspective, the question remains why both the NSB and the NSAP maintained its place in their symbolic order.

One answer must be that some fascist performances appeared unconvincing, artificial or even ridiculous without uniforms. Once uniforms had been established as a core part of the mythopoeic repertoire, their absence became noticeable, and an object of scorn for inimical analyses. When, in the aftermath of the Swedish uniform ban, Lindholm appeared at a large public meeting at the Stockholm Auditorium, newspapers made fun of the un-uniform impression that the fascists now made, a 'confusion of shirts'. Lindholm, the regional *Stockholms-Tidningen* reported, performed in a blue shirt, 'his SA-leader's colour was a screaming red, and the standard-bearing boys had both speckled and stripe-shirted torsos – indeed, it was such a motley selection of shirt fabrics you could notice the irony'.[190] Several other papers took similar delight in pointing out these veritable anti-uniforms.[191] Out of uniform, performances looked less organized, the collection of individuals less disciplined, and it heavily undermined the image of unity and competence the NSAP and NSB were so keen to maintain.

The contrast was at its most noticeable during a party convention, when the customary marches through the cities of Amsterdam, Gothenburg, 's-Gravenhage or Stockholm, made a rather dismal impression when the parties tried to maintain some kind of dignified and disciplined front, without the clothing to visually tie the ranks together, and lend coherence to the demonstration. At the 1935 Amsterdam convention, Mussert complained how they were forced 'to proceed through Amsterdam like prisoners-of-war, without flags, without music' – an obvious contrast to the ceremonial display in the RAI-building.[192] Photographs of the 'civilian' marches, even those made for fascist publications, are not instantly recognizable as displays of fascism. The contrast between the brown-shirted columns of the 1933 *årstingsmarsch* and its 1934 equivalent in the rain speaks volumes. Outside commentators were but all too aware of how fascism wanted to appear, and took much satisfaction in highlighting the contrast. Un-uniformed performances were far less photogenic, and made less of a spectacle: discursive and visual representations of large meetings tended to be much more focused on the indoors, private, aspect of the event, with all its ritual and ceremony, and less on the public procession which instead became about the martyrdom of the party, the heroic discipline of respectable men in the face of uncouth Bolshevik agitators.[193]

While the uniform lost its immediate mythopoeic strength in the face of the laws against political uniforms, and negative portrayals did not cease during the following years, both parties still benefitted from the indirect transmission of images of uniforms to the public, through their newspapers, propaganda and other publications. These had the advantage that, unlike the, doubtlessly more impressive immediacy of a physically present uniformed army, they were tightly controlled and selected, framed by discursive reconstructions which directed the beholder's interpretation. VoVa and DSN were a far more common point of encounter for outsiders with the fascist uniform than the physically present. They ensured it was always accompanied by the appropriate fascist commentary, and through selection manufactured the special character of the uniform. It was removed from the mundane, secular world, and preferentially staged in a ritual context. While such imagery was not immune to deconstruction by a critical gaze, fascist hermeneutics helped offset rival interpretations. The extent to which this was effective can only be surmised, but it was safer than physically present uniforms on the street, unprotected by discursive fascist interjections, precariously open to interpretation. Hence the uniform was, in spite of the risks and drawbacks, not necessarily from the outset a lost battle in the struggle for the meaning of fascism. The mythopoeic potential of the uniform was too powerful to be abandoned, and there were openings and opportunities to convey that mythopoeic force to the public.

Nor was this purely a matter of propaganda strategy. Neither Mussert nor Lindholm was in a position to simply abolish the uniform in the party. Apart from the ridicule of the press, they faced the devotion of the cadres to the garments, so that mythopoeic strategy was also tied up with their fetishistic commitment to the symbol. Attempts by the Haarlem Circle Leader to prohibit NSB-members from wearing the black shirt to IJmuiden celebrations of Queen Wilhelmina's birthday in 1933 (the event was ostensibly not meant to be exploited for propaganda purposes) were met with indignant responses.

> Some of our members will not go to IJmuiden, precisely because the black shirt has been forbidden to them; they say that they wish to bear witness to our loyalty to the Dynasty, and do that preferentially in a black shirt, the dress of our Movement [...] In my opinion every compromise is out of the question, and the wearing of black shirts ought to be encouraged under all circumstances, certainly not be prohibited, with perhaps as only exception in church.[194]

In the years after 1933 the desire to wear uniforms in public was partially satisfied by the wearing of uniform-like clothes whenever possible – this habit in the NSAP has already been noted, while in the NSB this was rather more difficult, but still possible on some occasions. For instance, the WA and NSB started infiltrating hiking organizations, and instructed members to participate in apolitical sport marches in identical clothing.[195] For the traditional Four-Day march (*vierdaagse*), NSB- and WA-members were informed of the desirability 'that everyone will be as similarly dressed as possible', giving a specific list of garments and colours to be worn (long-sleeved open-necked white shirt, short black trousers, orange lower socks, black upper socks, black shoes).[196] In Sweden, the NSAP insisted that the ban against uniforms was ultimately temporary in nature, and its regulations even prescribed a quasi-uniform for the period when uniforms were banned: '[d]uring periods of democratic uniform scares (uniform ban) a white shirt is worn (sport- or tennis shirt) as well as a brown motor cap. Note that boots and trousers are not [legally considered] uniform paraphernalia.'[197]

It is remarkable that when Lindholm in 1937–8 identified uniforms as one of the most problematic aspects of the party image, rather than getting rid of them, the colours and design were changed. When on 28 October 1938 Lindholm gathered the leading party functionaries to explain the New Direction, he argued that 'we have made a few mistakes. One of these mistakes is that we have used means and symbols which have scared off some of our countrymen (*folkkamrater*) and prevented them from joining us.'[198] Apart from a change in name and most crucially the party symbol, the swastika, he insisted that changing 'certain forms of presentation is absolutely necessary'.[199] This led to a breakaway faction being formed under the leadership of SA-functionary Nils Björkman, but Lindholm thought this was good riddance. 'If you who leave us are such friends of Germany, or if you want to go dressed in uniforms so badly, that you do not wish to follow me in the future, you are free to go.'[200] According to the police informant, about two-thirds of the audience immediately left in silence. But in the resulting circular sent out to all members on 1 November, notifying them of the changes, the idea of abolishing the uniform had been dropped. 'As you understand, sometimes the forms have to make way so that the content, *the ideas*, can be disseminated better,' but uniforms were not mentioned explicitly, and would continue to feature in the SSS.[201] NSAP/SSS-members were deeply committed to the uniform, as the Swedish and Dutch fascists generally were to their symbols. Only a few months earlier in the Netherlands, Mussert had tried to replace the party's triangular black-red symbol as displayed on flag and insignia with an encircled *wolfsangel*, but had to compromise after an outcry from the cadres.[202] One party veteran wrote to Mussert:

> Leader, our Black Red flag, was to me and tens of thousands of others, *everything*. [...] I know, that flag was only a symbol, but still, something has been *taken away* from me, and many other older comrades. And the emptiness has not been filled by the 'newcomer' by a long way yet. Us older ones MISS the good old Black-Red flag. [...] And then my insignia, that strong, angular sign of honour, which as workers in the Movement. you have lent to [us] ... ? Must I put away my NSB-memories and instead pin [on my clothing] this sweet round little thing [the wolf's hook] ... ?[203]

In the end Mussert had to concede that it was 'impossible' to be disloyal to the old symbols.[204]

But in the end one of the most remarkable aspects of the NSAP's and the NSB's attitude to their uniforms and associated symbols during this period is how the fetishistic commitment was not just continuously propagandized, and demanded by members, but deliberately sustained in spite of all disadvantages, and ultimately integrated even further into their mythologies. The bans were not to be an obstacle to the continued acquisition of uniforms, whole or in part,[205] and a uniformed show of force at meetings remained desirable.[206] The mythopoeic force of the uniform was pent up internally, only let out indirectly, through discursive reconstruction and visual representation. But in both parties' myths, the NSB's in particular, the struggle would one day conclude with a fascist victory, and that day the uniforms would appear on the

Figure 8 The NSB uniformed again. Mussert salutes five thousand marching WA-men in Amsterdam, November 1940. Photographer: NSB Fotodienst. *Voor Volk en Vaderland*, 2nd ed., edited by Cornelis Van Geelkerken, 1943.

streets of Sweden and the Netherlands again, and the fascists would march freely in their brown and black shirts for all to see. 'Our faith is not in our brownshirts or our uniforms. When there is nothing else to attack, *Social-Demokraten* attacks our boots. But truly we will not for the sake of *Social-Demokraten* put on any democratic slippers to seem more peaceful. […] One day the working people itself will annul this curious clothing-ban.'[207] The NSB promised: '[o]ne day the hour will strike, when we, bold and free in our uniforms, will march on the streets behind our storm flags in the service of the NSB; but when that hour comes we must be COMPLETELY prepared.'[208]

†††

Uniforms were a lynchpin in the symbolic order of both the NSAP and NSB, and fulfilled broadly the same function in both parties. They were powerful symbols and important aesthetic components of the external propaganda, a crucial part of the fascist myth, but their real importance was within the party, as an internal mobilizing and integrating force. It was directly tied up with several key themes of the same myth of a holy army under one leader, in a fated battle for the nation, and even Europe, destined to overcome its enemies. The narrative itself was trite for sure, but the uniform played a huge roll in allowing members to become protagonists in this myth. It enhanced the comportment of the wearer, and added a symbolic dimension to their very body, foregrounding its imagined masculinity.[209] This seems to have fuelled what can only be termed a uniform fetishism amongst the cadres, implicitly encouraged by the leadership. The uniform was part of an integrated network of symbols that constructed the fascist myth in various forms, with props like flags and insignia, and a distinct fascist corporeal repertoire, all being used in conjunction with clothing to further the mythopoeic project. It is curious to see just how similar the political culture around the uniform was in both Sweden and the Netherlands, underpinning a militaristic subculture of hierarchy and fantasy, more for the benefit of the members than propaganda.

The difference between the two parties was instead outsiders' reactions, as shaped by the political climate stemming from the respective uniform bans. In neither case did media opinion seem to be particularly amenable to political uniforms, but in Sweden attitudes were far more relaxed towards the NSAP's uniformed delinquency than in the Netherlands. The threat of civil war came up in both countries, but only the NSB faced actual rumours of coup d'états and illegal militia infiltration; correspondingly it also saw far more practical legal repression. In Sweden on the other hand, the mainstream press was quite happy to report on uniformed fascists with humour and light-hearted mockery, even in the left-wing press. While this made the NSAP seem far less dangerous than the NSB, it severely undermined its credibility: unlike the NSB, the NSAP was portrayed as childish and silly, which was probably worse than being dangerous.

In both cases the parties nevertheless throve on the associations of danger, violence and masculine bravado that was inherent to the uniform. Marches, fights, expeditions into 'red' neighbourhoods, and the carrying of weapons were a liability, but indispensable to maintaining the fascist myth in its fantastical dimensions. While patriotic symbols and imagery, and a discourse of law and order were enlisted to balance out other associations, the fascist movements were saddled with an awkward dilemma. The militaristic myth was essential to the appeal of fascism, to both the cadres and potential newcomers, but its props and paraphernalia were an affront to conservative respectability, and fuelled hostile discourses which undermined that myth. In a way the bans against political uniforms cut the Gordian knot, as they restricted the uniform to the party internally, satisfying members' desires and guising this dubious side of the party from the public. But through discourse and insubordination, the problem kept resurfacing throughout the decade. The allure of violence and power inherent to the uniform attracted and repelled, but was ultimately too ingrained in the fascist political cultures.

5

Making fascism in Sweden: Spectacle and the 1935 *årsting*

The centre piece of the NSAP's and the NSB's propaganda efforts every year was the party convention, the pinnacle of the parties' organizational capacities, and the greatest manifestation of the movements to the public. Fascist rallies have attracted the attention of historians before, the NSDAP's much-publicized *Nürnberg Parteitage* in particular. The fascist spectacles have been analysed quite extensively, with academic interest in the role of aestheticism in fascism,[1] going back to Walter Benjamin's 1935 essay *Das Kunstwerk im Zeitalter seiner technischen Reproduzierbarkeit* (the work of art in the age of mechanical reproduction). A great deal of attention has been paid to the real political value of such performances and its imagery, rather than being dismissed as merely totalitarian window-dressing.[2]

One angle through which such spectacle has been viewed is modernity and its technologies. Fascist rallies not only relied on modern technologies, but the format itself was symptomatic of modern mass politics. Bringing together ever larger numbers of people, in a single place to be ritually unified as an expression of political will, was perhaps a uniquely twentieth-century phenomenon, symptomatic of a new 'totalitarian' approach to politics.[3] Accordingly, fascist parties were not the only ones to organize such political spectacles, even if theirs have been most deeply impressed on historical memory.[4] In the Netherlands, the SDAP used mass rallies which symbolized the strength of the unified working class, replete with red flags and music. In 1936 the SDAP managed to gather as many as 40,000 demonstrators in the market halls of Amsterdam.[5] At the same time leading SDAP figures were keen to counter the fascists' exploitation of myths and aesthetics to woo the working classes, developing a 'festive culture' to create a sense of socialist community.[6] Nor were such spectacles, appealing to the audience through a heady mixture of sound, imagery and pregnant symbolism a preserve of the rising socialist Left and fascist Right. In 1921, the Dutch Jesuit Jacques van Genneken founded the Grail movement, which controversially relied heavily on modern technologies to orchestrate ritualistic mass performances, as well as processions through the streets of the Southern Netherlands in colourful uniforms, with battle cries, flags and standards.[7] Sweden on the other hand was not renowned for such modernistic spectacles; with its far more spread out population and isolated communities, political theatre of any kind was generally on a far smaller scale than in the Netherlands, with the possible exception of the famous 1914 Farmers' March (with the involvement of Elof Eriksson).[8]

Since the cultural and performative turn, the political spectacles of the interbellum have been analysed with the understanding that the propaganda of spectacle does not merely aim to deceive or blindfold its audience, but actively creates meaning. Inspired by theatre studies since the nineteenth century, historians and other academics have connected performativity to theatrical concepts of direction, stage, actors and mise-en-scène, and sociological discussions of ritual, as a means of furthering the understanding of political performances.[9] One notable theorist of theatre studies who has turned to historical approaches, Erika Fischer-Lichte, argued that the interwar period was a time of fusion between ritual and theatre – looking particularly at the Soviet Union and Nazi Germany's *Thingspiel* – giving rise to a new form of political mass spectacle that became ubiquitous in Europe.[10] Ritual is here understood as a scripted form of symbolic communication, which reaffirms the ties between spectators and performers, and their joint commitment to a shared symbolic order, reifying the bonds of the community. Fischer-Lichte points to a crucial historical moment in the late nineteenth and early twentieth centuries where research into ritual and theatre studies intersected,[11] producing discussion of how theatre could build communities, and theatre techniques could be applied to ritual.[12] She points to the political significance of mise-en-scène (*Inszenierung*) not just as an aesthetic criterion, manipulating *how* the performance is perceived, but whether it is perceived as staged in the first place.[13] This point about perceived authenticity has been picked up on by Jeffrey C. Alexander, who has also explored the interface between ritual and theatre, and the twin themes of authenticity and integration. The standard of 'a performative' in his reading is to be judged not by whether it is true or false, but felicitous or infelicitous, where the former is perceived as authentic, the latter as artificial, i.e. the audience is 'dis-enchanted' and perceives the performance for what it is: a staged performance.[14] Their theoretical framework is useful in the assessment of the impact of organized fascist performances, i.e. the conventions, and analysing the connection between the modern fascist party organization, the myth, the performance itself and the roles of actors and spectators – sometimes embodied by the same group.

Both Fischer-Lichte and Alexander rely on performativity as understood by Judith Butler, using her re-application of J.L. Austin's concept to apply not to just discursive, but especially bodily acts.[15] Butler's work has been applied extensively in the previous chapter, but is of continued relevance here, as she has gone on to apply ideas of bodily performativity to politics in her 2015 *Notes toward a Performative Theory of Assembly*. Verbalization is the norm for expressive political action, but, Butler argues, acting in concert in an embodied form can challenge this through the plural and embodied form of assembly.[16] While she specifically considers democratic and anti-authoritarian forms of assembly, there is no reason this notion cannot be applied to the politics of fascism. What her recent work highlights in this case is that there was a specific performativity of the collective and bodily presence of individuals, which could challenge political norms in unique ways. Previously William H. Sewell has argued for the significance of gathering large groups of people in specific spaces, to further political ends, but has rooted his analysis predominantly in how this collective presence changes the meaning of space, and the outlook and experience of participants, rather than analysing political assembly at the level of the immediate production of meaning.[17] As will be shown below, bodily presence was central to the mythopoeic potential of fascist conventions, and was important both for *how* it created meaning, and its emotional impact on participants.

The following two chapters will analyse the annual party conventions of the NSB and NSAP as a type of political spectacle that performatively constructed fascism through organized, collective, bodily performance. The party conventions of 1935 will be used as case studies, reconstructing their organization and implementation closely to analyse their mythopoeic effects. These theatrical performances, manifesting the party as a unified force in action, were an unparalleled act of mythopoeia. This was a holistic event, where not just the actual spectacle of the political theatre was propaganda, but also the very act of organizing it was performative, a construction of the strength and will of the party. At the same time the convention was an inimitable way of bringing otherwise isolated members together, reminding them of their greater purpose, and reinvigorating them for future activism through integration. In other words it was a mobilization exercise which had a tremendous impact on party morale, something especially important for the widely scattered NSAP formations who struggled for years with few signs of progress, unlike the mushrooming and comparatively urban NSB organization.

What made the conventions effective as mythopoeia was their overwhelming aesthetic and emotional appeal. The party organizations aimed to mobilize the party *en masse*, and valued the scale of the event perhaps more than anything else, enhancing the sense of collective belonging so important for morale. The participants themselves became objects of mythopoeia, tools in the grandiose performance, designed to impress members and outsiders. The nature of the spectacular was the result of the conventions' holistic nature: close organization and theatrical staging techniques, and the closely controlled and scripted nature of the performance, all contributed to creating a coherent narrative in which spectators and participants could be fully immersed. This analysis of fascist spectacle will show that, while the liturgical elements of a 'political religion' were doubtlessly present, this dimension was largely *ad hoc*, and in service of a more central aesthetic register. More than anything this was a cultural event for the immediate physical performance of fascism, rather than the mystical worship of a transcendent principle, no matter how religious the rhetoric. The analysis here also goes beyond the focal point of ritual and theatre studies, community and social integration, to foreground the fantastical.

This comparative analysis of the aesthetics of spectacle will bring out two functions of the Swedish and Dutch fascist conventions of 1935, but which were privileged in contrasting ways by the two parties. The function of rallies as propaganda is the most obvious; the other was as mobilization to boost morale. For the NSB, propaganda was clearly the most important, something that can be linked back to the trajectory of its success, and the scale of its organization. For the NSAP it was morale – the Swedish party did not enjoy the media attention of its Dutch counterpart, and its struggles with Swedish geography made the need to reify the bonds between the members more acute. These two approaches to the fascist convention made for quite different events, which brings out the importance of the national context for the nature of fascist mythopoeia – both in the character of its enactment and its aims. The following chapters aim to show

how and why circumstances pushed the NSAP and NSB to organize two very different spectacles, but both of which from different angles sought to construct a fantastic fascism that could punch above their immediate political weight. In the general analysis of fascist mythopoeia and respectability, this analysis unifies the examination of specific myths, practical party organization, fantasy, activism and national contexts and political cultures, in what served as the definitive performance of fascism, a holistic unity through embodiment. At the same time it will show that, no matter how spectacular, fascists were never in control of the public discourse about their events; even the greatest mythopoeic efforts could be unpicked.

Årsting and *landdagen*

When Lindholm broke away from the SNSP in January 1933, it took little time before party newspaper DSN announced the first NSAP party convention, the *årsting*.[18] As fascists whose first direct experience of National Socialism was as guests at the August 1929 Nuremberg rally of the NSDAP, Lindholm and the Party Leadership had an impressive idea of what such an event could be like, and its importance for the movement.[19] The trip had been arranged via Lindholm's friend and Himmler's associate Max Pferdekämper. Lindholm, as SNSP functionary, was to learn from the propaganda and organization of the Nazis. In the 1980s, he recalled the powerful impression the rally made on him:

> And it was then a perhaps mile-long column of members [came], first and foremost SA-troops from different parts of the country, with their standards and flags; masses of viewers, there were raised tribunes on the side, there stood masses of people, and in the windows and on the roofs, and waving with flags, shouting and screaming. It was something altogether indescribable, something like that simply doesn't happen in Sweden.[20]

With this formative experience in mind, the NSAP set about organizing its own annual party convention. The *årsting* was first held on 3 and 4 June 1933 in Gothenburg, where party headquarters were initially located and where fascists were most heavily concentrated in the country. Throughout the 1930s, it had a set structure. Over the course of two or three days around Pentecost, party members would gather for four main events: the 'leader day', a small-scale meeting on the first day of the congress for functionaries, which dealt with practical matters of organization and instruction; indoor party meetings focused on a series of speeches from the Party Leadership; an outdoor public meeting; and the *uppmarsch*, a ritual march through town in formation. These events were interspersed with a number of rituals and ceremonies, music and singing, while every evening was ended with a 'comrade evening', a festive occasion for the members to gather for food, drink and entertainment.

It took the NSB over a year to organize its first *landdag* (the Dutch term for a large, organized gathering), which took place on 7 January 1933, in Utrecht. While

Lindholm broke out of a pre-existing party and had a need to quickly consolidate his followers, Mussert used the first year of the party to lay the foundation of the organization and establish a small following. Just like the NSAP's first *årsting*, the first *landdag* was a small-scale affair to assert the presence and authority of the new party, to the public and to rivals, and instruct the members – a demonstration not of numbers, but of discipline.[21] These first conventions of the NSB and NSAP were remarkably similar in some of the features they included, such as uniformed marches through the city, instructive speeches of encouragement from the Leader and the affirmation of loyalty to his person. But the NSB conventions across the decade diverged from their Swedish counterpart in many ways. Rather than a strictly annual event, the *landdag* was organized whenever it was deemed opportune by the leadership. Instead of lasting several days, it was always a short, concentrated affair, lasting from afternoon until late evening. Quite unlike an *årsting*, it was not a time for celebration or entertainment, leaving only a break of about an hour for refreshments, while the rest of the day was typically scheduled with speeches. While a march through town from the railway station to the event building was always an important part of the convention, it never had the importance of the NSAP's *uppmarscher*, and was redundant by 1936. Strictly speaking the last *landdag* of the NSB was in October 1935, after which they were replaced by the *Hagespraak*, a *public* open-air convention on the party's grounds in Lunteren, on the Goudsberg. These *Hagespraken* made for a very different kind of event compared to the *landdagen*: the location of a hill-top meadow in the countryside made for a very different setting from the major Dutch cities, and threw up different organizational challenges.[22] Their public character was of particular significance for these conventions, as they prohibited the wearing of uniforms, but also enlarged the scale of the event, as they attracted people outside of the party. The kind of organization was also heavily altered to cater for this mixed public of members and curious outsiders. Nevertheless, the *Hagespraken* clearly fit in with the tradition of previous conventions, and retained their overall structure and ceremonial features, even if the purpose was rather altered.

In Sweden, the *årsting* were held once a year, bar 1936 when the party organization focused on the general election campaign instead. The first two were held in Gothenburg, but as the party's centre of gravity shifted to the east, they were subsequently held in Stockholm. The two largest cities were an appropriate location not just for their size, but also because they were situated (very) roughly in the middle of Sweden, making the travel distance more or less fair for the members in the countryside. However, 1939 saw the event held for the first time in Sweden's third largest city, Malmö. This too corresponded to a geographical shift of the party's propaganda and member concentration, this time focused on Scania in the south. The Malmö convention, or *Öresundstinget* as it was officially called, underlined the importance of access: for members in Norrland travel to Malmö was virtually impossible, and a separate *Norrlandsting* had to be organized in Östersund at Midsummer. Otherwise the convention was held on the weekend of Pentecost, generally a popular time for these kinds of events. They were perhaps the only time of the year when people were guaranteed to have the time off work, and could take the time to travel to the city and be back home by Monday. Apply for the convention, 'you're free anyway', as DSN put it.[23] Additionally the weather was likely to be good, something of some importance for the impression the *uppmarsch* made.

The NSB conventions were irregular: two in 1933, January and October; a regional convention in Amsterdam in 1934; another two conventions in 1935; and one *Hagespraak* a year at Pentecost in 1936–40. Plans had been made to have an urban *landdag* again in 1939, but this was cancelled due to the unavailability of extra trains; instead regional conventions were organized alongside the *Hagespraak*.[24] In terms of locality, there was a sharp divide between the urban gatherings in the major cities and the remote and difficult to access Lunteren in Gelderland. Why exactly Lunteren was chosen remains a matter of speculation – no relevant documents have been found pertaining to the party's purchase of the land. The symbolism of 'the centre of the Netherlands' is obvious, but it was very inconvenient; by 1941 it was literally impossible to organize conventions there due to fuel rationing, while railway access was almost non-existent.[25] The choice of place for the *landdagen* is rather self-evident: Utrecht was the place of the NSB headquarters, and conveniently situated within the *Randstad*. When the number of attendees grew too large to be contained by any public building in Utrecht, it moved on to Amsterdam and finally The Hague, the other major cities of the *Randstad*, easily accessible by rail from most places in the country. In Amsterdam it was the massive RAI-building which accommodated the event (also used for SDAP conventions), then in October 1935 a specially constructed tent in a field in The Hague outside the city centre was used, when the RAI-building also proved too small.

Attendance figures for the conventions are informative, and it is possible to reconstruct a great deal about the rising and falling fortunes of the NSAP and NSB through these. While both the first *årsting* and the first *landdag* saw some 500 attendees, in 1934 the *landdag* numbered 5000, and subsequently in the tens of thousands. NSAP *årsting* grew to a little over 2000 in 1935, but declined again thereafter. Comparing the figures, the most striking difference is the extremely rapid growth of the NSB conventions in its first years. The meteoric rise of the NSB has already been discussed, and the sense of mission and destiny that came with it – as well as the firm response from the authorities that it produced. The Dutch figures for 1936–8 need to be handled with caution, as these were public events attracting numerous non-party members. Moreover the figures were highly disputed, with wildly varying estimates depending on source. The NSB did not give a figure for 1939, only speaking of 'tens of thousands'. Regardless, these were some of the largest political rallies ever seen in the Netherlands, and even as the NSB's membership shrunk in the latter half of the decade, it still managed to get an ever-greater proportion of its cadres to attend the event.[26] By comparison the NSAP saw an initial increase as the party grew and consolidated its organization, before quickly stagnating, seeing only very modest growth until its collapse in 1939, partially caused by the unfortunate choice of location which effectively excluded the entire northern half of the country. In light of the party's loud insistence that each convention was to be bigger and better than the last, the attendance in Malmö was downright humiliating, and reflected poorly on the 'New Direction' of the SSS. The figures also indicate that the size of the NSAP peaked in the mid-1930s, at up to 12,000 members. The incremental growth of the *årsting* after that points to the improvements in the party apparatus in the later 1930s. The year 1935 was in many ways a 'year of consolidation' for the party's organization, and the years that followed bore fruit in this regard. One thing that is not borne out by these figures is attendance at the adjacent public meetings, which were a standard part of the NSAP *årsting*; freely accessible, these could attract impressive crowds of up to 8000 people.[27] Nevertheless, it is very striking that compared to the NSB, the NSAP at best managed to mobilize perhaps just under a fifth of its members at the conventions, the NSB closer to 80 per cent. This can largely be explained by the geographical and infrastructural context, discussed in Chapter 2.

The enormous amount of time, money and organizational skills that went into these conventions indicates their central role in the life of the movements. While the NSB and the NSAP had a particularly rich meeting culture, and were constantly engaged in bringing members together and the party to the public, these events stood out. The parties were convinced that 'the best propaganda is and remains the public meetings and marches, where the people can see and hear themselves what the National Socialists want, and through which the lies of the Popular Front press fall to the ground like empty shells',[28] an explicit statement that events like these served to push their own idea of fascism into public discourse.

Context and preparation of the *årsting*

In 1935, it was time for Lindholm's NSAP to demonstrate how far the fledgling movement had come in two years, and prove to the public and its rivals that the *lindholmare* were the only fascists in Sweden that mattered. The year 1935 was an eventful year for the party: the party headquarters in Gothenburg had been raided in February, starting a police investigation into illegal paramilitaries; Lindholm had been put on trial for libel as the editor-in-chief for DSN, and was sentenced to two months in prison, from March till May. The 17 March Stockholm city council elections (*stadsfullmäktigeval*) saw fascist parties increase their votes from 279 in 1931 to 6300; of these the NSAP accounted for just under half, the others going to Furugård's SNSP and Martin Ekström's National Socialist Block. To heighten the sense of change, the Communists gained their first seat in the city council at the expense of the Social Democrats.[29] By spring it was evident that the NSAP had managed to outgrow old and new fascist rivals, and gain a foothold in the capital, building up its organization in Stockholm from scratch to a local membership of thousands, at a time when radical parties briefly seemed to be gaining ground. As Lindholm wrote to his followers on the DSN front page before going to prison, the first storm had been endured successfully, and now '[t]he time of great trials for which we have been waiting has begun'.[30] It was with this sense of potential, new gains and new opportunities, and a gathering storm, that the Party Leadership decided to demonstrate the strength and mission of the movement, at the first fascist *årsting* ever to be held in Stockholm, named *Sveatinget*. To some extent the choice of Stockholm was a reward to the city branch for its success in the elections.[31]

The orchestration of the third *årsting* of the NSAP in 1935 will be reconstructed as closely as possible; sadly far from all documents pertaining to this convention have survived, so it is necessary to also rely on materials from other *ting*. The third NSAP convention was particularly interesting, as it was held at a time when the party apparatus was being consolidated, at the same time as its centre of gravity shifted from west to east. Finally, on account of Lindholm's prison sentence, it also shows the organization in action without the Party Leader – judging by his diary entries, he did not get involved with the preparations until 27 May.[32]

Centrally the convention was organized by Gunnar Svalander, one of the most influential members of the leadership, who until 1936 (when he was ousted for conspiring against Lindholm) acted as Deputy Leader, Party Secretary and Party Organizer: in other words he had considerable organizational experience.[33] The *årsting* was first announced in DSN on 3 April by Nils Dahlrot, the press chief, editor of DSN, and one of the party's most popular speakers. His announcement of the first Stockholm *ting* started with an invocation of the experience of the previous year's convention in Gothenburg, presenting readers with the myth of a classless *folkgemenskap* (national community, cf. *Volksgemeinschaft*) on the march. Notably he used the *uppmarsch* to evoke this myth, focusing immediately on the aesthetic impressions of the march. 'It was 20 May 1934. The music resounded between the rows of houses, the flags were flying in the wind. But this was not a Marxist proletarian demonstration, this was not the bourgeois jogging procession of the Right, it was an emerging people's movement which was marching forward.'[34] As will be shown below, the experience of being part of such a march was linked to the longing to once more tie the bonds of comradeship, and renew energy for the struggle. Instructions for the convention were subsequently issued predominantly via DSN.

The *årsting* was to start on 9 June, leaving the branch organizations less than two months to prepare and organize the attendees. The applications were due 25 May, but as was always the case, an additional week was conceded to slow members.[35] The main thing that needed time was organizing transport to the capital, which had the best railway connections in the country. However, long distance travel of this kind could be prohibitively expensive. Hiring extra trains to get formations to the city was an expense the party could not easily afford, and the party's travel leaders' organization had to siphon off the costs to the membership. In 1934 the extra train between Gothenburg and Stockholm, the best connection in the country, cost 20 kronor for a return ticket – a large portion of a worker's average monthly wage.[36] By 1938 if not earlier, transport organization was left specifically to the Circle Leaders, implying that local branches were too small to finance and organize travel for their members. Additionally it was much easier for the centre to control the few dozen Circle Leaders, rather than the countless local *avdelningar*.[37] In the end twenty-seven buses were hired for the 1935 *årsting*. There were also groups who travelled on the back of trucks, even if this meant standing up for the entire journey.[38] Finally there were always a handful of members who simply walked the distance, even from Norrland, where the party organization remained primitive, and railway infrastructure sparse. Beyond the details of organization, such a journey was for some members simply a part of the adventure; many of the young members had never been to the big cities before in which the *årsting* were held, and to cross hundreds of miles on foot to get to the fabled event only added to the excitement.[39]

Financing the *årsting* was always a challenge for the party, one which tellingly shaped the way it was organized. The largely decentralized organization of transport and reliance on branch initiative were a reflection of the fact that the NSAP was barely equipped to handle the large sums that would be involved in arranging this centrally – that they in 1935 attempted but failed to hire extra trains is symptomatic, even though this was blamed on the state railway company.[40] The entry ticket for the convention itself was priced at 1 krona, slightly higher than the 75 öre at previous conventions, but one which virtually all members could afford, and added some 2000 kronor to the organizers' funds, and may well have been enough to pay for the use of Stockholm's Auditorium building, the main venue. It seems the first Stockholm convention was rather more expensive than the party was used to, and members were encouraged to sort out accommodation at their own expense. Mass quarters were firstly reserved for female members, who could not be expected to sleep just anywhere.[41] The archives do not show what other expenses the NSAP had, but by mid-April it was evident that the party budget could not manage both the convention and the impending summer propaganda campaign with members' fees and tickets alone. Gunnar Svalander decided to start a short collection campaign for the party's 'war coffers' (*krigskassa*) from 20 April to 20 May, using a coupon system by which the cadres could collect money from sympathizers; it was deemed undesirable to demand money from the members themselves, who were already under strain.[42]

The main expense was probably hiring the various venues: apart from the main venue, Auditorium, the party hired the Victoria Hall (*Victoriasalen*) for its 'Leader day', and three other smaller venues across Stockholm for minor functions on the second day. Auditorium (renamed *Vinterpalatset* in 1942), a concert- and cinema hall at the central square Norra Bantorget, and one of the largest buildings of its kind, could seat 1751 in its main hall, and 1952 after being rebuilt in the mid-1920s. Auditorium provided an ideal space for the convention, an exciting two-tiered venue in which all members would be able to see the stage with ease, with its circular floor plan. The fact that the building was built specifically for viewing performances made it well-suited to this kind of political theatre. Additionally it was commonly used for public meetings by the Stockholm Local Group, especially when Lindholm visited. The Victoria Hall by comparison was a more mundane building, suitable for an audience of a few hundred, but like Auditorium centrally located, on the picturesque Norra Tunnelgatan. For one function the party hired the house of the Christian Union for Young Women, another rather ordinary venue. The other venues were the Workers' Union building, and lastly Manhem on Odengatan 42,[43] a property owned by Carl-Enfrid Carlberg, and one used extensively throughout the 1930s and 1940s for pro-Nazi lectures and meetings.[44] The choices of Auditorium and Manhem are obvious enough, and, in the absence of any direct evidence, one may wonder whether the NSAP got a good deal for using the property; Carlberg after all helped bankroll the movement in subsequent years. (Notably Manhem is also slightly further away from all the other venues – about 1.6 km from Auditorium, while the other venues were between 0.7 and 1.1 km away from Auditorium.) Regardless, the five venues were generally situated within a few hundred metres of each other, making it easy for the assembly to split up from the main venue and spread out to their respective functions within a quarter of an hour. Svalander and the other organizers then must have selected the venues firstly out of practicality, only secondly out of financial considerations, highlighting the importance of the *årsting* to the movement in spite of its perpetual financial problems.

As the 'most important action of the year' moved ever closer,[45] DSN harangued the cadres to apply for the convention, emphasizing the significance of the event for the party's propaganda efforts, as well as promising an unforgettable personal experience; '[a]t least once a year you have to see thousands of comrades around you and march in mighty columns, once a year defy the howls of the enemies', marking the event as a rite of passage.[46] These mobilizing messages underscore the mythopoeic potential of the *årsting*, bringing out the fantastic dimensions which the party leadership sought to evoke through their organization. They also show that the convention as a mythopoeic spectacle was not only propaganda, but that its established mythic qualities were retrospectively employed to mobilize cadres and public alike. 'It is not a small insider clique, which gathers in Stockholm this Pentecost, [rather] they are fighting battalions that march forward in the capital, to gather around their young chieftain.'[47] To emphasize the point in later years, DSN would reprint photographs from former conventions to show readers what kind of spectacle they could expect. The capital was the fortress of the enemy, of capitalism and Marxism, but the fascists would gather in greater numbers than ever before, from all parts of the country, from all classes,

> and you yourself [Stockholm inhabitants] will be able to conclude that the newspaper press lies, when it claims that Lindholm's militant organization is a small clique, that the newspaper press lies, when it claims that the NSAP consists only of school boys and offenders! Go out into the streets and behold the large marches on the first and second days of Pentecost.[48]

Locals were encouraged to watch the spectacle of the marches; the convention was not just for the benefit of members, but also a strike in the battle for the myth and image of the party, the meaning of fascism in Sweden, an explicit counter-attack against the media discourse about fascism. In the run-up to the event, posters were put up all around the city proclaiming the event, announcing the time and marching route of the party. Flyers were distributed depicting the marching route, encouraging people to protest with the fascists against the rotten system.[49]

The busy programme for the three-day event, with its rules and regulations, was published in DSN. Members were encouraged to cut them out and take them with them. The first day of Pentecost was officially the first day of the convention, but the evening prior was the Leader Day. Non-functionaries were encouraged to travel to Stockholm to arrive on Saturday night. To ensure all formations arrived in an orderly manner, any larger groups travelling by bus or train had to assign a commander responsible for the party. Given that members were attending as representatives for their local branches (circa 130 out of 300 were represented at the convention), it was crucial that they were organized accordingly. To this end each branch was absolutely obliged to bring the venerated symbol of each formation, the standard, a crucial prop to mark the organization and expansion of the movement across the country. For the two to three days each member was attending they had to bring their membership card, their own blanket (two if they were to sleep in mass quarters), toiletries and a bag for their own breakfast, as well as a copy of NSAP songs booklets and cash. Intriguingly for the overall impression the convention must have made, members were encouraged to dress in cheap civilian clothes (*sämre civila kläder*). Wearing a uniform in public was of course out of the question. Within Auditorium it was permitted, and the schedule left enough time for members to change if they so desired, but photographs show that in practice many members, apart from the leading functionaries, did not wear the full party uniform at these events.[50] On the other hand, the party supply service noted that orders for equipment and accessories tended to increase quickly before the annual convention.[51]

The *årsting*

Early on Saturday evening, the first members arrived in Stockholm. Most came by bus or train, but some walked or cycled from Sweden's northernmost communities within the arctic circle. Upon arrival members registered with the convention office, where they were greeted by Lindholm himself, who had travelled to Stockholm earlier that day with his trusted aide Per Dahlberg.[52] Members were then directed to the sleeping quarters. At 8 am the functionaries gathered in the Victoria Hall. For the first time these also included local branch functionaries including council members and independent Section Leaders; nevertheless no more than 125 functionaries managed to find their way to Stockholm by this time. This particular event does not appear to have been of much significance: after Svalander welcomed the functionaries, Lindholm gave guidelines for the party's strategy in the coming year, after which the Stockholm District Leader Sven Rhenström chaired a discussion with the functionaries. In practice the discussion was very short, and local and regional leaders had little input. DSN noted that 'National Socialists are not friends of discussion', but that the functionaries 'think and act in the spirit of Lindholm'.[53] After a short speech on state law, the event was wrapped up with party songs. The small, private gathering was in no way spectacular – Lindholm himself observed in his diary merely the order of events and that it was 'well-attended and with a good mood'.[54] Decorations were minimal (two banners with guards and a large flag) and did not give the impression of a particularly 'fascist space'. But as the 125 functionaries all sat politely in their chairs in the overly large Victoria Hall, listening to the representatives of the Party Leadership, an important function was fulfilled, that of reifying the bond of loyalty of the functionaries to Lindholm personally, and reinforcing his authority. Backed by a large yellow swastika on a blue background, the four speakers sat above the small group of functionaries, who were gathered at the front, intimately close. The intimacy of the event, held in the convention's atmosphere of general excitement before the opening day, may well have left the attendees with a renewed sense of loyalty to Lindholm. At the same time the short event, that can have lasted no more than two hours, heavily underlined the hierarchical structure of the NSAP, the Leadership dictating to the functionaries, while the cadres were left out to be summoned the following day.

It was on Pentecost Sunday that *Sveatinget* truly started. Busses and trucks were still arriving from all over the country when Lindholm, who was staying over at a friend's house just outside the city, drove in at 9 am. A large audience had already gathered at Auditorium.[55] People were arriving who had just come off the bus, others had stayed overnight in the houses and apartments of Stockholm party comrades, while a few hundred were walking from the mass quarters shared with NU on Regeringsgatan, a stone's throw away from Auditorium, on Tjärhovsgatan – nearly an hour's walk away on the other side of Stadsholmen, the central Stockholm island connecting the city districts.[56] According to Lindholm's diary and DSN, 1800 party members were present in Auditorium for the opening at 10 am, but this must be wrong – there are mentions of late groups, while just over 1800 is the total figure for the entire convention which DSN gives. Between 9 and 10 am people entered the salon of Auditorium, occupied the seats along the curved walls and in the centre of the floor, and the balconies above the stage, while a band played marching music. Outside it was sunny, but thunder rumbled in the distance.[57]

The stage was decorated with long blue banners on either side, a swastika superimposed in yellow.[58] Behind the centre stage was an enormous yellow flag, with a blue or red circle with a yellow swastika.[59] All along the balcony hung coats of arms of the Swedish landscapes, from Lapland to Scania, mixed with various fascist symbols, swastikas and runes. By 10 am the cylindrical domed hall was filled, not quite to capacity, with people, most in civilian clothes, some in uniform. Never before had so many of the NSAP gathered together. It was the largest fascist meeting ever to take place in Sweden at this point. At 10 am the band played some marching tunes – then, most likely to the cheerful sounds of the 'March of the Leader', Lindholm entered in full uniform, followed by his colleagues. The audience rose, and greeted *partiledaren* with an ovation, salutes and shouts of *hell Lindholm*, which must have been acoustically overwhelming. The almost traditional fascist Leader entry, where the Leader walks between his followers who make a path through which he can pass, was not possible here.[60] Lindholm must have used the front doors to make sure his entrance was not anti-climactically short, but as the floor plan shows, he would have had to rather awkwardly walk around the large shield-formed section of seats in the middle. Then one of the Party Leadership, Carl A. Alfredsson, member since 1931 (SNSP), DSN editor, District Leader for the West, and a party speaker, opened the *årsting* with a word of welcome; the exact contents of the short speech were not reported.

Then followed the second part of the opening ceremony. To the tune of Lindholm's *Friheten Leve!* the massed standards of the party marched in, carried by members of the A-group in full uniform, while the audience saluted the banners. Thanks to an irate circular a few months earlier, members had learned to stand up when the massed standards entered, salute them as they passed, and end the salute the moment the standards were on the stage, and placed on the floor in front of the guards (this last part had caused confusion before).[61] The lyrics of the song playing were a call to arms, proclaiming the imminent liberation of Sweden, employing imagery of marching ranks and raised banners, the Swedish landscape, and a youth army burning with passion in a struggle against bourgeois capitalist oppression.[62] By all accounts, the spectacle was electrifying; the militaristic symbols of the party joined together in formation were marched past the attendees, up the stage, where the uniformed guard took its place around the Leader, planting their standards on the floor. The Leader stood tall on the rostrum, his brown uniform contrasting with the surrounding sea of bright blues and yellows, all facing the audience, in an aesthetic performance of the party as a glorious, unified army destined for victory. The united party sat in the hall, looking up to a stage that showed a construction of the movement in mythic form, symbolized by the sensuous colours of the fabrics, the uniforms, the music, the Leader. Then Lindholm spoke to welcome the attendees to the *ting*, followed by another popular party song, *Folk i gevär* (A people in arms) (thematically identical to *Friheten leve!*, but with a more anti-Semitic emphasis) sandwiching the event opening between militaristic music dramatizing the party struggle, while the movement found itself gathered with its leaders in the capital for the first time, at a politically heady time of growth and opportunity.[63] The whole ceremony took a little over half an hour, an aesthetically intense moment which readied the audience for the drier parts of the *årsting* that followed. In Lindholm's diary it is this first half hour which he focuses on the 'heartfelt ovations, song and marching music'.[64]

For the next two hours the audience was subjected to statistical and financial reports from the Party Organizer Gunnar Svalander and the Party Secretary L.E. Dahlin, and a speech on Swedish youth (marking the growing importance of NU) by S. Ahnfeldt, before a lunch break at 12.40 pm. At this point the hundreds of party functionaries that had arrived by now split up to attend events in the four other venues: for NU-functionaries, propagandists, independent local leaders, study leaders, treasurers and women, a category of their own in the NSAP. Suffice to say that the convention continued with further speeches, with more song and music, until all members were joined together again in Auditorium at 5.30 pm, for the second spectacle of *Sveatinget*: the march.

The 1935 convention featured two marches, one on each day of Pentecost. The first march was the longest, from Auditorium on Norra Bantorget to Vitabergsparken, a public park on Södermalm, the southern island district of Stockholm, and generally considered a leftist area. The second march went from Norrmalm (northern district) to Östermalmstorg, a public square with a less circuitous route from the venue.[65] Interestingly there is one major difference between the marching route for the second day as described in the programme published in DSN on 29 May, and the flyers encouraging citizens to watch the march.[66] The latter includes the long, straight Karlavägen, a scenic avenue lined with blossoming trees at this time of the year, the former instead of curving north-east towards Östermalmstorg. Some sort of compromise had evidently been made, although none of the documents show why, and it would appear that the final, actual marching route was never published – a quite astounding piece of mis-organization if that was the case. As the party's 1938 rules and regulations point out, it was ultimately the police authorities who decided the final marching route, so that most likely a route change was enforced at short notice.[67] The march on the first day took circa two hours, the second about one hour and fifteen minutes, probably to make sure that the convention could be concluded in time for participants to travel home in good time.

The participants gathered on the square outside Auditorium, some 1800 NSAP-members, and for the first time also the NU, divided into six columns. In practice a march to the southern park to listen to a speech by Wilhelm Sterner, veteran speaker and Western District Leader, the action had high mythopoeic potential, which DSN would make the most of. In spite of the lack of uniforms, no one could have doubted that the marching columns festooned with blue, yellow and red swastika flags, as well as NU's 'Odin flags', was an army of sorts. In surviving copies of the party's rules and regulations (TF), emphasis was always placed on ostentatious order and discipline, more important than numbers, whereby the marching columns were meant to contrast with those of the Left.[68] The detailed 1938 IF instructions for *uppmarscher* give some indication of what the NSAP sought to achieve, although it does note that *årsting* had their own regulations.[69] The entire marching army was led by a marching leader – in this case former SA-leader and future Eastern District Leader, Karl Erik Ekegren, i.e. someone with ample experience of propaganda marches, and presumably someone not too 'screechy', which IF noted should be avoided[70] – a reminder of Judith Butler's dictum that speech acts too are implicated in embodiment.[71]

> Every National Socialist, who has participated in one of the marches organized by the party, knows what a great propaganda value a well-organized [march] has. [...] Since we National Socialists in all areas demand *order and discipline*, it is *a matter of honour* for us to order our propaganda actions of various sorts in such a way, that every *folkkamrat* who sees and hears us is *impressed* by the will to struggle, the *will to victory*, which suffuses each participant.[72]

At 5.30 pm the first column set in motion.

> There was pacing and precision, and one could *see* that those marching were *freedom fighters*. We understand very well that Stockholm's capitalists and Marxist bigwigs, Jews and other parasites, were terrified at the sight of these columns. They could see that these people would not let themselves be compromised away; one could see that they knew what they wanted, that they marched towards a decided destination, the freedom of Sweden.[73]

The columns, carrying seventy flags representing the NSAP districts and branches of Sweden, marched for the next two hours following a circuitous route. At the front marched Lindholm and the Party Leadership. All columns marched three abreast, which made the columns oddly narrow, reducing the visual impact somewhat much of the time, but which would also significantly lengthen the marching army, with a strong effect on the longer streets. *Sveatinget* marched south, with a route that took the army straight through Stadsholmen, the geographical and historic heart of Stockholm. Here the ranks of three filled the space neatly, while at the same time allowing the snaking march to uncurl to its full length all along the street. From the steeply elevated side streets and alleys east of Stora Nygatan, onlookers would have been able to look down

Figure 9 The NSAP marches from Stora Nygatan onto Slussen at the 1937 *årsting*. Photographer unknown. *Den Svenske Nationalsocialisten*, 1937, no. 38. Kungliga Biblioteket (National Library of Sweden).

on the marching fascists. Doubtless this, and the exit from Stadsholmen onto Slussen (the sluice), was the thought-out climax of the march. Slussen provided an excellent vantage point from which to watch the procession snake along the street towards the southern district, maybe the only point during the march from which one could see the army in its entirety. Evidently this part of the route was deemed good enough to repeat in its entirety at the 1937 *årsting*, when the party had clearly developed a better mise-en-scène to capture a shot of the mythic spectacle that the marching army created. (Evidently photographing their own spectacles was something the party took time to develop over several years.)

The resulting photograph displayed on DSN's front page also gives a good idea of what the 1935 march must have looked like. The booted fascists marched, shouting slogans and singing party songs, marching music played, and the scores of flags flew brightly in the wind.[74] Cutting through the old heart of the Swedish empire, towards the workers' quarters, this was the NSAP pulling out all the stops in a holistic mythopoeic action, making use of the full fascist repertoire.[75] This was intended as the ultimate manifestation of fascism in Sweden, a strong, disciplined and unified army against the historical backdrop of Stadsholmen, conquering the capital and the enraged Red workers, a narrative unfolding right before the eyes of the public.[76] A collective fantasy was being fulfilled in this moment.

> Column after column marched up, and one could see from the viewers, who by their thousands lined the pavements, that they were surprised. The newspaper press had not written anything about *that* freedom movement. 'Imagine that the little Lindholm sect was this big!' The Stockholmers truly got their conception of the National Socialists thoroughly corrected! After all, here they got to see with their own eyes that Sweden's National Socialists are not a few hundred Furugårdian drunkards, but thousands of farmers and workers from all the lands of Sweden.[77]

The final stage of the mythopoeic march took the army into Södermalmen, taking long roads in a round-about way to Vitabergsparken. A public park set on a hill top, against the background of the imposing Sofia church, it had a natural stage with elevated places for the crowds to watch the meeting in the style of an amphitheatre. The army marched up the hills to the stage, where the speaker, Sterner, was waiting from the back of a truck draped with party flags. Here the standards massed in front of the speaker's makeshift podium, making a wall of blue and yellow between him and the audience of around 3000 that had already assembled.[78] As a conclusion to this spectacle, Sterner held a speech of about one hour which attacked the evils of Bolshevism, in an obvious provocation of the Södermalm inhabitants, and a fitting end to the narrative that the march constructed. To complete the event, party speaker Ahnfeldt was attacked by two 'Marxist' opponents, but the fight was quickly dealt with before police arrived.[79] To the frustration of the NSAP, this was the main event of the convention dailies like DN picked up on, devoting about half or the entirety of their brief reports to the fight.[80] *Svenska Dagbladet* noted that '[t]he nazi meeting did not happen without one of the usual street disorders'.[81] The day was closed with a 'comrade evening' at 9.15 pm, giving the participants an opportunity to meet other members from all over the country and socialize, watch a recording of the previous year's convention, and participate in song and music.

A few observations are in order about the second day's march. Most notably this time NU was separated from the party, and instead the 270 or so youths gathered on Lovön, the palace island just outside the city. Here they were treated to an apparently downright fairy-tale-like speech by Lindholm, were rewarded distinctions and had their standards consecrated by the Leader.[82] From there on they marched back into Stockholm, past the royal Drottningholm palace, saluting as they went past in a sign of respect for the monarchy. Lindholm himself was evidently impressed by the march, which was recorded on film,[83] describing it as 'very stylish and colourful with all the standards and blue shirts'. He was so inspired by the young fascists he went home to write a poem about them.[84] The formal conclusion to the convention was Lindholm's speech of little more than an hour, but it was the public meeting following the final march to Östermalmstorg which provided the grandiose ending befitting *Sveatinget*.

Once again the party was organized in marching columns, and in an hour and fifteen minutes the procession made its way through the northern district, repeating the previous day's performance, but here they ran into more trouble. While the route was different, going past the party headquarters but avoiding Karlavägen, the same techniques were utilized.

The long, central street was much busier than Karlavägen, with its tram lines and two-way traffic, which detracted a great deal from the overall impression. It did have the advantage of a large picturesque bridge over the middle of the street, from which crowds could view the entire train as it extended across the street. Unfortunately for the party, the marching columns were significantly marred this day by what was afterwards described as sabotage by the police. Apparently this had also undermined the march somewhat on Sunday, but was even worse now. Police constables walked along with the marching columns, which were obliged to maintain the same pace as the constables. However, as the police men walked at different paces, the columns ended

Making Fascism in Sweden 139

Figure 10 The NSAP marches along Kungsgatan at the 1938 convention, while onlookers watch from the bridge. Photographer unknown. National Archives of Sweden, Marieberg, SO Lindholm's collection (SE/RA/720834).

up further and further apart, of a distance up to 200 m, something which seriously undercut the impression of a single unified army. According to the police this was so that traffic could continue to flow – particularly important for the northern city area, and police had trouble handling traffic problems at previous NSAP conventions when spectators blocked the roads entirely.[85] But as DSN bitterly pointed out, car drivers did not have a right to drive through marching columns. Nevertheless, in a show of respectability, the paper made sure to point out that they did not blame the police per se, but their political overlords.[86] It is impossible to gather what the public really did think of the NSAP's propaganda march, which was greeted with straight-arm salutes and leftist spit alike.[87] But when the convention arrived at the public square in Östermalm, a crowd of some 6000 people gathered. The numbers were doubtlessly boosted by the location in the north-eastern districts, instead of the working class south, and Lindholm's profile – 'our greatest propaganda resource', as Nils Dahlrot had called him earlier that day.[88]

The sky was clear, and the sun shone brightly on the large open space. Nils Dahlrot opened the meeting, then Lindholm commenced his speech, lasting an hour and a half. Unfortunately, after a march which already in several ways had not conformed to the NSAP's plans, the electronic speaker system now turned out to be inadequate. The party leader was forced to shout his entire speech, in an effort to make himself heard to several thousand people on one of the largest public squares of Stockholm.[89] DSN did not mention this defect, though it must have been obvious to everyone present. While Lindholm was a reasonably skilled orator, and had prior experience of crowds of this size, it is rather unlikely that he managed to make himself heard to the entire audience. The speech itself was filled with the usual fascist hobby horses, with attacks on capitalists, Marxists, Jews, the Social Democratic government and democracy, and comments on fascist social, economic and foreign policy. Stuffed with exclamatory statements (the transcript is littered with exclamation marks, though one wonders whether that is because of Lindholm's shouting), it was a rhetorically over-excited piece conveying little of substance. Nor was it meant to. Starting with a portrayal of the rise of the NSAP in the past two years, in the context of a supposedly faltering democracy, Lindholm ended the speech with an appeal to present sacrifice, and the power of fascism to grasp and alter the course of Swedish history.[90] In the rhetorical climax of the convention, Lindholm shouted:

> Yes – we wish to continue the history of Sweden, says the answer which resounds from the northern land's fells to Öresund – from the western – to the eastern land! Yes – we wish to confess to the people's will which flows in our own blood! Here we wish to found a free motherland for the workers, and here fight for that culture which can speak to Nordic hearts, to the people's own soul![91]

In an idiosyncratic move, he proceeded to recite two stanzas from a poem (*Grubblaren*, 'The Brooder') by Viktor Rydberg (1828–95), one of Sweden's most renowned Romantic poets.[92] One can only imagine the impact of shouting the stanzas across the crowd. Doubtless, the effect was unique.[93]

There are woven, circling in space, stars
and thoughts, circling in human brains,
there is woven generation, there is woven death,
and the shape of things and the destiny of peoples.
There patterns are made, shifting and bright,
like nerve threads, quivering in desire and pain,
but the pattern's theme is eternally set,
an unrelenting, ceaseless struggle for life.[94]

The poem, as Lindholm explained to his audience, compares human life to a weave spun through time and history, in which it is human action which forms the pattern. The interpretation linked the poem to core themes of fascist myth: nation, action, sacrifice and struggle. Intriguingly this was not Lindholm's own interpretation: the same stanzas are quoted by Are Waerland in his 1924 popular philosophical tract *Idealism och Materialism* (Idealism and Materialism), and Lindholm was actually citing Waerland almost verbatim in his interpretation.[95] (Conveniently Lindholm left out the stanza in between the two he recited, which emphasized the smallness of humans, and their lack of perspective in a pessimistic vein which is also present in *Grubblaren* – 'We believe ourselves to will, even to be able to [act], / but are mere thread figures in the weave'.)[96] Invoking the poem mythopoeically interweaved the party struggle with Rydberg's vision of human destiny and the search for meaning, elevating the actions of the past two days to a cosmic stage. At the same time it lent the party myth as presented here a touch of the glory and respectability that marked the national poet. After explaining the meaning of the poem to the NSAP, Lindholm ended his speech with a poem of his own, *Folket som slår* (The People That Strikes), a poem which was printed in full in DSN several weeks later: 'We shape Your destiny, Sweden, with the powerful voice of love, / and sing praise of your future, from thousands of young breasts! / Fly out, our freedom flags in the wakeful spring of struggle – / the dawn is rising – labour's people strike!'[97] It was, in his own words, 'a grandiose conclusion to the conference'.[98]

†††

As far as the NSAP organizers were concerned, *Sveatinget* was a success. Lindholm described a great mood at headquarters the following days, and DSN had enough material to celebrate the convention for weeks.[99] The next issue on 12 June headed the front page with a grand acclamation of the convention, '[a]gainst lies and oppression', calling it a 'tremendous freedom demonstration against the terror laws of capital-democracy'.[100] Apparently hundreds of photographs had been taken, though only eleven of those made it into the party newspaper, as the paper's finances did not permit for more to be printed.[101] DSN interviewed the organizers of the event, who were universally pleased with the outcome. Gunnar Svalander noted drily that: '[t]he convention has been executed in a desirable fashion in its organizational aspects. It is only pleasing to note that it in certain cases has exceeded all of our expectations. But nothing is so good it can't be better'.[102] The treasurer, Carl Kristern, thought the convention was the most impressive one yet, though he lamented that the organization could not afford as much music as desirable. The DSN's reporting is typical: simultaneously effusive in praise, portraying the event as exceedingly impressive, while at the same time leaving room to push members to do better. The interviews with the rank-and-file members all spoke of the fantastic atmosphere, the great propaganda, and the invigorating and inspiring effect of being together with so many comrades from all over the country, an excellent antidote to the isolation many experienced the rest of the year.[103] In a private letter from Svalander to District Leader Arvid Gerhardsson, who did not attend the convention, he noted that it was needless to say how other comrades had felt about the *årsting*, but one thing he could assure Gerhardsson. 'Never before has the militant spirit been so powerful and never before have the followers given their leader greater evidence of immortal loyalty and dedication [in all capitals]. It would have done you well to have been among us, comrade.'[104]

In the 1980s, Lindholm said that the party's outward activity in the second half of the decade largely followed a set pattern, of which *årsting* were one part.[105] Comparing the 1935 *Sveatinget* to its predecessors and successors this seems to indeed be the case, but it is important to note that these spectacles, as comments from the organizers imply, were not the same year-on-year, but developed over time. As the attendance figures show, until 1939 the party managed to mobilize more and more members for the *årsting*, even while absolute party membership figures declined. While the organization failed to get an extra-train from Gothenburg in 1935, the 1937 and 1938 conventions were far better served by public transport.[106] Another important improvement over the years was the presentation of the convention in party media. Specifically the photographs of the 1937–9 conventions are markedly better than those of 1933–5, paying far more attention to the framing of the shot, composition and timing. In fact 1935 appears to have been something of a low in this regard, with the 1934 Gothenburg *årsting* resulting in both more photographs in DSN, published in a special issue, with additional artists' representations, and more impressive ones. The pictures were a means for '[o]ur sympathisers around the country to get an impression of the massive following, the conditions, and maybe also the atmosphere. And through the photographs the convention participants get a valuable memory of the unforgettable days of struggle, a link which will tie them ever closer to [their] comrades, and urge them on to new and powerful efforts.'[107] But if the following Stockholm *årsting* were notable improvements on the 1935 success, this probably owed a great deal to repetition.[108] The 1937 convention's marching routes were almost identical to those of 1935,[109] and only the first march of the 1938 convention took a new route altogether.[110] In all other regards the proceedings followed a nearly identical structure and order to those of 1935, so that in some ways *Sveatinget* was trend-setting for the rest of the decade. This was a notable contrast to the more varied conventions of the Dutch NSB.

6

Making fascism in the Netherlands: Spectacle and the 1935 *landdag*

When, in October 1935, the Dutch *landdag* in The Hague began, the NSB already had an exhilarating year behind it. Membership had been growing steadily, if not quite as fast as in the two years before then, and the convention in March, in Amsterdam, had been a resounding success – in fact it claimed to be the largest political convention of its kind in the Netherlands ever. Even more beneficial for the confidence of the young movement were the results of the Provincial Elections in May that year, which rewarded the NSB with 7.94 per cent of the vote, an unprecedented first time result for a new party, confirming all the hopes of the leadership. At the end of the month, Mussert undertook his famous journey to the Dutch Indies, staged to elevate the Leader in the eyes of his followers. It was also a time of reflection for the party, as the Leadership conferred what steps to take next, to ensure continued growth and the hoped for seizure of power. The image of the party was at stake here. The NSB was at this point under heavy attack from the party-political press.[1] It was heavily associated, by much of the public but also many members, with the Italian and German regimes, just when public opinion was turning against these countries. In Germany the previous year's Night of the Long Knives massacre of the SA and other opponents disillusioned much of respectable opinion, while the *Kirchenkampf* unified confessional opinion against fascism.[2] As the convention speeches were prepared, the Catholic District Leader d'Ansembourg wrote to Mussert that it was crucial to show at this point that the NSB did not just go along with everything that happened in Germany.[3] At the same time the positive reputation which Mussolini had enjoyed in the Netherlands in the late 1920s was taking a turn for the worse,[4] particularly as the Colijn government struggled to respond to the controversial invasion of Abyssinia.[5] By 1935, in contrast to the NSAP's trajectory in the same period, the balance of the NSB membership was changing ideologically, reflected in increasingly explicit anti-Semitism, as more radical fascists started to join the cadres.[6] Internally, the Leadership was pondering how to mobilize the membership more effectively, worrying that the expanding party bureaucracy was stifling enthusiasm.[7] In summary, while the May elections had confirmed the party's remarkable growth, it was also running up against more and more obstacles and uncertainties; here too, as in Sweden, a creeping sense of crisis set the tune for the fourth national convention of the NSB.

Planning

In the summer, planning for the next *landdag* started at Headquarters in Utrecht. This meeting provides some interesting insights into how the event was shaped early on. Some of the present District Leaders (Limburg, Groningen, Friesland) reported that the attendees of the previous convention in Amsterdam were enthusiastic and satisfied with the event, although one, Bakker, thought that one convention per year was enough. However, the General Secretary and Deputy Leader, Van Geelkerken, had the impression that some attendees did not like the massive scale of the Amsterdam convention. It lacked the intimacy of previous events, and some had left complaints. But, Van Geelkerken noted, 'the members forget, that the convention is held to make an impression to the outside', not for the benefit of the participants. Mussert agreed: '[t]he massive character of the convention is necessary to show to the outside world how strong our Movement is, while the necessity is also felt to bring members, who live far away, amidst their comrades for once'.[8] The initial date suggested by Van Geelkerken was 31 August, to coincide with the Queen's birthday, but Mussert argued for the autumn, so that it could re-mobilize members after the lax summer period. A date was not decided on yet, but most likely it was the extra weeks required for the building of a tent which ultimately placed the date in October. In a foreboding comment, Mussert said that: '[h]olding a convention in October is, with an eye on the season, not feasible. [Even] if we were to do so in September, we would need to be lucky to get dry weather'.[9]

Later that same month Dutch intelligence services CI reported to the government that the NSB leadership was planning on organizing a convention in a field on the outskirts of The Hague, to be held in the beginning of October. For the event a colossal tent would be imported from Köln, to be constructed under the supervision of a German engineer. One hundred WA-members would be recruited to build the edifice in a work camp, over the course of approximately one month.[10] Requiring thirty train carriages to transport the tent materials, the final result would be 160 by 125 m, with seating space for 35,000 people. Two 45 m towers connected by a bridge would give the guards an overview of the entire terrain. The initial location did not work out for reasons not apparent from the documents, while the request to hire a second location from the city council was rejected.[11] The third option ended up being an hour's walk from the railway stations, meaning attendees were going to have to make their way back from the *landdag* late at night, in the dark. Located in the Escamppolder of Loosduinen, a meadow in 's-Gravenhage, provisions for clean water and electricity would also need to be installed at considerable expense. In the following years, these problems were circumvented by purchasing the Goudsberg ground in Lunteren for the *Hagespraken*.

The same organizer of the previous *landdagen*, Jacob de Vries, was in charge of organization, assisted by Johannis Sandberg. The Circle Leaders were in charge of collecting the funds, and recruiting members to attend the rally.[12] Documents from the district party administration of Limburg and North Brabant show detailed plans were made to ensure all outward aspects of the convention did not only proceed smoothly, but with militaristic discipline. Nothing could be left to chance. Headquarters issued instructions to the branches which insisted that '[i]t is for us fascists of the greatest importance, that the travel by extra-train and the marching through The Hague happens with the most consummate order and regularity'.[13] Circle and Group Leaders were instructed on how to lead their subordinates to the trains, signs were made to identify each Circle and their train carriages, a precise marching order was assigned, groups were to march in ranks of four, the trains to be entered from front to back, signs held at a specific height and so forth. A veritable hierarchy of train-leaders was created, with insignia designed for the purpose (a black band with a train wheel). The NSB *landdag* was remarkable for the centralization of its organization, and the micromanagement of the branches from Utrecht, not just in comparison to the NSAP's *Sveating* but in its own right. Circulars for other NSB conventions show that this was by no means unusual; instructions detailed to the point of inevitable confusion, complete with images and diagrams, seem to have been the norm.[14]

This level of organization required a great deal more financial muscle than the NSAP could ever manage – especially considering that the NSB had already organized a convention that year, and run an election campaign. The fact that it was all held in one day, instead of over the course of two or three days, generated its own costs and challenges. The single greatest expenditure was the special trains which this required – the NSB could not afford for buses and the like to turn up late as they did at *Sveatinget*. There was very limited local organization of transport to the convention; instead Mussert himself ensured that there were special trains for the entire country to bring the tens of thousands of members to The Hague and back in one day. The bill from the Dutch Railway Service came to 33,290.45 guilders, but was easily covered by the tens of thousands of travellers.[15] It also made train travel much cheaper compared to that of the Swedes. Whereas special trains in Sweden could cost as much as 20 kronor, the Hague convention tickets, which also served as train tickets, cost 1.25–2.50 guilders. The administration divided the country into five zones – the closer members lived to The Hague the more expensive the tickets, as a means of subsidizing those further away.[16] It was an excellent arrangement, but it did require conventions to be held during low-travel seasons, and within the central urban *Randstad*; when the *Hagespraken* were held during Pentecost in rural Gelderland, the railway services could not only not provide special trains, but discouraged the NSB from using the services at all.[17]

Actually getting the members to The Hague was left to the Block Leaders, under the supervision of the Circle Leaders. Mussert ordered the Circle Leaders to ensure at least two-thirds of the members were present – a rather more dictatorial approach to recruitment than the NSAP ever attempted – and they were to personally take charge of the party apparatus to achieve this goal.[18] Surviving functionary reports show that *landdag*-representatives were assigned to the branches, to ensure that sufficient members were recruited.[19] Within the branches, these representatives also sent circulars to mobilize the cadres: 'every "WAPENSCHOUW" [military review] of the movement is a mighty *Monument*, in which we, in sight of the entire people, show our determined will to, in spite of all resistance, as the Leader said: "win the soul of the Dutch People" for the National Socialist idea'.[20] Block Leaders subsequently walked the neighbourhoods and sold the tickets door-to-door; evidently a very effective method.

The first announcement of the convention in VoVa was on 10 August, and the tickets went on sale 12 August.[21]

To further encourage attendance VoVa, like DSN, periodically published articles to inspire members. On 17 August it promised a 'massive march' to the *landdag*, and in subsequent weeks articles describing the elaborate and impressive preparations of the tent were printed, offering members a look behind the scenes.[22] These were alternated with circulars from Headquarters, emphasizing the absolute importance of the convention, not just as propaganda, but for the future of the movement, and by extension the nation. 'This *Landdag* will be an event in the Netherlands, which does not know its equal. The *Landdag* will leave a mark on the Netherlands of 1935, which will experience how a will has come forth from the Dutch people, to escape from a regent-regime which threatens to suffocate this people.'[23] It was promised that everyone would be able to see the speaker's podium this time.[24] The stated purpose of the convention according to one circular from the party's Central Election Bureau was to awaken that part of the people that is not yet aware that the NSB is on the march to power. To encourage a maximum number of participants, the party Film Service did a report on the building of the tent at the work camp ('Behind the Screens of our 4th General *Landdag*'): '[f]or those who currently still hesitate, seeing this film will help them make up their mind, while it will encourage others to bring more interested parties to The HAGUE.'[25]

The tent was itself an attraction. It cost the NSB 3,414.66 guilders, arranged by the firm L. Stromeyer & Co from Konstanz, which specialized in these kinds of textile and wood constructions.[26] It would be a feat of engineering, and allow the NSB to hold the largest private political *landdag* in the Netherlands ever, if not the largest rally as such. Building the tent took weeks. The work camp at the Leyweg recruited unemployed NSB-members and WA-members, 200 in total according to camp documents, and between 65 and 175 at the same time, depending on the workload.[27] The construction was a propaganda effort, a sign of the party's dedication to honest work and a respectable manifestation of fascist order and discipline. Sadly for the NSB, this effort badly backfired when the Dutch autumn climate made itself felt a little more than usual – as Mussert had predicted months earlier.

On 19 September the organizer, de Vries, wrote to Mussert to inform him that constant rain had made the field exceedingly soggy, which forced the workers to labour in the mud. The city authorities managed to drain the waters enough to make conditions bearable, and even in the storm that followed the 'spirit among the comrades [was] excellent', but there was a silent longing that the Leader would visit them and eat with them at least once before the *landdag*. 'This would mean more to them, than speeches and tokens of gratitude.'[28] Then disaster struck as a second storm completely destroyed the tent, requiring the entire event to be postponed by one week, to 12 October. To compound the embarrassment of fascists trying to build a hubristically large tent in a soggy field in Holland during autumn, mutiny followed on the night of 3–4 October. Workers prevented the camp authorities from calling headquarters, there were instances of vandalism and the head guard was beaten up. Most of the WA-guards had joined the mutineers. Police and gendarmerie had to be called in, until the situation was defused by Van Geelkerken. Part of the workforce was evicted from the camp.²⁹ Apparently the trigger for the mutiny was Mussert himself, who was scheduled to visit the camp to raise morale, but cancelled on account of a cold. In an extensive disciplinary investigation into the mutiny which took the rest of the year, it came to light that workers were unhappy with the poor living conditions, arduous working hours, lack of decent uniforms or boots and perhaps above all the incompetent and antagonizing camp leaders.³⁰ Needless to say, the mutiny was widely reported on in the press, which rather undermined the propaganda value of the work camp, although it seems some of the worst incidents remained a secret to all except the CI.³¹ The fact that the workers were recruits from the WA, supposedly a model of discipline, made the whole episode even more embarrassing. 'The W.A. stands and falls with discipline; without discipline no guard, no troop, no banner. Discipline can only be maintained in a group when it is *in extremis* ensured that a given order is followed *unconditionally* by every man', as a reprimanding circular to all WA-commanders put it.³² An appeal had to be made to the cadres for further donations, so that the extra costs could be covered.³³

The tent and the mutiny were doubtless the biggest headaches for the organizers, but there were other difficulties as well. While holding the *landdag* on a Saturday made good sense in terms of members' availability, the scheduled closing of the convention late at night offended Calvinist members. The IJmuiden Circle wrote to de Vries, complaining that it ended far too late, and reminded him that 'the press, especially the Christian press, would probably exploit it as desecration of the Sunday, and use it as evidence for their readers that the N.S.B. is not all that concerned with the veneration of the Sunday'.³⁴ This was an issue that had already been raised previously in regard to NSB marches on Sundays, 'a stone of offence'.³⁵ Specific requests were made for the convention to be over at 10 pm, so that no one would be forced to travel past midnight, but the final schedule shows that the organizers did not meet this demand.³⁶ It was the kind of issue that holding the later *Hagespraken* on the second day of Pentecost avoided, except then the organizers ended up on the wrong side of the Catholic members, who had nowhere to attend Mass in the Reformed community of Lunteren, and had to make special arrangements in neighbouring towns like Ede and Barneveld.³⁷ The demands of Dutch confessional respectability could prove quite challenging to a *landdag* organization.

The *landdag*

The obstacles that the Hague convention threw in the organizers' path were ultimately surmountable for the quite large and experienced party apparatus, and on 12 October the *landdag* could go ahead. VoVa had been subjecting its readers with *landdag*-related material for weeks, with articles, drawings, instructions and poetry, and now they could finally experience the highly anticipated spectacle that had been promised.³⁸ Nor was it just the party that got to enjoy the event: more than a dozen newspapers, including all the major national dailies (bar *Het Volk*), had been invited to attend the convention, to ensure that they could report on it accurately and in their own words to their readers. Such invitations have survived for the *landdag* in Amsterdam earlier that year, but it is also evident that papers like the NRC, *Algemeen Handelsblad*, *De Standaard*, *De Telegraaf* and *De Maasbode* all accepted for the fourth General *Landdag*.[39] Where *Sveatinget* was above all a mobilization action with a Stockholm public, the fourth *Algemeene Landdag* was a propaganda event, principally staged for the benefit of the national public. With this in mind, the transition to the public *Hagespraken* was a natural one for the NSB.

As a silver lining to the postponement of the *landdag*, 12 October 1935 was a clear and sunny day. The performance started immediately when the first trains arrived at 3 pm at the twin Hague railway stations. A crowd had already gathered, aware that something major was afoot.[40] 'From the North and from the South, from all social strata, from all social ranks and professions, the pioneers of a new *volksgemeenschap* are come together.'[41] Photographers and film cameras were ready to document the arrival of the participants. As they arrived, they were immediately assembled by station and Circle, for the public march to Loosduinen. Thus long twin columns were formed, one from the HSM station, and one from the SS-station (closed since 1973).[42] The precise route that had been planned out has not survived, but from the station to the Leyweg is a fairly straightforward route, just under 5.5 km. Under ordinary circumstances such a march would have taken a little over an hour, but with more than 30,000 participants it was expected to take until right before the official opening of the convention, at 7.25 pm.[43]

The march itself was, in spite of its impressive size, not quite the fantastic spectacle that the organizers might have hoped for, although it was an improvement on the previous *landdag* march in Amsterdam, when participants were forced to roll up national flags in what was described as a walk of shame. The mayor of 's-Gravenhage had imposed considerable restrictions on the procession, on the basis that the NSB was on the list of dangerous revolutionary organizations. The police directed the members to their places on arrival, and they were only allowed to march on the condition that 'the aforementioned participants are not allowed to form speaking choirs, not allowed to sing, not allowed to play music, no banners and signs with slogans and no flags, with the exception of national flags'.[44] Combined with the lack of any (visible) uniforms the whole procession had a distinctly bourgeois appearance, not least with the marching leaders in long winter coats and Homburg and Fedora hats. Apart from Mussert's characteristic military-style jacket, only Van Geelkerken seemed to have tried constructing some sort of semi-uniform for the march, with a wide waist belt and shoulder strap, and shiny leather boots peeping out underneath his long coat. The white shirt rather undercut the whole impression however, making him look quite peculiar.

VoVa ultimately opted to describe it as 'an impressive procession of workers, for whom the streets had been kept free'.[45] If, apart from the sheer numbers, the march was not spectacular, at least it was thoroughly respectable, something much commented on in the conservative press, which admired the order and discipline of the organization, and the lack of unrest that accompanied this performative demonstration of the NSB.[46] A VoVa poem about the march exploited this impression, contrasting it with the image of the uncouth left-wing protesters that lined the streets, the real threat in the royal residence of The Hague.[47] In a reminder of the international context in which the NSB

Figure 11 The march leaders, Mussert walks second from the left, Van Geelkerken on the far-right. Photographer: NSB Fotodienst. *Het Landdag Gedenkboek*, 1935. IISG (International Institute for Social History): Bro N 188.

was viewed by the Dutch public, the procession was occasionally harassed with cries of 'Abyssinia!'[48] Quite unlike the NSAP's *uppmarscher*, what this march had in numbers, it lacked in style, with very few parts of the fascist mythopoeic repertoire being enacted. But then, the real spectacle was going to be in the giant tent, carefully staged in a controlled environment away from undisciplined and critical spectators, with no room for the spontaneous. (There is an interesting echo here of Fischer-Lichte's description of nineteenth-century theatre laws which sought to eliminate the uncertainty of audience interaction from the performance – rowdy audiences were a nuisance to be eliminated, and the emphasis was placed on quiet and emphatic watching.)[49]

As the procession entered the Leyweg just before 7 pm it had become dark, so that the marchers could from a distance see glowing letters at the entrance of the convention terrain, spelling out *HOU ZEE*, 'as a symbol of our radiant self-confidence, our hope for the future of the entire Dutch people'.[50] At the entrance the two columns split, and then divided into sixteen groups to be seated in designated places in the tent.[51] Party reports proudly mention how smoothly this occurred, and the detailed organization that was required. It would seem that the NSB realized that organization itself had mythopoeic potential. The tent was impressive. It created a majestic space, well-lit and festooned with endless rows of vertically suspended orange-white-blue flags. The stage was painted in black and orange, with an enormous golden rampant lion as backdrop

Figure 12 The tent on the inside as the *landdag* is about to begin. Note the wide central aisle. Photographer: NSB Fotodienst. Het Landdag Gedenkboek, 1935. IISG (International Institute for Social History): Bro N 188.

for the rostrum. A special podium had been constructed for the music band, orchestra and women's choir.

At 7.25 pm Van Geelkerken opened the *landdag*. The audience could follow the proceedings in their programme booklets, a high-quality production (in marked contrast to the cheap and flimsy booklets the NSAP used) of fifty pages, illustrated and consisting mostly of advertisements.[52] After ten minutes, Mussert entered. Here the large central aisle between the seats allowed the *Leider* to, now in an all-black uniform with the obligatory belt and shoulder strap, walk amongst his followers, saluting them as they thronged around him. The contrast with Stockholm's Auditorium is intriguing: the seating must have been purposefully arranged to set the stage for this fascist ritual. In other words the mise-en-scène had deliberately excluded a vast expanse of central seating that would have made the proceedings easier to see for the actual audience, for the sake of enacting aesthetically appealing and dramatic rituals, but paradoxically not necessarily ones observable to the spectators. Afterwards it was reported that some members were disappointed that they had not been able to see or hear enough of what was going on – but as propaganda it was a success.[53] It was a striking illustration of the priorities of the *landdag*: outward propaganda first, morale and mobilization second. Subsequently the audience listened to two short speeches, one by the dour *volkse* Calvinist E.J. Roskam on the idea of the Leader and the *Dietse* state,[54] one by d'Ansembourg on Church and State.[55] In less than an hour since Mussert's entry, it was time for the next ritual: the oath-taking ceremony.

Six-thousand new members of the NSB swore their oath to the Leader, in an impressive demonstration of the growing strength of the movement. More than two months before, the head of Department I (Organization and Statistics) had informed all districts and branches that it was Mussert's wish that several thousand new members would swear their oath to him personally at the next *landdag*. It was a striking use of physical bodies as a ritual resource, a mass imbued with fascist symbolism.[56] Consequently, from 1 August all new members were prohibited from taking the customary oath, so that these could happen during this ceremony instead. 'It is not necessary to tell you, that this massive oath-taking during the *Landdag* must be entirely successful and leave a grand impression on everyone present. Each administrative functionary must therefore do everything possible to make sure that no available member will miss this unforgettable solemnity.'[57] VoVa reported on the ceremony in its special *landdag* issue with great detail, giving Mussert's dramatic speech to the new members in full. Mussert embodied the priest-figure in this baptismal ritual, bathed in a patriotic orange light while looking down on this new addition to his growing army, presumably occupying the tent's central aisle which led up to his pulpit. Aesthetically it was a composition which fused a heady mixture of elements that constructed him simultaneously as fascist Leader, priest, general and patriot, framed by the myriad national flags, highlighting the connection between national and party destiny. Mussert spoke:

> History will elevate you to [be] saviours of our People and of our Fatherland [*ons Volk en ons Vaderland*], if you accept your part in the battle. Then may this hour remain in your memory for as long as you live, and may you at the end of your days remember with satisfaction the deed, which you perform today. Your people calls you, you report, and the N.S.B. accepts you. God be with you.[58]

After the Leader had brought out the transcendent significance of this moment in time, the anticipatory atmosphere was built up further as music started to play; photographs suggest the lights were dimmed.[59] As the tens of thousands of spectators watched in complete silence, 6000 initiates answered the Leader 'with a thunderous "Yes!"', arms raised in salute. The women's choir hummed the national anthem, again punctuating the national importance of the consecration.

> The solemnity with which our General Leader took the oaths of six-thousand new members, after a speech which made a profound impression not just for the way in which it was formulated, but which more than ever made the National Socialist sense of reality shine brightly, formed without a doubt one of the pinnacles of the *Landdag*. For it was not only a call [*appèl*] for these six-thousand men, standing with raised arm before their leader in the cleared space around the podium … It was also a call for the entire N.S.B.[60]

To further mark the occasion the following part of the schedule was dedicated to the collective singing of party songs, in what must have been an elated atmosphere after the tension of the grandiose liturgy – an outburst of joyful and triumphant music after the pressure of a carefully directed performance. The organization made sure to use this opportune moment to also collect funds for the party.[61] This was one of the twin pinnacles of the *landdag* – the other would follow after the break.

Thanks to a system by which coupons had been sold in advance for 15 cents, attendees could quickly get their food and drink without delay, and all 35,000 attendees were processed without any hiccups. Even *Het Volk* wrote that this part of the convention went smoothly, if only mockingly to cast aspersions on the rest of it.[62] The three hundred or so toilets that were installed just outside the tent seem to also have done their job.[63] It is a point of interest that only one hour had been assigned for the break. The attendees had little time to socialize; getting food and drink, using the toilet, and maybe buying something at the Nenasu stall would really have been all members had time for in the throng – a sharp contrast with the 'comrade evenings' of the NSAP.

At 10 pm everyone was seated again, for another indispensable fascist ritual: the paramilitary procession. This event had been prepared and practised months in advance; since August WA-commanders had been drilling the rank-and-file for this moment, under the oversight of J. Hogewind. The WA assembled in ranks of eight – something that proved to be a challenge as most troops had not done this before – carrying signs to denote their company. Six different 'model marches' were to be performed. The instructions were an instance of painstaking military discipline, detailing the precise positions of the fingers, angling of the head, arm movements, etc.[64] Diagrams were provided.[65] The whole performance was quite challenging for the actors, not least as many of the WA-companies did not have much space or opportunity to actually practise this style of marching.[66]

On the day, at the given sign, the WA-drums and horns started to play, and 1200 fully uniformed men entered the tent through the south entrance. For this moment Mussert was standing on a central podium from which he watched his troops, with Hogewind at his side. The audience applauded and cheered; with thumping steps the jackbooted WA marched past the Leader up to the north side, and turned around the corner to fully circle the platform. On account of the muddy soil that had been caused by the poor weather of previous weeks, wooden boards had been placed all over the ground. With evident satisfaction VoVa reported how this made the WA's leather boots resound all the louder as they marched, a fetishistic detail repeated by the commemorative *Landdag Gedenkboek*.[67] Admiringly the VoVa report described the uniforms, stature and appearance of the paramilitaries.[68] As they crossed the centre again, the music players separated from the rest of the group, before the whole army came to a halt as indicated by the *jaloneur* – an easy way of directing even inexperienced troops[69] – between Mussert's platform and the front stage on the west side. That way the whole procession, spectacularly outfitted in flawless black uniforms, with striking black-red standards, was arranged to be facing both Mussert and the audience simultaneously.[70] Finally at the very end came the WA camp workers and cooks in their own attire, carrying the tools of their trade over their shoulder, taking up position at the far back. According to VoVa the spectators watched the performance with great enthusiasm, in a 'spirit of young heroism'.[71] It was perhaps the most well-prepared and militaristic NSB performance yet, for a colossal crowd including film cameras and journalists, an ostentatious demonstration of fascist organization and discipline, unity and loyalty and of power. The more sinister implications of this mythopoeic spectacle could not have been lost on the audience: here was the NSB with an army of its own, a disciplined force of real, uniformed soldiers, absolutely loyal to their Leader who promised a rapid seizure of power. Given the ubiquity of propaganda images from Nazi Germany, displaying precisely these kinds of ranked 'black soldiers', the association must have been inevitable. The very bodies of the WA-men were symbolic,[72] the marriage of masculine body and black uniform infusing their presence with a mythopoeic potential, their every movement a promise and a threat of power and violence, of war.

Now, with Mussert in the middle of the tent, the audience on one side, and his paramilitary army on the other, he started his speech which would conclude the *landdag*. It went on for well over an hour (dashing any hopes that Reformed attendees would get home before midnight), using his return from the East Indies and the unexpected rise of the NSB which defied all expectations, symbolized by the arduous *landdag* preparations, as a starting point. Then followed a rather dry account of the political chaos and decline of the Netherlands and the incompetence of its governments, before offering a solution to these problems, and the coming task of the Movement. Aspects of the somewhat generic speech were reminiscent of Lindholm's a few months earlier. 'Great things are afoot; we feel the greatness of this time and our own insignificance, but also our responsibility and our determination and our faith, that we will be shown the way, if we take the truth and love for God and our neighbours as a guide line for our thinking and our actions.'[73] His last words for the audience were a pious encouragement to work harder for the Movement, closing with the words of William of Orange from the national anthem. 'But you workers, carriers of the Movement, you are also the protectors of the future of your people. Nothing may stop you from fulfilling your duty. Work and pray, and may God give us the power to lead our people out of its great distress. "Loyal to the Fatherland, I remain unto death."'[74] The speech was interrupted on numerous occasions by more or less spontaneous applause, and shouts of agreement from the audience. With the final thunderous ovation, the fourth *Algemeene Landdag* was at an end, and the tens of thousands of members made their way to the railway stations in the night. Apparently there were still some members of the public out to watch the procession back, but no particular efforts appear to have been made for this occasion. According to VoVa, everyone returned with an invisible bond, that this farewell was the promise of an even greater return to 'our Leader'.[75]

Perspectives and reactions

Unlike the Swedish 1935 convention, the *Algemeene Landdag* was subject to close media scrutiny, making a different kind of analysis possible. The aftermath of this grandiose political theatre, of a scale and type the Netherlands was hardly accustomed to, emphasizes two points. Firstly, the NSB had managed to largely fulfil the goal of creating a spectacle that made a lasting impression on the audience, directly and through the media. Secondly, the mythopoeic qualities of the spectacle were effective, but volatile – some were interpreted precisely as the party could have wanted, others backfired badly. There is no such thing as a homogenous audience, especially not in the Netherlands.[76] Ultimately, in spite of the Leadership's priorities, the *landdag* may well have been more effective as an exercise in morale and mobilization than propaganda.

Most remarked on was the orderly march from the train station through the city to the tent, bringing out the performative qualities of organization, in a way that gave the movement an aura of respectability, and was an antidote against accusations of political dilettantism.[77] The confessional dailies were invariably concerned with law and order and obedience to authorities in their reports, and could record with satisfaction that the march took place virtually 'without incident' – only three troublesome communists needed to be arrested. Catholic *De Maasbode* noted the military-style marching in ranks of four from the train station, and described in detail the extensive organization to it readers.[78] Local newspaper *De Haagsche Courant* took a similar approach to its report on the convention. Orthodox Calvinist *De Standaard* noted that, apart from the 'understandable' mutiny at the work camp, organization was good.[79] There were also some hints that these outsider newspapers were impressed with the spectacle: Catholic *De Tijd* wrote how '[a]cross these paths thousands went from all parts of our land – 35000 men and women in total – to the central point: a tent, so gigantic in dimensions as one has never seen in our country before.'[80] Evidently impressed the article continued to describe how the crowds chanted '*Hou Zee*' in a 'thunderous choir' while Mussert ascended the podium, until he, underneath the image of the great golden Dutch lion, greeted his devotees.[81]

Outsiders were by no means insensitive to the spectacle, and there is ample evidence that the ostentatiously detailed organization of the event made an impact, but it is also clear that little of this was taken at face value, and that none of the major dailies cared to emulate VoVa's rapturous discourse. While all approved of the orderliness of the event, there were hints of dissatisfaction that such a large police force was necessary in the first place. *De Standaard* remarked snidely that '[t]hanks to the cooperation of the authorities and organs of the democratic state, which the N.S.B. intensely hates and undermines, the participants arrived safely on the terrain',[82] while SDAP paper *Het Volk* noted how the large police force and gendarmerie ensured the complete isolation of the Nazis from their surroundings, symbolic of their social-political isolation. 'Once the Congress visitors were on the terrain ... there were no signs left in the city, that there at the Leyweg the gentleman Mussert and his compatriots celebrated a rather bleak party.'[83]

The report from the predictably hostile *Het Volk* shows that a positive predisposition towards the mass rally was required to read the spectacle the way the NSB intended it to be. Of course the organizers were not so foolish as to invite *Het Volk* reporters to the convention, but this did not prevent them from sneaking in. Their report revealed some distinctly farcical elements to the rally. Inspecting the tent during the break, apart from catering arrangements, the reporters also noticed the floor boards that had been required. These proved to be rather insufficient however, so that people were at constant risk of putting their feet in the mud. The secret reporters themselves ended up covered in filth up to the knees by the end of the night. Moreover:

We saw the Convention in the way the majority of the 35 000 present must have seen it: a forest of hundreds of posts, stretching into an unspecified distance, garlands of little lamps, metres of flag fabric, and somewhere, very far away, a brightly lit orange spot: that would be the podium ... [...] There was nothing to see. Mussert could appear and disappear, we didn't see him. ... yes, six-thousand members could be taking an oath, without any one of us even catching the slightest glimpse of what appeared in the beacons.[84]

Yet, *Het Volk* continued, this did not prevent their fascist neighbours from shouting and crying with zealous enthusiasm at the spectacle which they could not see any better. The reactions of the fascist audience were in fact one of the things that most baffled and alienated outsiders. *De Standaard* in particular found it 'peculiar' how the participants invariably required only a raising of the voice and a bit of rhetorical bombast before breaking out into applause and *hou zee*-chants. Judging Mussert's speech demagogical nonsense, *De Standaard* figured that 'any good speaker could get an equally powerful applause out of this ignorant public, if he directly after Mussert had proclaimed the precise opposite'.[85] 'That that free-thinking part of the population without principles [liberals] is enraptured by this is bad enough, but that people who want to be Christians let themselves be misled by these sophisms is tragic.'[86]

It turned out that it was precisely in its most successfully spectacular, its most impressive, aspects that the convention failed to strike the right note with outsiders, and greatly offended their sense of respectability. The militaristic, even aggressive values the rally demonstrated made a particularly bad impression on the Calvinist audience, especially the WA-procession. 'We experienced a procession of perhaps a thousand blackshirts, which reminded us a lot of the famous parades in Potsdam under a certain monarch. If grim faces and hard stomping are synonymous with heroic courage, then Mussert does indeed possess an elite corps.'[87] Sarcasm aside, the WA gave the impression of being a downright dangerous force. In an extra-large font the article noted how these troops could only mean the NSB was planning to take power illegally. Here, mythopoeia failed to mesh with respectability, and spilled outside its boundaries.

> Eye for an eye, a tooth for a tooth is the doctrine. We will only recommend these words in particular to *those participants* of the *Landdag*, who stayed over with 'comrades' in The Hague because they had religious objections to travelling back by train on the night of Saturday to Sunday. Such meticulous Christians really should try to harmonize this language and morality with that of Holy Scripture.[88]

NSB patriotism and royalism in particular were questioned by *De Tijd* in a front page article three days later, revealingly entitled 'Nürnberg in Holland: Everything Is German'.[89] It reported: 'In the Hague the N.S.B. had held a convention, which was a consummate imitation of the *Parteitag* in Nuremberg: processions, glorification of old Germanic society, condemnation of Jewish international Marxism, veneration of heroes and the dead with "Ich hatt' einen Kameraden" and finally a sort of deification of the leader, or at least of the *Führerprinzip*'.[90] The choice of performances, staging and rhetoric at the *landdag* were evocative – but of an example from abroad.

In articulating a certain myth of fascism the NSB had come rather close to its German counterpart, a likeness which antagonized Dutch Christian audiences dismayed by the Church Struggle in Germany, and undermined NSB claims to be respectably nationalist. At the same, legitimating rituals of respectability, like the singing of the national anthem, *De Tijd* deemed 'an aggravating usurpation of the song of Nassau for the advantage of Mussert's personal glory'.[91] The celebrated sending of telegrams proclaiming the loyalty of all participants to the Queen and Crown Princess during the rally, demonstratively printed on VoVa's front page, was termed 'propagandistic messing-about' (*propagandistisch gesol*). The Catholic newspaper was generally the most sensitive to and critical of these kinds of political theatre, and gave scathing and sarcastic reviews of NSB meetings throughout the decade, pointing to Germanic barbarisms and hypocritical Pharisaism.[92] In other words those performances which were bound to appeal only to the fascist cadres and did not conform to any more general (particularly Christian) notions of respectability could not simply be neutralized by ostentatious demonstrations of patriotism, religiosity and Orangism. Rather it seems that mixing these elements was an infelicitous choice, which to a critical audience marked the performance as inauthentic – a cynical display covering a sinister load.

Ultimately it was the members themselves on whom the whole event had made the greatest impression, in spite of how the mise-en-scène had been for the benefit of the press and cameras. Mussert received letters from his devotees to personally thank him for the *landdag*, with 'praise for the wonderful organization and order, and then praise for the incredible work such as the construction of the tent', and satisfaction at his speech.[93] Members and VoVa readers could not possibly have missed the great effort that had gone into this, and were probably less critical of the flaws in the organization, especially the mutiny and misdemeanours at the work camp, which remained largely a matter of internal discipline. Whether these few letters were representative at all is impossible to say. More may have been written, but they are but a small sample out of the 35,000 attendees. Combined with letters from other conventions, one can at least reconstruct how some members experienced the event, and what the myth it created meant to fascists. For instance a branch leader in Bremen, Germany, asked Headquarters if they could send some of the posters from the 1935 Amsterdam convention, 'such ones as hung up in the R.A.I.-building, since many of our Bremer Comrades have never seen such a thing [before]'.[94]

The desire for mementos, as well as the sale of illustrated convention albums, highlights what an extraordinary experience the spectacle was to many attendees. 'I feel the urge to prove my upright loyalty to you [Mussert] this way. A day like last Saturday gives you something which nothing else is capable of. It is a pity, that not all of our opponents can experience a day like that, maybe then they would change their minds.'[95] To these people the spectacle was not just propaganda, but a transcendent manifestation of fascism as it truly was, above the realm of everyday life and mundane politics, something that was difficult to put in words and could only be experienced through the senses and emotions, through bodily presence. A *landdag* was a moment when people were in the direct presence of mythopoeia as it happened. To some it exposed the seams of the process, undermining the performances. To others the spectacle was overwhelming, and the immediacy of it all chimed emotionally with their beliefs about what fascism was, what it meant to be part of the Movement. To them the performance was authentic, reifying the collective myth as constructed by the party.

The *landdag* and *årsting* compared

Comparing the 1935 Hague *landdag* and the NSAP's *Sveating* that year, what stands out is the completely different press reactions, or lack thereof. If the Dutch fascists got a rather mixed, not to say negative, response to their convention, the Swedes found that while press reports tended to be ostensibly neutral, they were also sparse and minimal to the point of non-existence. The lack of media attention was deeply frustrating to the NSAP, and contributed to the specific ways in which their conventions were organized. In 1935, as during the rest of the 1930s, newspapers generally reported only on the *lindholmare* when there were fights or breaches of the law; this convention was no different, with for instance *Dagens Nyheter*'s report focusing almost entirely on the minor fight with communists that broke out in Vitabergsparken. For the 1937 *årsting* the same paper only printed eleven lines for its report, while in 1938 no report was published at all.[96] For the 1939 *Öresundsting* the national daily only reported on the fact that the NU had broken the uniform law, when the youths famously removed their shirts in front of the embarrassed police, but made no mention at all of the actual convention.[97]

The voluminous reports on the NSB's conventions – consistent for the rest of the decade – are striking, but easily explained by the far greater size of the Dutch party, and the political furore it caused in the Netherlands. Much of Dutch politics in the 1930s was focused on the NSB, and how it should be dealt with, a key theme of both the 1935 and the 1937 elections, so that extensive media attention came naturally.[98] The fact that Mussert was already a known political figure when the party was founded also helped, and ensured the initial interest from the liberal press.[99]

Hence the NSAP *ting* had different priorities from the Dutch *landdagen*. While the NSAP kept angling for media attention, for instance through inclusion of the sometimes rowdy NU, or repeated (and repeatedly declined) invitations to journalists to attend,[100] it always recognized attention was at least currently limited, and organized conventions accordingly. In broad terms, if the Hague convention was above all staged for propaganda, the Stockholm convention was a rally to boost morale, mobilizing the members to strengthen the bonds of comradeship. *Sveatinget* was *for* the spectators, a spectacle put on to draw in the members, to strengthen their loyalty to Lindholm and to the party, remind them of the greater struggle to give them the willpower to continue, even in isolation. Even if the performance was dwarfed by its Dutch equivalent, it felt grandiose to the (mostly young) participants, who had often never been in Gothenburg or Stockholm before, let alone such a large political rally – perception counted for everything here. The fact that some members travelled as far as from Överkalix to Malmö (*c.* 1800 km) to enjoy these events is indicative.[101] In the Netherlands on the other hand, the audience was more *part of* the convention, i.e. a piece of the performance, itself propaganda.[102] This also explains the heavy emphasis on corporeal discipline in the NSB documents. The fact that members' complaints about poor seating and vision were repeatedly met with the emphasis on propaganda value speaks volumes. The point was the members' presence, not their enjoyment.[103] The drive to summon ever greater numbers to the *landdagen* and later *Hagespraken* as a symbol of strength and unity was central to the NSB's conventions. As indicated earlier, even as the NSB declined, year-by-year a greater proportion of members attended the conventions, while the mixing of members and non-members in Lunteren was a powerful symbol of the supposed equivalence between Movement and nation.

Beyond membership figures, organization and resources were crucial to managing these performances. Summoning the 35,000 or so members to The Hague in 1935, or the tens of thousands more to Lunteren in later years, required an elaborate organization, simultaneously centralized and with authority down to the smaller branches, and the financial structure to support it. The tent construction, transport arrangements and ticket system of the NSB demonstrated the efficiency and reach of the party apparatus, and demonstration was partially the point. Being able to manage such a large-scale event within three years of their first public appearance, after an election campaign, the NSB showed the party was capable, disciplined, ordered and a respectable force in politics: one of the real parties, not like the fascist dilettantes of rival parties who never acquired a single seat in parliament. NSB organization was performative, and in terms of mythopoeia as much part of the convention as the proceedings on the day itself. Rather than just presenting a 'natural' image of the event, hiding the underlying artifice, NSB discourse actually exposed the construction, work and organization that lay underneath the performance, proud of the modern technologies and skills it had harnessed, the organizational muscle and discipline it managed, the work ethic of its labourers. That the *landdag* programme booklet on its cover featured the workers of the camp, tools slung over one shoulder, is a clear statement of this point.[104]

By contrast the Swedes could not really visibly impress with their organization, and lacked the financial capacity and acumen, so instead put a characteristic emphasis on the will to sacrifice of the cadres that was required to mobilize the few thousand. The NSAP's inability to effectively gather its members for the convention, hampered by infrastructure and geography, prevented an emulation of the propaganda of scale of the NSB (or the example more likely on Swedes' minds, the Nazi state). But the Swedish party nevertheless did manage to put on a spectacle, and succeeded in places to put on a rather impressive performance with the limited resources at its disposal. The choice of the Auditorium, a space with which the party had ample experience from past meetings there, and the effective use of decorations created a good atmosphere for staging their rituals, and all accounts suggest participants were taken in by their surroundings, and enjoyed the intimacy. But most important, and impressive, was the *uppmarsch*. The emphasis on a public march as the principle piece of propaganda was interesting in light of the relatively few attendees, but made sense given the lack of press coverage. This was a way of bringing the spectacle directly to the public, without any intermediaries, a point emphasized in the party's own discourse. At the same time it was the kind of performance that financially required little more than the members' bodies on the street, and was effectively incorporated in the overall structure and schedule of the convention. As seen, the routes – paying close attention to space, setting and symbolism – as well as the discursive reconstruction of the march were used to great effect to maximize the mythopoeic potential of this political spectacle, and minimize the significance of low numbers.

The surprising efficacy of the *Sveatingsuppmarsch* is evident in comparison to the NSB's march through The Hague (they were no longer a feature with the *Hagespraken*). While the fifteen-minute WA-procession inside the tent demonstrated all the qualities of organization and discipline essential to fascist myth, the city march was unimaginative, and had little going for it but the sheer number of marchers. This is particularly obvious when comparing the photographs: even the NSB's own photographers failed to take any impressive or striking pictures of the march, while the NSAP's show that the party managed to fully utilize its greater freedom in the use of flags and symbols. While uniforms were as lacking in the NSAP march as in that of the NSB, the small Swedish contingent gave a far stronger impression of an army, while the NSB looked like a rather strange procession of bourgeois, be they very many.

The NSAP photographs point to the issue of technology and technique in presentation, which foregrounds how the fascist spectacles changed over time. The NSAP clearly improved its photography and staging after 1935, and subsequent photographs look much better than those of the first half of the decade. The party also managed to print more photographs in the party press in subsequent years. The year 1935 was a year when the NSAP was still consolidating its organization, while in 1936-8 the party moved to Stockholm and expanded financially, buying its own printing press (if never the elusory rotational press) and city properties to house the DSN offices. Capturing the moment on camera, and distributing the images to a wider audience, was an important part of the mythopoeic project, and in this regard the NSAP would not peak until 1937-8. The NSB by contrast had very quickly acquired the technological equipment and competence to record the spectacle, and its profitable printing presses were always equipped to produce myriad pictures for a wider audience. The party also sold gramophone recordings of the speeches in 1934.[105] The rather handsome and well-designed commemorative books for each of the *landdagen* and *Hagespraken* show off not only the financial capacity but also the commercial competence of the Leadership, advertising them as collector's objects, an investment even.[106] The point should not be exaggerated however: the books produced for the 1935 Amsterdam Landdag were still not sold out one year later, so that it is perhaps more a point about the NSB's willingness to commercialize its activities.[107]

NSB conventions did change significantly after 1935: whereas NSAP *årsting* seem to have remained surprisingly static in many respects, the Dutch party was developing the mise-en-scène for the *Hagespraken* every year, researched already in some detail by René van Heijningen. The large hilltop meadow was an excellent place for audiences of up to a hundred thousand people, albeit without shelter from the elements, though that never became a problem. Compared to the *landdagen* it had none of the viewing problems vis-à-vis the seating, as the audience could be freely gathered as one large mass in front of the large central tribune – that being said, managing the vantage of tens of thousands of people in a largely flat field presented its own difficulties. These were overcome over the years by the building of a large stone wall-like structure, heavily reminiscent of some of the Nuremberg structures, which was intended as a lasting monument to the national movement that had captured the Netherlands.[108] (The wall still stands to this day, be it heavily neglected.) The tall structure rising before the audience made an imposing stage on and before which to pose standard-bearers, and from which Mussert could speak, elevating his small figure before his devotees. The party also continued to experiment with other tall but impermanent structures with which to dominate the field of vision: seven enormous black-red banners behind the rostrum, and party flags encircling the grounds captured the eye in 1937, while 1938 saw the raising of a large mast, on which flags of the 'liberated' nations (Italy, Germany, Portugal, Spain) and the Netherlands were ritually raised. Grand and imposing structures remained a key element of the NSB's staging techniques, and to great effect in the open field.

†††

One sentiment that emerged from time to time in both Sweden and the Netherlands was the notion that if political opponents had been able to experience a convention in person, they would feel differently about fascism. This foregrounds the crucial point about the importance of physical presence to these spectacles. Unlike any other kind of propaganda, or any other kind of meeting, the spectacular *landdag* or *årsting* was an *overwhelming* appeal to the senses, a way of accessing the emotions through sensory stimulus: beautiful sights and sounds, the feeling of being part of a mass, the throng of bodies pressed together, the symbolism, uniforms, music, applause and shouts and chants, maybe even the smell, were all a way of conjuring the myth through an immersive spectacle.[109] The thing that made it all a spectacle was the holistic nature of the fascist conventions: this was mythopoeia through a tightly organized and prepared, carefully directed and staged performance, in which actors were closely following a script designed to draw in the audience. Without the interjection of critical hermeneutics, attendees were not only faced with a holistic performance of fascist myth, but were made into participants or fellow-actors – Fischer-Lichte has previously identified this co-participation of spectators in the acting, seeing it primarily as a means of social integration.[110] This was a rare moment for someone to actually *experience* the fascist myth, identifying with it by being part of its mythopoeia. This was the realization of a fantasy. Given that this moment depended on a harmonious entanglement of personal and party understanding of the fascist myth, it was hardly likely to have the kind of impact on outsider observers that fascists imagined, but it does cast a spotlight on the paramount importance of physical presence in fascist spectacle.

Only through physical presence could the spectator be immersed in the myth, which was perhaps the most effective way of communicating the authenticity of the performance. Discursive reconstruction in party organs, communicating the experience to the myriad absent, was ultimately a very flawed instrument in conveying the performance intact. Even if film and photography could add to the presentation, through framing and selection, sound and sense were omitted, largely lost in translation. Reports helped underpin and clarify the narratives that the performance meant to convey, but a textual reconstruction of jackboots rhythmically pounding the floor is a far cry from the experience of seeing, hearing and feeling it. Holistic sensory immersion required physical presence, and was ultimately needed to convey authenticity, that is to say to neutralize critical faculties and lead to an acceptance of the myth at face value.[111]

What this analysis of fascist conventions gets at is that spectacle had a decisive role to play in mythopoeia: spectacle is symbolic of the wider fascist mythopoeic project in Sweden and the Netherlands in the 1930s, and shines a spotlight on the fantastical elements of fascist myths. As has been noted repeatedly, fascist myth relied on fantasy, a personal and collective fantasy with multiple and sometimes conflicting dimensions. The fantasy was one of being a part of a grandiose narrative largely cast in a military and religious register. There were obvious parallels here to Gentile's understanding of political religion: the sense of communion inherent to the liturgical-style rituals, dedication to a common faith, etc.[112] But focusing on the religious aspects of this political theatre is misleading. While faith was psychologically an important part of this, secular concepts of fantasy and immersion are the key to understanding the construction and appeal of the Swedish and Dutch fascist spectacle. The sense of the sacred and divine was merely means to that end.[113]

Rather than religion, Jeffrey Alexander's notion of re-fusion is appropriate here: the performance re-fuses the disparate elements that constitute it into a seamless whole for the audience, and rather than appearing contrived conveys an aesthetic truth, allowing the psychological identification of the audience with the myth.[114] The analysis here also conforms to the ideas of a number of scholars of fascism about the importance of aesthetic impressions, and the concomitant emotional response, and the role it played in facilitating individual identification with a (collective) myth, which explains the impact on morale. Mabel Berezin argued that in Fascist Italy, public rituals were a liminal space in which identities could be formed, where emotion helped obliterate the old self and create a new one.[115] Anette F. Timm more recently made the point that emotion could lead to feelings of empowerment, blurring the distinction between emotions and ideology.[116] Rather than focusing on the religious aspects or liturgical nature of these rituals, these chapters have highlighted the corporeal and somatic factors that facilitated this identification: overwhelming sensory impressions, bodily presence and the literal incorporation of the audience.[117] The difference here is that political religion is ultimately an interpretation of ritual as referring to underlying ideology, rather than a cultural interpretation which sees meaning precisely at the level of the performance itself.[118] Within the framework of performativity theory, meaning cannot be understood beyond the performance – ontologically myth did not 'exist' outside of the performative-mythopoeic spectacle, because performative acts are by definition non-referential.[119]

While other performances on a smaller scale offered the observer glimpses of this myth, a spectacle was not just something bigger but qualitatively different. Spectacle was congruous with the fantastically grand proportions of the political myth – Lindholm and Mussert constructed the struggle in cosmic and divine terms respectively – but also offered the observer a way into *being part* of it.[120] The army metaphor is apt here: the observer becomes a soldier, a knight under the aegis of the Leader in a heroic battle against evil. Immersion was a gateway to participation, of fully going up in the narrative and becoming a protagonist in the story – 'achieving harmony through becoming a work of art oneself'.[121] Ideally the observer did not just witness fascism as myth, but became a fascist;[122] in this the fascist conventions offered something few if any other political parties did.[123]

Conclusion

Dénouement

Both Lindholm and Mussert would look back on the 1930s as something like the glory days of their parties. Considering the past five years in 1945, Mussert compared that period in the NSB's history to a *via dolorosa*, a great sacrifice on the altar of the Fatherland that only future generations would recognize.[1] For Lindholm the struggle was then not yet over, but marked the victory of communism in Europe. He gave up the Swedish struggle for fascism five years later.

The German invasion of Poland in September 1939 and particularly the April and May 1940 campaigns against Scandinavia and the Low Countries radically changed the circumstances of the two fascist movements, albeit in very different ways. The German invasion of Denmark, and Norway in particular, sharply altered Sweden's national security situation. With its neighbours occupied by one of the strongest military powers of the continent, Sweden doubled down on its neutrality policy, albeit with considerable *de facto* concessions to Germany.[2] For the SSS the new situation was disastrous: Nazi Germany's invasion of a brother nation translated into a considerable loss of what little sympathy Swedes possessed for Nazism, and Lindholm himself condemned the invasion, as well as Vidkun Quisling's collaboration, in no uncertain terms. Swedish military mobilization meant that many SSS members, including key functionaries and Lindholm himself, were forced to halt party activities in order to do military service. Yet many others, including Lindholm's advisor Sven Hedengren and Gösta Hallberg-Cuula, volunteered to fight in Finland against the Soviet Union, the latter killed in action in April 1942.[3] Lindholm himself was called in for military service again, and promoted to the rank of *styckjunkare* (also *fanjunkare*) in 1941. However, he was sent home again in the autumn of 1942 under pressure from the public and press when it came out he was essentially evolved in contingency plans in case of a Nazi invasion.[4]

The SSS was forced to devolve into a much simpler administrative structure, and did not contest any elections until 1944, when its support had dwindled to 0.1 per cent. This was partially out of necessity, as secret police monitoring of fascists and other groups considered 'politically unreliable' was sharply increased: the government closely considered banning the SSS several times.[5] Secret police files, including phone taps, show that this was a time of extreme financial crisis for the party, though it did manage to stay afloat for a few more years. This is not to say that the party came to a complete standstill. In mythopoeic terms, it still initiated new developments, perhaps most notably the creation of a new elite party formation, Sveaborg (after the fortress in Finland, built against Russia during the age of Sweden's Baltic empire), which incorporated military veterans from the Finno-Soviet war in particular, and amounted to a further elaboration of SSS's military subculture. The SSS volunteers killed in the war led to the formation of a martyrs' cult which included an annual pilgrimage to Hallberg-Cuula's grave, a tradition that would come to last to the present day.[6] As late as 1967 Lindholm still gave speeches to old comrades at the grave, even if his own political convictions had taken an extremely sharp turn to the Left.[7]

During the war the party continued to organize rallies and marches as it had in the previous decade, and which continued to cause unrest as they were often attacked by political opponents (now also including Norwegian refugees). Germany's surrender in the war caused the party to haemorrhage members, but at the end of May 1945 it was decided the SSS would not 'capitulate'. There were new recruitment campaigns and attempts to mobilize the remaining cadres, but the leadership struggled to keep the party together and publish DSF every week by the end of the 1940s, also facing discontent from younger members. In 1950 Lindholm decided to dissolve the party.[8]

Lindholm spent most of his post-fascist decades maintaining the purity of his and the party's motives, ever further distancing his Swedish fascism from German Nazism, which he retrospectively declared a corruption of the pure ideals of the early years, coming to a definitive end with the Night of the Long Knives in 1934.[9] While he went through an ideological metamorphosis that ended with him supporting the anti-Vietnam war protests in the 1960s and a supporter of the Swedish Left, he maintained contact with former party comrades through the NSAP/SSS veteran organization Sveaborg. His second wife, Vera (later Oredsson, after her marriage to Göran Oredsson), divorced Lindholm in 1962 over their political differences, two years after she joined Nordiska Rikspartiet (Nordic National Party) the most active neo-Nazi organization in postwar Sweden in the twentieth century.

If the Second World War marked a period of relative inertia and decline for the SSS, it was very much the opposite for Mussert and the NSB. On 10 May 1940 the Wehrmacht invaded the Netherlands, and after five days of fighting occupied the country. After the Dutch government and the royal family had fled to Britain, there followed an initial period of surprisingly lenient German government, as the Reichskommissariat of the Austrian Nazi Arthur Seyss-Inquart encouraged a more or less *laissez-faire* Dutch self-nazification, which included independent Dutch political organizations, most notably the Nederlandse Unie (Dutch Union).[10] The Germans soon resorted to a more hands-on strategy however, which led to all Dutch political organizations being banned, except for the NSB, putting the party in an unprecedented position to exercise power and influence. NSB-members were widely appointed mayors, the party proving an excellent source of collaborators.[11] By 1943 the party had become indispensable to the German occupiers, with Mussert informally declared 'Leader of the Dutch People' by Hitler the year before.[12] With the Occupation came the lifting of the bans on political uniforms and paramilitaries, making these the greatest years of mythopoeic expression for the NSB, in terms of resources and scale. The NSB mythopoeic project was also helped along by the massive influx of new members, over 100,000, approximately double the party's peace-time peak. Many of the most enduring images of the NSB after the war were those of the party during the Occupation, WA members marching in rank through the city streets, with little opposition from the public.

On the other hand war and occupation also involved considerable restrictions. War restrictions meant travel was sharply limited; for instance petrol rationing meant the party could no longer organize mass rallies in Lunteren after 1940.[13] Most importantly, the NSB was no longer operating in a liberal democratic public forum, and Mussert was under constant pressure from German organizations to adhere to Nazi policy. The NSB's continued desire to construct a peculiarly *Dutch* fascism, which came with an emphasis on Dutch culture and sovereignty, put it on a direct collision course with the SS. This led to some rather public confrontations between the two organizations, something the Dutch party was bound to lose.[14] While the NSB and Mussert ultimately proved to be impossible to remove from their position in the Occupied Netherlands, it produced a great factional split in the party between Mussert-loyalists and pro-SS adherents of a *gross-germanische* imperialism, with proponents among leading NSB functionaries such as Henk Feldmeijer and Rost van Tonningen. Under Heinrich Himmler's pressure, the NSB was soon supplying its own steady stream of martyrs for the cause in the form of Waffen-SS volunteers.[15]

The NSB's collaboration with German authorities fatally undermined the already unpopular party in the eyes of the Dutch public however, in a way no mythopoeic project could reverse. Mussert soon had the reputation of the most hated man in the Netherlands, while underground news and literature reviled NSB-members as traitors to the Fatherland. Far worse, the NSB provided ample collaboration in and profited from the murder of the Netherlands' Jewish community. During his 1945–6 trial for high treason, Mussert defended himself as having attempted to maintain Dutch independence under the worst possible conditions, in an act of sacrificial patriotism.[16] In his prison account of the history of the NSB, he maintained the same thing: 'The Movement has been sacrificed on the altar of the Fatherland'.[17] With the liberation of the Netherlands by the Allies and the return of the national government, the NSB was banned by the state and declared a criminal organization, and its membership prosecuted accordingly. Around 100,000 people had been a member of the party at that point, with another 22,000 in the SS. The denazification process saw between 120,000 and 150,000 people interned at some point, although prosecution sharply tailed off by the end of the decade. Nevertheless, to have been an NSB member remained a considerable stigma for decades to come. Studies have shown that even children of NSB-members suffered from the association – in the end the meaning of the NSB's fascism came to be indelibly associated with collaboration, treason and oppression.[18]

†††

This book has been about how the 'something new' that Lindholm's NSAP and Mussert's NSB attempted to create, and how they tried to convey it. The premise of the research was that the 'new' with which the fascists came did not reside in their message, but the form, that is to say the performances, and by extension the performative of their myth. While it has been impossible to verify the extent to which this actually attracted new members and voters, it is evident that this was a major reason for some members to stay and dedicate themselves to the party, and was a powerful tool in shaping party policy and image.

It has been shown throughout that fascist mythopoeia was a major mobilizing force, and improved cadre morale. Mythopoeia had the potential to create a feedback mechanism of ceaseless mobilization: identification with the myth raised morale and pushed the cadres to further activism and sacrifice, which could be used to enact mythopoeic performances that required those resources, and fed back into the cadres' identification. The evidence for this is the strongest in the Swedish NSAP, where the perpetually under-resourced party managed to overcome its small size and financial difficulties numerous times through the dedication of young fanatical activists who worked hard and with little sign of success in the foreseeable future. The NSB makes a less strong case, as there appeared to be a weaker activist spirit, and the branches were more tightly controlled by Headquarters.

This points to another finding, that while fascist mythopoeia seems in the first instance to be above all a matter of propaganda, in reality it was frequently for the benefit of the members themselves, who one may assume already believed in or identified with the myth. Different priorities are evident between Lindholm's and Mussert's parties, where the former was far more concerned with sustaining morale while the latter emphasized expansion and quick success – this can be explained almost entirely by the sharply divergent growth trajectories of the two parties in 1933–5. This is illustrated at its clearest by the completely different attitudes to the party conventions: while the NSB recognized the benefit of bringing members together and allowing them the experience of being part of a greater force than their local branch, it repeatedly prioritized appearances for the benefit of the press, and largely used the cadres as part of the performance, rather than the performance being for them. This was a peculiarity of these political performances, that the spectator was often also the actor.[19]

This again foregrounds the importance of identification to fascist mythopoeia. Identification was to be part of the 'something new', which was something that transcended everyday life and 'normal' politics. Integration with a collectively constructed myth was a means to realizing a fantasy, which can be seen as the personal dimension of political myth. A myth of a glorious army, led by a prophetic Leader, guiding his manly and disciplined troops to a predestined victory, was a narrative that permitted members to cast themselves as protagonists, actors following a script, in a myth that transcended fiction, a higher truth. The almost mystical aspects of this identification process left their evidence in the fetishism for the props which underpinned mythopoeia: the standards and symbols, the whole repertoire of salutes and slogans and marches, and of course the uniform. This explains how myth could generate quite such enthusiasm and self-sacrifice, without any tangible reward.[20] Functionaries could be quite explicit about the mobilizing instrumentality of myth, e.g. Arne Clementsson: '[t]o create a youth movement and advance it, there has to be an integrating, inciting element: *a myth*. A thought of incredible stature, which unites everyone and drives them forward in dedicated work for its realization.'[21] But what people like Clementsson perhaps did not anticipate was that in organizations prone to factionalism, internal groups developed vested interests in specific myths, which could be at odds with changing party tactics. Paradoxically, the means that generated cohesion and loyalty could end up also tearing the party apart, as we saw in the NSAP/SSS in 1938.

Fetishism revealed an interesting pressure behind the mythopoeic process, namely a grassroots demand for myth and its constituent performative elements. Embodied identification probably played a powerful role here: the invitation to 'live the myth' as it were, by integrating members physically into mythopoeic performances, was liable to produce strong personal (fetishistic) attachments. Much as the removal of beloved symbols was unacceptable to the cadres of both parties, and the uniform was considered indispensable by all, so a 'normal', respectable party leader could hardly be countenanced. While both Lindholm and Mussert showed signs of reluctance to act the part of the Leader in the style of Hitler or Mussolini, there was strong pressure from the rank-and-file to construct such a myth, and by extension sustain the collective fantasy that drove activism.

This is where the theme of respectability and its ambiguous relationship to fascist myth comes out strongly. These demands from below could push at the boundaries of respectability that the leadership was willing to transgress. To simplify, it has been clear that the NSAP and NSB started out in different places, and that the twin pressures of respectability and mythopoeic desire pushed them in opposite directions. The NSB, led by a bourgeois civil engineer, heavily appealed to Dutch conservative standards of political respectability, before giving in to internal pressures and introducing increasingly dubious elements (e.g. wolf's hook symbols, Germanic-pagan elements) which conformed to certain fascist myths, but undermined the image of respectability in the eyes of the public. The NSAP on the other hand started out as a left-oriented party emphasizing militarism and revolution, before embarking on a 'New Direction' that naturalized uniform paraphernalia, party name and symbols, to the dismay of the radicals. This confirms that respectability had a sort of limiting effect on fascist mythopoeia, with fascist parties moved by two forces that pushed in opposite directions. The image construction of fascist parties then seems guided by a dynamic paradox. Given that much of the disapproval of the public was from a patriotic angle – questioning the nationalist credentials of fascist myth that appeared imported from foreign countries – this is a problem quite specific to the fascist movements of Europe that operated within democratic societies, constantly pushing them towards an awkward compromise.

Yet the dynamic between myth and respectability was not a straightforwardly dialectical one. This is especially clear in the mythopoeia of Mussert's persona, which tried to mythicize precisely those dimensions that were symbolic of his respectability, such as his social status as civil engineer. His evolution into biblical prophet married myth and respectability in one figure, using positive Christian elements to elevate him to providential Leader. Other aspects of fascist myth had an inherently respectable dimension to them, and depended on perspective. The NSB tried to exploit this more than the NSAP. The paramilitaries were a cornerstone of the army myth, but they were also constructed as models of respectability: neat and trim, perfectly disciplined, and a bulwark of law and order against godless communism. Similarly the NSAP utilized the heavy military presence in its ranks as a demonstration of respectability, deliberately posting uniformed army supporters alongside its processions to not just reinforce the idea of the fascists as powerful army, but also one with the support of patriotic and respected soldiers and officers. Myth and respectability were not always clearly antagonistic in the mythopoeia of the NSB and NSAP.

It is precisely in these respects, where mythopoeia was susceptible to multiple layers of interpretation, that public debate was at its most intense. Shows of organization, discipline and power could be admired by the conservative Right especially – and where they were lacking the parties faced relentless mockery – but they also raised the spectre of violence. Street fights come out of this as a major problem which threatened to undermine the respectability of both parties, as it facilitated an interpretation of fascism as a force of disorder. Such opposing interpretations quickly led to a construction of fascism as neither mythic nor respectable, but grotesque. Fascists were depicted as uncouth thugs, their leaders as gangster bosses and Hitler-parodies, or in the Swedish case as undisciplined juveniles. It appears that in the small democracies fascist mythopoeia could never entirely divorce itself from respectable concerns, and carried an innate risk of undermining itself.

Perhaps respectability was by its nature always going to pose a dilemma for interwar fascists that could never be neatly resolved, pulling the fascists in opposing directions. The respectability of class was bound to create contradiction for national socialist parties, attempting to speak the language of socialism at the same time as appealing to traditional bourgeois values like nation and order. Interestingly this turned out to be perhaps more of an issue for the Swedish NSAP/SSS than the NSB. This was partially because Mussert was less interested in appealing specifically to Dutch workers, and preferred to speak of the dignity of and respect for traditional labour, rather than a revolutionary discourse. Here there was also an echo of the Catholic politicians' conception of labour in society, as constituting a fixed and dignified place in God's order, and one in which had succeeded reasonably in maintaining Catholic workers' support in the south. It was indeed precisely in the provinces of North Brabant and especially Limburg that the NSB managed to make inroads, where there was virtually no radical workers' political culture, and traditionally bourgeois values weighed heavily. On the other hand the point should not be exaggerated: there is no evidence the NSB managed to really contest SDAP control of the workers' vote at a national level. The elements of respectable (bourgeois) class presentation in the NSB's performative repertoire are thus not evidence of a strategy that was actually widely successful with Dutch workers, but rather of NSB priorities and alternative strategic considerations.

The party-political struggle across the class divides is instead ironically more evident in the NSAP/SSS, in spite of Lindholm's overt appeal to the working classes and manual labourers in particular. This prioritization came to the fore in both a revolutionary discourse, propaganda imagery of bare-chested and muscled factory workers, and party organizations like the national socialist trade union (Sveriges Fackliga Kamporganisation) – in essence a different type of class respectability. But the NSAP failed to win any major successes with this approach, as the party proved to be entirely incapable of contesting SSAP and LO dominance; it is worth noting that the only other parties able to win over some workers aside from the Social Democrats were the two Swedish communist parties. Thus, unlike the NSB, the NSAP made a major class shift towards a more (bourgeois) respectable performative, as seen in the 1938 makeover to the SSS. Support for the fascist project was significantly stronger in the upper ranks of Swedish society, not least in military and aristocratic circles, which were liable to be more susceptible to displays of bourgeois respectability.

Respectability, then, was not simply a limiting factor on mythopoeia, nor was the dynamic it produced consistent or predictable. This is not entirely unexpected, given the multifaceted nature of respectability (class, gender, religion, etc.) and hence fascists' ability to invoke some specific aspects while ignoring or contesting others. Its role in Sweden and the Netherlands was very different, and one can see from how the parties were founded that it played a crucial role in the initial cultural construction of the fascist parties, and their later development. Swedish and Dutch fascists were faced with rather different strategic requirements produced by their social-political environments, but in both cases, mythopoeic desire could overrule an arguably more sensible propagandistic strategy. The internal pressure to sustain mythopoeia was powerful, and overrode considerations of respectability and public image. The backlash against Lindholm's 'New Direction' is instructive: the leadership may have considered many of the mythopoeic props to be inimical to success, but to at least a core of the party they were the raison d'être of fascism. In the comparison both cadres are seen to have developed a specific fascist subculture, but more so in the NSAP than the NSB: the latter was always more outward looking, thriving on media attention from the very beginning, while the Dutch party apparatus was far better organized to instil discipline.

This characterization of Swedish and Dutch fascism as subcultural highlights how not just myth, but the particular performative methods of mythopoeia such as embodied identification are something that generated extraordinary loyalty to fascism, be it understood as the party, the Leader or 'the idea'. This research has shown that there was a personally transformative potential in participating in mythopoeia, which can explain the dedication of some members through all adversities. The wider significance is in explaining the initial emergence and persistence of minor fascist movements in unlikely places, not just Sweden and the Netherlands, and the fanatical loyalty of some of its cadres which allowed them to punch above their weight. The comparative angle shows that this was not just the fluke of a specific fascist party, but a feature that could potentially be generalized for fascism across Europe, however that might be understood. Their differences show that this is a point about survivability and persistence rather than success, at least in electoral terms – the NSB after all enjoyed exponentially better results than the NSAP could ever hope for. For 'stable democracies', it highlights that political failure in its own right was not enough to eliminate fascist challengers.

The implications for the study of neo-fascism could also be important. The brief glimpse of the last five years of the SSS already amply demonstrates the extraordinarily difficult circumstances under which postwar fascists operated. The total military defeat of fascism's regime representatives in 1945, the reality of Soviet occupation in eastern and central Europe, denazification processes in most European countries, and the comprehensive moral-political renouncement of fascism – especially as symbolized by the extreme and unusual violence of the Holocaust – made life all but impossible for those who choose to continue to associate themselves with the fascist legacy after 1945. But crucially, small groups did continue to invoke that legacy, often though by no means always denying their identification with fascism, and continued to create lasting fascist subcultures essentially comparable to those studied here.[22] From the zealot parties of the 1950s and 1960s which attempted to carry on fascist party organization in precisely the same vein as the interwar period in the postwar era,[23] to the altogether different white supremacist skinhead movement that formed in the 1970s and 1980s,[24] small groups of (neo-)fascists continued to survive, and more recently, sadly even thrive. The loyalty and will to charismatized Leaders, the fetishization of mythically charged props and symbols (perhaps now with a double charge with the enhanced taboo character of these objects), and the fantasy of embodying a sacred vanguard or resistance cell against the liberal order can all help explain why the fascist signifier continued to find adherents who had little real hope of political success in the foreseeable future. Political success, at least in terms of electoral victories, was by no means the only thing that fascist activists were interested in. Likewise, how various radical-Right groups confronted the dilemma of respectability, or indeed rejected it altogether, is another feature of postwar politics that deserves scrutiny in these terms.

The observant reader cannot have failed to notice the striking absence of anti-Semitism and racist ideology throughout the analysis. The NSAP/SSS subscribed wholeheartedly to the biological racism and race mysticism that was such a prominent aspect of German Nazism, but which was also firmly rooted in Swedish culture since the nineteenth century. Party membership was restricted on the basis of race, and the Swedish socialist *folkgemenskap* was exclusive to the Nordic-Aryan race – race was the basis of social progress.[25] Sweden was proclaimed the most racially pure nation in the world, a racial hygiene to be preserved at all costs. Swedish fascist racism took on more cultural undertones in the mid-1930s, as Lindholm started to more self-consciously draw on his literary inspirations, but this can in no sense be described as a moderation of the party's position on race.[26] Only with the makeover at the end of 1938 can there be any talk of some kind of mellowing of race ideology, for instance when anti-Semitism was justified on the basis of the Jews' supposed political, cultural and economic dominance. Later Lindholm argued, misleadingly, that while the ideology of racial hygiene was Swedish, anti-Semitism was a German import, though this ignores the prevalence of anti-Semitism since the days of the SFKO in the 1920s, and sidelines the prevalence of radical anti-Semites in the membership.[27]

Racism was notably marginal to official NSB ideology at first, permitting the membership of mixed-race colonial subjects, particularly boosting membership in the Dutch East Indies where Indo-European rightists saw their interests well-represented by fascism's defence of the existing imperial order. (Foreign fascists such as Heinrich Himmler were particularly affronted by this policy.) With the growing strength of the *volkse* current in the NSB racism became increasingly central to party ideology, but a study of earlier party correspondence shows more typical racist tenets were held by much of the rank-and-file and functionaries from the beginning, even if they were not prominent in party discourse. While the exclusion of Indo-Europeans from the membership was a direct result of the influence of new *volkse* leaders in the late 1930s, this race ideology should not be confused with the prevalence of racist imperialistic chauvinism that coloured NSB politics from the outset. While the likes of Roskam and Feldmeijer were concerned with the blood and soil of the Aryan-Germanic race, for Mussert and his kind race was about empire, Western civilization, and white supremacy over inferior Asian, African and South-American peoples. As the collision between the NSB and the SS during the Occupation showed, different fascist tenets of race could not only diverge, but be irreconcilable, as *gross-Germanische* ideology clashed with ideas of a sovereign Dutch empire.[28]

Anti-Semitism was a core part of NSAP/SSS ideology, and attendees of party meetings or readers of the party paper would have been unable to close their eyes to the overt and persistent singling out of Jews as the primary enemy of the Swedish people. The NSB had a more ambiguous stance on the role of the Jews, and one which changed over the decade. It seems that Mussert had no particular personal ill-feeling towards Jews, while he and his wife were known to be quite close friends to one Jewish couple with whom they regularly played bridge.[29] But while the first NSB party programme explicitly eschewed anti-Semitism, the movement attracted a great deal of anti-Semites all the same, and the party paper was not above the occasional anti-Jewish rhetoric and dog whistle tropes. The ambiguity is amply demonstrated by a matter brought to Mussert's attention in the mid-1930s: rank-and-file members were objecting to having to serve under Jewish party functionaries, revealing a movement strongly divided on the question of race. Within a few years the anti-Semites had decidedly won the battle, and Jews were banned from the NSB.

All the same, the endemic and official anti-Semitism in both cases barely featured in their mythopoeia, in spite of tolerance functioning as a signifier of respectability, particularly in the Netherlands, where religious tolerance still functioned as a marker of national identity since the days of the Dutch Republic. In the Dutch case then, the absence may be taken as itself an exercise in respectability – an effort to make audiences forget about the grim underbelly of the national socialist movement, when presenting them with a mythic image of the same. However, the comparison with Sweden is elucidating. The NSAP/SSS placed anti-Semitism front and centre in its party programme, and relished the use of grotesque Jewish stereotypes in word and image, yet for all that anti-Semitism had no more prominent a place in its mythopoeia as in the Dutch NSB. The disjunction here is partially explained by a distortion caused by the focus on performance over discourse. But this also highlights mythopoeia's propensity for positive images and constructions of identity, in other words a natural introversion. Fascists then did not typically construct fascism in relation to others, the 'antis' that are so prominent in some analyses of fascism (anti-liberalism, anti-socialism, anti-conservatism, etc.), but rather on its own terms, and against certain role models (both regimes, other fascist movements, as well as institutions such as the military). Obviously this raises crucial questions about fascism's appeal that could be explored further through the mythic lens, not least to what extent its attraction resided in positive narratives and images rather than negative ideological positions like anti-Semitism, and in how far followers in fact embraced one while ignoring the other.

This has raised a number of further questions and venues for future research. Fascist endurance and loyalty were not in any way universal; member turnover could be high, and branches disappeared over time. Mapping out the persistence and activism of the NSB and NSAP in specific regions would add valuable nuance to the picture painted here. The comparison of localities over time, such as the disproportionately NSB-supportive urban centres and the NSAP-dominated villages of Norrland, or the ephemeral outposts containing only a handful of activists, would add another important dimension.[30] One area left open for research by this book is the social dimension of mythopoeia. We can speculate that fantastical myths were more likely to appeal to some social groups than others (such as youth and students), but this needs to be verified. Second to this, what myths appealed to what social groups is another important question: can we trace these in internal party factionalism over mythopoeic projects, and can we see propaganda apparatuses targeting specific groups with specific myths? It is not unlikely that a social perspective could shed further light on why mythopoeic tactics changed the way they did over time. There is also more to be learned about the relationship between myth and respectability legally. Local court records could shed light on whether mythopoeia continued in the court room, and how defendants and prosecutors portrayed the clash with respectability.[31]

One important aspect of fascist mythopoeia only very imperfectly touched upon here is gender. There were specifically masculine fantasies that evidently drove the construction of certain myths, not least militaristic ones. Women very rarely featured in the myths that have been explored in this book, and indeed there are precious few others one could identify in which they did play a role, though they participated in the mythopoeia like other members. But while some research has been done in specifically female participation in the Dutch fascist movement, such research for the Swedish case is long overdue. It would be particularly interesting to know how women specifically related to fascist myths of masculinity; while they were formally excluded from militant groups like the SA or WA, they did partake of many of the same rituals and ceremonies, with the same props and symbols of fascist mythopoeia in other regards, not least the uniform of course. The NU deserves more attention too to this end; as a highly militant daughter organization that did not exclude girls, research has the opportunity of producing new knowledge about the gender dynamics in fascist mythopoeia in Sweden otherwise not available. This again raises an interesting dilemma vis-à-vis respectability: modes of dress and behaviour which were respectable for men could be quite the opposite for women. Notably in the present volume there has been little note of how political outsiders regarded fascist women, simply because they were never mentioned in any of the material used. Studies of female fascists elsewhere, such as Julie V. Gottlieb's *Feminine Fascism* in the British case, offer clues about what the perspectives on and impact of fascist women might have been, but national as well as local contexts differed sharply, so one cannot trivially extrapolate from other countries.

†††

The NSB and NSAP/SSS have here been compared in their nature as relatively small movements, both participating in a shared transnationally circulating repertoire of fascist cultural elements, with particularly strong currents from Germany. They emerged in 1931–3 at the initiative of part-time politicians with very different experiences of politics since the mid-1920s: Mussert's action on the Belgian Treaty proposed by the Dutch parliament, and Lindholm's activism as a functionary in the SFKO. The former was a civil engineer in a relatively prestigious state position, the latter a younger, low-ranking army man, but both decided to dedicate more and more of their time to the cause of fascism in their countries, becoming full-time party leaders in the next decade. Both parties were created in response to specific national concerns, but also participated in the sense of a new era, that of Europe or even the world overthrowing the old system of international democracy to be replaced by a new order of nationalist states. Like most fascist movements they set a very high bar for themselves as political newcomers: only a complete seizure of power and transformation of the state and nation, on the basis of massive popular support, would do.[32]

The NSAP was a break-away faction from Furugård's SNSP, and as such a product of the internecine squabble that plagued many European fascist movements, but outgrew its predecessor within two years, but not spectacularly so – over 10,000 members. Mussert tried to bypass the several pre-existing conflicting fascist groups that already existed, and successfully established a rapidly growing organization that soon attracted members from his rivals, probably benefiting from standing outside the sordid and petty political milieu of 1920s Dutch fascism. By 1935 the NSB was several orders of magnitude larger than any other fascist group, and one of the largest parties in the Netherlands by membership, with over 50,000 members, even if that membership proved to be highly unstable. Socially the NSB and NSAP/SSS looked quite different, reflecting national and ideological differences: the middle class was more prevalent among Dutch fascists, workers more so in the NSAP/SSS, though still underrepresented nationally, in spite of the proletarian ideological focus. Both were still more notable for their cross-class composition compared to other parties, more than the prevalence of one class over another. A notable social pattern in the NSB was its limited hold on Catholics, and to a lesser extent Protestants, with former liberals appearing over-represented: socially, the party's appeal was strongest on those outside of strongly established pillars. In the NSAP/SSS military and security personnel were particularly prevalent, perhaps an echo of the SFKO's origins in the military, and Lindholm's army background – that being said, colonial army veterans such as Hogewind played important roles in the NSB, with its hard-line imperialist stance. The NSB stands out for the large group of Indo-European supporters in the Dutch East Indies as well, providing crucial financial assistance to the Netherlands. Age differences stand out too: while both the NSB and NSAP/SSS had young cohorts compared to the established political parties, the NSAP/SSS had a far larger youth contingent, with youth wing NU providing a highly productive and visible activist section.

The most striking outward difference was the resources and organization at the movements' disposal. The NSB was much larger, and spread out over a far smaller geographical area, with much larger funds at its disposal, receiving the support of businesses and the colonies, in sharp contrast to the NSAP/SSS, which could count on only a very few wealthy donors such as C-E Carlberg. All evidence suggests neither received financial assistance from foreign sources during the 1930s; during the

Second World War SSS received money from its foreign branch in Germany, but no contribution from the Nazi regime it appears. The NSB, which actively collaborated with the German occupiers, is a different matter, though the relevant records were deliberately destroyed at the end of the war. NSB organization was consequently better executed, more consistent, and on a larger scale than that of the NSAP/SSS. While both used a variant of the charismatic-hierarchical party structure of the NSDAP, they deployed it very differently, with it being conspicuously more decentralized in Sweden. Both had strongholds in the countries' larger cities, particularly Amsterdam and Gothenburg.

Fundamentally different leadership styles shaped the characters of the two parties. Painting with a very broad brush, there was the centralized and bureaucratic administration of the NSB, powerfully directed by Mussert from Utrecht, capable of putting on nationally coordinated spectacles and campaigns. Mussert, while rather malleable on key ideological issues, reflected in the party's ambiguous and changing stance on matters such as race, religion and the royal family, provided (constructed) charismatic leadership (itself going through several mutations), maintaining his power position and cadre loyalty. (That loyalty was later tested significantly by outside powers such as the SS which were capable of contesting Mussert's hold on the party.) Lindholm never truly left behind his activist days in the SFKO and SNSP, and continued to lead the cadres by example as party leader, something that was perhaps causative or symptomatic of the weaker and less centralized leadership organization. It moved from Gothenburg to Stockholm, with growing attention to Malmö and the South in the second half of the thirties. Lindholm's ideological leadership was firmer than Mussert's, providing a clear stance on matters like the centrality of workers in the Swedish fascist state, racial hygiene, anti-Semitism and capitalism. Overall the NSAP/SSS was a less coherent and coordinated movement, reflecting both a smaller and more dispersed organization, and Lindholm's lack of ability in this regard, as well as lack of financial competence. Rival ideological factions were less prevalent in the NSAP/SSS compared to the NSB (though the turbulence caused by the 1938 *nyorientering* shows up differences beneath the surface) – but dynamic and coherent movement could not be achieved through unity of purpose alone. In both cases leadership and unity were maintained through charismatic mythopoeia rooted in a fascist principle of authoritarian leadership, be it in the costume of military leader, an omnicompetent civil engineer of the nation, Nordic chieftain or high priest.

The NSB and NSAP/SSS modus operandi included many shared elements from the transnationally circulating fascist repertoire, with public meetings and rallies front and centre in attracting new members and spreading the gospel. For the NSAP/SSS the organization and composition of these were learned directly from Nazi Germany, where Lindholm and other party functionaries had learned directly during educational visits. More specific characteristics and variable emphases, e.g. a Swedish penchant for torch-lit processions absent in the Netherlands, or the NSB's infiltration of militias and hiking organizations or 'apolitical' participation in royal festivities, were connected to their larger respective mythopoeic projects. A construction of fascism as youthful and revolutionary, proletarian and socialist underpinned the NSAP/SSS repertoire. Clichés of law and order, cross-confessional unity, Orangism and imperialistic strongmanship defined much of the NSB's inflection on a familiar European fascist methodology. Specific strategic considerations in achieving and maintaining both an attractive mythic charge and respectability likewise informed movement tactics, propaganda and activism. In all this both parties were dependent on purely pragmatic considerations of resources as well, though the NSAP/SSS was always manifestly more constrained in this regard than the NSB.

The NSB and NSAP/SSS underwent constant change over the decade – organizationally, ideologically, culturally. The NSB in 1940 was a rather different creature from the party in 1932, the SSS at the same time was no longer the NSAP of 1933 in more than just name, facts that we have been able to trace through their mythopoeic development. Yet both remained at all times recognizable as participating in the same European, and even global, political currents that they and their contemporaries understood as fascism and national socialism. Their political trajectories were different, and at times went in opposite directions to each other. In fact the NSAP/SSS's attitude to the NSB was hostile throughout the 1930s, largely on account of the Dutch party's initial rejection of anti-Semitism; the NSAP/SSS maintained contacts with C.J.A. Kruyt's NSNAP instead, a small Dutch rival. The NSB mostly just looked down on the Swedish party. Nevertheless, even these hostile connections and disagreements demonstrate the joint participation in a shared political space that crossed their national boundaries. They used and contributed to the same transnationally circulating repertoire of fascist myths, ideas and tactics. There was no limit to how far they could diverge from or alter these elements, to the point of complete and open hostility to other self-described fascists, or de facto departure from the 'fascism' signifier, but it is this fact of shared participation in a transnational network that made them comparable as fascists.

These relatively small fascist parties, which seem not to have played much of a role in the wider European context, have here been studied as independent and critical agents. Their failures and relative mediocrity were not the result of unthinkingly copying German or Italian methods. Rather they adopted and adapted fascist cultural techniques and strategies reflexively, and forged their own myths and identities.[33] While much was copied from other models, the copycat stereotype is a crude dismissal of the complexities of such adoption, and the possibilities, the open-endedness, of fascist political culture. Working against the grain of their national social and political cultures, the NSAP/SSS and NSB created new structures and performances to convey their own myths to the public, but perhaps especially to their own members. These parties come out looking surprisingly introverted.

Fascist myth was far more open-ended and varied than some historians have suggested. The myths of fascism emerge as multiple, without a core, and mutable.[34] Fascist myth was not static.[35] The study of fascist myth as a performative, operating in time, has shown that mythopoeia was a site of mutation and innovation, highly susceptible to internal and external pressures. Whatever the 'something new' that fascists brought to modern European politics, we cannot make *a priori* assumptions about its nature.

Instead, the core concept of mythopoeia as a performative emphasizes instability, contingency and mutability in fascist myth and practices. The semiotic character of fascism as an empty signifier made it prey to a ceaseless and dynamic interplay between national, international and transnational influences, which constantly changed the terms of the public discourse around fascism. It is evident that in the fascist *movements*, there was reflexive engagement with their foreign counterparts – in the form of foreign regimes, movements, as well as an international phenomenon – both in their own right and *through* the often hostile national press with which they debated, with a central preoccupation with respectability. Mutation in the mythopoeic trajectory of the NSB and NSAP/SSS shows that whatever difficulties they faced, these were not caused by any kind of stagnation that has been attributed to 'mimetic' fascist organizations. Instead, how the fascist regimes reflected back on the movements, and the national discussion thereof, was a constant force for fascist change. In a transnational perspective, interaction with the prominent fascist regimes was fraught and complex, and something that forced malleability and change on the radical Right of interwar Europe, not simply fixity through adoption.

All chapters in this book have demonstrated the constant involvement of the grassroots of the two parties in fascist mythopoeia, including where the subject was specifically on matters of party leadership. While fascist leaders clearly had their own specific visions, and steered the party in a certain direction, and while those leaders possessed immense authority within the organization and commanded adulation, they were nevertheless subject to pressure from the cadres. Myth was something that, by its partial nature as a tool of mobilization, necessarily generated a great deal of passion, and as such could not be handled carelessly or dismissed by fascist leaders. Cadres and activists arguably had the greatest stake in fascist myths, and they ended up playing a surprisingly powerful and influential role in mythopoeia, even if the leadership formulated the mythic substance. Leaders who sought to change or do away with myths and the props that sustained them faced resistance; members pushed for and defended their interests in the mythopoeic project. Even the NSB, where Mussert's administration was heavily centralized and sought to erase local autonomy, grassroots demands and pressures mattered. The understanding of fascism and fascist subjectivities was not just shaped by leaders and ideologues then, but to a significant extent from the bottom-up by the rank-and-file and activists. What fascism was or how it was understood then appears constructed in a dynamic exchange between leaders and members, an exchange of strategy and desire, propaganda and fantasy, in which the wider political and social context pushed for constant adaptation and change.

This argument can be extended to the study of fascism generally. In Swedish and Dutch scholarship Griffin's 'palingenetic ultra-nationalism' is still somewhat in vogue.[36] But debates about the definition of fascism are fortunately well on their way out, and some historians have called for examining how contemporaries understood their own political categories as a mode of inquiry instead, which is precisely what mythopoeia has done here.[37] Some scholars have defended their definitions of fascism from accusations of essentializing tendencies, describing them as 'heuristic' or unavoidable 'working definitions', but this has not avoided severely limiting how we understand the historic horizons of fascism. A definition of fascism has not been required for this study, which has allowed us to see the contested nature of that sign, and by extension the open-ended trajectory of that sign's political devotees, who in the 1930s, year-on-year, could still go in different directions.[38]

This is also an important insight for the recent transnational turn in fascism studies, and demonstrates some of the usefulness of the performative-mythopoeic approach to myth. Conceptualizing fascism as performative and predicated on a contingent and diachronic process is one way to situate fascism at an intersection of national and international contexts, and be sensitive to the transnational exchange of ideas – myths, specific mythopoeic techniques, competencies, resources and so forth. Marrying cultural approaches to fascist myth with the transnational turn, mythopoeia allows us to see the diachronic (semiotic) construction of fascism by contemporaries, paying attention to the transfer and exchange of specific myths and techniques in doing so. The transnational approach has a penchant for understanding fascism as a contingent and ever-developing phenomenon, constantly changing as it crosses borders, and mythopoeia and performativity are tools which match that approach neatly. The relationship of the Italian Fascist and Nazi regime to the NSB and NSAP/SSS has already hinted a little at what transnational influences on the European development of fascism (as understood by contemporaries) could look like, but there is the potential for research to uncover much more extensive networks of transfer and exchange, especially between movements (the Netherlands and Belgium, and the Scandinavian countries come to mind).

I have here assumed that myth was central to fascist politics, but what has been brought out of this is the value of recognizing the place of myth in fascism as a performative process, which in these terms can be shown to drive fascist strategy and tactics, responding to various contexts and influences. In other words, mythopoeia made fascist politics highly contingent.[39] It was in the nature of myth that it could change and be deliberately manipulated, and here it has been shown how in practice the modern party organization after the First World War had found new ways of doing so. What was quite unusual for fascism is that it operated as an empty signifier, which allowed self-styled fascists to treat the process of the creation of cultural meaning with the cavalier disregard for 'truth' that so concerned Johan Huizinga.

Huizinga's concerns about the immediate political future of Europe in the 1930s went beyond fascism. This study of the relationship between mythopoeia and respectability is situated in the greater context of the new forms of politics that emerged in the interbellum, and its intersection with the new Right. The expansion of the franchise, the experience of mass mobilization, the recent emergence of the modern mass party organization, and the development or democratization of media technologies, all fed into the new dynamics and functions of mythopoeia in politics. The consequences for political organizations, tactics and cultures were not limited to fascism. As such, the conclusions of this research open up venues of enquiry for the wider study of interwar European history. The examination of the semiotic construction of political concepts at the interface of myth and practical organization in dynamic relation to public discourse is surely a fertile field more generally. At the same time the historical application of new political techniques in Sweden and the Netherlands has shown there were no hard borders around these countries that made them into impregnable 'peaceful islands'. Rather, even if physical political violence was limited here, the politics of violence, its rhetoric, aesthetics and tactics,[40] easily made their way into the 'stable democracies', demonstrating a spill-over effect which ought to make us attentive to the political-cultural integration of these countries with their more tumultuous neighbours. Even if new political forms were not necessarily wielded effectively or even competently, it is worth noting how these were transferred and exchanged across Europe. The making of fascism was diverse, changeable and unpredictable. Ultimately it knew no boundaries, national or otherwise.

Notes

Introduction

1. Otto Michael Knab, *Kleinstadt Unterm Hakenkreuz: Groteske Erinnerungen Aus Bayern* (Luzern: Räbert, 1934), 13.
2. Ibid. 15; The episode is also reproduced and translated in: George L. Mosse, *Nazi Culture: Intellectual, Cultural and Social Life in the Third Reich* (New York: Schocken Books, 1986), 371.
3. Raymond Williams, *Culture* (Glasgow: Fontana, 1981), 87–8.
4. David D. Roberts, *Fascist Interactions: Proposals for a New Approach to Fascism and Its Era, 1919–1945* (New York: Bergahn, 2016), 53.
5. Daniel Chandler, *Semiotics: The Basics*, 2nd ed. (London: Routledge, 2002), 78–80.
6. Much as expectations of the NSDAP in Germany were conditioned by prior perceptions of Fascist Italy: Hans Woller, 'Machtpolitisches Kalkül Oder Ideologische Affinität? Zur Frage Des Verhältnisses Zwischen Mussolini Und Hitler Vor 1933', in *Der Nationalsozialismus: Studien zur Ideologie und Herrschaft*, ed. W. Benz and H. Mommsen (Frankfurt am Main: Geschichte Fischer, 1993), 47.
7. On the transnational reading of national comparative histories, see: Philipp Ther, 'Beyond the Nation: The Relational Basis of a Comparative History of Germany and Europe', *Central European History* 36, no. 1 (2003): 67–70.
8. Roger Eatwell, 'The Nature of "Generic Fascism": Complexity and Reflexive Hybridity', in *Rethinking Fascism and Dictatorship in Europe*, ed. António Costa Pinto and Aristotle Kallis (Basingstoke: Palgrave Macmillan, 2014), 70.
9. For a definition of culture as a site for the struggle over the terms of (collective) meaning, see: David Chaney, *The Cultural Turn: Scene-Setting Essays on Contemporary Cultural History* (London: Routledge, 1994), 11–23.
10. Introduction to: Victoria E. Bonnell, Lynn Hunt and Richard Biernacki, eds., *Beyond the Cultural Turn: New Directions in the Study of Society and Culture* (London: University of California Press, 1999), 17.
11. 'Central to all forms of cultural history, is the process of symbolic mediation through which human beings make sense of their world.' Anna Green, *Cultural History, Theory and History* (Basingstoke: Palgrave Macmillan, 2008), 9.
12. Mary Vincent, 'Political Violence and Mass Society: A European Civil War?', in *The Oxford Handbook of European History, 1914–1945*, ed. Nicholas Doumanis (Oxford: Oxford University Press, 2016), 394.
13. Ernst Nolte, *Three Faces of Fascism: Action Française, Italian Fascism, National Socialism* (New York: Times Mirror, 1965), 21.
14. The contemptuous association of staid respectability with the bourgeois is both well-established, and ill-defined, see: Raymond Williams, *Keywords: A Vocabulary of Culture and Society*, Revised ed. (Oxford: Oxford University Press, 1983), 47.
15. And indeed the Swedish fascist organizations barely dwelled on religious issues at all: Lena Berggren, 'Completing the Lutheran Reformation: Ultra-Nationalism,

Christianity and the Possibility of "Clerical Fascism" in Interwar Sweden', *Totalitarian Movements and Political Religions* 8, no. 2 (2007): 303–14.
16 George L. Mosse, *The Image of Man: The Creation of Modern Masculinity* (Oxford: Oxford University Press, 1998), 155, 167.
17 'Opbouwende Staatkunde', *Opbouwende Staatkunde*, no. 78, 3 January 1924, 537.
18 John F. Pollard, *The Papacy in the Age of Totalitarianism, 1914–1958* (Oxford: Oxford University Press, 2014), 16–20.
19 L. M. H. Joosten, *Katholieken en Fascisme in Nederland 1920–1940*, 2nd ed. (Utrecht: HES, 1982), 18–43.
20 Eric Wärenstam, *Fascismen och Nazismen i Sverige 1920–1940: Studier i den svenska nationalsocialismens, fascismens och antisemitismens organisationer, ideologier och propaganda under mellankrigsåren* (Stockholm: Almqvist & Wiksell, 1970), 27–9, 40; Karl N. Alvar Nilsson, *Svensk Överklassnazism, 1930–1945* (Stockholm: Carlsson, 1996), 95.
21 Lena Berggren, *Nationell Upplysning: Drag i den svenska antisemitismens idéhistoria* (Stockholm: Carlsson Förlag, 1999), 132.
22 Robert Gerwarth, *Die Grösste aller Revolutionen: November 1918 und der Aufbruch in eine neue Zeit* (Munich: Siedler, 2018), 150–1.
23 Robert Gerwarth and John Horne, 'Bolshevism as Fantasy: Fear of Revolution and Counter-Revolutionary Violence, 1917–1923', in *War in Peace: Paramilitary Violence in Europe after the Great War*, ed. Robert Gerwarth and John Horne (Oxford: Oxford University Press, 2013), 44–5.
24 George L. Mosse, *Fallen Soldiers: Reshaping the Memory of the World Wars* (Oxford: Oxford University Press, 1991).
25 Conny Kristel, *De Oorlog van Anderen: Nederlanders en Oorlogsgeweld, 1914–1918* (Amsterdam: De Bezige Bij, 2016), 9.
26 'In fact, it could be argued that the dislocation of economic relationships caused by the war was far more serious than actual physical destruction.' Derek H. Aldcroft and Steven Morewood, *The European Economy since 1914*, 5th ed. (London: Routledge, 2013), 21.
27 Remieg Aerts et al., *Land van Kleine Gebaren: Een politieke geschiedenis van Nederland 1780–1990* (Nijmegen: SUN, 1999), 194.
28 Christian Goeschel, *Mussolini and Hitler: Forging the Fascist Alliance* (Yale: Yale University Press, 2018).
29 Nathaniël Kunkeler, 'The Evolution of Swedish Fascism: Self-Identification and Ideology in Interwar Sweden', *Patterns of Prejudice* 50, no. 4–5 (2016), 390.
30 Aristotle Kallis, 'Fascism and the Right in Interwar Europe: Interaction, Entanglement, Hybridity', in *The Oxford Handbook of European History, 1914–1945*, ed. Nicholas Doumanis (Oxford: Oxford University Press, 2016), 304. Julia Adeney Thomas, 'Introduction; A Portable Concept of Fascism', in *Visualizing Fascism: The Twentieth-Century Rise of the Global Right*, ed. Julia Adeney Thomas and Geoff Eley (Durham, North Carolina: Duke University Press, 2020), 1–20.
31 Peter Burke, *History and Social Theory*, 2nd ed. (Cambridge: Polity, 2005), 113.
32 Mosse, *Nazi Culture*, 93.
33 Patrick Brantlinger, 'Mass Media and Culture in Fin-de-Siècle Europe', in *Fin de Siècle and Its Legacy*, ed. Mikuláš Teich and Roy Porter (Cambridge: Cambridge University Press, 1990), 99–104.
34 Stefan Jonsson, *Crowds and Democracy: The Idea and Image of the Masses from Revolution to Fascism* (New York: Columbia University Press, 2013), 7–17.

35 George L. Mosse, *The Nationalization of the Masses: Political Symbolism and Mass Movements in Germany from the Napoleonic Wars through the Third Reich* (New York: Howard Fertig, 1975), 2–9.
36 Ibid., 207–10; Jimmy Vulovic, *Reform eller Revolt: Litterär propaganda i socialdemokratisk, kommunistisk och nationalsocialistisk press* (Halmstad: Ellerströms, 2013), 82.
37 Introduction to: George Sorel, *Reflections on Violence*, ed. Jeremy Jennings (Cambridge: Cambridge University Press, 1999), xiii–xiv.
38 Ibid. 140.
39 Vincent, 'Political Violence and Mass Society', 388.
40 Myths are a particularly relevant form of symbol in the emergence of mass political movements, as Edelman argued: Murray Edelman, *Politics as Symbolic Action: Mass Arousal and Quiescence* (Chicago: Markham, 1971), 53.
41 'Zoover is het in de beschaafde wereld gekomen. Men meene niet, dat de verwording van het oordeel zich beperkt tot de landen, waar het extreme nationalisme heeft gezegevierd. Wie om zich heen ziet kan herhaaldelijk waarnemen, hoe bij ontwikkelde personen, veelal jongeren, een zekere onverschilligheid voor het waarheidsgehalte van de figuren van hun ideeënwereld is ingetreden. De categorieën fictie en historie ... worden niet duidelijk meer onderscheiden. Het intresseert niet meer, of de geestelijke stof op haar waarheidsgehalte beproefd kan worden. De opgang van het begrip mythus is hiervan het belangrijkste voorbeeld. Men aanvaardt een verbeelding, waarin de elementen wensch en fantazie bewust worden toegelaten ... ', Johan Huizinga, *In de Schaduwen van Morgen: Een Diagnose van het Geestelijk Lijden van onzen Tijd*, 6th ed. (Haarlem: H.D. Tjeenk Willink & Zoon N.V., 1936), 93.
42 Robert O. Paxton, *The Anatomy of Fascism* (London: Penguin, 2005), 9.
43 Peter Fritzsche, *Rehearsals for Fascism: Populism and Political Mobilization in Weimar Germany* (Oxford: Oxford University Press, 1990), 6–10.
44 Mark Neocleous, *Fascism* (Buckingham: Open University Press, 1997), 20.
45 Adolf Hitler, *Mein Kampf: Eine kritische Edition*, vol. 1 (Munich & Berlin: Institut für Zeitgeschichte, 2016), 193/507.
46 For the connection between fascist propaganda, aesthetics and self-identity, see also: Thomas J. Saunders, 'A "New Man": Fascism, Cinema and Image Creation', *International Journal of Politics, Culture, and Society* 12, no. 2 (1998), 235–6.
47 David E. Apter, 'Politics as Theatre: An Alternative View of the Rationalities of Power', in *Social Performance: Symbolic Action, Cultural Pragmatics, and Ritual*, ed. Jeffrey C. Alexander, Bernhard Giesen, and Jason L. Mast (Cambridge: Cambridge University Press, 2006), 223.
48 Cf.:Paul Betts, 'The New Fascination with Fascism: The Case of Nazi Modernism', *Journal of Contemporary History* 37, no. 4 (2002), 544.
49 Arnd Bauerkämper, *Der Faschismus in Europa 1918–1945* (Stuttgart: Reclam, 2006), 173–4.
50 See the startling table of all the various definitions of fascism given by scholars in: Daniel Woodley, *Fascism and Political Theory: Critical Perspectives on Fascist Ideology* (London: Routledge, 2010), 4–5.
51 'Interpretations of Fascism by Marxists', in *Fascism*, ed. Roger Griffin(Oxford: Oxford University Press, 1995), 260–6.
52 Roger Griffin, *The Nature of Fascism* (Oxon: Routledge, 1993); Bauerkämper, *Der Faschismus in Europa 1918–1945*; Constantin Iordachi, ed., *Comparative Fascist*

Studies: New Perspectives (London: Routledge, 2010); Henrik Arnstad, *Älskade Fascism: De Svartbruna Rörelsernas Ideologi Och Historia* (Stockholm: Norstedts, 2013); Roberts, *Fascist Interactions*; Roger Griffin, *Fascism* (London: Polity Press, 2018).

53 Nolte, *Three Faces of Fascism*, 22, 40.
54 Roberts, *Fascist Interactions*, 290.
55 Gilbert Allardyce, 'What Fascism Is Not: Thoughts on the Deflation of a Concept', *The American Historical Review* 84, no. 2 (1979): 367–8.
56 Mosse, *Nazi Culture*, xix.
57 George L. Mosse, *The Fascist Revolution: Toward a General Theory of Fascism* (New York: Howard Fertig, 1999), x–xi.
58 Nolte, *Three Faces of Fascism*, 39.
59 Modris Eksteins, *Rites of Spring: The Great War and the Birth of the Modern Age* (New York: Mariner Books, 2000), 304–12.
60 Gerhard Paul, *Aufstand der Bilder: Die NS-Propaganda vor 1933* (Bonn: J.H.W. Dietz Nachf., 1990), 12–3.
61 See, for instance, Henning Eichberg and Robert A. Jones, 'The Nazi Thingspiel: Theater for the Masses in Fascism and Proletarian Culture', *New German Critique*, no. 11 (1977), 133–50.
62 Ingemar Karlsson and Arne Ruth, *Samhället som Teater: Estetik och politik i tredje riket* (Stockholm: Liber, 1983), 16–24.
63 George L. Mosse, 'Fascist Aesthetics and Society: Some Considerations', *Journal of Contemporary History* 31, no. 2 (1996), 245–52.
64 Jeffrey T. Schnapp, *Staging Fascism: 18 BL and the Theater of Masses for Masses* (Stanford: Stanford University, 1996), 6.
65 Simonetta Falasca-Zamponi, *Fascist Spectacle: The Aesthetics of Power in Mussolini's Italy* (London: University of California Press, 1997), 1–4.
66 Mabel Berezin, 'The Organization of Political Ideology: Culture, State, and Theater in Fascist Italy', *American Sociological Review* 56, no. 5 (1991): 639.
67 Mabel Berezin, *Making the Fascist Self: The Political Culture of Interwar Italy* (London: Cornell University Press, 1997), 5–7, 19–28.
68 Emilio Gentile, *The Sacralization of Politics in Fascist Italy* (London: Harvard University Press, 1996), ix; Emilio Gentile, *Politics as Religion* (Oxford: Princeton University Press, 2006), 36–7.
69 Martin Baumeister, 'Faschismus als "politischer Religion"', in *Der Faschismus in Europa: Wege der Forschung*, ed. Thomas Schlemmer and Hans Woller (München: Oldenbourg Wissenschaftsverlag, 2014), 67–9.
70 Introduction to: Bonnell, Hunt and Biernacki, *Beyond the Cultural Turn*, 8.
71 Griffin, *The Nature of Fascism*, 32–55.
72 Roger Griffin, 'The Primacy of Culture: The Current Growth (Or Manufacture) of Consensus within Fascist Studies', *Journal of Contemporary History* 37, no. 1 (2002): 34.
73 Bauerkämper, *Der Faschismus in Europa 1918–1945*, 35; Baumeister, 'Faschismus als "politischer Religion"', 11; David D. Roberts, 'Myth, Style, Substance and the Totalitarian Dynamic in Fascist Italy', *Contemporary European History* 16, no. 1 (2007): 1–7.
74 Michael Mann, *Fascists* (Cambridge: Cambridge University Press, 2004), 12.
75 Ibid. 21–2.

76 Sven Reichardt, 'Faschistische Tatgemeinschaften: Anmerkungen zu einer praxeologischen Analyse', in *Der Faschismus in Europa: Wege der Forschung*, ed. Thomas Schlemmer and Hans Woller (München: Oldenbourg Wissenschaftsverlag, 2014), 75–8.

77 Sven Reichardt, 'Praxeologie und Faschismus. Gewalt und Gemeinschaft als Elemente eines Praxeologischen Faschismusbegriffs', in *Doing Culture: Neue Positionen zum Verhältnis von Kultur und Sozialer Praxis*, ed. Karl H. Hörning and Julia Reuter (Berlin: De Gruyter, 2004), 129–53.

78 Sven Reichardt, *Faschistische Kampfbünde: Gewalt und Gemeinschaft im Italienischen Squadrismus und in der Deutschen SA* (Köln: Böhlau, 2002), 11–9.

79 Griffin, *The Nature of Fascism*, 44.

80 E.g.: H.R. Kedward, *Fascism in Western Europe, 1900–45* (Glasgow: Blackie, 1969), 222.

81 David Roberts, 'Fascism and the Framework for Interactive Political Innovation during the Era of the Two World Wars', in *Rethinking Fascism and Dictatorship in Europe*, ed. António Costa Pinto and Aristotle Kallis (Basingstoke: Palgrave Macmillan, 2014), 44–7.

82 Friedrich Nietzsche, *Zur Genealogie der Moral: Ein Streitschrift* (Leipzig: C.G. Naumann Verlag, 1907), 2: 13.

83 Jan Melin, Alf W. Johansson, and Susanna Hedenborg, *Sveriges Historia: Koncentrerad uppslagsbok: Fakta, årtal, kartor, tabeller* (Stockholm: Rabén Prisma (Tiden Athena), 1997), 227–30.

84 Louise Drangel, *Den Kämpande Demokratin: En studie i antinazistisk opinionsrörelse 1935–1945* (Stockholm: LiberFörlag, 1976); Jan Peters, *Exilland Schweden: Deutsche und Schwedische Antifaschisten, 1933–1945* (Berlin: Akademie-Verlag, 1984).

85 Perhaps the first academic research on Swedish fascism was produced by Kurt Mall in Germany, at the University of Heidelberg. His 1936 doctoral thesis is however not very elaborate, and arguably somewhat marred by certain ideological biases. Kurt Mall, *Der Nationalsozialismus in Schweden im Spiegel seiner Kampfpresse*, PhD Thesis (Heidelberg, 1936).

86 Heléne Lööw, *Hakkorset och Wasakärven: En studie av nationalsocialismen i Sverige 1924–1950* (Magnus Mölner & Jörgen Weibull, 1990); Heléne Lööw, *Nazismen i Sverige, 1924–1979: Pionjärerna, partierna, propagandan* (Stockholm: Ordfront Förlag, 2004).

87 Lena Berggren, 'Den svenska mellankrigsfascismen – ett ointressant marginalfenomen eller ett viktigt forskingsobjekt?', *Historisk Tidskrift*, no. 3 (2002): 427–44.

88 Lena Berggren, 'Swedish Fascism: Why Bother?', *Journal of Contemporary History* 37, no. 3 (2002): 398.

89 Lena Berggren, 'Intellectual Fascism: Per Engdahl and the Formation of "New-Swedish Socialism"', *Fascism: Journal of Comparative Fascism Studies*, no. 3 (2014): 69–92.

90 Klas Åmark, *Att Bo Granne med Ondskan: Sveriges förhållande till nazismen, Nazityskland och Förintelsen* (Stockholm: Bonniers, 2011).

91 See also recent research on German infiltration of Swedish clubs and corporations, e.g.: Birgitta Almgren, 'Svensk-Tyska Föreningar: Mål för Nazistisk Infiltration', *Historisk Tidskrift* 135, no. 1 (2015), 63–91; Sven Nordlund, '"Tyskarna själva gör ju ingen hemlighet av detta." Sverige och ariseringen av tyskägda företag och dotterbolag', *Historisk Tidskrift* 125, no. 4 (2005), 609–41.

92 Arnstad, Henrik, *Älskade Fascism: De svartbruna rörelsernas ideologi och historia* (Norstedts: Stockholm, 2013), esp. 345–99.
93 Per Svensson, *Vasakärven och Järnröret: Om den långa bruna skuggan från Lund* (Stockholm: Weyler, 2014).
94 Henrik Dammberg, *Nazismen i Skaraborgs Län 1930–1945* (Bolum Förlag, 2009), 87–109.
95 Victor Lundberg, *En Idé Större än Döden: En fascistisk arbetarrörelse i Sverige, 1933–1945* (Stockholm: Gidlunds Förlag, 2014), 35–9.
96 Erik Hansen, 'Fascism and Nazism in the Netherlands, 1929–39', *European Studies Review* 3, (1981): 355–85, is one example of English work on the subject, and much better than the average chapters or articles that have appeared on the subject, but is very dated at this point.
97 'In wezen zijn Nederlandsche en Duitsche nationaal-socialisten kinderen ééns geestes.' P. A. Diepenhorst, *Het Nationaal-Socialisme* (Kampen: J.H. Kok, 1935), 8.
98 Annemieke van Bockxmeer, *De Oorlog Verzameld: Het ontstaan van de collectie van het NIOD* (Amsterdam: De Bezige Bij, 2014), 21.
99 Konrad Kwiet, *Reichskommissariat Niederlande: Versuch und Scheitern Nationalsozialistischer Neuordnung* (Stuttgart: Deutsche Verlags-Anstalt, 1968).
100 E.g.: Werner Warmbrunn, *The Dutch under German Occupation, 1940–1945* (Stanford: Stanford University Press, 1963); Gerhard Hirschfeld, *Nazi Rule and Dutch Collaboration: The Netherlands under German Occupation 1940–1945* (Oxford: Berg, 1988); Jennifer L. Foray, *Visions of Empire in the Nazi-Occupied Netherlands* (Cambridge: Cambridge University Press, 2012).
101 Foray, *Visions of Empire in the Nazi-Occupied Netherlands*, 9.
102 G. A. Kooy, *Het Echec van een 'Volkse' Beweging: Nazificatie en Denazificatie in Nederland 1931–1945* (Utrecht: HES, 1982).
103 L. M. H. Joosten, *Katholieken en Fascisme in Nederland 1920–1940*, 2nd edn (Utrecht: HES, 1982).
104 A. A. de Jonge, *Crisis en Critiek der Democratie: Anti-democratische stromingen en de daarin levende denkbeelden over de staat in Nederland tussen de wereldoorlogen* (Utrecht: HES, 1982); A. A. de Jonge, *Het Nationaal-Socialisme in Nederland: Voorgeschiedenis, Ontstaan en Ontwikkeling*, 2nd edn (Den Haag: Kruseman, 1979).
105 Konrad Kwiet, 'Zur Geschichte Der Mussert-Bewegung', *Vierteljahrshefte für Zeitgeschichte* 18, no. 2 (1970), 164–95, 164–5.
106 Ronald Havenaar, *De NSB tussen Nationalisme en 'Volkse' Solidariteit: De vooroorlogse ideologie van de Nationaal-Socialistische Beweging in Nederland* ('s-Gravenhage: Staatsuitgeverij, 1983).
107 Gerard Groeneveld, *Zwaard van de Geest: Het Bruine Boek in Nederland, 1921–1945* (Nijmegen: Vantilt, 2001), 57–68.
108 Gerard Groeneveld, *Zo Zong de NSB: Liedcultuur van de NSB 1931–1945* (Nijmegen: Vantilt, 2007).
109 Josje Damsma and Erik Schumacher, *Hier Woont een NSB'er: Nationaalsocialisten in bezet Amsterdam* (Amsterdam: Boom, 2010), 29–30, 71–2; see also: Josje Damsma and Erik Schumacher, '"De Strijd om Amsterdam": Een nieuwe benadering in het onderzoek naar de NSB', *BMGN – Low Countries Historical Review*, 124.3 (2009), 329–48; Josje Damsma, *Nazis in the Netherlands: A Social History of National Socialist Collaborators, 1940–1945*, PhD thesis (Amsterdam: University of Amsterdam, 2013).
110 Damsma and Schumacher, *Hier Woont een NSB'er*, 51.
111 Ibid. 71–2.

112 René van Heijningen, *De Muur van Mussert* (Amsterdam: Boom, 2015).
113 Kiran Klaus Patel, 'In Search of a Transnational Historicization: National Socialism and Its Place in History', in *Conflicted Memories: Europeanizing Contemporary Histories* (Oxford: Bergahn, 2007), 98.
114 Michael Kellogg, *The Russian Roots of Nazism: White Émigrés and the Making of National Socialism, 1917–1945* (Cambridge: Cambridge University Press, 2005).
115 Roland Clark, *Holy Legionary Youth: Fascist Activism in Interwar Romania* (New York: Cornell University Press, 2015); Rory Yeomans, ed., *The Utopia of Terror: Life and Death in Wartime Croatia* (Suffolk: University of Rochester Press, 2015).
116 Roger Griffin, 'Decentering Comparative Fascist Studies', *Fascism: Journal of Comparative Fascism Studies* 4, no. 2 (23 November 2015): 103–18.
117 Arnd Bauerkämper, 'Transnational Fascism: Cross-Border Relations between Regimes and Movements in Europe, 1922–1939', *East Central Europe*, no. 37 (2010): 214–46.
118 António Costa Pinto and Aristotle Kallis, eds., *Rethinking Fascism and Dictatorship in Europe* (Basingstoke: Palgrave Macmillan, 2014).
119 Roberts, *Fascist Interactions*, 3, 16, 22–3, 44–5.
120 Arnd Bauerkämper and Grzegorz Rossolinkski-Liebe, eds., *Fascism without Borders: Transnational Connections and Cooperation between Movements and Regimes in Europe from 1918 to 1945* (Oxford: Bergahn, 2017).
121 Probably the best recent critique of definitions of fascism and alternative approaches was Michel Dobry, 'Desperately Seeking "Generic Fascism": Some Discordant Thoughts on the Academic Recycling of Indigenous Categories', in *Rethinking the Nature of Fascism: Comparative Perspectives*, ed. António Costa Pinto (Basingstoke: Palgrave Macmillan, 2011), 85–116.
122 Kevin Passmore, 'Fascism as a Social Movement in a Transnational Context', in *The History of Social Movements in Global Perspective*, ed. S. Berger and H. Nehring (Basingstoke: Palgrave Macmillan, 2017), 583–4.
123 Ángel Alcalde, 'The Transnational Consensus: Fascism and Nazism in Current Research', *Contemporary European History*, 2020, 9, https://doi.org/10.1017/S0960777320000089.
124 Ibid.
125 Yeomans, *The Utopia of Terror*, 7.
126 Sven Reichardt, 'Fascist Marches in Italy and Germany: Squadre and SA before the Seizure of Power', in *The Street as Stage: Protest Marches and Public Rallies since the Nineteenth Century*, ed. Matthias Reiss (Oxford: Oxford University Press, 2007), 170.
127 For the performative connotations of the concept of repertoire, see: Eitan Y. Alimi, 'Repertoires of Contention', in *The Oxford Handbook of Social Movements* (Oxford: Oxford University Press, 2015), 410–2.
128 Maiken Umbach, 'Selfhood, Place, and Ideology in German Photo Albums, 1933–1945', *Central European History* 48, no. 3 (2015): 365.
129 Michel Foucault pointed out that 'what happens in someone's mind, or in the minds of a series of individuals, actually does belong to history: to say something is an event. The formulation of a ... discourse is not situated above history or off to the side: it's as much a part of history as a battle or the invention of a steam engine, or an epidemic.' Interview with Michel Foucault, 1978 w. D. Trombadori, orig. published in Il Contributo, 1980, in: Michel Foucault, *Essential Works of Foucault, 1954–1984: Power*, ed. James Faubion, vol. 3 (London: Penguin, 2001), 277.

130 Gabrielle M. Spiegel, ed., 'Introduction', in *Practicing History: New Directions in Historical Writing after the Linguistic Turn* (London: Routledge, 2005), 7, 11–4, 22; Green, *Cultural History*, 62.

131 William H. Sewell, 'The Concept(s) of Culture', in *Practicing History: New Directions in Historical Writing after the Linguistic Turn*, ed. Gabrielle M. Spiegel (London: Routledge, 2005), 83.

132 Jeffrey C. Alexander, 'Cultural Pragmatics: Social Performance between Ritual and Strategy', in *Social Performance: Symbolic Action, Cultural Pragmatics, and Ritual*, ed. Jeffrey C. Alexander, Bernhard Giesen and Jason L. Mast (Cambridge: Cambridge University Press, 2006), 32.

133 Erika Fischer-Lichte, 'Performance, Inszenierung, Ritual', in *Geschichtswissenschafft und 'Performative Turn': Ritual, Inszenierung und Performanz vom Mittelalter bis zur Neuzeit*, ed. Jürgen Martschukat and Steffen Patzold (Köln: Böhlau, 2003), 33–55.

134 Alexander, 'Cultural Pragmatics: Social Performance between Ritual and Strategy', 55.

135 Ibid., 68–76.

136 Judith Butler, 'Performative Acts and Gender Constitution: An Essay in Phenomenology and Feminist Theory', *Theatre Journal* 40, no. 4 (1988): 519–39; Judith Butler, *Gender Trouble: Feminism and the Subversion of Identity* (London: Routledge, 2007); Judith Butler, *Bodies That Matter* (London: Routledge, 2011).

137 Erika Fischer-Lichte, *The Transformative Power of Performance: A New Aesthetics* (London: Routledge, 2008), 26–7.

138 JL Austin, *How to Do Things with Words* (Oxford: Clarendon Press, 1962), 4–6.

139 Ibid. 12–8; See also the excellent summary in: James Loxley, *Performativity* (London: Routledge, 2007), 1–9.

140 Loxley, *Performativity*, 13.

141 Ibid. 74–5; Jacques Derrida, 'Signature Event Context', in *Margins of Philosophy* (Chicago: Chicago University Press, 1982), 324–5.

142 Derrida, 'Signature Event Context', 320.

143 Ibid. 321.

144 Butler, 'Performative Acts and Gender Constitution', 520.

145 Ibid.

146 Amy Hollywood, 'Performativity, Citationality, Ritualization', *History of Religions* 42, no. 2 (2002): 94–5.

147 Butler, *Gender Trouble*, 185.

148 Butler, 'Performative Acts and Gender Constitution', 520.

149 Butler, *Gender Trouble*, 191.

150 Ibid. 192–3.

151 Henning Grunwald is a notable exception, and has used specifically Butler's theory of performativity in his work, see: Henning Grunwald, *Courtroom to Revolutionary Stage: Performance and Ideology in Weimar Political Trials* (Oxford: Oxford University Press, 2012).

Chapter 1

1 Stig Hadenius, *Svensk politik under 1900-talet: Konflikt och samförstånd*, 4th ed. (Stockholm: Tiden Athena, 1996), 9; Per T. Ohlsson, *Svensk Politik* (Lund: Historiska Media, 2014), 7.

2   Bengt Owe Birgersson et al., *Sverige efter 1900: En modern politisk historia* (Stockholm: Bonniers, 1981), 11.
3   Geert Mak et al., *Verleden van Nederland* (Amsterdam: Olympus, 2015), 356–7.
4   J.J. Woltjer, *Recent Verleden: Nederland in de Twintigste Eeuw* (Amsterdam: Balans, 2005), 68–71.
5   Ohlsson, *Svensk Politik*, 113.
6   Nils Stjernquist, *Tvåkammartiden: Sveriges riksdag 1867–1970* (Lund: Sveriges Riksdag, 1996), 82–91.
7   Mak et al., *Verleden van Nederland*, 363–9.
8   Woltjer, *Recent Verleden*, 50.
9   Jan L. Van Zanden, *The Economic History of the Netherlands, 1914–1995: A Small Open Economy in the 'long' Twentieth Century* (London: Routledge, 1998), 10–1.
10 Reichardt, 'Faschistische Tatgemeinschaften', 80.
11 In fact, it could be argued that the dislocation of economic relationships caused by the war was far more serious than actual physical destruction. Aldcroft and Morewood, *The European Economy since 1914*, 21.
12 Pertti Haapala and Marko Tikka, 'Revolution, Civil War, and Terror in Finland in 1918', in *War in Peace: Paramilitary Violence in Europe after the Great War*, ed. Robert Gerwarth and John Horne (Oxford: Oxford University Press, 2013), 73, 84; Juha Siltala, 'Dissolution and Reintegration in Finland, 1914–1932: How Did a Disarmed Country Become Absorbed into Brutalization?', *Journal of Baltic Studies* 46, no. 1 (n.d.), 20–1.
13 Mak et al., *Verleden van Nederland*, 382–3.
14 Paul Arblaster, *A History of the Low Countries* (Basingstoke: Palgrave Macmillan, 2006), 212.
15 Louis de Jong, *Het Koninkrijk der Nederlanden in de Tweede Wereldoorlog, 1: Voorspel* ('s-Gravenhage: Martinus Nijhoff, 1969), 38–9.
16 Kristel, *De Oorlog van Anderen*, 35–49.
17 Jong, *Het Koninkrijk der Nederlanden in de Tweede Wereldoorlog, 1: Voorspel*, 36–8; Kristel, *De Oorlog van Anderen*, 117–8.
18 Ohlsson, *Svensk Politik*, 178–9.
19 Lars Gyllenhaal and Lennart Westberg, *Svenskar i Krig, 1914–1945* (Stockholm: Historiska Media, 2008), chap. I kaiserns tjänst, 1914–8.
20 Kwiet, 'Zur Geschichte Der Mussert-Bewegung', 167.
21 Ohlsson, *Svensk Politik*, 174–81.
22 Arblaster, *A History of the Low Countries*, 215–6.
23 Jong, *Het Koninkrijk der Nederlanden in de Tweede Wereldoorlog, 1: Voorspel*, 45–8.
24 Stjernquist, *Tvåkammartiden*, 82–91; Ohlsson, *Svensk Politik*, 195.
25 Stjernquist, *Tvåkammartiden*, 91–4.
26 J.C.H. Blom and E. Lamberts, eds., *Geschiedenis van de Nederlanden* (Rijswijk: Nijgh & Van Ditmar, 1993), 334–5.
27 Frans Verhagen, *Toen de Katholieken Nederland Veroverden: Charles Ruijs de Beerenbrouck 1873–1936* (Amsterdam: Boom, 2015), 212.
28 Tobias Berglund and Niclas Sennerteg, *Finska Inbördeskriget* (Stockholm: Natur och Kultur, 2017), 67–108.
29 Olle Larsson and Andreas Marklund, *Svensk Historia* (Lund: Historiska Media, 2012), 333; Berglund and Sennerteg, *Finska Inbördeskriget*, 175–80.
30 Ingvar Flink, 'Svenska Krigsförluster i Finland År 1918', in *Norden och Krigen i Finland och Balticum, 1918–19* (Helsingfors: Statsrådets kansli, 2004), 27.

31 Gyllenhaal and Westberg, *Svenskar i Krig, 1914–1945*, 83–5.
32 J.O., 'Samhallsrota', *Bageriarbetaren* [fr. *Metallarbetaren*], no. 6–7, June–July 1918, newspaper clipping in: Swedish Brigade archive, Military Archives of Sweden, Marieberg, vol. E:35.
33 Kristel, *De Oorlog van Anderen*, 251–2, 269.
34 Tessell Pollmann, *Mussert & Co: De NSB-Leider en zijn Vetrouwelingen* (Amsterdam: Boom, 2012), 111–2.
35 Koen Vossen, *Vrij Vissen in het Vondelpark: Kleine Politieke Partijen in Nederland 1918–1940* (Amsterdam: Wereldbibliotheek, 2003), 17, 67–73.
36 Frank van Vree, *De Nederlandse Pers en Duitsland, 1930–1939: Een Studie over de Vorming van de Publieke Opinie* (Groningen: Historische Uitgeverij, 1989), 52.
37 Ibid. 343.
38 Heijningen, *De Muur van Mussert*, 156–7.
39 Marjet Derks, '"Stralende strijdlust, taaie zelfverloochening": De dynamiek van traditie en moderniteit in de Graalbeweging', in *Moderniteit: Modernisme en massacultuur in Nederland, 1914–1940*, ed. Sophie Tates and Madelon De Keizer (Zutphen: Walburg Pers, 2004).
40 van Zanden, *The Economic History of the Netherlands, 1914–1995*, 10–8.
41 Ibid. 21–5.
42 Verhagen, *Toen de Katholieken Nederland Veroverden*, 26–7.
43 Woltjer, *Recent Verleden*, 90.
44 Chris Cook and John Paxton, *European Political Facts of the Twentieth Century*, 5th ed. (Basingstoke: Palgrave Macmillan, 2001), 259–60.
45 Aerts et al., *Land van Kleine Gebaren*, 205–6.
46 Vossen, *Vrij Vissen in het Vondelpark*, 67–70.
47 Aerts et al., *Land van Kleine Gebaren*, 206–7.
48 Ibid. 207.
49 Verhagen, *Toen de katholieken Nederland veroverden*, 53–4; Woltjer, *Recent Verleden*, 130.
50 Woltjer, *Recent Verleden*, 88, 101.
51 Jonge, *Crisis en Critiek der Democratie*.
52 Woltjer, *Recent Verleden*, 117–8.
53 Ibid. 127.
54 van Zanden, *The Economic History of the Netherlands, 1914–1995*, 109–14.
55 Friso Wielenga, *A History of the Netherlands: From the Sixteenth Century to the Present Day* (London: Bloomsbury, 2015), 214; Ronald Havenaar, *Anton Adriaan Mussert: Verrader voor het Vaderland* (Den Haag: Kruseman, 1984), 45–6; Robin Te Slaa and Edwin Klijn, *De NSB: Ontstaan en Opkomst van de Nationaal-Socialistische Beweging, 1931–1935* (Amsterdam: Boom, 2010), 56.
56 Vree, *De Nederlandse Pers en Duitsland, 1930–1939*, 33.
57 J.C.H. Blom, *De Muiterij op de Zeven Provinciën: Reacties en Gevolgen in Nederland* (Utrecht: HES, 1983), 49–55.
58 Jonge, *Crisis en Critiek der Democratie*, 185.
59 Willem Huberts, *In de Ban van een Beter Verleden: Het Nederlandse Fascisme, 1923–1945* (Nijmegen: Vantilt, 2017), 141–6.
60 Wielenga, *A History of the Netherlands*, 204.
61 Slaa and Klijn, *De NSB*, 251.
62 J. P. Stoop, *Om het Volvoeren van een Christelijke Staatkunde: De Anti-Revolutionaire Partij in het Interbellum* (Hilversum: Verloren, 2001), 152.

63 Arblaster, *A History of the Low Countries*, 226–7.
64 Mark Mazower, *Hitler's Empire: Nazi Rule in Occupied Europe* (London: Penguin, 2009), 397; Richard J. Evans, *The Third Reich at War: How the Nazis Led Germany from Conquest to Disaster* (London: Penguin, 2009), 386.
65 Adrian Vickers, *A History of Modern Indonesia* (Cambridge: Cambridge University Press, 2005), 11–3.
66 Ethan Mark, 'Fascisms Seen and Unseen: The Netherlands, Japan, Indonesia, and the Relationalities of Imperial Crisis', in *Visualizing Fascism: The Twentieth-Century Rise of the Global Right*, ed. Julia Adeney Thomas and Geoff Eley, (Durham, North Carolina: Duke University Press, 2020), 183–201; Slaa and Klijn, *De NSB*, 679–82.
67 Jonge, *Crisis en Critiek der Democratie*, 52.
68 Joosten, *Katholieken en Fascisme in Nederland 1920–1940*, 29–30.
69 J. L. Van Der Pauw, *De Actualisten: De Kinderjaren van het Georganiseerde Fascisme in Nederland 1923–1924* (Amsterdam: Sijthoff, 1987), 26–7, 53, 97–9.
70 Havenaar, *Anton Adriaan Mussert*; for a comprehensive history of the treaty, with a summary in English, see: R. L. Schuursma, *Het Onaannemelijk Tractaat: Het Verdrag met België van 3 April 1925 in de Nederlandse Publieke Opinie* (Groningen: H. D. Tjeenk Willink, 1975).
71 Aerts et al., *Land van Kleine Gebaren*, 220.
72 Slaa and Klijn, *De NSB*, chap. 22.
73 Dietrich Orlow, *The Lure of Fascism in Western Europe: German Nazis, Dutch and French Fascists, 1933–1939* (Basingstoke: Palgrave Macmillan, 2009), 51.
74 ' … moeilijk beslissend uit te maken, in hoever verschillende fascistische of nationaal-socialistische stroomingen te ontzend dezen "totalen staat" aanvaarden. […] … vroeg of laat zeer zeker onder den invloed van deze staats- of natievergoding zullen geraken. De groote gedachtenstroomingen toch in het wereldgebeuren beïnvloeden elkaar meestal op onweerstaanbare wijze … […] Een zekere gematigdheid bij de hoofdleiding is dus niet de minste waarborg voor de toekomstige ontwikkeling eener beweging. […] Bovendien is het meer dan waarschijnlijk, dat elk fascisme en nationaal-socialisme in Nederland op den duur zal beheerscht worden door een groep personen, die in meerderheid onze wereldbeschouwing niet deelen', Brochure, Pastoral letter from the Archbishop and the Bishops of the Netherlands to their committed Clergy and Faithful, *Zaligheid in den Heer*, Utrecht, 2 February 1934, National Archive, The Hague, 2.19.49: 10.
75 Orlow, *The Lure of Fascism in Western Europe*, 106–8.
76 Stjernquist, *Tvåkammartiden*, 82–94.
77 Claes-Göran Holmberg, Ingemar Oscarsson, and Per Rydén, *En Svensk Presshistoria* (Solna: Esselte studium, 1983), 86–143.
78 Arne Halvarson, *Sveriges Statsskick: En faktasamling* (Stockholm: Norstedts, 1986), 7.
79 Ohlsson, *Svensk Politik*, 219.
80 Francis Sejersted, *The Age of Social Democracy: Norway and Sweden in the Twentieth Century* (Princeton: Princeton University Press, 2011), 35–40.
81 Birgersson et al., *Sverige efter 1900*, 117; Aldcroft and Morewood, *The European Economy since 1914*, 55.
82 Halvarson, *Sveriges Statsskick*, 6–8.
83 Ohlsson, *Svensk Politik*, 163–4, 219.
84 Birgersson et al., *Sverige efter 1900*, 103–4.
85 Larsson and Marklund, *Svensk Historia*, 335.
86 Birgersson et al., *Sverige efter 1900*, 107.

87　John Gilmour, *Sweden, the Swastika and Stalin: The Swedish Experience in the Second World War* (Edinburgh: Edinburgh University Press, 2010), 7–8.
88　Ohlsson, *Svensk Politik*, 230–1.
89　Sejersted, *The Age of Social Democracy*, 132.
90　Larsson and Marklund, *Svensk Historia*, 342.
91　Birgersson et al., *Sverige efter 1900*, 125–8.
92　Larsson and Marklund, *Svensk Historia*, 341.
93　Halvarson, *Sveriges Statsskick*, 8.
94　Klaus Misgeld, Karl Molin and Klas Åmark, eds., *Creating Social Democracy: A Century of the Social Democratic Labor Party in Sweden* (Pennsylvania: Pennsylvania State University Press, 1992), 449–52.
95　Ohlsson, *Svensk Politik*, 240.
96　Ibid. 265–8.
97　Ibid. 268–71.
98　Oula Silvennoinen, 'Demokratins framgångshistoria? Skogsindustrin, arbetsmarknaden och en fascistisk samhällssyn 1918–1940', in *Demokratins drivkrafter: Kontext och särdrag i Finlands och Sveriges demokratier 1890–2020*, ed. Henrik Meinander, Petri Karonen, and Kjell Östberg (Stockholm: Appell, 2018), 193.
99　Berggren, *Nationell Upplysning*, 10, 73.
100　Maria Björkman and Sven Widmalm, 'Selling Eugenics: The Case of Sweden', *Notes and Records of the Royal Society of London* 64, no. 4 (2010), 380; see also: Paul Weindling, 'International Eugenics: Swedish Sterilization in Context', *Scandinavian Journal of History* 24, no. 2 (1999), 179–97.
101　Åmark, *Att Bo Granne Med Ondskan*, 367.
102　Svensson, *Vasakärven och Järnröret*, 96–7.
103　Bernt Hagtvet, 'On the Fringe: Swedish Fascism 1920–1945', in *Who Were the Fascists?*, ed. Stein U. Larsen (Oslo: Universitetsförlaget, 1980), 719–20.
104　Svensson, *Vasakärven och Järnröret*, 62–87; Nilsson, *Svensk Överklassnazism, 1930–1945*, 12, 43–57.
105　Åmark, *Att Bo Granne Med Ondskan*, 288.
106　Wärenstam, *Fascismen och Nazismen i Sverige 1920–1940*, 13–5; Hagtvet, 'On the Fringe: Swedish Fascism 1920–1945', 719–21; Stein U. Larsen, 'Conservatives and Fascists in the Nordic Countries: Norway, Sweden, Denmark and Finland, 1918–45', in *Fascists and Conservatives: The Radical Right and the Establishment in Twentieth-Century Europe*, ed. Martin Blinkhorn (London: Unwin Hyman, 1990), 243–4.
107　Wärenstam, *Fascismen och Nazismen i Sverige 1920–1940*, 65.
108　Police investigation protocol, Otto Meijer, 18 February 1948, P1279:1 (police file on Sven Olov Lindholm), SRA, Arninge.
109　Lööw, *Nazismen i Sverige, 1924–1979*, 15–6.
110　Sven Olov Lindholm, Lindholm Interview, tape recording, 1980, sec. 256: B, SO Lindholm's Collection, vol. 4, SRA, Marieberg.
111　Wärenstam, *Fascismen och Nazismen i Sverige 1920–1940*, 91–3.
112　Lundberg, *En Idé Större än Döden*, 56–7.
113　3 January 1933, Sven Olov Lindholm, Diary, SO Lindholm's collection, vol. 2, National Archives of Sweden, Marieberg.
114　E.g. 'Nazistbråk i Göteborg', *Svenska Dagbladet*, 20 December 1933.
115　14 January 1933, Lindholm Diary.
116　One morning Furugård opened the party newspaper, *Vår Kamp*, to read to his surprise the front page announcement that he had nobly chosen to resign. 'Furugård avgår! Nationalsocialistisk enhetsfront!', *Vår Kamp*, 7 October 1933, 1.

117 Sivert Wester, *Martin Ekström: Orädd frivillig i fem krig* (Västervik: Militärhistoriska Förlaget, 1995), 111–23.
118 Memorandum concerning NSAP, 10 March 1938, Arninge, 2B: Theses, programmes, summons, etc. folder 9, 1.
119 Kunkeler, 'The Evolution of Swedish Fascism', 391–2.
120 Lundberg, *En Idé Större än Döden*, 60.

Chapter 2

1 Jeffrey C. Alexander and Jason L. Mast, 'Introduction: Symbolic Action in Theory and Practice', in *Social Performance: Symbolic Action, Cultural Pragmatics, and Ritual*, ed. Jeffrey C. Alexander, Bernhard Giesen, and Jason L. Mast (Cambridge: Cambridge University Press, 2006), 5–6.
2 E.g. the work done in: Dietrich Orlow, *The History of the Nazi Party, 1919–33*, vol. 1, 2 vols (Newton Abbot: David & Charles, 1971).
3 Damsma and Schumacher, '"De Strijd om Amsterdam": Een nieuwe benadering in het onderzoek naar de NSB'; Damsma and Schumacher, *Hier Woont een NSB'er*.
4 A notable exception is: Lööw, *Hakkorset och Wasakärven*, chap. 4, especially 117–9.
5 E.g.: Pauw, *De Actualisten*, 22; Wärenstam, *Fascismen och Nazismen i Sverige 1920–1940*, 55.
6 For an account of how the NSDAP power structure was centralized and personalized, see Orlow, *The History of the Nazi Party, 1919–33*, vol. 1, chap. 3.
7 Memorandum concerning police raid, 22 May 1935, 23–4, Swedish National Archives (*Riksarkivet*): Arninge (Security Service archive), dossier 2H1.
8 Measure of the Administration No. 1: Regarding the organization, Utrecht, 1 February 1932, Amsterdam: NIOD (Dutch Institute for War Documentation), Archive 123 (NSB Party Archive), 1.1 (Leadership): dossier 3.
9 Lindholm interview, sec. 00258: B.
10 Booklet, Tjänsteföreskrifter för NSAP (TF), 15 January 1937, 1, Arninge: 2B1: 1.
11 'Meddelande från plg', *Den Svenske Nationalsocialisten (DSN)*, no. 6, 8 February 1934, 2.
12 'Meddelanden', DSN, no. 80, 17 October 1936, 2.
13 Lindholm interview, 1980–1, 260: A, 1 min.
14 'Erik Fahl fast anställd i Göteborg: Blir talare och organisatör för Västra Landsdelen', DSN, no. 6, 25 January 1939, 1.
15 Lindholm interview, 1980–1, 260: A, 4 mins.
16 Pollmann, *Mussert & Co*, 110. While Van Geelkerken and Mussert cooperated closely throughout the interwar period, they came to oppose each other during the German Occupation.
17 Zonneke Matthée, *Voor Volk en Vaderland: Vrouwen in de NSB 1931–1948* (Amsterdam: Balans, 2007), 51–63.
18 Hogewind was briefly preceded by artillery officer Raimond Nazaire de Ruyter van Steveninck as WA-leader, who handed in the post in February 1933 on account of the prohibition against military personnel holding membership in revolutionary organizations.
19 'Mussert sticht zich een dagblad en benoemt Rost van Tonningen tot hoofredacteur', *Volk en Vaderland* (VoVa), no. 34, 21 August 1936, 1.

20 The term *Randstad*, 'border city', first started being used in the interwar period, referring to the central-western conurbation of the Netherlands where the cities of Utrecht, Amsterdam, The Hague and Rotterdam and their surrounding urban regions were growing together.
21 3 February 1935, Lindholm diary.
22 List of meetings, *Vergaderingen*, January–June 1934, 6–14, NIOD: 123, 2.01: 534.
23 Minutes for meeting 11 July 1935, §1, 23–4, in: Book, meeting minutes *Algemeene Raad*, NIOD: 123, 1.3: 276.
24 See e.g.: Minutes, Meeting of Disciplinary Council, case HP 85, Comrade T. [name restricted], Doetinchem, Hilversum, 26 May 1936, 2, NIOD: 123, 2.30: 1341; Minutes, Meeting of Disciplinary Council, case Dordrecht Circle, 19 May 1937, 1–2, NIOD: 123, 2.56: 2026.
25 'Een nieuw hoofdkwartier: Gebouw aan de Maliebaan', VoVa, no. 7, 15 February 1936, 6; 'Het Willem de Zwijgerhuis: Stichting der Haagsche afdeeling van het Hoofdkwartier', VoVa, no. 41, 8 October 1937, 1.
26 'De NSB marscheert, ook in Indië', VoVa, no. 5, 3 February 1934, 4.
27 *Voor Volk en Vaderland*, 2nd ed., ed. Cornelis Van Geelkerken (Utrecht: Nenasu, 1943), part II, ch. 6.
28 The name was clearly copied from the office introduced into the NSDAP by Gregor Strasser in 1932: Orlow, *The History of the Nazi Party, 1919–33*, 1:259–61.
29 'Meddelanden', DSN, no. 86, 7 November 1936, 2.
30 'Meddelanden', DSN, no. 19, 9 March 1938, 2.
31 'Partiledaren … ', DSN, no. 41, 14 June 1939, 4.
32 Photo negative, Diagram of the party hierarchy, Tjänsteföreskrifter för NSAP, Arninge: 2B1: 1.
33 Odd, 'Björn Dalström partipropagandachef: I ett samtal med Den Svenske drar han upp riktlinjerna för den närmaste tidens verksamhet', DSN, no. 86, 16 November 1938, 1, 8.
34 Diagram, 'Centrale Propagandadienst', NIOD: 123, 2.01: 394.
35 Measure of the Administration, no. 8: 'Regeling der Propaganda', Utrecht, February 1932, NIOD: 123, 1.1: 3. For an example of such circulars, see: Message no. 64, C. van Geelkerken to all Circle Leaders, Utrecht, 27 May 1937, National Archive, The Hague, 2.19.049 (NSB Gewest III): folder 11.
36 Circular, District South-South-Holland, Rotterdam, 2 January 1936, NIOD: 123, 2.01: 504; Guideline no. 3, for the Documentation Service, 10 August 1933, 1–2, NIOD: 123, 2.01: 526.
37 Report: Documentation, J.C. Scholtz, Amsterdam, 29 September 1933, 1, NIOD: 123, 2.01: 542.
38 Booklet, Mussert, *Instructie voor de propaganda in den kring*, Utrecht, 1 September 1934, 4A, p. 5, NIOD: 123, 2.01: 526.
39 Circular no. 100, Ortsgruppschef Ragnar Lind, Stockholm, 25 April 1938, Arninge: 2A: 2.
40 E.g. Letter, to Ach Gagner, Ronneby, 15 September 1935, Marieberg: NSAP/SSS Archive, vol. 5, Ronneby (1934–8).
41 3–15 May 1933, Lindholm diary.
42 *Porg*, no. 10, October 1935, 55, Arninge: 2B: 5.
43 See the letter of complaint from a District Leader: Dch to Ps, Kalmar, 11 February 1935, Marieberg: NSAP/SSS, vol. 3, Södra Distriktet (1934–6).

44 For a rather exultant analysis of the significance of DSN, see Mall, *Der Nationalsozialismus in Schweden im Spiegel seiner Kampfpresse*, 61–9.
45 Jonge, *Het Nationaal-Socialisme in Nederland*, 4; Slaa and Klijn, *De NSB*, 183, 521.
46 Mussert, Order no. 2, to Circle Leaders, Utrecht, 30 December 1935, NIOD: 123, 1.1: 39.
47 Booklet, *Tjänsteföreskrifter för NSAP*, 15 January 1937, 27, 2B1: folder 1, Arninge.
48 Ibid. 7, 26.
49 Monthly Report April, Fridlevstad, 5 May 1934, Marieberg: NSAP/SSS, vol. 6; *Porg*, no. 9, September 1935, 53–4, 2B: 5, Arninge.
50 'Idag flyttar Den Svenske till Stockholm!', DSN, no. 55, 30 July 1938, 3.
51 Lindholm interview, sec. 00259: B.
52 Report, Sven Hagströms Revisionsbyrå, inquiry into SSS bookkeeping, 5 May 1948, P1279: 1, Arninge.
53 Secret Memorandum, concerning National Socialism in Sweden, 16 June-15 July 1937, Arninge: 2B: 7, 1–3; Memorandum, Retrospect of the NSAP, 10 March 1938, Arninge: 2B: 9, 4.
54 ' ... men vi "fast anställda" levde på existensminimum.' 19–30 January 1933; 3–5 January 1935, Lindholm diary.
55 See, for instance, the financial reports for 1936–37, in: NIOD: 123, 2.02: 688.
56 Booklet, *Financieel Verslag*, 31 March 1936, NIOD: 123, 2.02: 688.
57 Pollmann, *Mussert & Co*, 67–70.
58 Police memorandum, 'Översikt över nationalsocialismen i Sverige', 5 October 1935, 59, 2B1: 4, Arninge.
59 12 July 1938, Lindholm diary.
60 E.g. 'Meddelande från P.L.', DSN, no. 13, 11 Juni 1933, 2. See also the letter instructing Bertil Brisman to put the rules for the annual party congress in DSN: Letter, Herbert Hultberg to Bertil Brisman, 8 May 1937, Marieberg: NSAP/SSS, vol. 1, Herbert Hultberg, Partisekreterare, 1937–8.
61 Letter, Dep. 29 Secretary & Cashier, Karl-Axel Söderström, to DSN Financial Department, Karlstad, 17 February 1938, Marieberg: NSAP/SSS, vol. 2; MS, Stadscolportageleider to Otto van Leersum, 'Schema colportage met VoVa in Amsterdam', 12 July 1934, 1, NIOD: 123, 2.01: 394; Form, 'Weekrapport van den plaatselijken vertegenwoordiger van "Volk en Vaderland"', NIOD: 123, 1.1: 3.
62 See the correspondence between VoVa and the *Driehoek*, in: NIOD: 173 (Driehoek, Boekhandel en sigarenbedrijf), 27.
63 Letter, Herbert Widén to Helge Söderström, Stockholm, 1 March 1938, Marieberg: NSAP/SSS, vol. 2.
64 Measure of the Administration, no. 9: 'Instructie voor de plaatselyke vertegenwoordigers van "Volk en Vaderland"', Mussert, Utrecht, May 1933, NIOD: 123, 1.1: 3.
65 Letter, Frans Lindell to DSN, Kalmar, 18 March 1938, Marieberg: NSAP/SSS, vol. 2.
66 Ibid. 4.
67 DSN, no. 97, 31 December 1938, 2.
68 Mussert, Speech MS, Fifth anniversary gathering, RAI Amsterdam, 12 December 1936, 6, NIOD: 123, 1.1: 49.
69 G.J.A. Broek, *Weerkorpsen: Extreemrechtse strijdgroepen in Amsterdam, 1923–1942* (Amsterdam: University of Amsterdam, 2014), 102.
70 E.g.: 'Relletjes in west: Communisten contra fascisten', *Algemeen Handelsblad*, no. 34750, 6 November 1933, 2.

71 'Aanslag op een N.S.B.-colporteur', *De Standaard*, no. 19464, 1 October 1935, 1.
72 'Op Zon- en Christelijke feestdagen mag niet gecolporteerd worden en nimmer in de onmiddelijke nabijheid van kerken. Alles wat in strijd is met den goeden smaak, moet worden vermeden, zooals uitdagend en provoceerend optreden en colporteeren vlak naast colportage van tegenstanders. Er moet vooral voor worden gezorgd, dat het publiek niet, door opdringend of hinderlijk optreden, noodeloos wordt geirriteerd.' Booklet, Alterations to Circle Propaganda Instructions, III: 'Dienst C. – Colportage', 4, The Hague: 2.19.049: 2. See the same in: Booklet, Mussert, *Instructie voor de propaganda in den Kring*, Utrecht, 1 September 1934, 7, NIOD: 123, 2.01: 526.
73 Circular no. 17, Guideline for house visits during the electoral campaign, Amsterdam, 4 January 1935, NIOD: 123, 2.01: 502.
74 'Frontmannen behöver ej vara något helgon eller asket, men han får ej ryckas med av den osunda nöjesvirvel, varmed judiska profitörer vill fördärva vårt folk. [...] Tidningsförsäljare måste iakttaga ett sådant uppträdande, att han tilldrager sig allmänhetens intresse men *utan* att på något vis vara "uppseendeväckande", än mindre förargelseväckande.' Booklet, *Instruktion för Frontavdelningar (I.F.) inom NSAP*, NSAP Organisationsskrift no. 2, 1938, 6, 11, Arninge: 2H1.
75 E.g.: Circular no. 40, from the Local Group Administration, 4 January 1935, Arninge: 2B1: 2.
76 'obrottslig disciplin', ' ... som påverkar svenska människor fördelaktigt och vederlägger lögnen om, att vi skulle vara några utländska legoknektar.' Booklet, *Instruktion för Frontavdelningar (I.F.) inom NSAP*, NSAP Organisationsskrift no. 2, 1938, 5–6, Arninge: 2H1.
77 'vi sträva efter att få en elit av duktiga pålitliga medlemmar, som ej blott äro kunniga i idéerna utan även hängivna sin ledare.' Extract from: *Porg*, January 1935, 2, Arninge: 2B: 5.
78 Confidential police report, Kort redogörelse över den nationalsocialistiska rörelsens i Sverige utveckling under år 1933, 11, 19, Arninge: 2B1: 1.
79 E.g. Interrogation of Stig Karl Erik Witt, in: Police memorandum, 20 July 1934, Arninge: 2C: 2.
80 Letter, Dpch. Gunnar Agnér to NSAP A.69, Kristianstad, 9 March 1935, Marieberg, NSAP/SSS, vol. 4, Kristianstad (1935–8).
81 'Det är absolut nödvändigt att funktionärerna omgående besvara brev angående mötsverksamheten och inte vänta tills sista minuten eller rent av strunta i det.' Transcript of *Porg*, no. 3, May-June 1937, 7, Arninge: 2B: 7.
82 Circular, Message no. 3, Central Election Bureau to Group Leaders, Amsterdam, 11 January 1935, 1, NIOD: 123, 2.01: 514. Cf.: Turlach O Broin, 'Mail-Order Demagogues: The NSDAP School for Speakers, 1928–34', *Journal of Contemporary History* 51, no. 4 (1 October 2016), 728, https://doi.org/10.1177/0022009415609681.
83 Booklet, *Propaganda-instructie voor den Kring*, Utrecht, 1 September 1934, 9–11, NIOD: 123, 2.01: 526.
84 Booklet, *Tjänsteföreskrifter för NSAP*, 15 January 1937, 28, Arninge: 2B1: 1.
85 E.g. *Vetlanda-Posten*, no. 92, 19 November 1935, 1.
86 Circular no. 22, 'Kamporder', Stockholm, 16 March 1934; transcript of: Circular no. 24, 'Kamporder', Stockholm, 12 February 1934, Arninge: 2B: 1.
87 21 April 1939, Lindholm diary.
88 Memorandum to Police Constable, reg. NSAP meeting, 16 November 1934, Arninge: 2C: 2.
89 Circular, 'Bericht' no. 1/1936, Amsterdam. 8 January 1936, NIOD: 123, 2.01: 516.

90 E.g.: Memorandum, re. Gösta Hallberg-Cuula and propaganda, November 1934, 1–2, Arninge: 5, vol. 28, f. 2; Report, regarding pasting, 9 July 1937, Arninge: 2C: 8; Memorandum, re. report of pasting, 20 June 1935, Arninge: 2C: 3.
91 Message from Ragnar Lind, in: Transcript of memorandum, regarding NSAP, 24 March 1938, 2 [821], Arninge: 2B: 9.
92 'ty det är *polisens sak*, att uppspåra vilka som klistrat', [underlined in original], Letter, Lindholm to Lundahl, Ljusdal, 21 August 2935, Marieberg: NSAP/SSS, vol. 1.
93 ' … een bijeenkomst van N.S.B.ers iets anders is dan een vergadering van democraten. Onze bijeenkomsten dienen te getuigen van den nieuwen geest der Nat.Soc. Beweging; de belangstellende of slechts nieuwsgierige bezoeker, zoowel als de tegenstander … dient vanaf het betreden van het gebouw … voortdurend in aanraking te komen met dien nieuwen geest … Daartoe dient echter een ieder, die in het voorbereiden, dan wel tijdens of na de bijeenkomst een taak ten uitvoer te brengen heeft, deze te vervullen met alle strijdlust, toewijding en zorg, die een goed N.S.B.er kenmerken.' Booklet, *Uitvoeringsbepalingen voor de Propaganda*, VI.1, The Hague, 2.19.049: 2.
94 'De versiering dient uitdrukking te geven aan een wel opgewekte, doch overigen ernstige, min of meer stram-vastberaden sfeer.' ibid. VI.5.
95 Ibid. VI.4–7.
96 'Möteslokalen bör så gott sig göra låter vara dekorerad med fanor, nationalsocialistiska kampparoller o. dyl.' *Tjänsteföreskrifter för NSAP*, 15 January 1937, 30, Arninge: 2B1: 1.
97 *Porg*, no. 11, November 1935, 63, Arninge: 2B: 5.
98 Sven Olov Lindholm, 'Soldatliv och Politik, vol. 2' (Photocopy, n.d.), 19, SO Lindholm's Collection, vol. 4, SRA, Marieberg.
99 'Det yttre arbetet är ju oerhört viktigt, ty utan nytt folk så bliver det stagnation, för att kunna få nytt folk fordras talare och sådana hava vi ingen uppsjö på precis.' Letter, Dch. Gerhardsson to Po. Gunnar Svalander, 18 June 1935, Kalmar, 1, Marieberg: NSAP/SSS, vol. 3, Southern District (1934–6).
100 Letter, Kpch. [name illegible] to Ppch., Vittsjö, 20 July 1938, Marieberg: NSAP/SSS, vol. 3, Skåne (1938).
101 Letter, [name illegible] to Erik Fahl, Hässleholm, 8 February 1937, Marieberg: NSAP/SSS, vol. 4, Hässleholm (1937–8).
102 Lindholm more than once strained his voice during his extensive propaganda tours, e.g.: 12 June 1937, Lindholm diary.
103 'Det har nämligen kommit därhän, att några enstaka av partiets talare hålla på att arbeta ut sig, under det att de nya talarna aldrig ordentligt kunna komma igång. […] Är det inte fortfarande så på de flesta håll, att *om icke den önskade talaren kan erhållas, så låter man bli att anordna möten?*' Emphasis in original. *Porg*, no. 9, September 1935, 52, Arninge: 2B: 5.
104 Alg. Propaganda Leider, 'Instructie voor Sprekers', Hilversum, 1 September 1934, 1–2, NIOD: 123, 2.01: 501.
105 Circular, Mussert to the Regional Leaders, Propaganda Inspectors, et al., Utrecht, 6 September 1934, NIOD: 123, 1.1: 23. See also: Booklet, *Diensten Afdeeling III*, I.1–5, NIOD: 123, 2.01, 394.
106 As elaborated in a later version of the arrangements, see: Booklet, *7: Diensten Afdeeling 3*, Utrecht, 25 July 1936, Spr.D.1–8, NIOD: 123, 2.01: 527.
107 *Instructie voor de propaganda in den Kring*, Utrecht, 1 September 1934, 11, NIOD: 123, 2.01: 526.

108 Addition to 'Instructie voor de Propaganda in den Kring', VIII, 8-9, NIOD: 123, 2.01: 526. *Tjänsteföreskrifter för NSAP*, 15 January 1937, 30, Arninge: 2B1: 1.
109 See e.g.: Letter, Tjf. Ps. to Sten Liljeborg, Hallsberg, 15 April 1935, Marieberg: NSAP/SSS, vol. 4, Hallsberg (1935).
110 See, for instance, one local leader's enthusiastic report of the 'conquest' of Katwijk in the first years: Letter, Haarlem Circle Leader to Mussert, Haarlem, 9 May 1933, NIOD: 123, 1.1: 16. See also the need to start meetings in Zeelandic Flanders: Letter, D. Bruis to H.J. van Houten, ter Neuze, 25 February 1933, NIOD: 123, 2.01: 395.
111 Report, W.A. Driessen, Re. Meeting 24 November 1934 at den Burg (Texel), Amsterdam. 26 November 1934, NIOD: 123, 2.55: 2003.
112 *Instructie voor de propaganda in den Kring*, Utrecht, 1 September 1934, 9-12, NIOD: 123, 2.01: 526.
113 *Tjänsteföreskrifter för NSAP*, 15 January 1937, 27-31, Arninge: 2B1: 1.
114 E.g.: Transcript of meeting programme, Norrtälje, 20 February 1938, 3pm, Arninge: 2B: 9; Meeting programme, Auditorium, Stockholm, 13 November 1933, 8 pm, Arninge: 2C: 1a.
115 E.g. 10 July, 19 July, 7 August, 8 August, 14 August 1933, Lindholm diary.
116 Letter, A.S. Plekker to Head Dep. III, Heemstede, 7 January 1938, 2, NIOD: 123, 1.4: 284, which emphasizes that the point of gravity of the party was in North- and South-Holland.
117 Damsma and Schumacher, *Hier Woont een NSB'er*, 15; Jonge, *Het Nationaal-Socialisme in Nederland*, 101.
118 See the report summary of all travel for the 1935 convention: 'Uittreksel uit rapporten van reizen gemaakt ten behoeve der landdagorganisatie', Amsterdam, April 1935, 1-6, NIOD: 123, 1.1: 36. For the convention in The Hague that year, Mussert demanded at least two-thirds of all members be present: Order, Mussert to Circle Leaders, Utrecht, 12 September 1935, NIOD: 123, 1.1: 39.
119 Appendix to financial report for NSB HQ for 1936, Accountancy Office J. van Beek, Haarlem, 6 April 1937, 3 (Lasten), NIOD: 123, 1.1: 69.
120 'de autonomie der kringen volledig opheffen'. Report, B.H. Faddegon, 'Eenige beschouwingen naar aanleiding van de uitslag van de verkiezingen, gehouden voor de Provinciale Staten', Bussum, 28 April 1935, 6, NIOD: 123, 2.55: 2003.
121 Police memorandum, Overview of National Socialism in Sweden, NSAP, 5 May 1935, 15-7, Arninge: 2B: 4.
122 Letter transcript, Lindholm to Lööw, Rönninge, 20 January 1986, 1, Marieberg: SO Lindholm, vol. 5.
123 E.g.: Letter, Dk to A. Persson, 26 June 1934, Marieberg: NSAP/SSS, vol. 3, Södra Distriktet (1934); or, Letter to H. Emilsson, 29 June 1937, Marieberg: NSAP/SSS, vol. 3, Värmland (1936-8).
124 '*Botilsäter* tycks vara alldeles borta. Sedan formationen bildades har vi icke hört något dårifrån [sic]. Intet meddelande, ingen redovisning: På brev svarar icke formationschefen. Han är lantbrukare och just nu ha ju dessa visserligen mycket att stå i, men det är att lägga märke till att formationen bildades redan den 3.2.37, varför man tycker han haft tillfälle att låta höra av sig åtminstone någon gång.' Letter, Herbert Hultberg to H. Emilsson, 29 June 1937, Marieberg: NSAP/SSS, vol. 3, Värmland (1936-8).
125 Lindholm mentioned to his brother that they were used to terrible finances by 1935: Letter, Sven Olov Lindholm to Sigfrid Lindholm, Mjölby, 8 October 1935, Marieberg: NSAP/SSS, vol. 1, Lindholm (1935-8).

126 E.g.: Minutes protocol, meeting Fridlevstad, 29 April 1934, and Monthly Report, May, Fridlevstad, Marieberg: NSAP/SSS, vol. 6.
127 Lindholm Interview, sec. 00259: B.
128 When the NSAP broke away from the SNSP, the latter attacked Lindholm as despotic, unchivalrous and lacking in basic organizational ability. SNSP Circular no. 6, G. Ringström to all SNSP members, Gothenburg, [1933], Marieberg: Otto Hallberg's archive, vol. 2 (NS parties, 1927–63).
129 '1e overstroomt de afd. Organisatie de geheele N.S.B. med circulaires, verbeterende circulaires, aanvullende circulaires, circulaires die elkaar op vitale punten tegen spreken. En door deze waterval van papier worden de plaatselyke instanties verward en geremd in hun eigen werk ... ', Letter, van der Goes van Naters, J.J.C. Schreuder, E. Horsting, and P.J.S. Visser to Van Geelkerken, Apeldoorn, 4 July 1934, NIOD: 123, 1.6: 341.
130 'instede een centrum van bezieling te zyn, dat de *heele* Beweging voortstuwt en opzweept, merkt men er niet veel anders van dan boekenleggers in verschillend formaat en met verschillende opdruk: een klein burgerlyk lapjes winkel gedoe, dat voor buitenstaanders alleen maar belachelyk is, en de aandacht van de N.S.Bers afleidt van het groote doel en de groote taak naar prutserige byomstandigheden.', ibid. 4.
131 As discussed at a HQ meeting in 1936 for instance: Minutes for meeting 19 August 1936, 33–4, in: Book, meeting minutes *Algemeene Raad*, NIOD: 123, 1.3: 276.
132 'Er is niets wat lamlendiger werkt en den goeden geest meer aantast dan gekanker en kletspraatjes ... ' Booklet, *NSB-126a*, 'Plichten van den Weerman', 36, NIOD: 123, 2.14: 1005.
133 'Bergen op Zoom en gekanker is synoniem.' Inspection report regarding Brabant, John Boddé, Eindhoven, 14 September 1934, 2, NIOD: 123, 2.55: 2000.
134 Some described this as a historical flaw in the Dutch character, e.g: Letter, W. de Rijke to Mussert, Haarlem, 3 March 1934, 1, NIOD: 123, 1.1: 22.
135 Letter, Head Dep. I to G.J.K. Baron van Lynden van Horstwaerde, Amsterdam, 25 July 1935, 1–2, NIOD: 123, 2.30: 1337.
136 'Vroeger heb ik eens geklaagd over de betrekkelyke wanorde op het Hoofdkwartier, doch ik schreef er dan tevens by, dat ik het er zoo gezellig vond. Ik genoot van de enthousiaste verhalen, over colportage, etc. Telkens, wanneer ik in Utrecht geweest was, gevoelde ik mij tevens enthousiaster N.S.B.er. Er was élan, geestdrift, doch er werd niet gewerkt. Nu, nu wordt er gewerkt, doch er is geen enthousiasme, zooals toen, een bezoek aan het Hoofd-kwartier [sic] heeft nu op my den zelfden invloed als een bezoek aan een Bureau voor Vreemdelingenverkeer. Ik heb antwoord gekregen, op de vragen, die ik stelde. [...] Wy worden momenteel van uit Utrecht "beadministreerd", en wy wenschen van uit Utrecht aangevoerd te worden, en aangevuurd.' Letter, T. van de Weide to Mussert, Overveen, 20 June 1933, 1–2, 3, NIOD: 123, 1.1: 16.
137 'Laat ons hopen, dat de idee – het organisme – NIET ONDERGAAT door de organisatie. [...] Want de 80 of 90% dooie leden – zijn dood gemaakt – door organisatie en op andere wijze – want ieder, werd lid met en door enthousiasme.' Letter, to G. van Duyl, Amsterdam, 9 May 1936, 1, 4, NIOD: 123, 2.04: 719.
138 'Man torde icke inom något annat politiskt parti kunna finna en större självuppoffring från medlemmarnas sida att utan någon som helst ersättning helt hängiva sig åt partiets verksamhet. Detta kan till stor del förklaras härmed, att partiets huvudkader utgöres av ungdomar, som med glödande entusiasm använda

största delen av sin fritid för partiets framgång.' Police memorandum, 'Översikt över nationalsocialismen i Sverige', 5 October 1935, 53, Arninge: 2B: 4.
139 Police memorandum, 'angående nationalsocialismens utveckling i Sverige', 1924–40, 4, Arninge: 2B: 14.
140 'det är svårt att få "pojkarna" att arbeta självständigt och det måste till för att vi skall kunna hålla det hela igång. [...] Då jag hemkommer från en turné har man endast skött det allra nödvändigaste emedan man ej förstår att handla på egen hand.' Letter, Gerhardsson to Gunnar Svalander, Kalmar, 18 June 1935, Marieberg: NSAP/SSS, vol. 3, Södra Distriktet (1934–6).
141 Dammberg, Nazismen i Skaraborgs Län, 21.
142 Letter, Formation 225 to Ppch. Erik Fahl, Arvika, 18 September 1937, Marieberg: NSAP/SSS, vol. 4, Arvika (1937).
143 E.g.: Letter, H. Wennberg to Gunnar Svalander, Lund, 9 January 1934, Marieberg: NSAP/SSS, vol. 1, Gunnar Svalander; Letter, Helge Burman to Prag, Härnösand, 4 June 1934, Marieberg: NSAP/SSS, vol. 1, Helge Burman.
144 Letter to G.V. Jönsson [Southern District Leader], 22 February 1938, Marieberg: NSAP/SSS, vol. 3, Skåne (1938).
145 Secret memorandum, regarding National Socialism in Sweden, 16 June–15 August 1937, 5, Arninge: 2B: 7.
146 See, for instance, Police memorandum, regarding 4th *landsting* in Uppsala, 3, Arninge: 2C: 8.
147 Makt, 1936, cited in: Armas Sastamoinen, *Hitlers Svenska Förtrupper* (Stockholm: Federativs, 1947), 21.
148 ' ... vi här helt kunna taga upp konkurrensen med motståndarna och även överträffa dem.' NSAP experience memorandum, Gothenburg elections, October 1934, 141a-43, in: Report concerning NSAP SA-troops, 1935, Marieberg: Eric Wärenstam, vol. 35.
149 'Vi måste nämligen komma ihåg, att vi av motståndarna utmålas och betraktas som barnsliga upptågsmakare. Det kan därför vara onödigt att underblåsa denna uppfattning.' ibid. 143.
150 Lindholm later claimed the party leadership never seriously considered a violent overthrow of the government: Lindholm interview, 00262: B.

Chapter 3

1 Stanley G. Payne, *A History of Fascism, 1914–1945* (Wisconsin: University of Wisconsin Press, 1995), 7.
2 E.g. Roger Eatwell, 'The Concept and Theory of Charismatic Leadership', *Totalitarian Movements and Political Religions* 7, no. 2 (2006), 141–56.
3 Martin E. Spencer, 'What Is Charisma?', *The British Journal of Sociology* 24, no. 3 (1973), 341–5.
4 J. P. Stern, *Hitler: The Führer and the People* (London: Flamingo, 1984), 28–9.
5 R. J. B. Bosworth, *Mussolini* (London: Arnold, 2002), 314–5.
6 Ian Kershaw, *The 'Hitler Myth': Image and Reality in the Third Reich* (Oxford: Clarendon, 1987), 2–3.
7 Johan Stenfeldt, *Renegater: Nils Flyg och Sven Olov Lindholm i gränslandet mellan kommunism och nazism* (Lund: Nordic Academic Press, 2019); see also his article from the same year in: Johan Stenfeldt, 'The Fascist Who Fought for World

Peace: Conversions and Core Concepts in the Ideology of the Swedish Nazi Leader Sven Olov Lindholm', *Fascism: Journal of Comparative Fascism Studies* 8, (2019): 9–35.
8   Jan Meyers, *Mussert: Een Politiek Leven* (Amsterdam: Uitgeverij De Arbeiderspers, 1984).
9   Wärenstam, *Fascismen och Nazismen i Sverige 1920–1940*, chaps 4–5.
10 Victor Lundberg, 'Within the Fascist World of Work: Sven Olov Lindholm, Ernst Jünger and the Pursuit of Proletarian Fascism in Sweden, 1933–1945', in *New Political Ideas in the Aftermath of the Great War*, ed. Salvador Alessandro and Anders G. Kjøstvedt (Basingstoke: Palgrave Macmillan, 2016), 199–217.
11 Havenaar, *Anton Adriaan Mussert*, 41–4.
12 Philip Rees, *Biographical Dictionary of the Extreme Right since 1890* (New York: Harvester Wheatsheaf, 1990), 274.
13 Pollmann, *Mussert & Co*, chap. 1.
14 Groeneveld, *Zwaard van de Geest*, 128–31.
15 Maurizio Bach, 'Mussolini und Hitler als charismatische Führer', in *Der Faschismus in Europa: Wege der Forschung*, ed. Thomas Schlemmer and Hans Woller (München: Oldenbourg Wissenschaftsverlag, 2014), 109.
16 Cf. Stein U. Larsen, 'Charisma from below? The Quisling Case in Norway', *Totalitarian Movements and Political Religions* 7, no. 2 (2006), 235–44.
17 Lindholm, 'Soldatliv och Politik', I,1.
18 Ibid. 1–3.
19 Report [copy in abstract], Gothenburg Detective Police (Criminal Department), 19 March 1935, B.D. nr. 342, P1279: 1, Arninge.
20 December 1932, Lindholm diary. Lindholm's visit came right at the moment of Strasser's break with Hitler in a disagreement over political strategy – Strasser was ousted as Organization Leader before the end of the month, and denounced as a traitor by January: Orlow, I, 291ff.
21 Lindholm, 'Soldatliv och Politik', I, 96–101.
22 Lindholm, 'Lindholm Interview', 00256: B.
23 Lindholm, 'Soldatliv och Politik', II, 12–3.
24 Ibid. 30.
25 Especially after Vera became involved with Göran Oredsson, leader of the neo-Nazi *Nordiska Rikspartiet* (Nordic National Party) – Vera herself briefly became leader of this successor to the SSS.
26 Esaias Tegnér (1782–1846) and Viktor Rydberg (1828–95) were highly regarded as the two greatest Swedish poets of the nineteenth century, with patriotic themes strongly focused on the Old Nordic era (Viking era). Verner von Heidenstam (1859–1940) was an important contemporary writer of patriotic poetry in the same tradition. Johan Runeberg (1804–77) and Bertel Gripenberg (1878–1946) were both Finno-Swedish (*svekkomen*) writers. The former was renowned for his Finnish epic *The Tales of Ensign Steel*, popular among soldiers; the latter was a nationalist poet who fought in the White Army during the Finnish Civil War, and joined the Lapua movement in the late 1920s.
27 Lundberg, 'Within the Fascist World of Work'.
28 Nathaniël Kunkeler, 'Sven Olov Lindholm and the Literary Inspirations of Swedish Fascism', *Scandinavian Journal of History* 44, no. 1 (2019), 77–102.
29 Sejersted, *The Age of Social Democracy*, 125.
30 'Bevare oss, gamla soldater, för all längtan efter bekvämlighet och för alla kinkigheter. Men det är bara *ordning* vi vill ha i allt.', Note from Lindholm, 1935 (Spring), Marieberg: NSAP/SSS Archive, vol. 1.

31   Police memorandum, S. Fransson regarding splits in the NSAP, 27 February 1937, 1, Arninge: XII 64: 1.
32   1 November 1936; 9-13 November 1936, Lindholm diary.
33   Pollmann, *Mussert & Co*, 28.
34   Because of a lung infection, acquired after bathing in a frozen lake mid-winter. Anton's father was, though severe and stately, also prone to occasional recklessness.
35   Meyers, *Mussert*, 15-8.
36   Havenaar, *Anton Adriaan Mussert*, 13-4.
37   Meyers, *Mussert*, 32-4.
38   For a critical account of Mussert's career as civil engineer, see 'Mussert als waterstaatsingenieur, 1920-1934', in Pollmann, *Mussert & Co*, 28-50.
39   Meyers, *Mussert*, 36-8.
40   For further detail and the political background to this treaty, see: Schuursma, *Het Onaannemelijk Tractaat*; Jonge, *Crisis en Critiek der Democratie*, 279-82.
41   Anton Mussert, *Nagelaten Bekentenissen: Verantwoording en Celbrieven van de NSB-Leider*, ed. Gerard Groeneveld (Nijmegen: Vantilt, 2005).
42   *Het Proces Mussert* (Amsterdam: Rijksinstituut voor Oorlogsdocumentatie, 1987), xii.
43   Bauerkämper, 'Fascism Without Borders', 219.
44   Havenaar, *De NSB tussen Nationalisme en 'Volkse' Solidariteit*, 15, 86-8, 131.
45   Kunkeler, 'Narratives of Decline in the NSB', 213-7.
46   As noted by one commentator, in: 'S.O. Lindholm nazistledaren', *Göteborgs-Posten*, no. 283, 5 December 1933, 11.
47   Anton Mussert, *Richtlijnen voor een Nederlandsch-Belgische Overeenkomst* (Utrecht: A. Oosthoek, 1927).
48   Huberts, *In de Ban van een Beter Verleden*, 105-6.
49   Kwiet, 'Zur Geschichte der Mussert-Bewegung', 174; Lindholm interview, 262: A, *c.* 30 mins. Lindholm did read Thomas Carlyle's *On Heroes* in 1935.
50   Hitler, *Mein Kampf*, 1:1139 [88] ff.
51   'Ty en ledare kan ej framtrollas genom reklam eller tomma deklamationer, han verkar genom *makten av sin personlighet*', Per Dahlberg, 'Ledning och efterföljelse: Nationalsocialismens grundprinciper', DSN, no. 3, 15 February 1933, 1.
52   *Het Proces Mussert*, 309.
53   Meyers, *Mussert*, 72.
54   Letter, Hofman to d'Ansembourg, Roermond, 5 July 1937, The Hague: 2.19.49: 5.
55   Again, opinions are divided on Lindholm's qualities as a public speaker: Stenfeldt, *Renegater*, 165.
56   E.g.: GHC, 'Nordisk Ungdom på marsch i Stockholm: Clementsson talar', DSN, no. 24, 24 March 1936, 8.
57   E.g.: 'De Landdag: De marsch door Amsterdam', VoVa, no. 14, 6 April 1935, 3.
58   E.g.: 'Där vi kämpa: Nytt storstilat kampmöte med Pl. på Auditorium', DSN, no. 17, 3 March 1937, 5.
59   'Ledarens stabsflagga', DSN, no. 45, 14 June 1936, 5; Minutes for meeting 19 August 1936, in: Book, meeting minutes *Algemeene Raad*, 35, NIOD: 123, 1.3: 276.
60   'Mussert solliciteert: Voor .... reclamepop', *De Tijd*, no. 28699, 24 March 1936, 2.
61   ' ... de napoleontische gestalte met den imposanten kop, waarin de mond als een zware groef de wilskracht accentueert', gkj [George Kettmann Jr], 'Geestdrift in Utrecht: "In het teeken van den driehoek"', VoVa, no. 41, 14 October 1933, 3.
62   'Meddelande från Plg', DSN, no. 47, 19 June 1935, 2.
63   *Porg*, no. 11, November 1935, 66, Arninge: 2B: 5.

64 E.g.: VoVa, no. 39, 29 September 1934, 1.
65 DSN, nos 21–6, 24 May-28 June 1934.
66 'Militärdisciplin inom grupperna', Gothenburg SA-inquiry police report, 1935, 141.
67 'Årstinget: en kraftig manifestation av nordisk frihetsvilja! Femhundra deltagare. Värdefulla föredrag. Imponerande uppmarsch. Lindholm ovationsartat hyllad', DSN, no. 13, 11 June 1933, 1, 8.
68 Gefem, 'Frihetsfacklor i Stockholm: Stor uppmarsch med massmöte! Partiledaren talar', DSN, no. 12, 13 February 1935, 1, 6.
69 'Som en hotande åska fyllde applådernas dån den väldiga cirkuslokalen! Ledaren hade talat och följet hade smitts samman till en kampberedd enhet! Under det Lindholm talat hade all tvekan försvunnit, problem, som man funderat på i veckor, hade lösts, linjerna had klarnat, kampmålen stodo tydliga och konkreta för ens ögon och viljan till fortsatt kamp hade blivit mera järnhård än någonsin!', Munin, 'Stormöte i Göteborg! Lindholm anklagar och kräver svensk neutralitetspolitik', DSN, no. 89, 13 November 1935, 5.
70 Newspapers created fictionalized narratives of a narrow range of enthusiastic emotions, while the reality of it was rather more complicated: Berezin, *Making the Fascist Self*, 97.
71 Branch report, Örebro, September 1935, Marieberg: NSAP/SSS, vol. 6, Västra Distriktets Rapporter (1935).
72 gkj [George Kettmann Jr], 'Mussert spreekt te Amsterdam: Een avond van strijdbare geestdrift', VoVa, no. 37, 16 September 1933.
73 'De Landdag – De marsch door Amsterdam', VoVa, no. 14, 6 April 1935, 3.
74 'Dan maakte Mussert's bekende gebaar, als maaide hij met één streek het rijpe koren – de luide ovaties verklonken', ibid.
75 'Mussert in Amsterdam', VoVa, no. 6, 8 February 1936, 1.
76 Maarten Cornelis van den Toorn, *Wij Melden U den Nieuwen Tijd: Een Beschouwing van het Woordgebruik van de Nederlandse Nationaal-Socialisten* ('s-Gravenhage: SDU, 1991), 9.
77 On the 'charismatic bond', see: Aristotle Kallis, 'Fascism, "Charisma" and Charismatisation: Weber's Model of "Charismatic Domination" and Interwar European Fascism', *Totalitarian Movements and Political Religions* 7, no. 1 (2006): 25–43.
78 'Kunnen we er zeker van zyn, dat de N.S.B. eene fascistische organisatie bedoelt te zyn.' [underlined in original], Letter, T. van de Weide to Mussert, 20 June 1933, Overveen, 1, NIOD: 123, 1.1: 16.
79 'De fascistische wereldbeschouwing stelt tegenover het dood gewicht van meerderheden, de levenwekkende kracht van de persoonlijkheid. Zij wenscht een sterk gezag; zij wenscht persoonlijke leiding. Wij zullen in eigen organisatie daarin natuurlijk het voorbeeld moeten geven', 'Onze Leider aan het woord: De richtlijnen uitgestippeld'. VoVa, no. 2, 14 January 1933, 4.
80 This point was reiterated several times throughout the 1930s, e.g.: 'Het leidersbeginsel', VoVa, no. 6, 8 February 1936, 2.
81 'Maar de massa wil persoonsvereering, de massa wil een symbool; zou er "begeisterung" uit kunnen gaan van van [sic] een dagelyks bestuur van b.v. 3 personen, een driemans-schap? [...] En zoo moet ook U het symbool voor onze Beweging zyn, ook U moeten de de [sic] menschen niet kennen, ze moeten U niet kennen als een gewoon sterveling, ze moeten U alleen zien en hooren op het podium, of voor de troep.' Letter, T. van de Weide to Mussert, 20 June 1933, Overveen, 2, NIOD: 123, 1.1: 16.

82 'Naar aanleiding van het feit, dat wy in U het voorbeeld zien van een goed Vaderlander en een oprecht fascist en tevens hopende, dat hem dit voorbeeld een leiddraad moge zyn in zyn verder leven, hebben wy de vryheid genomen hem naar U ANTON, ADRIAAN te noemen', Letter, Group Leader van de Waal, to Mussert, 4 December 1933, Hillegersberg, NIOD: 123, 1.1: 16.
83 ' ... jag var inte så särdeles förtjust i det, men jag måste tyvärr acceptera. Faktum är nämligen att det gjorde starkt intryck på både anhängare och åskådare – de ville ha sådant.' Lindholm interview, 00259: B, c. 7 mins.
84 Letter, Gustaf Johansson to Lindholm, 27 July 1934, Björkeryd, 1, Marieberg: NSAP/SSS, vol. 3, Södra Distriktet (1934).
85 Letter, Dpch to Apch Agnér (branch 69), 27 April 1935, Kristianstad, Marieberg: NSAP/SSS, vol. 4, Kristiandstad (1935–8).
86 'De hade inga ideal att hylla, / de hade ingen Lindholm, de, – som vi.' 'En visa om Tinget', DSN, 1934, transcript in Arninge: 2A: 1.
87 Durandal, 'Mussert naar Indië', VoVa, no. 29, 20 July 1935, 1.
88 ' ... het onbelangrijke feit, dat iemand, die Indië bezoekt, ook weer terugkomt ... ', 'Mussert kwam aan: Partij-poezie', De Tijd, no. 28370, 10 September 1935, 5.
89 Paulus, 'De trommels van Mussert', VoVa, no. 33, 17 August 1935, 6; Gabriel Geelmuijden, 'Het woord van den leider', VoVa, no. 8, 22 February 1936, 6.
90 E.g.: Sven-Olov, 'Svensk Morgon', DSN, no. 9, 1 March 1934, 6; S. L-m, 'Norrskensbön', DSN, no. 12, 13 February 1935, 5; Sven Olov, 'Folket som slår', DSN, no. 51, 3 July 1935, 4; S. L-m, 'Tre år i kamp', DSN, no. 7, 25 January 1936, 5; Sven Olov, 'Ett sommarminne', DSN, no. 88, 14 November 1936, 6.
91 See, for instance, 15 March and 24 November 1935, Lindholm diary.
92 'Propagandanyhet!', DSN, no. 18, 6 March 1937, 3. Originally the party leadership seems to have considered the production company Edition da Capo instead, who would have produced the records in Germany, at a total cost of c. 1,300 kronor. Most likely the final product cost a little less than that, so that the NSAP could profit a little over 1,000 kronor from this endeavour.
93 Lindholm postcard, 'S.O. Lindholm: Ledare för N.S.A.P.', Arninge: 2C: 6.
94 E.g.: Circular no. 13, Van Bilderbeek (Dep. VII), to Chief of Materials et al., Utrecht, 5 June 1936, The Hague, 2.19.49: 4.
95 Lindholm admitted that he generally did not have any understanding of party finances: Lindholm interview, 00259: B, c. 16 mins.
96 Brochure, Programme for the third Landdag, Amsterdam, 30 March 1935, 49, NIOD: 123, 2.55: 2004.
97 'Door de blaadjes vlug na elkaar door de vingers te laten gaan, ontstaat een levend beeld van den Algemeen Leider', Circular no. 66, Hilversum, 23 July 1934, NIOD: 123, 2.01: 501.
98 Brochure, Programme for the fourth Landdag, The Hague, 5 October 1935, 19, NIOD: 123, 1.1: 37.
99 Circular, Publisher H. Hoogewoud Jr., to all participants of the Regional Landdag, Amsterdam, 28 April 1934, NIOD: 123, 1.1: 25.
100 Cf. Hitler and the NSDAP 1924–6, in: Orlow, The History of the Nazi Party, 1919–33, 1:53–5.
101 ' ... en aldrig sviktande, sin ledare orubbligt tillgiven stamptrupp av hakkorskämpar', 'Speciellt regelemente för SA, SAR', Gothenburg SA-inquiry police report, 1935, 14.
102 Transcript and extract from: Porg, 1/1935, 2, Arninge: 2B: 5.

103 'Förväntansfulla se kämparna ute i bygderna mot Stockholm i pingst. Efter ännu ett år av kamp, trohet och offer skola de nu få tillfälle att komma tillsammans med kamrater från hela landet och få möta sin Ledare ... ', Ragnar Lind, NSAP circular, no. 100, 25 April 1938, Arninge: 2A: 2.

104 ' ... det är kämpande bataljoner som marschera upp i huvudstaden för att samlas kring sin unge hövding', -rot [Nils Dahlrot, most likely], 'NSAP samlas till ting: Stockholm står i hakkorsets tecken under pingstdagarna', DSN, no. 44, 8 June 1935, 1.

105 'Lindholm hade försökt avstyra personliga hyllningar, men det var det enda på tinget som misslyckades – fullkomligt spontant brusade hellropen emot honom ur tusende hjärtans djup', '"Judeväldet och utplundringen över vårt svenska folk skall brytas!" Årstingets enda men viktiga beslut!', DSN, no. 22, 31 May 1934, 8.

106 'En utomstående kan inte förstå den hjärtliga kontakt som vid ett tillfälle som detta råder mellan Ledare och följe, men vi vet att denna naturliga frivilliga solidaritet, grundad på själarnas frändskap endast finnes hos oss', 'Genom nationalsocialismen vinnes frihet och bröd', DSN, no. 45, 12 June 1935, 5.

107 Lindholm interview, 00259: B, *c.* 6 mins.

108 'Onze Gewestelijke Landdag', VoVa, no. 18, 5 May 1934, 8–9.

109 'Het wordt dan geen hulde aan den Leider, geen mensch vergoding. Integendeel wij scharen ons rond onzen Leider, wij zweeren trouw, en de Leider neemt dat aan en stelt zich *daarom juist* met ons voor het aangezicht van den Schepper', Letter, John Boddé, [date and place unknown, probably 1935, Hilversum], NIOD: 123, 1.1: 37.

110 'Wilt heden nu treden voor God den Heere, / Hem boven al loven van herten seer'.

111 'Dan beleven wij een moment waar men een jaar mee vooruit kan en wat ze nooit meer vergeten. We moeten toch pakken in hun doepste [*sic*] wezen', Letter, John Boddé, [date and place unknown, probably 1935, Hilversum], NIOD: 123, 1.1: 37.

112 'Onze Beweging is te groot dat dat wij, hoe graag ik het ook zou willen, persoonlijk contact kunnen onderhouden. Maar al kan dat dan niet dan wil dat daarom nog niet zeggen dat er geen mistieke band zou zijn die ons samenbindt en samen houdt', Letter, E.J. Roskam (Raad voor Volksche Cultuur) to Mussert, Amsterdam, 1 November 1936, 2.

113 Ibid. 3.

114 27 March, 19–20 April 1935, Lindholm diary.

115 Letter, Sven Olov Lindholm to Sigrid Lindholm, Härlanda, 19 April 1935, Marieberg: NSAP/SSS, vol. 1, Sven Olov Lindholm (1935–8).

116 17 May 1935, Lindholm diary.

117 ' ... persoonlijk, uiting te geven van mijn gevoelens van oprechte vereering', Letter, B.W.F. Paauwe to Mussert, 's-Gravenhage, 1 April 1935, 1, NIOD: 123, 1.1:36.

118 ' ... de gloedvolle woorden die U tot ons hebt gesproken [...] mijn heele wezen in dienst stellen der N.S.B. om als vrouw U zoveel mogelijk mee te helpen aan het grootsche werk tot heil van ons Vaderland', Letter, J. Stoop to Mussert, The Hague, 1 April 1935, 1–3, NIOD: 123, 1.1:36.

119 'Het hoogtepunt was voor ons allen echter wel de figuur van onze Algemeen Leider heel in de verte te zien staan, fel belicht en hoog boven zijn duizenden getrouwen, als op de voorplecht van zijn admiraalschip!', Letter, H.J. Raad to Mr and Mrs Mussert, Hilversum, 'Sunday evening', NIOD: 123, 1.1: 36.

120 Circular (summons), 'MUSSERT roept zijn getrouwen op', Utrecht, September 1937, NIOD: 123, 1.1: 71.

121 Heijningen, *De Muur van Mussert*, 109; 'De negende october: De getrouwen op den Goudsberg', VoVa, no. 42, 15 October 1937, 4.

122 Newspaper clipping, 'Mussert geeft rekenschap van zijn daden: Rede op de Hagespraak te Lunteren', *De Telegraaf*, 10 October 1937, NIOD: KA II, 1702.
123 Newspaper clipping, 'De crisis in de N.S.B.: De derde "hagespraak" te Lunteren', *Dordrechts Dagblad*, 11 October 1937, NIOD: KA II, 1702.
124 Circular, Mussert, Utrecht, NIOD: 123, 1.1: 71.
125 ' ... betuigen hiermede hun onwankelbare trouw aan den Leider', 'Trouw tot in de dood!', Booklet, 'Bijeenkomst 9 October 1937 Lunteren', Kring 23 Groep 1, NIOD: 123, 1.1: 71.
126 As Willem Huberts points out, the NSB was the only one of the dozens of fascist movements in the Netherlands which had the same leader throughout its entire existence. Huberts, *In de Ban van een Beter Verleden*, 196–7.
127 'Ofta förekommer i våra motståndares propaganda agget mot den nordiska ledarprincipen. Han förväxlar vår ledare med orientaliska avgudar och småtyska gauführer. Vår ledare är en svensk folkledare och ingenting annat. Den främste bland kamrater', Circular, Stockholm, 18 September 1938, in: Police memorandum, concerning NSAP, 1, Arninge: 2B: 11.
128 'Våroffensiven begynner! Lindholm och Landahl i främsta linjen!', DSN, no. 5, 15 March 1933, 5.
129 'Med Lindholm i fält: Genom arbete o. försakelse till seger!', DSN, no. 20, 21 August 1933, 1, 8; 'Lindholm erövrar Norrland!', DSN, no. 9, 1 March 1934, 6; 'Lindholm till Norrland', DSN, no. 7, 26 January 1935, 1, 6; 'Lindholms fälttåg: Genom socialistisk offervilja förmår NSAP:s propaganda nå hela landet', DSN, no. 51, 3 July 1935, 1, 6; 'Drag ut i fält! Sommarkriget börjar – anmäl dig till närmaste propagandalag!', DSN, no. 40, 26 May 1937, 1, 6; 'Under Tyrsflaggan: Med propagandalaget i fält', DSN, no. 61, 11 August 1937, 1, 6; 'Ut i fält! Skänk livsmedel åt våra aktiva frontmän!', DSN, no. 43, 15 June 1938, 5.
130 ' ... i sista hand är vår kamp en vilje sak, det är viljan till liv som tvingar oss till hart när hur stora offer som helst, och i detta liksom alla andra fall är det Lindholm som är vårt föredöme', Letter, Do. to Oscar Larsson, 6 November 1934, 2, Marieberg: NSAP/SSS, vol. 3, Södra Distriktet (1934).
131 IF. 5–6.
132 'Av *ledningen* för detta nat. soc. parti måste man fordra inte bara att de äro ärliga, dugliga och med sin politiska uppgift väl förtrogna män, utan även att de i sitt personliga föredöme *representera* idéerna. Av en *ledare* själv slutligen, fordrar man, att han *personifierar* idéerna även i sitt liv och sina handlingar ... ', Lindholm, 'Till Sveriges Nationalsocialister!', DSN, no. 1, 25 January 1933, 2.
133 'NSAP och Lindholm äro ett', DSN, no. 38, 19 May 1937, 1.
134 Md, 'Frihetsrörelsens årsdag', DSN, no. 3, 12 January 1935, 2.
135 'Den man, som stått i ledningen för dem, hade svikit – på dem som nu kände sitt ansvar inför folket berodde det nu, om allt skulle störta samman, om offren hitintills skulle varit förgäves. De visste, att de måste handla, och i den dystra januaridagen kom revolutionen. Lindholm höjde sin hand till slag. Lindholm höjde sin hand till förnyad kamp. Kring Lindholm samlades de, den svenska nationalsocialismens äldsta och ärligaste kämpar', Torsten G:son Elg, 'Två år i kamp', DSN, no. 3, 12 January 1935, 1.
136 ' ... han framhöll Lindholm som den man "som skall frälsa svenska folket från deras förtryckare"', Police memorandum, concerning NSAP *kamrataftan*, 30 March 1937, 1, Arninge: XII 64: 1.
137 '*Lindholm* ledar'n skall föra folket ur nöd och sorg', Letter, Gösta Ståhlvärn, Uddevalle, 10 July 1935, Marieberg: NSAP/SSS, vol. 1, Sven Olov Lindholm (1935–8).

138 E.g.: Letter, J.L.S. [name restricted] to C. van der Voort van Zijp, Antwerp, 11 January 1933, NIOD: 123, 2.01: 395; Press release, 'Landestagung der Niederländischen National-Sozialistischen Bewegung', NIOD: 123, 1.1: 86.
139 Mussert, 'Landdagrede van Mussert', VoVa, no. 41, 14 October 1933, 1.
140 Note, Mussert to Her Majesty the Queen, Utrecht, January 1933 at the first *Landdag*; Letter, Secretary of HM the Queen to Mussert, no. 1663, 's-Gravenhage, 7 May 1934, NIOD: 123, 2.01: 2173.
141 'Er is uit zijn verleden als waterstaatsingenieur niets dan goeds bekend. Zijn liefde voor land en volk is onverdacht. Hij is ook niet begonnen met bombardie in een theoretische leegte, doch methodisch als een conscientieus ambtenaar heeft hij het eerste optreden naar buiten voorbereid. Het moet werkelijk allemaal keurig in orde zijn geweest', Newspaper clipping, Oudeis, 'Van Mussert tot Veraart', *M.E.*, 23 January 1933, in: NIOD: KA II, 1701.
142 Newspaper clipping, 'Nationaal-Socialistische Beweging', *Algemeen Handelsblad*, 8 October 1933, NIOD: KA II, 1701.
143 Mussert, 'Uit het ambt ontzet', VoVa, no. 9, 3 March 1934, 1.
144 Homan van der Heide, *Mussert als Ingenieur* (Utrecht: Nenasu, 1944).
145 'Deze jonge hoofd-ingenieur van Rijkswaterstaat, die overdag wegen bouwt en al zijn vrijen tijd besteedt aan den opbouw van een beweging, waarvan hij groote verwachtingen heeft, is een persoonlijkheid, een geboren leider en organisator', L. P., 'In het hoofdkwartier der Nationaal-socialisten', from *Utrechtsch Provinciaal en Stedelijk Dagblad*, quoted in: VoVa, no. 5, 4 February 1933, 3.
146 'De komst van den leider wordt aangekondigd; onder daverend houzee-geroep begeeft Mussert zich door het midden van de zaal naar het podium. In alles betoont Mussert zich de ingenieur: de rechte lijn is de korste weg tusschen twee punten ... ', 'Mussert in Amsterdam', VoVa, no. 6, 8 February 1936, 1.
147 Mussert, 'Mussert blijft ons trouw: Een schrijven van Mussert aan de Provinciale Staten van Utrecht', VoVa, no. 8, 24 February 1934, 1.
148 E.g. The riots in the Jordaan in 1934, and more carefully the Night of the Long Knives in Germany, see Mussert's articles in: VoVa, no. 28, 14 July 1934, 1–2.
149 '*erkent ten volle het Christelijk karakter der natie*' [italicized in original], Mussert, 'Landdagrede van Mussert', VoVa, no. 41, 14 October 1933, 2.
150 Letter, van der Goes van Naters et al. to Cornelis Van Geelkerken, Apeldoorn, 4 July 1934, 3, NIOD: 123, 2.01: 341.
151 Pollmann, *Mussert & Co*, 18. It was precisely in the first years that members and outsiders worried about an insufficiently *Christian* programme in the NSB, see e.g. the Jesuit letter demanding the rejection of atheism: Letter, A. de Lang Jz. to Mussert, Amsterdam, 20 September 1933, NIOD: 123, 1.1: 398.
152 MS speech, Mussert, Lunteren, 'Bergopwaarts', 1937, 8, NIOD: 123, 1.1: 70.
153 'Wie dit al overdenkt voor hem is het geen wonder dat het rommelt ook in ons vaderland. Dit is een wonder, dat de Almachtige het nog langer draagt, dat een goddeloos staatsbestel de wetten van zijn Schepper vertreedt en veracht', MS speech, Mussert, 'De Nood van het Landvolk en het Rechtsherstel dat komt', 1, 6, NIOD: 123, 1.1: 94.
154 E.g.: Newspaper clipping, 'Ir. Mussert aan het woord', *Nieuwe Rotterdamsche Courant*, 9 April 1937, NIOD: KA II, 1702.
155 'Aan het einde van ieder menschenleven komt het er geen steek op aan of het afscheid geschiedt in de gevangenis of in een praalbed ... het komt er alleen op aan, of gij naar eer en geweten uw plicht hebt gedaan tegenover God en de menschen', Mussert, 'De weg omhoog', VoVa, no. 1, 4 January 1936, 1.

156 Cf. Otto Dietrich, 'A Flight Through the Storm and Hitler's Mission', in Mosse, *Nazi Culture*, 291–3.
157 Minutes for meeting 19 August 1936, 32, in: Book, meeting minutes *Algemeene Raad*, NIOD: 123, 1.3: 276.
158 'Welkom!', VoVa, no. 36, 7 September 1935, 1.
159 Hoofd Afd. X, 'Vijf jaar oud', VoVa, no. 2, 8 January 1937, 2.
160 Roger Griffin, *Modernism and Fascism: The Sense of a Beginning under Mussolini and Hitler* (Basingstoke: Palgrave Macmillan, 2007), 4.
161 'Wij staan midden in het tijdvak waarin geschiedenis gemaakt', Mussert, quoted in: Message of the NSB Press-Service, 'De Tweede Hagespraak der N.S.B', 6, NIOD: 123, 2.01: 2006.
162 'dat er een Beweging is ontstaan in ons volk … die haar onverwoestbaarheid heeft getoond en zich geleidelijk gereed maakt om haar historisch aan de orde zijnde roeping in ons volk te vervullen … ', Mussert, 'Stormloop 1938: Wij dringen naar het licht', VoVa, no. 1, 7 January 1938, 1.
163 'Een nieuwe tijd is komende: die tijd is Mussert. Onweerhoudbaar. Hij is de stem van het wordende Nederland … ', 'Om het vertrouwen in Mussert', VoVa, no. 4, 28 January 1938, 3.
164 ' … dat zich een Godsgericht voltrekt over datgene wat ondeugdelijk is gebleken, zoowel in den enkeling als in het volk', MS speech, Mussert, 'Herdenkingsbijeenkomst RAI', 12 December 1936, 1, NIOD: 123, 1.1: 49.
165 'Wij vragen niet dat ons in de komende jaren leed en zorgen en moeite bespaard zullen blijven; / Wij vragen niet, dat het ons goed zal mogen gaan; / Wij vragen niet, dat onze wenschen en onze verlangens in vervulling mogen gaan, / want niet onze wil zal geschieden. / Maar wij vragen op dezen avond aan het begin der nieuwe strijdperiode slechts dit eene: / dat God ons geve het inzicht, den moed, de vastberadenheid, de eerlijkheid, den goeden trouw, die noodig zijn om een goed werktuig te zijn in Zijn hand, dienende tot wederopstanding van dit volk, dat wij liefhebben, opdat het Vaderland, opdat het Imperium niet verloren zal gaan, maar behouden zal blijven en de weg naar omhoog doelbewust zal worden betreden volgens Zijnen wil. / Zingen wij te zamen: Wilt heden nu treden', MS speech, Mussert, 'Herdenkingsbijeenkomst RAI', 12 December 1936, 1, NIOD: 123, 1.1: 49.
166 Letter [transcript], H.J. Leeuwenberg to John Boddé, [1937], p. 1, NIOD: 123, 2.39: 1379.
167 ' … dat zijn ware aard wel onder schooner woorden tracht te verbergen. Soms ook zijn het vrome woorden, die echter onmiddellijk verraden, dat het slechts woorden en begrippen zijn, gehanteerd door hen, die den christelijken zin er van niet kennen … Het is een gruwelijk misbruik, een weerzinwekkende methode om eenvoudigen te misleiden. Desondanks (goed beschouwd moet er o.i. staan "dientengevolge" doc.) is het nationaal-socialisme van Mussert even heidensch en verwerpelijk in zijn principieelen grondslag als het Duitsche, dat door hem wordt nagebootst. Onchristelijk, onhistorisch en revolutionair, concludeerde Prof. Anema. En terecht', *De Rotterdammer*, 19 February 1937, quoted in: NSB weekly overview (press summary, District Propaganda Chamber), 2: 10, Rotterdam, 8 March 1937, 50, NIOD: 123, 2.49: 1529.
168 Circular no. 59, Van Geelkerken, Utrecht, 24 December 1936, NIOD: 123, 2.01: 516.
169 The Socialist press complained of the party's ceaseless insults of the national press: Newspaper clipping, 'N.S.B. beledigd opnieuw de dagbladpers', *Het Volk*, 9 April 1937, NIOD: KA II, 1702.
170 'De leugenpers', VoVa, no. 34, 21 August 1936, 7.

171 E.g.: Jac., 'Nazisträdsla i den "svenska" systempressen: Fruktar demokratin öppen discussion?', DSN, no. 17, 21 July 1933, 3.
172 See, for instance, report of a speech attacking the bishops, in: -rr-, 'Nazistleve i Cirkus för revolutionen: Hr Lindholms parti skall deltaga i göteborgsvalet', Göteborgs-Posten, no. 65, 18 March 1936, 8; or Lindholm letter to his sister Margit, 20 February 1935, Marieberg: NSAP/SSS, vol. 1 (Sven Olov Lindholm, 1935–8).
173 'Västeråspolisen måste dra blankt vid nazistmöte', Dagens Nyheter, 12 September 1935, 6.
174 'äkta göbbelsk', Neuer Vorwärts, quoted in: -rot [Nils Dahlrot], 'Lindholm samlar trasproletariatet: "Hitlerapor i Sverige"', DSN, no. 55, 17 July 1935, 1.
175 Cf. Roger Griffin, 'Der Grösste Verführer aller Zeiten?', in Attraktion der NS-Bewegung, ed. Gudrun Brockhaus (Essem: Klartext Verlag, 2014), 215–6.
176 'En de heer Mussert speelde voor Hitler ... ', NRC quoted in: 'Het groenehout aan de rottetronk', VoVa, no. 42, 21 October 1933, 4.
177 'Zoo heer, zoo knecht!', Newspaper clipping, Het Volk, 29 October 1933, in NIOD: KA II, 1701.
178 De Maasbode, 29 October 1935, in: NSB weekly overview, Rotterdam, 8 November 1935, 4, NIOD: 123, 2.49: 1529.
179 ' ... vele NSB'ers komen al tot hun bezinning ... ', NRC, 21 February 1937, quoted in: NSB weekly overview, 2: 9, Rotterdam, 1 March 1937, 46, NIOD: 123, 2.49: 1529.
180 'Hij (ir. Mussert) bleef de leider van een werkstuk; wat hij niet was: de profeet die de menigte buiten zich zelf zou brengen', quoted in: 'Boekbespreking: Over Mussert, P.H. Ritter Jr', VoVa, no. 29, 21 July 1934, 7.
181 Newspaper clipping, Per Gyberg, 'Nazistisk möteskultur: På diskussion hos "Lindholmarna"', Tidningen Freden, 1933, no. 1, 21, Arninge: 2C: 1a.
182 -rr-, 'S.O. Lindholm nazistledaren', Göteborgs-Posten, no. 283, 5 December 1933, 11.
183 'hoe het mogelijk is, dat duizenden Nederlanders "zich opwerken tot hysterische aanbidding van een dood-gewonen burgerman"', quoted in: 'Henri roert de trom – Kroniekschrijver van den Mussert-"cultus"', VoVa, no. 16, 17 April 1936, 3.
184 ' ... de heer Mussert is een heel doodgewone, gemiddelde mijnheer; ... hij draagt allernaarste zwarte broeken, die zijn kleine gestalte niet op haar voordeeligst doen uitkomen ... ', 'Cosmopolitica: Mussert', De Tijd, no. 28535, 16 December 1935, 1.
185 'Op 19 September 1917 huwde ANTON ADRIAAN MUSSERT, oud 23 jaar, zonder beroep, op het gemeentehuis te de Steeg, met Maria Witlam, met de zuster van zijn moeder, van beroep verpleegster, tweemaal zoo oud als hij. ... Moeders van zonen, gij moet U zooiets eens indenken. Uw zoon met Uw zuster!!', Propaganda leaflet, PH. H. ter Meulen, 'Dàt is MUSSERT!', NIOD: 123, 2.01: 619.
186 Police memorandum, concerning SSS, 1 September 1939–1 December 1940, Arninge: 2B: 2.
187 Police memorandum, S. Fransson, concerning factionalism in the NSAP, 27 February 1937, 1, Arninge: XII 64: 1.
188 Letter, Gösta Larsson to Hermann Göring, 9 November 1940, transcript in: Police memorandum, concerning the Nazi movement in Gothenburg, John Westlin, 19 November 1940, 1–2, Arninge: 2B: 1.
189 Minutes, Meeting Disciplinary Council, case HP 68, The Hague, Hilversum, 14 March 1936, 2, NIOD: 123, 2.30: 1342.
190 Secret memorandum, concerning the national socialists' activities in Stockholm, 15 April-15 June 1937, Arninge, XII 64: 1.

191 'Lindholm slutade sitt anförande med att utbringa ett fyrfaldigt leve för N.S.A.P.!? Nu var det en del medlemmar, som hurrade, en del som "hellade" och en del som teg. Var Lindholm full eller hade han blivit borgare? Det hade förut aldrig hänt i N.S.A.P.:s historia, att ens en vanlig medlem utbringat "ett leve", och nu gjorde själva ledaren detta. [...] Mötet avslutades under en mycket underlig – för att icke säga betryckt – stämning', Confidential police informant memorandum, 14 October 1938, 2, Arninge: XII 64: 2.

192 'Jag varnade redan i början av vår kampgemenskap för att ni skulle betrakta mig som någon sorts övermänniska eller trollkarl, men jag har lovat att ärligt strida och ställa mig främst i ledet för vår heliga sak ... ', 'Partiets 6-årsdag firad i Stockholm', *Den Svenske Folksocialisten* (DSF), no. 6, 25 January 1939, 5.

193 'Vi nationalsocialister äro lojala mot vår ledare, så länge denne är lojal mot oss. En för alla – alla för en', Police memorandum, concerning *Solkors* meeting, 13 February 1939, 2, Arninge: 4A: 1.

194 Kunkeler, 'Narratives of Decline in the NSB', 223–4.

195 See notification of Clementsson's removal: 'Meddelanden: Meddelande från Plg', DSN, no. 3, 14 January 1939, 5.

196 George L. Mosse, *The Culture of Western Europe* (Chicago: Rand McNally, 1974), 335–6.

Chapter 4

1 Helmuth Auerbach, 'Nationalsozialismus Vor Hitler', in *Der Nationalsozialismus: Studien zur Ideologie und Herrschaft*, ed. W. Benz and H. Mommsen (Frankfurt am Main: Geschichte Fischer, 1993), 22.
2 Paul, *Aufstand der Bilder*, 174–5.
3 Reichardt, *Faschistische Kampfbünde*, 576–86.
4 Eichberg and Jones, 'The Nazi Thingspiel'.
5 Vincent, 'Political Violence and Mass Society', 395.
6 Nadine Rossol, 'Performing the Nation: Sports, Spectacles, and Aesthetics in Germany, 1926–1936', *Central European History* 43, no. 4 (2010), 622; Carl Levy, 'Fascism, National Socialism and Conservatives in Europe, 1914–1945: Issues for Comparativists', *Contemporary European History* 8, no. 1 (1999), 107.
7 For a critique of Theweleit's book and its significance, see Sven Reichardt, 'Klaus Theweleits "Männerphantasien" – ein Erfolgsbuch der 1970er-Jahre', *Zeithistorische Forschungen/Studies in Contemporary History* 3, (2006), 401–21.
8 Jessica Benjamin and Anson Rabinbach, foreword to Klaus Theweleit, *Male Fantasies, II: Male Bodies: Psychoanalyzing the White Terror* (Cambridge: Polity, 1988), xvii.
9 Ibid. 153, 155.
10 The Swedish law was in force from 1 August 1933, the Dutch law 23 September 1933.
11 'Bärande av uniform eller liknande klädedräkt, som tjänar att utmärka bärarens politiska meningsriktning, vare förbjudet.' Booklet, Organization document no. 2, *Instruktioner för Frontavdelningar (I.F.) inom NSAP*, 1938, 24–5, Arninge: 2H1.
12 Thomas Bull and Anders Heiborn, 'Uniformsförbudet, tiden och grundlagen', *Svensk Juristtidning*, no. 4 (1996), 329.
13 See especially August 1933, Lindholm diary.
14 Newspaper clipping, 'De overheid contra de georganiseerde wanorde', *Algemeen Handelsblad*, 28 July 1933, NIOD: KA II, 2296.

15 'Hij die in het openbaar kleedingstukken of opzichtige onderscheidingsteekenen draagt of voert, welke uitdrukking zijn van een bepaald staatkundig streven, wordt gestraft met hechtenis van ten hoogste twaalf dagen of geldboete van ten hoogste honderd vijftig gulden.' Addition to the Penal Code, Session 1933–231, Law Draft no 2 ('Aanvulling van het Wetboek van Strafrecht met het oog op kleedingstukken en onderscheidingsteekenen, welke uitdrukking zijn van een bepaald staatkundig streven'), NSB newspaper clippings collection, NIOD: Amsterdam, KA II: 1701.
16 See, for instance, the Anti-Revolutionary commentary of 'Het Uniformverbod', *De Standaard*, no. 18 833, 8 September 1933, p. 1.
17 Verhagen, *Toen de Katholieken Nederland Veroverden*, 291.
18 See, for instance, the case against John Boddé and his wearing of the party insignia in a court of law in 'Ons insigne voor den Hoogen Raad', VoVa, no. 2, 12 January 1935, 3.
19 As many scholars have argued, violence could be cathartic and liberating for the perpetrators: Mann, *Fascists*, 29; it could also bind the perpetrators together, united by mutual participation in a transgressive act: Reichardt, *Faschistische Kampfbünde*, 39–40; Aristotle Kallis, 'Fascism, "Licence" and Genocide: From the Chimera of Rebirth to the Authorization of Mass Murder', in *Rethinking the Nature of Fascism: Comparative Perspectives*, ed. António Costa Pinto (Basingstoke: Palgrave Macmillan, 2011), 257.
20 Cf.: Kunkeler, 'The Evolution of Swedish Fascism'.
21 'Blusarna voro förfärdigade av brunt khakityg, försedda med axelklaffar ... ' Inventory after raid of NSAP's treasury office, in: Gothenburg SA police report, 1935, 49–50.
22 NSAP, SA, and A-Group confiscated documents, in: Gothenburg SA-inquiry police report, 1935, 66.
23 As well as the occasions for any public meeting. E.g.: Booklet, Programme for the Third Party Convention, Amsterdam, 30 March 1935, 28, 49, NIOD: 123, 2.55: 2004.
24 Ibid. 64.
25 Concept, WA Inspector, 5 July 1935, 1, NIOD: 123, 1.1: 50.
26 NSAP, SA, and A-Group confiscated documents, in: Gothenburg SA-inquiry police report, 1935, 65.
27 Concept, WA Inspector, 5 July 1935, 1, NIOD: 123, 1.1: 50, 3.
28 Interrogation SO Lindholm, 15 February 1935, in Gothenburg SA-inquiry police report, 1935, 164, Wärenstam's archive.
29 E.g.: Letter, Ove Adamsson to Southern District, Karlskrona, 25 [month illegible] 1934, Marieberg: NSAP/SSS, vol. 4, Karlskrona (1934–8).
30 E.g. Lundins paper store in Stockholm: NSAP circular, Stockholm, 15 April 1937, Arninge: XII 64: 1.
31 *Tjänsteföreskrifter* (TF), 1937, 36.
32 'Meddelande från Plg', DSN, no. 3, 18 January 1934, 2.
33 A note on prices and wages: the average annual wage for servants in Sweden and similar 'unskilled' workers in 1930 was around 500 kronor. While living costs were lower in the 1930s than the previous decade, a pair of boots could consume most or all of someone's monthly wage. In the Netherlands, a trained worker could earn typically around 1000 guilders/annum, though this figure would typically be less during the economic depression. It is important to bear in mind that many did not necessarily have stable or regular work, while unemployment was high for most of the period.

34 Letter, Ds. to Ove Adamsson, 22 January 1934, Marieberg: NSAP/SSS, vol. 3, Södra Distriktet (1934).
35 It is intriguing how closely photographed these boots were at times, with what Maiken Umbach has termed 'an intensity bordering on fetishisation'. Umbach, 'Selfhood, Place, and Ideology in German Photo Albums, 1933–1945', 350.
36 Booklet, *Prijslijst van Materiaal*, Utrecht, August 1936, NIOD: 123, 2.10: 857.
37 E.g. see the advertisement in VoVa, no. 3, 21 January 1933, 3; or VoVa, no 21, 27 May 1933, 3.
38 See, for instance, the advertisements in: Brochure, *Programma van den Gewestelijken Landdag*, Amsterdam, 28 April 1934, p. 16, NIOD: 123, 1.1: 25. To a lesser extent the same happened in Sweden: DSN, no. 12, 22 March 1934, 5.
39 Minutes for meeting 11 July 1935, in Book, meeting minutes *Algemeene Raad*, §1, p. 29, NIOD: 123, 1.3: 276.
40 Booklet, WA Organization, *NSB-126a*, §64, NIOD: 123, 2.14: 1005.
41 Interrogation SO Lindholm, 15 February 1935, in: Gothenburg SA-inquiry police report, 1935, 165–6.
42 See Concept, WA Inspector, 5 July 1935, 1, NIOD: 123, 1.1: 50, 1; Circular no. 30, 'Kamporder' 3 October 1934, Arninge: 2B1: 2.
43 ' … gäller alltjämt och än *mera nu*, när det offentliga bärandet är förbjudet.' Emphasis in original. *Porg*, no. 12, December 1935, Arninge: 2B: 4.
44 Circular, J. Hogewind to all WA and RWA commanders, Utrecht, August 1935, 1, NIOD: 123, 2.14: 1046.
45 Circular, 'Kamporder' 3 May 1934, Arninge: 2B: 1.
46 Circular no. 26, Central Bureau of Propaganda to all Circle Leaders, Amsterdam, 7 May 1936, The Hague: 2.19.49: 4.
47 'Orders W.A. en R.W.A.', in: Circular, J. Hogewind to all Circle Leaders, Utrecht, 8 March 1935, 1, The Hague: 2.19.49: 3.
48 'Vooral het effect van den a.s. Landdag-optocht door Amsterdam's straten zal, indien deze zeer kleurige beschermers veel worden gedragen, verhoogd worden en de stoet zal er een fleurig aanzien door krijgen.' Circular, to all Circle Leaders and Independent Group Leaders, Utrecht, 18 February 1935, The Hague: 2.19.49: 3.
49 See, for instance, Police memorandum concerning NSAP meeting, 3 September 1936, Arninge: 2C: 6.
50 'Det finns alltför många partikamrater som inte kan sträcka upp handen, inte bära partimärket … ', *Porg*, no. 12, December 1935, Arninge: 2B: 4.
51 'Ik persoonlijk hecht niet de minste waarde aan het speldje en het zwarte hemd.' Minutes, Meeting of High Disciplinary Council, case HP 81, Comrade L. [name restricted], Hilversum, Hilversum, 20 April 1936, 5, in NIOD: 123, 2.30: 1343.
52 Schnapp, *Staging Fascism*, 6.
53 'Nationalsocialisternas tjänstedräkt är ett symboliskt uttryck för den kamp vi föra. För oss är den icke någon militäruniform utan en arbetsskjorta som gör oss alla lika i plikterna för samma sak.' NSAP, SA, and A-Group confiscated documents, in: Gothenburg SA-inquiry police report, 1935, 66.
54 'De Beweging is haar strijd voor de wederopstanding van ons Volk begonnen met als uiterlijke teekenen: het zwarte hemd en den fascistengroet, de zwart-roode vlag en het insigne. Het zwarte hemd is onze officieele dracht, aangenomen ter eere van Mussolini en zijn zwarthemden, die het sein hebben gegeven voor de wederopstanding van Europa, aanvaard als uitdrukking van onze kameraadschappelijke verbondenheid in den strijd voor Volk en Vaderland. […]

Niemand onzer zal ooit er aan denken, deze uiterlijke kenteekenen van onzen strijd weg te nemen.' Mussert order, 'Uit de Beweging: ORDER van den Leider ten aanzien van vlaggen, insignes en zwart hemd', 14 June 1938, NIOD: 123, 1.1: 79.

55 Sven Reichardt has previously noted the effect of the uniform as a metaphor for militaristic violence: Reichardt, *Faschistische Kampfbünde*, 40.

56 'När någon i dessa förfallets dagar i Sverige nämner ordet *soldat*, ryggar alla tillbaka och se inom sig de militariserade diktaturerna marschera upp, hotfullt beredda att krossa kulturens sista utpost – det demokratiska Norden.' Arne Clementsson, DSN, no. 10, 7 February 1937, 5.

57 r, 'De Nationaal-Socialistische tucht: Disciplinair, niet militair', VoVa, no. 43, 28 October 1933, 6.

58 Slaa and Klijn, *De NSB*, chap. 22.

59 'Mitt besök i Tyskland gjorde mig ännu mer övertygad om att din tanke att ändra uniformen så att den får en mer markant svensk prägel är önskvärd. Trots att förhållandena där nere endast gör proppaganda [sic] för ideen [sic] så skulle en tydlig skillnad i uniform starkare markera vår vilja till självständigt nationellt liv.' Letter, Land Inspector for the Eastern Region to Lindholm, Birka, 23 July [hay month] 1937, Marieberg: NSAP/SSS, vol. 1, Sven Olov Lindholm (1935–8).

60 For a seminal analysis of the political role of Charles XII's history in this period, see Sverker Oredsson, 'Stormaktsdrömmar och Stridsiver: Ett tema i svensk opinionsbildning och politik 1910–1942', *Scandia* 59, no. 2 (1993), 257–96.

61 W. Jason Mast, 'The Cultural Pragmatics of Symbolic Action', in *Performance and Power*, ed. Jeffrey C. Alexander (Cambridge: Polity, 2011), 7.

62 Butler, 'Performative Acts and Gender Constitution', 521.

63 'Hij zal zich er steeds van bewust zijn zich daarbij met trots en waardigheid te gedragen.' Concept document NSB membership, 2, NIOD: 123, 1.1: 3.

64 'Iedere N.S.B.-er bedenke, dat hij (zij) in uniform gekleed, getuigt voor de N.S.B. en dat hij (zij) dan nog meer dan anders het geval zou zijn, een voorbeeld moet zijn van netheid, stiptheid, beleefdheid en kameraadschap.' Concept, WA Inspector, 5 July 1935, 1, NIOD: 123, 1.1: 50, 3.

65 'Varje medlem skall bära sin brunskjorta med stolthet och iklädd densamma mer än någonsin vinnlägga sig om god hållning.' TF, 197, 35.

66 'Een *actief lid* is verplicht in alle gevallen, waarin zulks zal worden bevolen, het zwarte hemd, de uniform, het insigne te dragen en den N.S.B. groet te brengen. Hij zal zich er steeds van bewust zijn zich daarbij met trots en waardigheid te gedragen.' Ibid. 'Verplichtingen der leden', 5.

67 ' … icke härstammar från judar eller "färgade" raselement. Den inträdessökande måste dessutom vara känd för redlighet och får ej ha uppträtt osolidariskt mot arbetskamrater under berättigade sociala lönekonflikter.' Booklet, *Utdrag ur NSAP:s föreskrifter och reglementen*, 1, 2B: 4. Arninge.

68 'Nationalsocialistiska Arbetarepartiet bildades just genom en moralisk revolution, som rensade ut streberdömet och korruptionen inom de egna leden. Och nu gäller det för oss, att inte bara få med så *många anhängare* som möjligt, utan det viktigaste är att vi få *redliga* medkämpar, sådana som kunna arbete för *sakens* seger, för sina *folkbröders* skull och ej för sin egen.' Ibid. 3.

69 Circular no. 38, 17 December 1934, Arninge: 2B1: 2.

70 Police memorandum regarding NSAP, 17 December 1936, 2–3, Arninge: 2B: 6.

71 7 January 1934; 28 October 1934, Lindholm diary.

72 Reichardt, 'Praxeologie und Faschismus', 133.

73 'De som icke kunna försaka nöjen för arbete i partiets tjänst äro icke värda namnet nationalsocialist. Genom sin idéella offervilja och oförskräckta handlingskraft, goda hållning och ett klanderfritt uppträdande skall A-gruppsmannen ingjuta aktning för idéerna och N.S.A.P.' Appendix B to circular no. 40, Local group administration to members, 4 January 1935, Arninge: 2B1: 2.

74 'Nationalsocialismen är icke blott en politisk åsikt utan en världsåskådning, som först och främst avser att förändra människorna och giva dem nya mål. Denna åskådning måste sätta sin prägel på sina bärare, ej blott ifråga om föredömet utan också levnadssättet och hållningen. Det strider mot vår åskådning att begagna det borgerliga samhällets vanor. Nationalsocialister böra icke deltaga i det moderna samhällets urartade nöjesliv eller vara kända som restaurangbesökare o. dyl.' TF, VI: 212, 33.

75 Jürgen Martschukat and Steffen Patzold, 'Geschichtswissenschaft und "Performative Turn"', in *Geschichtswissenschaft und 'Performative Turn': Ritual, Inszenierung und Performanz vom Mittelalter bis zur Neuzeit*, ed. Jürgen Martschukat and Steffen Patzold (Köln: Böhlau, 2003), 11.

76 Butler, *Gender Trouble*, 185.

77 See, for instance, Tilman Allert, *The Hitler Salute: On the Meaning of a Gesture* (New York: Metropolitan Books, 2008), 5.

78 'Soldat är hållning, stil', Arne Clementsson, DSN, no. 10, 7 February 1937, 5.

79 'Hugg och mothugg', DSN, no. 6, 23 January 1935, 3. Compare to the Italian myth of the New Man, and Mussolini's rejection of a bourgeois mentality: Jorge Dagnino, 'The Myth of the New Man in Italian Fascist Ideology', *Fascism: Journal of Comparative Fascism Studies*, no. 5 (2016), 143–5.

80 'Verslag van de colporatagetocht naar Bussum op Maandag 24 Juli 1933', VoVa, no. 31, 5 August 1933, 1.

81 ' … här är ingen skillnad på samhällsklass, *idéerna* förena och brunskjortan förenar dem', DSN, no. 13, 11 June 1933, 3.

82 William H. Sewell, 'Space in Contentious Politics', in *Silence and Voice in the Study of Contentious Politics* (Cambridge: Cambridge University Press, 2001), 58.

83 'Naar buiten werkt uniformkleeding, gekozen als teeken van bepaald staatkundig streven, op zich zelf, ook als van verdere organisatie wordt afgezien, imponeerend op het publiek. Deze werking pleegt ook allereerst beoogd te worden door wie de uniform invoeren. Men wil zijn aanhangers duidelijk doen onderkennen en door hun aantal indruk maken. Intusschen blijft het veelal niet hierbij en gaat men daarnevens gezamenlijk, in organisatorisch verband, optreden … ', Minister of Law Van Schaik, Memorandum no. 3, Session 1933-231, ('Aanvulling van het Wetboek van Strafrecht met het oog op kleedingstukken en onderscheidingsteekenen, welke uitdrukking zijn van een bepaald staatkundig streven'), 1, NSB newspaper clippings collection, NIOD: Amsterdam, KA II: 1701.

84 Booklet, Organization document no. 2, *Instruktioner för Frontavdelningar (I.F.) inom NSAP*, 1938, 24–5, Arninge: 2H1.

85 [Photocopy] *Porg*, no. 2, March 1936, §244, 12, Arninge: 2B: 5.

86 ' … genom att marschera upp på gatorna i fast och disciplinerad styrka, med frimodig blick och sång, med stil. Dessa ungdomar komma med musik och lysande hakkorsfanor, i händerna hålla de flammande facklor, och de marschera med rättning och beslutsam vilja … ', 'Där vi kämpa: Nytt storstilat kampmöte med Pl. på Auditorium', DSN, no. 17, 3 March 1937, 5.

87 'Skällsord, spott och knytnävar från de röda, kommunisternas råa provokationsförsök, intet bekom dem, de marscherade lugnt i sina led, sjöngo kampsångerna och höjde rungande hellrop.' 'Hysteriska kvinnor främst vid Masthuggskravallerna', DSN, no. 21, 24 May 1934, 5.
88 E.g.: Message, Van Deinse, 'Instructies voor den landdag', 1933, NIOD: 123, 1.1: 10.
89 Letter, Mussert to Amsterdam mayor, Utrecht, NIOD: 123, 1.1: 36; Letter transcript, Mayor of 's-Gravenhage, Ag. Nr. 19383, Afd. KZ, NIOD: 123, 2.55: 2004.
90 E.g., Circular, Van Geelkerken to all Circle Leaders, Utrecht, 18 December 1936, NIOD: 123, 2.01: 346; Circular, de Blocq van Scheltinga to all District Leaders, Utrecht, 26 August 1938, NIOD: 123, 2.01: 283.
91 See e.g.: Report on CHI meeting, Circle Electoral Leader to Farwerck, Amsterdam, 29 March 1935, 2, NIOD: 123, 2.01: 534.
92 Brochure, *Wat iedere Nederlander van zijn Vlag moet weten*, Bussum, April 1937, NIOD: 123, 2.55: 2006.
93 See, for instance, the anti-revolutionary paper: 'Wat de "Beste" Nederlanders beweren', *Nederland Waakzaam*, February 1937, in 'Weekly overview', Dep. III, no. 8, 27 February 1937, 4, NIOD: 123, 2.01: 561.
94 Letter, Farwerck to Mussert, Hilversum, 6 July 1936, NIOD: 123, 1.1: 48; Circular no. 5, Van Geelkerken to all Circle Leaders, Utrecht, 30 January 1937, The Hague: 2.19.49: 11.
95 '... het strijdbare geestelijke leger ... ', Speech notes, Mussert, Third Party Congress, 1935, 15, NIOD: 123, 1.1: 36.
96 '... een politiek leger, dat gelooft in de roeping van de N.S.B. Gij zijt de soldaten van dat leger.' Speech notes, Mussert, 'Gelofte-Aflegging', 1935, Fourth Party Congress, NIOD: 123, 1.1: 37.
97 'Ook wy zyn een leger en wel een leger, dat zou zyn te vergelyken met dat der verschillende Kruistochten. [...] Ook wy <u>doen</u>, zonder te vragen, zonder te morren, zonder te kankeren; omdat wy weten, dat de Leider ons voorgaat in den stryd voor een machtig idéaal! – Ook wy zyn bezield. Bezield door het voorbeeld van onzen Leider, door het zien van onzen Standaard.'
98 '... blir soldat i framtidens armé för socialistisk folkgemenskap ... ', Lindholm speech, Stenographic transcript of NSAP meeting, Stockholm Auditorium, 24 October 1933, 30, Arninge: 2C: 1a.
99 '... en ungdomsarmé med fanatisk tro och järnhård vilja.' -rot, [Nils Dahlrot], 'Krig!', DSN, no. 15, 23 February 1935, 6.
100 'Din plats är i frihetshären, / ett svärd har du snart dig smitt [...] Ditt Sverige ropar dig an: / Din plats är i frihetshären, / gå med, bli en kämpe, en man!', Gunnar Henningsson, 'Frihetshären', DSN, no. 39, 23 May 1936, 5.
101 'Med uniformen följer alltid en friskare kampanda, som förhöjer intrycket av mötet och gör gott på nya kamrater.' *Porg*, no. 12, December 1935, Arninge: 2B: 4.
102 Magnus, 'Kamratskap och segervilja präglade Hökerumslägret – Nordisk Ungdom på frammarsch', DSN, no. 53, 10 July 1935, 1, 6.
103 Letter, E.L. to Pl. S.O. Lindholm, Sydfronten, [place & date unknown], Marieberg: NSAP/SSS, vol. 1, Sven Olov Lindholm (1935-8); Letter, Haarlem Circle Leader to Mussert, 9 May 1933, 1, NIOD: 123, 1.1: 16; 'De N.S.B. in den aanval', VoVa, no. 39, 29 September 1934, 1-2; 'Lindholm till Norrland', DSN, no. 7, 26 January 1935, 6; VoVa, no. 23, 8 June 1935, 8.

104 'Vår strid är revolutionär och den föres med blanka vapen. Du behövs vid fronten.' Election information pamphlet, Stockholm, 3 February 1935, Arninge: 2J: 1.
105 Reichardt, *Faschistische Kampfbünde*, 40.
106 'Sie vermittelten das sensuelle Bild eines uniformierten Nationalismus, von dynamischer Jugendlichkeit, Männerdominanz und kompromissloser Gewaltsamkeit ... ', Reichardt, 14.
107 Havenaar, *Anton Adriaan Mussert*, 34.
108 'Bij de foto's: Tegenstellingen', VoVa, no. 20, 15 May 1936, 4.
109 ' ... kranig gelid na gelid, de gezichten strak en den stormriem om de kin. Daar gaan ze martiaal in het zwarte uniform met breeden koppel en schouderriem: de manhafte jeugd ... ', 'Onze Gewestelijke Landdag', VoVa, no. 18, 5 May 1934, 9.
110 'De bära blåa speglar på kragen, det är Stockholms SA under sin ledare Hermann – taktfasta gossar, vana att "göra gatan fri" för sig. [...] det är Göteborgs hurtiga SA med sin gruppledare Linder i spetsen. De igenkännas på sina gula kragspeglar och sin morska uppsyn – folk som ingen skrämmer.' DSN, 11 June 1933, cited in Confidential police memorandum, 'Kort redogörelse över den nationalsocialistiska rörelsens i Sverige utveckling under år 1933', 15, Arninge: 2B: 5.
111 Letter, WA-Inspector (Hogewind) to [name restricted], The Hague, 14 November 1933, NIOD: 123, 2.14: 1006.
112 ' ... dat in onze Beweging een zekere draag [sic] naar distinctieven bestaat, daarbij de wensch uitsprekende, dat zulks niet zijn oorzaak vindt, om door het distinctief een zekere machtswellust te kunnen botvieren.' Letter, Head Department I to Mussert, Amsterdam, 27 February 1936, 1–2, NIOD: 123, 1.1: 50.
113 'Mij werd gevraagd, of het niet-leden van de W.A. geoorloofd is koppels met schouderriem te dragen en of dit b.v. voor bepaalde functionarissen voorgeschreven is. Het dragen van het zwarte hemd met een zwarte of donkergrijze broek vereischt tenminste een zwarte riem en daarom wordt door velen in plaats daarvan het W.A. koppel met schouderriem gedragen. [...] Bestaat hiertegen bezwaar?' Letter, District Commissar Inspection III (d'Ansembourg) to General Secretary (Van Geelkerken), Amstenrade, 15 September 1934, NIOD: 123, 1.6: 341.
114 Letter, General Secretary to d'Ansembourg, [Utrecht], 20 September 1934, NIOD: 123, 1.6: 341.
115 Police memorandum regarding an NSAP meeting, 10 October 1933, Arninge: 2C: 1a; Police memorandum regarding an NSAP meeting, 3 September 1936, Arninge: 2C: 6; Police memorandum regarding SSS meeting, 3 December 1940, 1, Arninge: 2C: 1 [Äldre Aktsystemet].
116 ' ... en del herrar i kostym', 'Första maj firad i strålande sol', *Dagens Nyheter*, 2 May 1934, 5.
117 'Demonstration i Masthugget gav starkt eko. – Nazisterna sjunga och marschera', *Göteborgs-Posten*, no. 115, 22 May 1934, 1.
118 S. [most likely Lindholm], 'Ungdomen i Göteborg under hakkorsfanan!', DSN, no. 9, 1 May 1933, 5; 'Brunskjortekolonner genom Göteborg!', DSN, no. 13, 11 June 1933, 5; -rot [Nils Dahlrot], 'Till tings!', DSN, no. 12, 22 March 1934, 4; Torsten G:son Elg, ' ... och så börjar livet', DSN, no. 50 (Christmas issue), 2; Munin, 'Lindholm fri från fångenskapen', DSN, no. 38, 18 May 1935, 1; 'De Landdag', VoVa, no. 14, 6 April 1935, 3.
119 Eichberg and Jones, 'The Nazi Thingspiel', 146.
120 ' ... vapenrock och spetsbyxor fullständigt lika arméns senaste modell och i samma färg.' Police memorandum, retrospect of the NSAP, 10 March 1938, 12–3, Arninge: 2B: 9.

121 'Den vid livremmen med *karbinhakor* fästade *axelremmen* är även användbar.' According to interrogation of Gunnar Svalander, Gothenburg SA-inquiry police report, 1935, 104. Emphasis in original.
122 Shoulder straps were also used as weapons by the Dutch WA: Broek, *Weerkorpsen*, 116.
123 Letter, Lindholm to Sven Hedengren, cited in: Kunkeler, 'The Evolution of Swedish Fascism', 391.
124 'Ons hemd', VoVa, no. 38, 23 September 1933, 2.
125 See August 1933, Lindholm diary.
126 Letter photocopy, Lindholm to Lennart Westberg, Rönninge, 24 October 1977, 6, Marieberg: SO Lindholm, vol. 5.
127 Heléne Lööw, *Nazismen i Sverige 1980-1999: Den rasistiska undergroundrörelsen: musiken, myterna, riterna*, 2nd ed. (Stockholm: Ordfront Förlag, 2000), 439-42.
128 Håwe, 'Minnen från flydda kampår', DSN, no. 42, 11 June 1938, 5.
129 Confidental police memorandum, 'angående Nationalsocialistiska Arbetarepartiets 5:te årsting i Stockholm', 1938, 7, Arninge: 2A: 2.
130 'Tungt tramp / och ståltärningars rassel / ljuder i mina öron. / Tigande går ödet / över Rubicons älv / och det stora bokslutet nalkas.' Bertil Brisman, 'S.A.' DSN, no. 43, 7 June 1936, 2.
131 Mosse, *The Nationalization of the Masses*, 7.
132 'Op den Landdag zal ik zijn / als duizenden die met mij kwamen / in dien bruizenden golfstroom: klein, zonder rangen en zonder namen; één enkele stem in 't "hou zee!" / dat juichen zal over de straten, / één man slechts in Mussert's armee, / één der onbekende soldaten. / In mijn zwart hemd tusschen het zwart / dat anderen gansch'lijk verloren, / zal ik tot den klop van mijn hart / in den hartslag der massa hooren. / En één zal ik zijn in macht, / in volharden in beminnen, / één zijn in moed en in kracht, / en méé zal ik overwinnen!', Rob Delsing, 'Als één man', VoVa, no. 40, 5 October 1935, 4.
133 Alexander and Mast, 'Introduction: Symbolic Action in Theory and Practice', 15.
134 'Uniformsskräck – Klappjakt på statsfientliga klädespersedlar!', DSN, no. 19, 11 August 1933, 1, 8; see also: 'Även underkläder statsfientliga?', DSN, no. 22, 11 September 1933, 2.
135 Social Democratic politician Beukema argued that 'a fascist in uniform has an irritating effect', according to *Algemeen Handelsblad*, citing in: Reference-material, 2nd week, 5, NIOD: 123, 2.01: 542; Swedish politicians argued much the same thing: P.D. [Per Dahlberg], 'Uniformsförbudet', DSN, no. 12, 1 June 1933, 5.
136 'Lindholmsnazisternas pingstmöte – Agitationsmöte i Vitabergsparken med slagsmål som efterspel', *Stockholms-Tidningen*, 11 June 1935, 5; 'Polismästeren slogs i gatan vid nazisttåg – Allvarligt kommunistupplopp i Göteborg', *Svenska Dagbladet*, 21 May 1934; 'Uppträden i Malmö vid nazistmöte – Bråkiga ungsocialister och kommunister i farten', *Sydsvenska Dagbladet*, no. 259, 23 September 1935, 7.
137 Confidential police report, 'Kort redogörelse över den nationalsocialistiska rörelsens i Sverige utveckling under år 1933', 19-20, Arninge: 2B: 1.
138 29 August 1935, Lindholm diary.
139 'Communisten contra fascisten', *Algemeen Handelsblad*, no. 34563, 2 May 1933, 13.
140 ' … dat een zoodanige, min of meer militaire, machtsontwikkeling van politieke richtingen naast het wettig gezag – al kleedt men haar, wellicht in den aanvang te goeder trouw, in den vorm van hulpverleening aan dit gezag – in een geordenden staat niet kan worden geduld.' Van Schaik, Memorandum no. 3, Session 1933-231,

('Aanvulling van het Wetboek van Strafrecht met het oog op kleedingstukken en onderscheidingsteekenen, welke uitdrukking zijn van een bepaald staatkundig streven'), 1, NSB newspaper clippings collection, NIOD: Amsterdam, KA II: 1701.
141 'Iedere poging om den legalen weg af te snijden voor een nieuwe geestesstrooming in een volk, die historisch aan de orde is, is in wezen een poging tot burgeroorlog.' Mussert, quoted on the front page of: VoVa, no. 39, 29 September 1934.
142 E.g. Secret memorandum, concerning a NS revolution, Astrid Ström, 17 April 1940, Arninge: 3B: 1.
143 Lööw, *Hakkorset och Wasakärven*, 370-1.
144 Berglund and Sennerteg, *Finska Inbördeskriget*, 135.
145 See also 'Munck ensam ansvarig för skyddskåren', *Svenska Dagbladet*, 23 January 1932, 5.
146 Åke Nerby, Secret composition of a P-file regarding Sven Hedengren, 16 August 1946, 1, Arninge: P4770: 2.
147 Lindholm, *Svensk Frihetskamp*, 14.
148 Wärenstam, *Fascismen och Nazismen i Sverige 1920-1940*, 68-71; Ohlsson, *Svensk Politik*, 251-2.
149 Newspaper clipping, 'J.K. ingriper för nazisternas beväpning', *Ny Dag*, 12 November 1935; Newspaper clipping, 'Åklagaren struntade i Lindholmsnassarnas innehav av vapen!', Arninge: 2E: 1.
150 Military uniforms in political contexts were not forbidden: 'Politiska uniformer förbjudas', *Göteborgs-Posten*, no. 85, 12 April 1933.
151 'Verbod van particuliere weerkorpsen', *De Tijd*, no. 28 806, 29 May 1936, 3.
152 'Kort en bondig! – W.A. niet opgeheven', *De Tribune*, 11 September 1936, 5.
153 See, for instance, the report on the NSB procession before the regional party congress in Loosduinen: 'N.S.B. landdag in Loosduinen', *De Maasbode*, no. 26 419, 13 October 1935, 3.
154 'Mussert en de Burgerwachten: Is het hem om cellenvorming te doen?' *De Tijd*, no. 27746, 1 September 1934, 3.
155 ' ... wapenen zijn gemakkelijk te verkrijgen.' Newspaper clipping, 'Het uniformverbod', *Nieuwe Rotterdamsche Courant*, 1 August 1933, NIOD: KA II, 2296.
156 'De verboden N.S.B. – Ontoelaatbare Weerbaarheidsafdeelingen naar buitenlandsch model', *De Tijd*, no. 27 367, 20 January 1934, 2.
157 Report for Reichsführer-SS, 24 February 1938, in: Preliminary investigation protocol, Lindholm, 18 February 1948, 19, Arninge.
158 ' ... een, min of meer belachelijke, zucht tot nabootsing van buitenlandsche methoden ... ', Van Schaik, Memorandum no. 3, Session 1933-231, ('Aanvulling van het Wetboek van Strafrecht met het oog op kleedingstukken en onderscheidingsteekenen, welke uitdrukking zijn van een bepaald staatkundig streven'), 1, NSB newspaper clippings collection, NIOD: Amsterdam, KA II: 1701.
159 'het uiterlijk militaristisch gedoe "wel erg on-Nederlandsch" noemt voor een zoo patriottisch doende groep.' *Het Volk*, no. 11 895, 11 January 1933, evening edition, p. 5; the charge of un-Dutch NSB behaviour recurred regularly, see for instance: 'De Landdag van de N.S.B', *De Standaard*, no. 19 475, 14 October 1935, 3.
160 'En het fascisme is de groote strooming van den nieuwen tijd.' 'Interview met Mussert', VoVa, no. 30, 27 July 1935, 4.
161 Kunkeler, 'The Evolution of Swedish Fascism', 387-95.
162 Newspaper clipping, 'Nazistbekymmer', *Ny Dag*, 2 October 1933, Arninge: 2C: 1a.
163 E.g., 'Polisen tog 5 nazister', *Dagens Nyheter*, no. 233A, 28 August 1936, 1.

164 Sven Olov Lindholm, *Döm Ingen Ohörd*, 2nd ed., 1968, p. 16, Marieberg: SO Lindholms Samling, vol. 8 (Print media).
165 Lindholm, Lindholm Interview, sec. 259:A.
166 'Det skulle dock säkerligen icke skada om nazisterna lämnade sina stövlar hemma när de höllo sina utomhusmöten då det troligen är den uniformsliknande klädseln som retar galla på särskilt söderborna. Vore nazisterna klädda "som vanligt" folk kunde ju heller inte bråkstakarna veta vilka som voro nazister eller icke när de lämnade mötena och hade då inga att ofreda som nu alltid är fallet.' Police memorandum regarding National Socialism in Sweden, 16 October–15 November 1937, Arninge: 2B: 8.
167 For an assessment of Clementsson's character and the Clarté theft, see: Interrogation of Gunnar Johanssen, 9 March 1939, 3, Arninge: 2G1: 2.
168 Newspaper clipping, 'Ganska ruskig samling', *Ny Dag*, 6 February 1939, Arninge: 2G1: 2.
169 'Onze eerste landdag', VoVa, no. 2, 14 January 1933, 3.
170 Broek, *Weerkorpsen*, 105–25.
171 ' ... nette welwillende Vaderlanders, maar die als de dood er voor zyn, dat hun ruiten ingeworpen zouden worden, die her verschrikkelyk zouden vinden, als een schoenmaker hun met "kameraad" zou aanspreken, die misschien wel eens een zwart hemd zullen aantrekken, na zich tevoren telefonisch overtuigd te hebben, dat de vrienden en kennissen het ook doen. [...] Heilsoldaten noemde een Ymuider Kerkblad ons, en dat moeten we zijn, heil*soldaten*, die stryden voor het heil van Volk en Vaderland ... ', Letter, T. van de Weide to Mussert, Overveen, 20 June 1933, 4, NIOD: 123, 1.1: 16.
172 Letter, WA-Inspector Hogewind to Reydon, Amsterdam, 4 July 1933, NIOD: 123, 2.55: 1768.
173 'Verslag van de colportagetocht naar Bussum op Maandag 24 Juli 1933', VoVa, no. 31, 5 August 1933, 1.
174 Letter, WA-Inspector (Hogewind) to General Leader of Propaganda, Hilversum, 21 September 1934, NIOD: 123, 2.14: 1006.
175 E.g., Letter, J.L.S. [name restricted] to C. van der Voort van Zijp, Antwerpen, 11 January 1933, NIOD: 123, 2.01: 395.
176 Letter, P.F.v.Z. [name restricted] to Mussert, Mombasa, 13 March 1933, 2, NIOD: 123, 2.01: 395.
177 'Maar in plaats daarvan waren het welgeteld dertig geüniformeerde mannetjes en de omstandigheid, dat zij door "leider" Mussert met de noodige bereddering geïnspecteerd werden, nam niet weg dat het heele fascistische "leger" uit dertig man bestond', 'Keurig fascism – Maar in wezen even grof.' *Het Volk*, no. 11 890, 9 January 1933, 5.
178 ' ... ook deze groep zich inspireert op het weerzinwekkend moordfascisme met zijn grove, bombastische optreden en zijn jammerlijk lage verstandelijke peil ... ', ibid.
179 Tjalve, 'Dahlrot skrämde TT', DSN, no. 46, 15 June 1935, 1.
180 'Demonstration i Masthugget gav starkt eko', *Göteborgs-Posten*, no. 115, 22 May 1934, 1, 6.
181 'Bärande av nat.-soc. *uniformspersedlar är absolut förbjudet* ... ', DSN transcript, Instructions for *Årstinget*, 1935, Arninge: 2A: 1.
182 Damsma and Schumacher, *Hier Woont Een NSB'er*, 121.
183 Transcript of Composition and Procedure of the Regional Disciplinary Councils, NIOD: 123, 2.30: 1337.

184 E.g., Minutes, case comrade G.P. [name restricted], Rotterdam, 11 November 1936, 1, in NIOD: 123, 2.30: 2026; Minutes, Meeting High Disciplinary Council, case HP 106, concerning comrade F. [name restricted], Amsterdam, Utrecht, 24 July 1937, NIOD: 123, 2.30: 1342; Minutes, Meeting Disciplinary Council, case comrade M. [name restricted], Druten, Hilversum, 20 July 1935, NIOD: 123, 2.30: 1343; Minutes, Case comrade V. [name restricted], Schiedam, 14 November 1936, NIOD: 123, 2.30: 2026; Advisory letter, case comrade G.J.G. [name restricted], Rotterdam, 8 December 1935, NIOD: 123, 2.30: 2026.

185 'Battonger får ni allt skaffa individuellt, enär det inte hör till utrustningen.' Letter, DK [Nils Wenchert] to Ove Adamsson (avd. 39), 8 January 1934, Marieberg: NSAP/SSS, vol. 3, Södra Distriktet (1934).

186 Lindholm, Lindholm Interview, sec. 258: B; 15 July 1932, 19 July 1933, 4 July 1934, Lindholm diary.

187 As instructed in the directives for colporteurs: Directive, 'Richtlyn no. 2: Instructie straat colportage', 1, NIOD: 123, 2.01: 526.

188 *Het Volk*, no. 12 169, 24 June 1933, 13; 'Gewapende Mussert-fascisten', *Het Volk*, no. 12 273, 24 August 1933, 1.

189 '… maar zeker is, dat Mussert een zweep bij zich had, toen hij partijgenooten in de als zeer communistisch bekende wijk per auto ging bezoeken, terwijl zijn chauffeur een revolver droeg.' 'De held van het "Blauwe Zand"', *De Tijd*, no. 29 399, 15 May 1937, 6.

190 'hans SA-ledares färg var skriande röd och de fanbärande gossarna voro både sträckliga och randiga på skjortöverkroppen – ja, det var en så brokig uppsättning av skjorttyger, att man rent av märkte ironien.' 'Partiledare Lindholm vill ej bli utnämnd av Hitler', *Stockholms-Tidningen*, 25 October 1933.

191 Newspaper clipping, Per Gyberg, 'Nazistisk möteskultur', *Tidningen Freden*, no. 121, 1933, 1, Arninge: 2C: 1a.

192 Mussert quote: 'Wij zijn door Amsterdam getrokken als krijgsgevangenen, zonder vlaggen, zonder muziek.' 'De landdag der N.S.B', *Algemeen Handelsblad*, no. 35 254, 31 March 1935, 6.

193 E.g., 'Hysteriska kvinnor främst vid Masthuggskravallerna', DSN, no. 21, 24 May 1934, 5.

194 'Enkele onzer leden gaan niet naar Ymuiden, juist omdat men hun het zwarte hemd verbiedt; ze zeggen wy wenschen te getuigen van onze trouw aan het Vorstehuis [sic] en doen dat by voorkeur in een zwart hemd, de dracht van onze Beweging […] M.i. is elk compromis uit den booze, en dient het dragen van zwarte hemden onder alle omstandigheden aangemoedigd te worden, in geen geval verboden met misschien als eenigste uitzondering: in de Kerk.' Letter, T. v.d. Weide to Gen. Leader of Propaganda, Overveen, 27 August 1933, NIOD: 123, 2.01: 397.

195 Broek, *Weerkorpsen*, chap. 5.

196 Circular, WA-Inspector (Hogewind), Utrecht, 28 May 1934, NIOD: 123, 2.14: 1046.

197 'Under perioder av demokratisk uniformsskräck (uniformsförbud) bäres vit skjorta (sport- el. tenniskortja) samt brun motormössa. Obs. Stövlar och byxor äro icke uniformspersedlar.' NSAP, SA, and A-Group confiscated documents, in: Gothenburg SA-inquiry police report, 1935, 65.

198 '… vi ha gjort en del misstag. En del av dessa misstag äro att vi använt medel och symboler som avskräckt en hel del av våra folkamrater att ansluta sig till oss [sic].' Lindholm, qu., Police memorandum regarding NSAP, 3 November 1938, 3, Arninge: XII 64: 2.

199 'samt visa former för framträdandet är absolut nödvändig.' Ibid. 4.
200 'Om ni som lämna oss äro sådana tysklandsvänner, eller om ni så gärna vill gå klädda i uniformer att ni därför inte vill följa mig i fortsättningen då må ni gärna gå.' Ibid. 6.
201 'Som du förstår måste ibland formerna vika för att innehållet, *idéerna*, bättra skall kunna utbredas.' Circular, Sven-Olov Lindholm and Party Leadership to all members, Stockholm, 1 November 1939, Arninge: XII 64: 2.
202 Order concept, Mussert, Utrecht, June 1938, NIOD: 123, 1.1: 79.
203 'Leider onze Zwart Roode vlag, was my en tienduizenden wellicht met my *alles*. [...] Ik weet het, die vlag was slechts een symbool; maar toch, van my, van zoo heel velen met my, oudere kameraden is iets wèggenomen. En de leegte is door de "nieuwelinge" nog ganschelyk niet opgevuld. Wy ouderen MISSEN onze oude goede Zwartroode vlag. [...] En dan myn insigne, dat sterke hoekige eereteeken my, en ons, door U als werkers in de Beweging verleend..? Moet ik dat by myn NSB-herinneringen opbergen en ervoor in de plaats dat zoete ronde dingske spelden...?' Letter, A.P. Hengeveld to Mussert, Laren, 8 June 1938, NIOD: 123, 1.1.: 79.
204 Order from the Leader regarding flags etc., for publication in VoVa, 14 June 1938, 3–4, NIOD: 123, 1.1.: 79.
205 'Meddelande från Plg', DSN, no. 2, 11 January 1934, 2.
206 Police memorandum, regarding NSAP comrade evening, 30 March 1937, 1, Arninge: XII 64: 1.
207 'Vår tro fanns inte i våra brunskjortor eller i vår uniformering. När det inte finns något annat att angripa, angriper man i Social-Demokraten våra stövlar. Vi ämna sannerligen inte för Social-Demokratens skull anlägga några demokratiska tofflor för att verka mera fredliga. [...] En dag skall det bli det arbetande folket självt som upphäver detta kuriösa klädselförbud', -uu-, 'Stövelskräck i Social-Demokraten!', DSN, no. 39, 23 May 1936, 7.
208 'Eens zal het uur slaan, waarop wy fier en vry in onze uniformen acter onze stormvlaggen in dienst der N.S.B. op straat zullen marcheeren; maar op dat uur moeten wy ook VOLLEDIG klaar zyn.' Circular, J. Hogewind, regarding the recent *Landdag*, Utrecht, 15 October 1935, NIOD: 123, 2.14: 1046.
209 Mosse, 'Fascist Aesthetics and Society', 248.

Chapter 5

1 Mosse, George L., 'Fascist Aesthetics and Society: Some Considerations', *Journal of Contemporary History* 31, (1996), 245–7.
2 Paul, *Aufstand der Bilder*, 13.
3 David D. Roberts, *The Totalitarian Experiment in Twentieth-Century Europe: Understanding the Poverty of Great Politics* (New York: Routledge, 2006), 430–7.
4 Eichberg and Jones, 'The Nazi Thingspiel', 143–50.
5 R. Abma, 'Het Plan van de Arbeid en de SDAP', *Low Countries Historical Review* 92, no. 1 (1977), 67.
6 Bernard Rulof, 'Selling Social Democracy in the Netherlands: Activism and Its Sources of Inspiration during the 1930s', *Contemporary European History* 18, no. 4 (2009), 484–6, 495–6.
7 Derks, '"Stralende strijdlust, taaie zelfverloochening": De dynamiek van traditie en moderniteit in de Graalbeweging', 284–93.

8 Elof Eriksson, *Bonderörelsen: En historisk återblick*, vol. 1 (Stockholm: Nationens Förlag, 1946), 35–48.
9 Martschukat and Patzold, 'Geschichtswissenschaft und "Performative Turn"'.
10 Erika Fischer-Lichte, *Theatre, Sacrifice, Ritual: Exploring Forms of Political Theatre* (London: Routledge, 2005), 89–95, 128.
11 Fischer-Lichte, 'Performance, Inszenierung, Ritual', 33.
12 Fischer-Lichte, *The Transformative Power of Performance*, 51–2.
13 Fischer-Lichte, 'Performance, Inszenierung, Ritual', 44–5.
14 Alexander and Mast, 'Introduction: Symbolic Action in Theory and Practice', 3–6.
15 Andrew Parker and Eve Kosofsky Sedgwick, eds., *Performativity and Performance* (London: Routledge, 1995), 1–2.
16 Judith Butler, *Notes toward a Performative Theory of Assembly* (Cambridge, Massachusetts: Harvard University Press, 2015), 9–19.
17 Sewell, 'Space in Contentious Politics'.
18 'Meddelande från P.L.', DSN, no. 5, 15 March 1933, 2.
19 Nilsson, *Svensk Överklassnazism, 1930–1945*, 98.
20 'Det var då en milslång kolonn med medlemmar, först och främst SA-trupper från olika delar av landet, med sina olika standarer och fanor; åskådarmassor, det var läktare på sidorna, uppbyggda, där stod massor av folk, och i fönstrena och hustaken, och viftade med vimplar och flaggor, ropade och skrek. Det var nånting alldeles obeskrivligt, och sånt förekommer bara inte i Sverige.', Lindholm interview, 00256: B, c. 12 min.
21 'Congres te Utrecht: Niet het aantal, maar de kracht', VoVa, no. 1, 7 January 1933, 2.
22 The Hagespraken have been researched in some detail recently in: Heijningen, *De Muur van Mussert*.
23 'Du är ändå ledig under Pingsten!', 'Upp till TINGS!', DSN, no. 17, 26 April 1934, 10.
24 Circular, de Blocq van Scheltinga to District Leaders, Utrecht, 18 September 1939, 1–2, NIOD: 123, 2.01: 505.
25 Heijningen, *De Muur van Mussert*, 81–3, 142–3.
26 Ibid.
27 The biggest meeting Lindholm ever spoke at had an audience of reportedly 12,000 people. 19 September 1936, Lindholm diary.
28 'Den bästa propagandan för nationalsocialismen är och förblir alltjämt de offentliga mötena och uppmarscherna, där befolkningen själv kan se och höra vad nationalsocialisterna vilja, och varigenom folkfrontspressens lögnskriverier falla till marken som tomma skal.', Transcript and excerpt from *Porg*, no. 5, November 1937, Arninge: 2B: 8.
29 'Väldig frammarsch för nat.-soc. i Stockholm: 6300 röster', DSN, no. 22, 20 March 1935, 1, 6.
30 'Den tid av stora prövningar, som vi väntat på, har nu börjat.', Sven Olov Lindholm, 'Kamrater och medkämpar!', DSN, no. 22, 20 March 1935, 1.
31 Munin, 'Og. 2 Stockholm', DSN, no. 44, 8 June 1935, 4.
32 27 May 1935, Lindholm diary.
33 Tjalve, 'Vad de tyckte', DSN, no. 46, 15 June 1935, 4.
34 'Det var den 20 maj 1934. Musiken genljöd mellan husraderna, fanorna fladdrade i vinden. Men det var ingen marxismens proletärdemonstration, det var inte högerns lunkiga borgartåg, det var en folkrörelse i vardande som marscherade fram.', -rot [Nils Dahlrot], 'Till tings: I pingst samlas vi i Stockholm', DSN, no. 26, 3 April 1935, 5.

35 'Meddelande från Plg', DSN, no. 41, 29 May 1935, 2.
36 Advertisement, 'Extratåg! Res Stockholm-Göteborg i pingst!', DSN, no. 19, 10 May 1934, 2.
37 'Meddelanden', DSN, no. 37, 21 May 1938, 2.
38 'Efterskörd från årstinget', DSN, no. 46, 15 June 1935, 5.
39 NSAP monthly branch report, Fridlevstad, May 1934, Marieberg: NSAP/SSS, vol. 6.
40 Tjalve, 'Dahlrot skrämde TT: Vägrade extratåg minskade tingsdeltagarna med flera hundra!', DSN, no. 46, 15 June 1935, 1, 6.
41 'Till tings!', DSN, no. 29, 13 April 1935, 2.
42 Letter, Acting Party Secretary to Enar Häll, Gothenburg, 15 April 1935, Marieberg: NSAP/SSS, vol. 3, Västra Distriktet (1935–8).
43 'Program vid NSAP:s tredje årsting i Stockholm', DSN, no. 41, 29 May 1935, 5.
44 Wärenstam, *Fascismen och Nazismen i Sverige 1920–1940*, 140–1; Nilsson, *Svensk Överklassnazism, 1930–1945*, 154.
45 Sven-Olov Lindholm, 'Mot judefront och världsdemokrati! Samling till årstinget i Malmö!', DSN, no. 21, 19 April 1939, 3.
46 'Minst en gång om året måste du se tusentals kamrater omkring dig och marschera fram i mäktiga kolonner, en gång om året trotsa fiendernas skrän!', Sven Olov Lindholm, 'Till Stockholm i pingst! Kring landet går signalen', DSN, no. 33, 7 May 1938, 6.
47 'Det är ingen liten invigd klick, som samlas i Stockholm i Pingst, det är kämpande bataljoner som marschera upp i huvudstaden för att samlas kring sin unge hövding', -rot [Nils Dahlrot], 'NSAP samlas till ting: Stockholm står i hakkorsets tecken under pingstdagarna: Möt upp till de offentliga massmötena!', DSN, no. 44, 8 June 1935, 1.
48 ' ... Du skall själv kunna konstatera att tidningspressen ljuger, när den påstår att Lindholms kamporganisation är en liten klick, att tidningspressen ljuger, när den påstår, att NSAP utgöres endast av skolpojkar och förbrytare! Gå ut på gatorna och se på de stora uppmarscherna på Pingstdagen och Annandag Pingst.', -rot [Nils Dahlrot], 'NSAP samlas till ting: Stockholm står i hakkorsets tecken under pingstdagarna: Möt upp till de offentliga massmötena!', DSN, no. 44, 8 June 1935, 4.
49 Flyer, Marching route for NSAP *Sveatinget*, Gernandts Boktryckeri: Stockholm (1935), Arninge: 2A: 1.
50 'Årstinget 1935 (Bör utklippas av tingsdeltagarna)', DSN, no. 42, 1 June 1936, also found as a newspaper clipping in: Arninge: 2A: 1; 'Program vid NSAP:s tredje årsting i Stockholm', DSN, no. 41, 29 May 1935, 5.
51 'Meddelanden', DSN, no. 14, 20 February 1937, 4.
52 8 June 1935, Lindholm diary.
53 'nationalsocialisterna äro inga vänner av diskussioner'; 'som tänker och handlar i Lindholms anda', 'Genom nationalsocialismen vinnes frihet och bröd: Sakkunskap och kampvilja präglade tingsföredragen på Auditorium', DSN, no. 45, 12 June 1935, 5.
54 ' ... välbesatt o. på bästa humör.', 8 June 1935, Lindholm diary.
55 9 June 1935, Lindholm diary.
56 'Efterskörd från årstinget', DSN, no. 46, 15 June 1935, 4.
57 'Genom nationalsocialismen vinnes frihet och bröd', DSN, no. 45, 12 June 1935, 5.
58 Stage decoration was largely the same every year in Stockholm, and probably handled by a decoration team the night before or in the morning, see: Letter, Bertil Brisman to Lindholm, Gothenburg, 16 March 1937, Marieberg: NSAP/SSS, vol. 1, Lindholm (1935–8).

59 Photograph, 'Det tredje årstinget', DSN, no. 47, 19 June 1935, 4.
60 Cf. Mosley's entrance as mentioned in: Julie Gottlieb, 'Body Fascism in Britain: Building the Blackshirt in the Inter-War Period', *Contemporary European History* 20, no. 2 (2011), 124–5.
61 Circular no. 46, 1 March 1935, Arninge: 2B1: 3.
62 For the lyrics of 'Friheten leve!', see: Programme, *NSAP:s 5:te årsting*, Stockholm (1938), 3, Arninge: 2A: 2.
63 Ibid. 5.
64 '… hjärtliga ovationer, sång o. marschmusik.', 9 June 1935, Lindholm diary.
65 'Program vid NSAP:s tredje årsting i Stockholm', DSN, no. 41, 29 May 1935, 5.
66 Flyer, Marching route for NSAP *Sveatinget*, Gernandts Boktryckeri: Stockholm (1935), Arninge: 2A: 1.
67 IF, 1938, 19.
68 TF, 1937, 31–2; IF, 1938, 18–9.
69 IF, 1938, 19.
70 Ibid. 22.
71 Butler, *Notes toward a Performative Theory of Assembly*, 9.
72 'Varje nationalsocialist, som deltagit i en av partiet anordnat uppmarsch, vet vilket stort propagandavärde en välordnad dylik har. [...] Då vi nationalsocialister på alla områden kräva *ordning och disciplin* är det *en hederssak* för oss att ordna våra propagandaaktioner av olika slag så, att varje folkkamrat som ser och hör oss blir *imponerad* av den kampvilja, den *vilja till seger*, som präglar varje deltagare.', IF, 1938, 18–9.
73 'Det var takt och rättning och man kunde *se* på de marscherande att det var *frihetskämpar*. Vi förstår så innerligt väl att Stockholms kapitalister och marxistpampar, judar och andra parasiter blev förskräckta vid åsynen av dessa kolonner. De kunde se att dessa människor inte skulle låta sig bortkompromissas; man såg att de visste vad de ville, att de marscherade mot ett bestämt mål, Sveriges frihet.', 'Två stora massmöten och glänsande uppmarscher: 3000 åhörare i Vitabergsparken och 6000 å Östermalmstorg. Marxistöverfall', DSN, no. 45, 12 June 1935, 1.
74 9 June 1935, Lindholm diary.
75 Cf. SA marches through proletarian quarters, Reichardt, 'Fascist Marches in Italy and Germany', 181.
76 'Efterskörd från tinget', DSN, no. 46, 15 June 1935, 4.
77 'Om den frihetsrörelsen hade tidningspressen ingenting skrivit. "Tänk på att den lilla Lindholmssekten var så stor!" Stockholmarna fick sannerligen sin uppfattning om nationalsocialisterna grundligt korrigerade! Här fick de ju se med egna ögon att Sveriges nationalsocialister inte är ett hundratal furugårdska dyllkajor utan tusende bönder och arbetare från allt Sveriges land.', 'Två stora massmöten och glänsande uppmarscher', DSN, no. 45, 12 June 1935, 1, 4.
78 Audience figure as estimated by the police: 'Lindholmsnazisternas pingstmöte: Agitationsmöte i Vitabergsparken med slagsmål som efterspel', *Stockholms-Tidningen*, 11 June 1935, 5.
79 'Två stora massmöten och glänsande uppmarscher', DSN, no. 45, 12 June 1935, 4.
80 'Nazistmöte med litet gruff', *Dagens Nyheter*, 11 June 1935, 26; 'Lindholmsnazisternas pingstmöte', *Stockholms-Tidningen*, 11 June 1935, 5.
81 'Nazistkongress met åtföljande gatuuppträden: Lindholmarna ha hållit sin tredje årskongress', *Svenska Dagbladet*, 11 June 1935.

82 'Nordisk Ungdom har svår och härdande uppmarsch', DSN, no. 45, 12 June 1935, 4.
83 Sadly it is unclear whether the film has survived.
84 '... mycket stiligt o. färgrikt med alla standard o ljusblå skjortor.', 10 June 1935, Lindholm diary.
85 Extract from minutes, Over-Governorship [Överståthållarämbetet] for police matters before the police commissioner [för polisäranden inför polismästaren], 24 July 1933, Arninge: 2C: 3.
86 'Hade polisen fått order att förstöra NSAP:s marschkolonner?', DSN, no. 46, 15 June 1935, 3.
87 'Efterskörd från årstinget', DSN, no. 46, 15 June 1935, 4.
88 '... vår bästa propagandistiska tillgång ...', 'Annandagens förhandlingar', DSN, no. 45, 12 June 1935, 8.
89 10 June 1935, Lindholm diary.
90 Frank-Lothar Kroll, 'Endzeit, Apokalypse, Neuer Mensch – Utopische Potentiale im Nationalsozialismus und im Bolschewismus', in *Rechtsextreme Ideologien in Geschichte und Gegenwart*, ed. Uwe Backes (Köln: Böhlau, 2003), 139, 155.
91 'Ja – vi vill fortsätta Sveriges historia säger svaret som skallar från nordlandets fjäll till Öresund – från väster- till österland! Ja – vi vill bekänna oss till den folkvilja som strömmar i det egna blodet! Här vill vi upprätta ett arbetarnas fria fosterland och här kämpa för den kultur som kan tala till nordiska hjärtan, till folkets egen själ!', Sven Olov Lindholm, '"Svensk frihet är vår lösen": Lindholms tal på Östermalmstorg i Stockholm', DSN, no. 48, 23 June 1935, 4.
92 The figure of the brooder was probably a reference to Odin, see: Viktor Rydberg, *Fädernas Gudasaga, m.m.*, Skrifter av Viktor Rydberg, XII (Stockholm: Albert Bonnier, 1918), 39.
93 The translation is my own – no English translation has been published to date, to my knowledge.
94 'Där vävas, kretsande i rymden, stjärnor / och tankar, kretsande i mänskohjärnor, / där väves alstringen, där väves döden, / och tingens skepnader och folkens öden. / Där inslås mönster, skiftande och bjärta, / som nervgarn, dallrande i lust och smärta, / men mönstrets ämne är för alltid givet, / en hejdlös, oupphörlig kamp för livet.', DSN, ibid.
95 Are Waerland, *Idealism och Materialism* (Uppsala: J.A. Lindblads Förlag, 1924), 29–30.
96 'Vi tro oss vilja, tro oss kunna även, / men äro trådfigurer blott i väven.', 'Grubblaren', in: Viktor Rydberg, *Dikter* (Stockholm: Albert Bonnier, 1929), 201.
97 'Vi forma Ditt öde, Sverige, med kärlekens starka röst / och sjunga Din framtids lovsång ur tusende unga bröst! / Flyg ut, våra frihetsfanor i kampens vakna vår – / det är morgendagen som randas – det är arbetets folk som slår!', Sven Olov, 'Folket som slår', DSN, no. 51, 3 July 1935, 4.
98 10 June 1935, Lindholm diary.
99 13 June 1935, Lindholm diary.
100 'Mot lögn och förtryck! NSAP:s tredje årsting blev en väldig frihetsdemonstration mot kapitaldemokratiens terrorlagar', DSN, no. 45, 12 June 1935, 1.
101 'Det tredje årstinget', DSN, no. 47, 19 June 1935, 4.
102 'Tinget har genomförts på önskvärt sätt i organisatorisk avseende. Att det i vissa fall överträffat allas våra förväntningar är ju enbart roligt att konstatera. Men inget är ju så bra att det inte kan bli bättre.', Tjalve, 'Vad de tyckte', DSN, no. 46, 15 June 1935, 4.
103 See especially the response from Ivar Johansson from Götene, ibid.

104 'ALDRIG TILLFÖRE HAR KAMPGEISTEN VARIT SÅ KRAFTIG OCH ALDRIG HAR VÄL FÖLJET GIVIT SIN LEDARE STÖRRE BEVIS PÅ ODÖDLIG TROHET OCH HÄNGIVENHET. Det skulle stärkt Dig att vara med kamrat.', Letter, GS [Gunnar Svalander] to Dch. A[rvid] Gerhardsson, Stockholm, 14 June 1935, Marieberg: NSAP/SSS, vol. 3, Sydöstra Distriktet (1936–8).
105 Lindholm interview, 00259: A, 1 min.
106 'Två extratåg till Stockholm i pingst: Fjärde årstinget skall överglänsa de tidigare', DSN, no. 27, 10 April 1937, 3.
107 'Våra sympatisörer landet runt kunna härigenom få föreställning om massanslutningen, förhållandena och kanske även stämningen. Och tingsdeltagarna få i fotografierna ett värdefullt minne från de oförglömmeliga kampdagarna, ett band som skall knyta dem fastare samman med kamraterna och egga dem till nya och kraftfulla ansträngningar.', DSN, no. 22B, 31 May 1934, 3.
108 In his 1943 book Lindholm declared the 1937–8 Sveating the most impressive of the decade: Lindholm, *Svensk Frihetskamp*, 39.
109 Transcript, Programme for NSAP's fourth *årsting* in Stockholm, 2, 1937, Arninge: 2A: 2.
110 Programme booklet (Lindholm private copy), *N.S.A.P.s 5:te årsting: Stockholm 4–6 juni 1938*, 4–5, Marieberg: SO Lindholms samling, vol. 8.

Chapter 6

1 Paul Stoop, *Niederländische Presse unter Druck: Deutsche Auswärtige Pressepolitik und die Niederlande 1933–1940* (München: Saur, 1987), 71.
2 Ger van Roon, *Zwischen Neutralismus und Solidarität: Die evangelischen Niederlande und der deutsche Kirchenkampf, 1933–1942* (Stuttgart: Deutsche Verlags-Anstalt, 1983), chap. 7.
3 Letter, District Leader [d'Ansembourg] to Mussert, Amstenrade, 1 October 1935, NIOD: 123, 1.1: 37.
4 Huberts, *In de Ban van een Beter Verleden*, 65; Verhagen, *Toen de Katholieken Nederland Veroverden*, 288–9.
5 Orlow, *The Lure of Fascism in Western Europe*, 67.
6 Havenaar, *De NSB tussen Nationalisme en 'Volkse' Solidariteit*, 101–6.
7 Minutes for meeting, 11 July 1935, §1, 22–3, in: Book, meeting minutes *Algemeene Raad*, NIOD: 123, 1.3: 276.
8 '... de leden vergeten, dat de landdag wordt gehouden om indruk naar buiten te maken ... '; 'Het massale van den landdag is noodig om naar buiten te kunnen toonen hoe krachtig onze Beweging is en ook de noodzakelykheid wordt gevoeld om de leden, die ver af wonen eens te midden van hun overige Kameraden te brengen', Minutes for meeting, unknown date, Utrecht, §6, 47–8, ibid.
9 'Een landdag houden in October is met het oog [op] het jaargetij niet uitvoerbaar. Zouden wij dat in September doen, dan moet het geluk met ons zijn om droog weer te hebben ... ', ibid. 49.
10 CID report, 'Landdag N.S.B.', C.I. no. 22787, 's-Gravenhage, 23 July 1935, The Hague: Ministry of Internal Affairs cabinet archive 1918–1935, 2.04.26.02: 612, 22787a.
11 Letter, Mayor of 's-Gravenhage to Minister of Internal Affairs, 's-Gravenhage, 31 July 1935: The Hague, 2.04.26.02: 612, 22787a.

12 CID report, 'Landdag N.S.B.', C.I. no. 24348, 's-Gravenhage, 16 September 1935, The Hague: 2.13.70 (General Staff archive, 1914–1940): 1574, 24348a.
13 'Het is voor ons fascisten van het grootste belang, dat het reizen per extra-trein en het marcheeren door Den Haag in de meest volmaakte orde en regelmaat geschiedt', Circular, 'Organisatie 4e Algemeene Landdag. Algemeene instructies', Utrecht, 5 October 1935, The Hague: 2.19.049: 3.
14 Cf. the *Landdag* document-bundle, 'Landdag', Utrecht, The Hague: 2.19.049: 3.
15 Letter, Dutch Railway Service (Dienst der Exploitatie) to J. de Vries, Utrecht, 24 October 1935, NIOD: 123, 2.55: 2004.
16 Circular no. 1, 'Verkoop van deelnemerskaarten', Organization of the 4th General *Landdag*, The Hague, NIOD: 123, 2.55: 2004.
17 Letter, Dutch Railway Service (Dienst der Exploitatie) to Mussert, Utrecht, 18 April 1936, NIOD: 123, 1.1: 53.
18 Letter [model], Musser to Circle Leader, Utrecht, 12 September 1935, NIOD: 123, 1.1: 39.
19 Week report, 26–31 August 1935, Zaandam et al., NIOD: 123, 2.55: 2004.
20 Circular, A. Groeneveld to Circle 20 West-Betuwe, Tiel, [no date], NIOD: 123, 2.55: 2004.
21 '4e Algemeene Landdag te 's-Gravenhage', VoVa, no. 32, 10 August 1935, 1.
22 'Vierde Algemeene Landdag: Een massale opmarsch', VoVa, no. 33, 17 August 1935, 10; 'De N.S.B. aan het werk: De dag van vijf October in voorbereiding', VoVa, no. 35, 31 August 1935, 5; 'Het werkkamp der N.S.B.: Voor den Landdag in Den Haag', VoVa, 7 September 1935, 8–9.
23 'Deze Landdag wordt een gebeurtenis in Nederland, die haar weerga niet kent. De Landdag zal een stempel drukken op Nederland van 1935, die beleeft hoe uit het Nederlandsche Volk de wil naar voren is gekomen om zich te ontworstelen aan een regenten-régime, dat dit volk dreigt te verstikken.' Circular no. 7, NSB Central Election Bureau to all Circle leaders, Amsterdam, 30 August 1935, The Hague: 2.19.049: 3.
24 Circular, Provincial *Landdag* representative to District III (Limburg & North-Brabant), The Hague: 2.19.049: 1.
25 'Voor hen die thans nog twijfelen, zal het zien van deze film den doorslag geven, terwijl anderen er door opgewekt worden meerdere belangstellenden naar Den HAAG mede te brengen.' Circular no. 1, Service 5 (Film) to all Convention representatives, The Hague, 28 August 1935, The Hague: 2.19.049: 3.
26 Letter, Dutch Clearing Institute to NSB *Landdag* Organization, 's-Gravenhage, 8 October 1935, NIOD: 123, 2.55: 2004.
27 Diagram, 'Werkkamp', 7 September–26 October, NIOD: 123, 2.55: 2004.
28 'De geest onder de kameraden is voortreffelyk.'; 'Dit zal voor hen meer beteekenen, dan toespraken en dankbetuigingen.', Letter, Jacob de Vries to Mussert, The Hague, 19 September 1935, NIOD: 123, 1.1: 37.
29 CI report, 'Revolutionaire actie bij een werkkamp van de N.S.B.', C.I. no. 25160, 's-Gravenhage, 11 October 1935, The Hague: 2.13.70: 1574.
30 Report, 'on the investigation into the unrest at Leiweg, The Hague, evening of 3 to 4 October 1935', 2–3, NIOD: 123, 2.56: 2020.
31 'Ontevredenheid in N.S.B.-werkkamp', *Algemeen Handelsblad*, no. 35443, 08 October 1935, 3; 'Moeilijkheden in N.S.B.-werkkamp', *De Tijd*, 4 October 1935, 2.
32 'Met discipline staat en valt de W.A.; zonder discipline geen wacht, geen troep, geen vendel. Slechts dan kan discipline in een afdeeling gebracht worden, indien er *tot het*

33 *uiterste* de hand aan gehouden wordt, dat een gegeven order *onvoorwaardelyk* door "iederen" man wordt opgevolgd.' Message, WA-inspector to all WA-commanders, 'Discipline', Utrecht, 23 October 1935, The Hague: 2.19.049: 3.
33 Letter [copy for Mussert], Slinkert to Jacob de Vries, Nymegen, 18 September 1935, 1.1: 37.
34 'Vermoedelyk zal de pers, vooral de Chr. pers het als zynde Zondagsontheiliging, uitbuiten en het haar lezers voorhouden, als een bewys dat de N.S.B. het zoo nauw niet neemt met de Zondagsheiliging', Letter, *Landdag* organizer of the IJmuiden Circle to the *Landdag* organizer [de Vries], IJmuiden, 20 August 1935, NIOD: 123, 2.55: 2004.
35 'steen des aanstoots', Letter, M.J. Bomers to Mussert, 's-Gravenhage, 4 April 1934, NIOD: 123, 1.1: 22.
36 Letter, Circle Leader 15 IJmuiden to Jacob de Vries, IJmuiden, 29 August 1935, NIOD: 123, 2.55: 2004.
37 Urgent circular, to Circle papers, Amsterdam, 26 May 1936, NIOD: 123, 2.01: 504.
38 E.g.: VoVa, no. 39, 28 September 1935, 1, 4; Rob Delsing, 'Als één man ... ', VoVa, no. 40, 5 October 1935, 4.
39 See letters of acceptation and rejection from the various newspapers in: NIOD: 123, 2.55: 2004.
40 *Het Landdag Gedenkboek: ter herinnering aan den 4den Algemeenen Landdag der N.S.B. gehouden te Den Haag op 12 October 1935*, (Hobera: Amsterdam-Zuid, 1935), 6, International Institute for Social History (IISG), Amsterdam, Bro N 188.
41 'Van het Noorden en het Zuiden, uit alle sociale lagen, uit alle maatschappelijke standen en beroepen zijn de pioniers van een nieuwe volksgemeenschap bijeengekomen', Programme booklet, *N.S.B.: 4e Landdag, 5 October 1935*, 33, NIOD: 123, 1.1: 37.
42 Diagram marching column, 'Samenstelling van den optocht', The Hague: 2.19.049: 3.
43 'De N.S.B. marcheert: Vierde Landdag in Den Haag', VoVa, no. 42, 19 October 1935, 5.
44 ' ... bovengenoemde deelnemers geen spreekkoren mogen vormen, niet mogen zingen, geen muziek mogen maken, geen doeken en borden met leuzen en geen vaandels en vlaggen, met uitzondering van nationale vlaggen ... ', Letter transcript, Mayor of 's-Gravenhage, Ag. No. 19 383, NIOD: 123, 2.55: 2004.
45 'De N.S.B. marcheert', VoVa, no. 42, 19 October 1935, 5.
46 Cf. Matthias Reiss, 'Introduction', in *The Street as Stage: Protest Marches and Public Rallies since the Nineteenth Century* (Oxford: Oxford University Press, 2007), 15–6.
47 De B., 'Langs de straten van Den Haag', VoVa, no. 42, 19 October 1935, 2.
48 'De N.S.B. marcheert', VoVa, no. 42, 19 October 1935, 5.
49 Fischer-Lichte, *The Transformative Power of Performance*, 38–9.
50 'De N.S.B. marcheert', VoVa, no. 42, 19 October 1935, 5.
51 Ground plan and diagram of tent and marching procession entry, NIOD: 123, 2.55: 2014.
52 Programme booklet, *N.S.B.: 4e Landdag, 5 October 1935*, NIOD: 123, 1.1: 37.
53 Report, meeting District Council North-South-Holland, The Hague, 5 November 1935, 1, NIOD: 123, 2.01 534.
54 *Volks* (i.e. of the people, but with racialist connotations, cf. German *Völkisch*) refers to the race-oriented faction of the NSB, characterized by a desire for close ties with Nazi Germany, conceptions of a single Germanic race and culture, and anti-Semitism. The *Dietse* state was the goal of uniting all Dutch-speaking regions (principally understood as the Netherlands, Flanders and the Boers of South Africa) in one

state, Dietsland. The *volkse* current of NSB ideology became increasingly associated with a pro-German politics, and under the German Occupation specifically with collaboration with the SS and its greater-Germanic agenda, while the goal of Dietsland became a proponent of those wishing for a sovereign and independent Dutch state separate from the German Reich, including Mussert in particular.

55 Programme booklet, *N.S.B.: 4e Landdag, 5 October 1935*, 24, NIOD: 123, 1.1: 37.
56 Berezin, *Making the Fascist Self*, 116.
57 'Onnoodig U te zeggen, dat deze massale gelofte-aflegging op den Landdag volledig zal moeten slagen en een grootschen indruk op alle aanwezigen zal moeten achterlaten. Ieder administratief functionaris dient dus alles in het werk te stellen, opdat aan geen daarvoor in aanmerking komend voorloopig lid deze onvergetelijke plechtigheid zal kunnen ontgaan.' Circular no. 6/1935, Head of Department 1 to all Circle Leaders, Amsterdam, 3 August 1935, The Hague: 2.19.049: 3.
58 'De geschiedenis zal u verheffen tot redders van ons Volk en van ons Vaderland, indien gij uw aandeel in den strijd aanvaardt. Moge dan dit uur u in herinnering blijven zoolang ge leeft en moogt gij aan het einde uwer dagen met voldoening kunnen terugzien op de daad, die gij heden verricht. Uw volk roept u, gij meldt u, de N.S.B. aanvaardt u. God zij met u.', Mussert speech MS, 'Gelofte-aflegging', 5, NIOD: 123, 1.1: 37; also printed in: 'Gelofte-aflegging: De Toespraak van den Algemeen Leider', VoVa, 19 October 1935, no. 42, 4.
59 *Het Landdag Gedenkboek* (1935), 53.
60 'De plechtigheid, waarbij onze Algemeen Leider zesduizend nieuwe leden de gelofte afnam na het houden eener toespraak, welke niet slechts om de wijze, waarop zij was geformuleerd, diepen indruk maakte, maar meer dan ooit den realiteitszin van het nationaal-socialisme helder deed uitstralen, vormde ongetwijfeld een der hoogtepunten van den landdag. Want het was niet slechts een appèl voor deze zesduizend man, met geheven arm staande vóór hun leider in de vrijgemaakte ruimte rondom het podium en tot ver in doorloop. Het was een appèl voor heel de N.S.B.', 'De N.S.B. marcheert', VoVa, 19 October 1935, 5.
61 Programme booklet, *N.S.B.: 4e Landdag, 5 October 1935*, 25, NIOD: 123, 1.1: 37.
62 'Nazi's hielden hun landdag: Kil hoogtijfeest', *Het Volk*, no. 13582, 14 October 1935 3.
63 Ground plan and diagram of tent and marching procession entry, NIOD: 123, 2.55: 2014.
64 Circular, J. Hogewind to all WA & RWA Commanders, Utrecht, August 1935, NIOD: 123, 2.14: 1046.
65 WA marching diagram, 'Schets van de opstelling', accompanying Hogewind's circular, NIOD: 123, 2.14: 1046.
66 Circular, Hogewind to all WA & RWA Commanders, Utrecht, 15 October 1935, NIOD: 123, 2.13: 1046.
67 *Het Landdag Gedenkboek* (1935), 16.
68 'De N.S.B. marcheert', VoVa, 19 October 1935, 5.
69 Or Guide, see: William Duane, *A Military Dictionary, or, Explanation of the Several Systems of Discipline of Different Kinds of Troops*, (Philadelphia: William Duane, 1810), 244, 'Guides'.
70 Diagram of the procession, NIOD: 123, 2.13: 1046.
71 ' ... dien geest van jonge heroïek ... ', 'De N.S.B. marcheert', VoVa, 19 October 1935, 5.
72 Cf.: Paul, *Aufstand der Bilder*, 174–7.
73 'Groote dingen zijn er op komst; wij gevoelen de grootheid van dezen tijd en onze eigen nietigheid, maar tevens onze verantwoordelijkheid en onze vastberadenheid en

ons geloof, dat ons den weg zal worden gewezen, als wij de waarachtigheid en de liefde tot God en onze medemenschen als richtsnoer voor ons denken en handelen willen nemen.', Mussert speech MS, '4e Landdag 5 October 1935', 5, NIOD: 123, 1.1.: 37.
74 Ibid. 28.
75 'De N.S.B. marcheert', VoVa, 19 October 1935, 5.
76 Kennedy, *The Spectator and the Spectacle*, 3–14.
77 E.g.: 'In de politiek: De dilettanten', *De Tijd*, no. 27785, 24 September 1934, 1.
78 'N.S.B.-landdag in Loosduinen', *De Maasbode*, no. 26419, 13 October 1935, 3.
79 'De Landdag van de N.S.B.', *De Standaard*, no. 19475, 14 October 1935, 3.
80 'Over deze paden trekken duizenden uit alle deelen van ons land – 35 000 mannen en vrouwen in totaal – naar het centrale punt: een tent, zoo reusachtig in afmetingen als men er in ons land nog geen heeft gezien.', 'N.S.B.-Landdag: Ir. Mussert over den buitenlandschen toestand en over Ned.-Indië', *De Tijd*, no. 28427, 13 October 1935, 2.
81 Ibid.
82 'Dank zij de medewerking van de Overheid en organen van den democratischen staat, dien de N.S.B. vurig haat en ondermijnt, kwamen de deelnemers veilig op het terrein ... ', *De Standaard*, ibid.
83 'Toen de landdagbezoekers eenmaal op het terrein waren ... was in de stad aan niets meer te merken, dat daarbuiten aan de Leyweg de heer Mussert en zijn volksgenoten een overigens tamelijk kil hoogtijfeest vierden.', 'Nazi's hielden hun landdag: Kil hoogtijfeest', *Het Volk*, no. 13582, 14 October 1935, 3.
84 'Wij zagen de landdag dus zoals de meerderheid van de 35 000 aanwezigen haar moeten hebben gezien: een mastbos van honderden palen, verlopend in een onbestemde verte, guirlandes van kleine lampjes, meters vlaggedoek en ergens, héél ver weg, een hel verlichte oranje-plek: dat zou het podium zijn.. .... [...] Iets te zien was er niet. Mussert kon verschijnen en verdwijnen, wij zagen hem niet ... ja, zesduizend leden konden worden beëdigd, zonder dat iemand onzer ook maar een glimpje vatten kon van wat daarvoor in het licht der schijnwerpers voorviel.', *Het Volk*, ibid.
85 'Ik durf zeggen, dat elk goed spreker een even krachtig applaus uit deze menigte, die geen kennis heeft, gehaald had als hij direct na Mussert precies het tegenovergestelde had betoogd.', *De Standaard*, ibid.
86 'Dat het beginsellooze, vrijzinnige volksdeel zich daardoor laat vangen is al erg, dat menschen, die Christenen willen zijn zich door zulke drogredenen laten misleiden is droevig.', ibid.
87 'Wij hebben een défilé meegemaakt van misschien duizend zwarthemden, dat veel herinnerde aan de beroemde parades in Potsdam onder een zeker vorst. Als grimmige gezichten en hard stampen synoniem zijn met heldenmoed, dan beschikt Mussert inderdaad over een keurkorps.', ibid.
88 'Oog om oog en tand om tand, is de leer. Alleen bevelen we deze woorden nog een bijzondere ter overweging aan, bij *die deelnemers* van den Landdag die in Den Haag bij "kameraden" werden ondergebracht omdat ze godsdienstige bezwaren hadden tegen terugreizen per trein in den nacht van Zaterdag op Zondag. Zulke nauwgezette Christenen mogen deze taal en moraal wel eens toetsen aan de Heilige Schrift', ibid.
89 'Nürnberg in Holland: Alles Duitsch wat de klok slaat', *De Tijd*, 15 October 1935, 1.
90 'In Den Haag heeft de N.S.B. een landdag gehouden, die volslagen een nabootsing was van den Parteitag in Neurenberg: défilé's, verheerlijking van de oude Germaansche samenleving, veroordeeling van het Joodsche internationale Marxisme,

helden- en doodenvereering met "Ich hatt' einen Kameraden" en ten sloote een soort vergoddelijking van den leider, althans van het Führerprinzip.', ibid.
91 'Dit is een ergerlijke usurpatie van het lied der Nassau's ten voordeele van de persoonlijke glorie van Mussert.', ibid.
92 See also: 'Fascisme: Contra Nationaal-socialisme', *De Tijd*, no. 28103, 2 April 1935, 1; 'De groote mond: De N.S.B. vergadert', *De Tijd*, no. 29040, 13 October 1936, 1.
93 ' ... hulde voor de prachtige regeling en orde dan hulde voor het ontzaggelijken werk zoaals bouw van tent ... ', Letter, [signature illegible] to Mussert, Rotterdam, 15 October 1935, NIOD: 123, 1.1:37.
94 ' ... zooals zij in het R.A.I. gebouw hingen, daar vele van onze Bremer Kameraden zooiets nooit hebben gezien.', Letter, W.R. van de Loo Jr to the NSB, Bremen, 2 April 1935, NIOD: 123, 2.55: 2004.
95 'Ik voel me gedrongen, U langs deze weg mijn oprechte trouw te bewijzen. Een dag als Zaterdag j.l. geeft je iets wat niets anders in staat is te geven. Het is jammer, dat niet al onze tegenstanders een dergelijke dag meemaken, misschien zouden zich dan hun gedachten ... ', Letter, [signature illegible] to Mussert, Groningen, 15 November 1935, NIOD: 123, 1.1: 37.
96 'Kommunisterna och nazisterna ha firat pingst', *Dagens Nyheter*, 18 May 1937, 11.
97 'Uniformsåtal mot nazister', *Dagens Nyheter*, 31 May 1939, 13.
98 Aerts et al., *Land van Kleine Gebaren*, 218.
99 Meyers, *Mussert*, 72.
100 1935 was no exception: Tjalve, 'Dahlrot skrämde TT: Vägrade extratåg minskade tingsdeltagarna med flera hundra!', DSN, no. 46, 15 June 1935, 1.
101 'Vad de sade om Öresundstinget: Alla var av en mening: Det bästa tinget hittills!', DSN, no. 38, 4 June 1939, 4.
102 Cf.: Eichberg and Jones, 'The Nazi Thingspiel', 139.
103 Heijningen, *De Muur van Mussert*, 38.
104 Programme booklet, *N.S.B.: 4e Landdag, 5 October 1935*, NIOD: 123, 1.1: 37.
105 'Gramofoonplaten landdag', VoVa, no. 19, 12 May 1934, 6.
106 Advertisement circular, '"De Hagespraak" Geïllustreerd Gedenkboek', NIOD: 123, 2.55: 2005.
107 Monthly report, Alb. van Leeuwen Jr, Chief of Materials Circle 67 (The Hague South), 4 April 1936, 3, NIOD: 123, 2.10: 855.
108 Heijningen, *De Muur van Mussert*, 31–2.
109 Cf.: Eichberg and Jones, 'The Nazi Thingspiel', 141.
110 Fischer-Lichte, *Theatre, Sacrifice, Ritual*, 23–30.
111 Cf.: Grunwald, *Courtroom to Revolutionary Stage*, 173–5.
112 Gentile, *The Sacralization of Politics in Fascist Italy*, 25–6.
113 This does correspond to the more watered down notion of political religion, as simply 'a political religiosity', 'the acknowledgment of a divine meaning in history and life': Gentile, *Politics as Religion*, 36–7.
114 Alexander, 'Cultural Pragmatics: Social Performance between Ritual and Strategy', 29–54.
115 Berezin, *Making the Fascist Self*, 28.
116 Annette F. Timm, 'Mothers, Whores, or Sentimental Dupes?', in *Beyond the Racial State: Rethinking Nazi Germany*, ed. Devin O. Pendas, Mark Roseman, and Richard F. Wetzell (Cambridge: Cambridge University Press, 2017), 344–5.
117 For a further discussion of the limited heuristic use of 'political religion', see: Baumeister, 'Faschismus als "politischer Religion"', 67.

118 Roberts, 'Myth, Style, Substance and the Totalitarian Dynamic in Fascist Italy', 6.
119 Fischer-Lichte, *The Transformative Power of Performance*, 27.
120 Mosse, *The Nationalization of the Masses*, 7.
121 Karlsson and Ruth, *Samhället som Teater*, 16.
122 This parallels what Berezin argued the Italian Fascist regime attempted to achieve with its public rituals and festivals: Berezin, *Making the Fascist Self*, 7, 19-20.
123 Introduction to: Gudrun Brockhaus, ed., *Attraktion der NS-Bewegung* (Essen: Klartext, 2014), 8.

Conclusion

1 Letter, Scheveningen, 6 May 1946, Mussert, *Nagelaten Bekentenissen*, 240.
2 Åmark, *Att Bo Granne med Ondskan*, 326.
3 Gyllenhaal and Westberg, *Svenskar i Krig, 1914-1945*, 246-52.
4 Lindholm, *Soldatliv och Politik*, II, 10-8.
5 Lööw, *Hakkorset och Wasakärven*, 420-8, 435.
6 Lööw, *Nazismen i Sverige 1980-1999*, 439-40.
7 Stenfeldt, *Renegater*, 226-9; see also: Stenfeldt, 'The Fascist Who Fought for World Peace: Conversions and Core Concepts in the Ideology of the Swedish Nazi Leader Sven Olov Lindholm'.
8 Lööw, *Hakkorset och Wasakärven*, 71-3.
9 Lindholm, *Döm Ingen Ohörd*, 2nd ed., 12-26.
10 Wichert Ten Have, *De Nederlandse Unie: Aanpassing, Vernieuwing En Confrontatie in Bezettingstijd 1940-1941* (Amsterdam: Prometheus, 1999).
11 Peter Romijn, *Burgemeesters in Oorlogstijd: Besturen tijdens de Duitse Bezetting* (Amsterdam: Balans, 2006), 17-9.
12 Jonge, *Het Nationaal-Socialisme in Nederland*, 174.
13 Heijningen, *De Muur van Mussert*, 142-3.
14 Kunkeler, 'Narratives of Decline in the NSB', 220-3; N. K. C. A. in 't Veld, ed., *De SS en Nederland: Documenten uit SS-Archieven 1935-1945*, 2 vols ('S-Gravenhage: Nijhoff, 1976).
15 Sytze Van Der Zee, *Voor Führer, Volk en Vaderland Sneuvelde ... : De SS in Nederland, Nederland in de SS* (Den Haag: Kruseman's, 1975).
16 *Het Proces Mussert*, 10, 112-50.
17 'De Beweging is geofferd op het altaar van het Vaderland.' Mussert, *Nagelaten Bekentenissen*, 58.
18 Ismee Tames, *Besmette Jeugd: De Kinderen van NSB'ers na de Oorlog* (Amsterdam: Balans, 2009), 13.
19 Cf.: Grunwald, *Courtroom to Revolutionary Stage*, 173-4.
20 The great potential for mobilization in fascist myth has also been observed by scholars of totalitarian regimes, see: Roberts, *The Totalitarian Experiment in Twentieth-Century Europe*, 437-8.
21 'För att skapa en ungdomsrörelse och föra den vidare framåt måste finnas ett sammankittande, eggande element: *en myt*. En tanke av väldig resning, vilken förenar alla och driver dem framåt i hängivet arbete för dess förverkligande', Arne Clementsson, 'Vår myt', DSN, no. 93, 1 December 1937, 6.

22 Nigel Copsey, "'Fascism … but with an Open Mind." Reflections on the Contemporary Far Right in (Western) Europe', *Fascism: Journal of Comparative Fascism Studies* 1, no. 2 (2013), 10–7.
23 E.g. the American Nazi Party of George Lincoln Rockwell, or the likes of Colin Jordan and John Tyndall in Britain with the National Socialist Movement and World Union of National Socialists. Nicholas Goodrick-Clarke, *Black Sun: Aryan Cults, Esoteric Nazism, and the Politics of Identity* (New York: New York University Press, 2002), 8–40.
24 John F. Pollard, 'Skinhead Culture: The Ideologies, Mythologies, Religions and Conspiracy Theories of Racist Skinheads', *Patterns of Prejudice* 50, no. 4–5 (2016), 398–419.
25 Extracts from NSAP rules and regulations, 2B: 4, SRA, Arninge.
26 Kunkeler, 'Sven Olov Lindholm and the Literary Inspirations of Swedish Fascism', 88–92.
27 Interview, 257:a. Kunkeler, 'Sven Olov Lindholm and the Literary Inspirations of Swedish Fascism'.
28 Kunkeler, 'Narratives of Decline in the Dutch National Socialist Movement, 1931–1945', 220–2. See also: Emerson Vermaat, *Anton Mussert en zijn conflict met de SS* (Soesterberg: Aspekt, 2011).
29 Meyers, *Mussert*, 131.
30 Some of this research has been done for Amsterdam, but not in a comparative way: Damsma and Schumacher, '"De Strijd om Amsterdam": Een nieuwe benadering in het onderzoek naar de NSB'.
31 Cf.: Grunwald, *Courtroom to Revolutionary Stage*.
32 Aristotle Kallis, 'The "Fascist Effect": On the Dynamics of Political Hybridization in Inter-War Europe', in *Rethinking Fascism and Dictatorship in Europe*, ed. Aristotle Kallis and António Costa Pinto (Basingstoke: Palgrave Macmillan, 2014), 15.
33 Bauerkämper, 'Fascism Without Borders', 215.
34 Roberts, 'Myth, Style, Substance and the Totalitarian Dynamic in Fascist Italy', 10, 18; Roberts, 'Fascism and the Framework for Interactive Political Innovation during the Era of the Two World Wars', 47–8.
35 Cf.: Introduction to: Arnd Bauerkämper and Grzegorz Rossolinkski-Liebe, *Fascism without Borders*, 4–5.
36 E.g.: Huberts, *In de Ban van een Beter Verleden*, 8–11; Lundberg, *En Idé Större än Döden*, 48–53.
37 Dobry, 'Desperately Seeking "Generic Fascism": Some Discordant Thoughts on the Academic Recycling of Indigenous Categories', 59–61. See also the ongoing European Fascist Movements project led by Roland Clark and Tim Grady, with Michaela Moriarty.
38 Roberts, *Fascist Interactions*, 16–7.
39 What has been identified as the ephemerality and hollowness of fascism, see: Ibid. 274.
40 Vincent, 'Political Violence and Mass Society', 390–400.

Bibliography

Archives

Amsterdam, NIOD Institute for War, Holocaust and Genocide Studies
Krantenknipsels, (KA II, newspaper clippings)
NSB, (123)
Driehoek, Boekhandel en sigarenbedrijf (173)
The Hague, National Archives
NSB, Gewest III (2.19.049)
Ministry of Internal Affairs (2.04.26.02)
General Staff (1574)
Arninge, Stockholm, National Archives of Sweden (Allmänna Säkerhetstjänstens arkiv)
SNSP
Kongresser, konferenser, ting
Teser, program, stadgar
Nybildade organisationer
Aktiviteter och propaganda
SSS ungdomsorganisation
Polisrazzian hos NSAP
SSS valverksamheten
Nat.soc. illegal verksamhet
XII 64
Den Svenske Folksocialisten
Nazism
Sven Olov Lindholm
Sven Hedengren
Marieberg, Stockholm, National Archives of Sweden
Eric Wärenstams arkiv
Kopiesamlingen III
Martin Ekströms arkiv
NSAP/SSS arkiv
Otto Hallbergs arkiv
SO Lindholms samling
Stockholm, Military Archives of Sweden (National Archives of Sweden)
Svenska Brigaden

Newspapers

Algemeen Handelsblad
Arbetar-Tidningen
Dagens Nyheter
De Maasbode

De Nederlander
Nieuwe Rotterdamsche Courant
Ny Dag
Social-Demokraten
De Standaard
Stockholms-Tidningen
Den Svenska Folksocialisten
Den Svenske Nationalsocialisten
Svenska Dagbladet
Sydsvenska Dagbladet
De Telegraaf
De Tijd
De Tribune
Utrechtsche Courant
Het Volk
Volk en Vaderland
(*Dutch newspapers accessed online, at* www.delpher.nl)

Other published primary sources

Geelkerken, Cornelis Van, ed. *Voor Volk en Vaderland*. 2nd Edition. Utrecht: Nenasu, 1943.
Heide, Homan van der. *Mussert als Ingenieur*. Utrecht: Nenasu, 1944.
Het Proces Mussert. Amsterdam: Rijksinstituut voor Oorlogsdocumentatie, 1987.
Hitler, Adolf. *Mein Kampf: Eine kritische Edition*. Vol. 1. 2 vols. Munich & Berlin: Institut für Zeitgeschichte, 2016.
Huizinga, Johan. *In de Schaduwen van Morgen: Een Diagnose van het Geestelijk Lijden van onzen Tijd*. 6th Edition. Haarlem: H.D. Tjeenk Willink & Zoon N.V., 1936.
Knab, Otto Michael. *Kleinstadt unterm Hakenkreuz: Groteske Erinnerungen aus Bayern*. Luzern: Räbert, 1934.
Lindholm, Sven Olov. *Svensk Frihetskamp*. Stockholm, 1943.
Mussert, Anton. *Nagelaten Bekentenissen: Verantwoording en Celbrieven van de NSB-Leider*, edited by Gerard Groeneveld. Nijmegen: Vantilt, 2005.
Mussert, Anton. *Richtlijnen voor een Nederlandsch-Belgische Overeenkomst*. Utrecht: A. Oosthoek, 1927.
Rydberg, Viktor. *Dikter*. Stockholm: Albert Bonnier, 1929.
Rydberg, Viktor. *Fädernas Gudasaga, m.m.* Skrifter av Viktor Rydberg, XII. Stockholm: Albert Bonnier, 1918.
Sorel, George. *Reflections on Violence*. Edited by Jeremy Jennings. Cambridge: Cambridge University Press, 1999.
Veld, N. K. C. A. in 't, ed. *De SS en Nederland: Documenten uit SS-Archieven 1935–1945*. 2 vols. 'S-Gravenhage: Nijhoff, 1976.
Waerland, Are. *Idealism och Materialism*. Uppsala: J.A. Lindblads Förlag, 1924.

Secondary literature

Abma, R. 'Het Plan van de Arbeid en de SDAP'. *Low Countries Historical Review* 92, no. 1 (1977): 37–68.

Adema, Janneke. 'Verzuiling als metafoor voor modernisering'. In *Moderniteit: Modernisme en massacultuur in Nederland 1914–1940*, edited by Madelon de Keizer and Sophie Tates, 265–83. Zutphen: Walburg Pers, 2004.

Aerts, Remieg, Herman de Liagre Böhl, Piet De Rooy and Henk Te Velde. *Land van Kleine Gebaren: Een politieke geschiedenis van Nederland 1780–1990*. Nijmegen: SUN, 1999.

Alcalde, Ángel. 'The Transnational Consensus: Fascism and Nazism in Current Research'. *Contemporary European History* (2020). https://doi.org/10.1017/S0960777320000089.

Aldcroft, Derek H., and Steven Morewood. *The European Economy since 1914*. 5th Edition. London: Routledge, 2013.

Alexander, Jeffrey C. 'Cultural Pragmatics: Social Performance between Ritual and Strategy'. In *Social Performance: Symbolic Action, Cultural Pragmatics, and Ritual*, edited by Jeffrey C. Alexander, Bernhard Giesen and Jason L. Mast, 29–90. Cambridge: Cambridge University Press, 2006.

Alexander, Jeffrey C. 'On the Social Construction of Moral Universals: The "Holocaust" from War Crime to Trauma Drama'. In *The Meanings of Social Life: A Cultural Sociology*, 28–85. Oxford: Oxford University Press, 2003.

Alexander, Jeffrey C. *Performance and Power*. Cambridge: Polity, 2011.

Alexander, Jeffrey C., and Jason L. Mast. 'Introduction: Symbolic Action in Theory and Practice'. In *Social Performance: Symbolic Action, Cultural Pragmatics, and Ritual*, edited by Jeffrey C. Alexander, Bernhard Giesen and Jason L. Mast, 1–16. Cambridge: Cambridge University Press, 2006.

Alimi, Eitan Y. 'Repertoires of Contention'. In *The Oxford Handbook of Social Movements*, edited by Donatella della Porta and Diani. P. Mario, 411–20. Oxford: Oxford University Press, 2015.

Allardyce, Gilbert. 'What Fascism Is Not: Thoughts on the Deflation of a Concept'. *The American Historical Review* 84, no. 2 (1979): 367–88.

Allert, Tilman. *The Hitler Salute: On the Meaning of a Gesture*. New York: Metropolitan Books, 2008.

Almgren, Birgitta. 'Svensk-Tyska Föreningar: Mål för nazistisk infiltration'. *Historisk Tidskrift* 135, no. 1 (2015): 63–91.

Althusser, Louis. *Essays on Ideology*. London: Verso, 1984.

Åmark, Klas. *Att Bo Granne med Ondskan: Sveriges förhållande till nazismen, Nazityskland och Förintelsen*. Stockholm: Bonniers, 2011.

Antliff, Mark. *Avant-Garde Fascism: The Mobilization of Myth, Art, and Culture in France, 1909–1939*. Durham: Duke University Press, 2007.

Apter, David E. 'Politics as Theatre: An Alternative View of the Rationalities of Power'. In *Social Performance: Symbolic Action, Cultural Pragmatics, and Ritual*, edited by Jeffrey C. Alexander, Bernhard Giesen and Jason L. Mast, 218–56. Cambridge: Cambridge University Press, 2006.

Arblaster, Paul. *A History of the Low Countries*. Basingstoke: Palgrave Macmillan, 2006.

Arnstad, Henrik. *Älskade Fascism: De svartbruna rörelsernas ideologi och historia*. Stockholm: Norstedts, 2013.

Arnstad, Henrik. 'Fascismens föränderlighet 1919–2014: De svartbruna rörelserna i ett kontextuellt perspektiv', *Historisk Tidskrift* 134, no. 2 (2014): 259–66.

Auerbach, Helmuth. 'Nationalsozialismus vor Hitler'. In *Der Nationalsozialismus: Studien zur Ideologie und Herrschaft*, edited by W. Benz and H. Mommsen. Frankfurt am Main: Geschichte Fischer, 1993.

Austin, J. L. *How to Do Things with Words*. Oxford: Clarendon Press, 1962.

Bach, Maurizio. 'Mussolini und Hitler als charismatische Führer'. In *Der Faschismus in Europa: Wege der Forschung*, edited by Thomas Schlemmer and Hans Woller, 107–21. München: Oldenbourg Wissenschaftsverlag, 2014.
Baker, David. 'The Extreme Right in the 1920s'. In *The Failure of British Fascism*, edited by Mike Cronin, 1–28. Basingstoke: Macmillan Press, 1996.
Barret, Neil. 'The Anti-Fascist Movement in South-East Lancashire'. In *Opposing Fascism: Community, Authority and Resistance in Europe*, edited by Tim Kirk and Anthony McElligott, 48–62. Cambridge: Cambridge University Press, 1999.
Barthes, Roland. *Mythologies*. London: Paladin, 1973.
Bauerkämper, Arnd. *Der Faschismus in Europa 1918-1945*. Stuttgart: Reclam, 2006.
Bauerkämper, Arnd. 'Transnational Fascism: Cross-Border Relations between Regimes and Movements in Europe, 1922–1939'. *East Central Europe* 37, no. 37 (2010): 214–46.
Bauerkämper, Arnd, and Grzegorz Rossolinkski-Liebe, eds. *Fascism without Borders: Transnational Connections and Cooperation between Movements and Regimes in Europe from 1918 to 1945*. Oxford: Bergahn, 2017.
Baumeister, Martin. 'Faschismus als "politischer Religion"'. In *Der Faschismus in Europa: Wege der Forschung*, edited by Thomas Schlemmer and Hans Woller, 17–33. München: Oldenbourg Wissenschaftsverlag, 2014.
Berezin, Mabel. *Making the Fascist Self: The Political Culture of Interwar Italy*. London: Cornell University Press, 1997.
Berezin, Mabel. 'The Organization of Political Ideology: Culture, State, and Theater in Fascist Italy'. *American Sociological Review* 56, no. 5 (1991): 639–51.
Bergen, Marcel and Irma Clement. *Kopstukken van de NSB*. Mokumbooks, 2019.
Berggren, Lena. 'Completing the Lutheran Reformation: Ultra-Nationalism, Christianity and the Possibility of "Clerical Fascism" in Interwar Sweden'. *Totalitarian Movements and Political Religions* 8, no. 2 (2007): 303–14.
Berggren, Lena. 'Den svenska mellankrigsfascismen - ett ointressant marginalfenomen eller ett viktigt forskingsobjekt?' *Historisk Tidskrift* 122, no. 3 (2002): 427–44.
Berggren, Lena. 'Intellectual Fascism: Per Engdahl and the Formation of "New-Swedish Socialism"'. *Fascism: Journal of Comparative Fascism Studies* 3, no. 3 (2014): 69–92.
Berggren, Lena. *Nationell Upplysning: Drag i den svenska antisemitismens idéhistoria*. Stockholm: Carlsson Förlag, 1999.
Berggren, Lena. 'Swedish Fascism: Why Bother?' *Journal of Contemporary History* 37, no. 3 (2002): 395–417.
Berglund, Tobias, and Niclas Sennerteg. *Finska Inbördeskriget*. Stockholm: Natur och Kultur, 2017.
Betts, Paul. 'The New Fascination with Fascism: The Case of Nazi Modernism'. *Journal of Contemporary History* 37, no. 4 (2002): 541–58.
Birgersson, Bengt Owe, Stig Hadenius, Björn Molin, and Hans Wieslander. *Sverige efter 1900: En modern politisk historia*. Stockholm: Bonniers, 1981.
Björkman, Maria, and Sven Widmalm. 'Selling Eugenics: The Case of Sweden'. *Notes and Records of the Royal Society of London* 64, no. 4 (2010): 379–400.
Blom, J. C. H. *De Muiterij op de Zeven Provinciën: Reacties en Gevolgen in Nederland*. Utrecht: HES, 1983.
Blom, J. C. H., and E. Lamberts, eds. *Geschiedenis van de Nederlanden*. Rijswijk: Nijgh & Van Ditmar, 1993.
Bockxmeer, Annemieke van. *De Oorlog Verzameld: Het ontstaan van de collectie van het NIOD*. Amsterdam: De Bezige Bij, 2014.

Bonnell, Victoria E., Lynn Hunt and Richard Biernacki, eds. *Beyond the Cultural Turn: New Directions in the Study of Society and Culture*. London: University of California Press, 1999.
Bosworth, R.J.B. *Mussolini*. London: Arnold, 2002.
Bosworth, R.J.B. *Mussolini's Italy: Life under the Dictatorship*. London: Penguin, 2006.
Brantlinger, Patrick. 'Mass Media and Culture in Fin-de-Siècle Europe'. In *Fin de Siècle and Its Legacy*, edited by Mikuláš Teich and Roy Porter, 98–114. Cambridge: Cambridge University Press, 1990.
Brendon, Piers. *The Dark Valley: A Panorama of the 1930s*. London: Jonathan Cape, 2000.
Brockhaus, Gudrun, ed. *Attraktion der NS-Bewegung*. Essen: Klartext, 2014.
Broek, G.J.A. *Weerkorpsen: Extreemrechtse Strijdgroepen in Amsterdam, 1923–1942*. Amsterdam: University of Amsterdam, 2014.
Brustein, William, and Marit Berntson. 'Interwar Fascist Popularity in Europe and the Default of the Left'. *European Sociological Review* 15, no. 2 (1999): 159–78.
Bull, Thomas, and Anders Heiborn. 'Uniformsförbudet, tiden och grundlagen'. *Svensk Juristtidning*, no. 4 (1996): 328–47.
Burke, Peter. *History and Social Theory*. 2nd Edition. Cambridge: Polity, 2005.
Burke, Peter. *What Is Cultural History?*. Cambridge: Polity, 2004.
Butler, Judith. *Bodies That Matter*. London: Routledge, 2011.
Butler, Judith. *Gender Trouble: Feminism and the Subversion of Identity*. London: Routledge, 2007.
Butler, Judith. *Notes toward a Performative Theory of Assembly*. Cambridge, MA: Harvard University Press, 2015.
Butler, Judith. 'Performative Acts and Gender Constitution: An Essay in Phenomenology and Feminist Theory'. *Theatre Journal* 40, no. 4 (1988): 519–39.
Butt, Wolfgang. *Mobilmachung des Elfenbeinturms: Reaktionen auf d. Faschismus in d. schwed. Literatur 1933–1939*. Neumünster: Wachholtz, 1977.
Chandler, Daniel. *Semiotics: The Basics*. 2nd Edition. London: Routledge, 2002.
Chaney, David. *The Cultural Turn: Scene-Setting Essays on Contemporary Cultural History*. London: Routledge, 1994.
Clark, Roland. *Holy Legionary Youth: Fascist Activism in Interwar Romania*. New York: Cornell University Press, 2015.
Conway, Martin and Peter Romijn. 'Belgium and the Netherlands'. In *Twisted Paths: Europe 1914–1945*, edited by Robert Gerwarth, 84–110. Oxford: Oxford University Press, 2007.
Cook, Chris, and John Paxton. *European Political Facts of the Twentieth Century*. 5th Edition. Basingstoke: Palgrave Macmillan, 2001.
Copsey, Nigel. '"Fascism … but with an Open Mind." Reflections on the Contemporary Far Right in (Western) Europe'. *Fascism: Journal of Comparative Fascism Studies* 1, no. 2 (2013): 10–7.
Cronin, Mike. *The Failure of British Fascism: The Far Right and the Fight for Political Recognition*. Basingstoke: Macmillan, 1996.
Dagnino, Jorge. 'The Myth of the New Man in Italian Fascist Ideology'. *Fascism: Journal of Comparative Fascism Studies* 5, no. 5 (2016): 130–48.
Dahlberg, Hans. *I Sverige under 2: a Världskriget*. 3rd Edition. Stockholm: Bonniers, 1984.
Dammberg, Henrik. *Nazismen i Skaraborgs Län 1930–1945*. Bolum: Bolum Förlag, 2009.
Damsma, Josje. *Nazis in the Netherlands: A Social History of National Socialist Collaborators, 1940–1945*. PhD thesis. Amsterdam: University of Amsterdam, 2013.

Damsma, Josje, and Erik Schumacher. '"De Strijd om Amsterdam": Een nieuwe benadering in het onderzoek naar de NSB'. *BMGN – Low Countries Historical Review* 124, no. 3 (2009): 329–48. https://doi.org/10.18352/bmgn-lchr.7009.
Damsma, Josje, and Erik Schumacher. *Hier Woont een NSB'er: Nationaalsocialisten in Bezet Amsterdam*. Amsterdam: Boom, 2010.
Derks, Marjet. '"Stralende strijdlust, taaie zelfverloochening": De dynamiek van traditie en moderniteit in de Graalbeweging'. In *Moderniteit: Modernisme en massacultuur in Nederland, 1914–1940*, edited by Sophie Tates and Madelon de Keizer, 284–99. Zutphen: Walburg Pers, 2004.
Derrida, Jacques. 'Signature Event Context'. In *Margins of Philosophy*, 307–30. Chicago: Chicago University Press, 1982.
Diepenhorst, P.A. *Het Nationaal-Socialisme*. Kampen: J.H. Kok, 1935.
Dijck, Teun A. van. 'Ideology and Discourse'. In *The Oxford Handbook of Political Ideologies*, edited by Michael Freeden and Marc Stears, 176–95. Oxford: Oxford University Press, 2013.
Dobry, Michel. 'Desperately Seeking "Generic Fascism": Some Discordant Thoughts on the Academic Recycling of Indigenous Categories'. In *Rethinking the Nature of Fascism: Comparative Perspectives*, edited by António Costa Pinto, 85–116. Basingstoke: Palgrave Macmillan, 2011.
Drangel, Louise. *Den Kämpande Demokratin: En studie i antinazistisk opinionsrörelse 1935–1945*. Stockholm: LiberFörlag, 1976.
Duane, William. *A Military Dictionary, or, Explanation of the Several Systems of Discipline of Different Kinds of Troops*. Philadelphia: William Duane, 1810.
Eatwell, Roger. 'The Concept and Theory of Charismatic Leadership'. *Totalitarian Movements and Political Religions* 7, no. 2 (2006): 141–56.
Eatwell, Roger. 'The Drive towards Synthesis'. In *International Fascism*, edited by Roger Griffin, 189–204. London: Arnold, 1998.
Eatwell, Roger. *Fascism: A History*. London: Vintage, 1996.
Eatwell, Roger. 'The Nature of "Generic Fascism": Complexity and Reflexive Hybridity'. In *Rethinking Fascism and Dictatorship in Europe*, edited by António Costa Pinto and Aristotle Kallis. Basingstoke: Palgrave Macmillan, 2014.
Edelman, Murray. *Politics as Symbolic Action: Mass Arousal and Quiescence*. Chicago: Markham, 1971.
Eichberg, Henning, and Robert A. Jones. 'The Nazi Thingspiel: Theater for the Masses in Fascism and Proletarian Culture'. *New German Critique*, no. 11 (1977): 133–50.
Eksteins, Modris. *Rites of Spring: The Great War and the Birth of the Modern Age*. New York: Mariner Books, 2000.
Ensel, Remco. 'Dutch Face-ism: Portrait Photography and Völkisch Nationalism in the Netherlands'. *Fascism: Journal of Comparative Fascism Studies* 2, (2013): 18–40.
Eriksson, Elof. *Bonderörelsen: En historisk återblick*. Vol. 1. 2 vols. Stockholm: Nationens Förlag, 1946.
Evans, Richard J. *The Coming of the Third Reich: How the Nazis Destroyed Democracy and Seized Power in Germany*. London: Penguin, 2004.
Evans, Richard J. *The Third Reich at War: How the Nazis Led Germany from Conquest to Disaster*. London: Penguin, 2009.
Falasca-Zamponi, Simonetta. *Fascist Spectacle: The Aesthetics of Power in Mussolini's Italy*. London: University of California Press, 1997.
Fischer-Lichte, Erika. 'Performance, Inszenierung, Ritual'. In *Geschichtswissenschafft und 'Performative Turn': Ritual, Inszenierung und Performanz vom Mittelalter bis zur*

Neuzeit, edited by Jürgen Martschukat and Steffen Patzold, 33–55. Köln: Böhlau, 2003.

Fischer-Lichte, Erika. *Performativität: Eine Einführung*. Bielefeld: Transcript Verlag, 2012.

Fischer-Lichte, Erika. *The Transformative Power of Performance: A New Aesthetics*. London: Routledge, 2008.

Fischer-Lichte, Erika. *Theatre, Sacrifice, Ritual: Exploring Forms of Political Theatre*. London: Routledge, 2005.

Flink, Ingvar. 'Svenska Krigsförluster i Finland År 1918'. In *Norden och Krigen i Finland och Balticum, 1918–19*, edited by Lars Westerlund, 25–37. Helsingfors: Statsrådets kansli, 2004.

Foray, Jennifer L. '"Clean" Wehrmacht in the German-Occupied Netherlands, 1940–45'. *Journal of Contemporary History* 45, no. 4 (2010): 768–87.

Foray, Jennifer L. *Visions of Empire in the Nazi-Occupied Netherlands*. Cambridge: Cambridge University Press, 2012.

Foucault, Michel. *The Archaeology of Knowledge*. London: Routledge, 2002.

Foucault, Michel. *Essential Works of Foucault, 1954–1984: Power*, edited by James Faubion. Vol. 3. 3 vols. London: Penguin, 2001.

Fritzsche, Peter. *Rehearsals for Fascism: Populism and Political Mobilization in Weimar Germany*. Oxford: Oxford University Press, 1990.

Gentile, Emilio. *Politics as Religion*. Oxford: Princeton University Press, 2006.

Gentile, Emilio. *The Sacralization of Politics in Fascist Italy*. London: Harvard University Press, 1996.

Gerwarth, Robert. *Die Grösste aller Revolutionen: November 1918 und der Aufbruch in eine neue Zeit*. Munich: Siedler, 2018.

Gerwarth, Robert, and John Horne. 'Bolshevism as Fantasy: Fear of Revolution and Counter-Revolutionary Violence, 1917–1923'. In *War in Peace: Paramilitary Violence in Europe after the Great War*, edited by Robert Gerwarth and John Horne, 40–51. Oxford: Oxford University Press, 2013.

Gilmour, John. *Sweden, the Swastika and Stalin: The Swedish Experience in the Second World War*. Edinburgh: Edinburgh University Press, 2010.

Goeschel, Christian. *Mussolini and Hitler: Forging the Fascist Alliance*. Yale: Yale University Press, 2018.

Goodfellow, Samuel Huston. 'Fascism as a Transnational Movement: The Case of Inter-War Alsace'. *Contemporary European History* 22, (2013), 87–106.

Goodrick-Clarke, Nicholas. *Black Sun: Aryan Cults, Esoteric Nazism, and the Politics of Identity*. New York: New York University Press, 2002.

Gottlieb, Julie. 'Body Fascism in Britain: Building the Blackshirt in the Inter-War Period'. *Contemporary European History* 20, no. 2 (2011): 111–36.

Gottlieb, Julie. *Feminine Fascism*. London: I.B. Tauris, 2003.

Green, Anna. *Cultural History. Theory and History*. Basingstoke: Palgrave Macmillan, 2008.

Griffin, Roger. 'Decentering Comparative Fascist Studies'. *Fascism: Journal of Comparative Fascism Studies* 4, no. 2 (23 November 2015): 103–18.

Griffin, Roger. 'Der Grösste Verführer aller Zeiten?' In *Attraktion der NS-Bewegung*, edited by Gudrun Brockhaus, 213–26. Essem: Klartext Verlag, 2014.

Griffin, Roger, ed. *Fascism*. Oxford: Oxford University Press, 1995.

Griffin, Roger. *Fascism*. London: Polity Press, 2018.

Griffin, Roger. 'Fascism and Culture: A Mosse-Centric Meta-Narrative (or How Fascist Studies Reinvented the Wheel)'. In *Rethinking the Nature of Fascism: Comparative*

Perspectives, edited by António Costa Pinto, 85–116. Basingstoke: Palgrave Macmillan, 2011.
Griffin, Roger. *Modernism and Fascism: The Sense of a Beginning under Mussolini and Hitler*. Basingstoke: Palgrave Macmillan, 2007.
Griffin, Roger. *The Nature of Fascism*. Oxon: Routledge, 1993.
Griffin, Roger. 'Palingenetischer Ultranationalismus: Die Geburtswehen einer neuen Faschismusdeutung'. In *Der Faschismus in Europe: Wege der Forschung*, edited by Thomas Schlemmer and Hans Woller. München: Oldenbourg Wissenschaftsverlag, 2014.
Griffin, Roger. 'The Primacy of Culture: The Current Growth (or Manufacture) of Consensus within Fascist Studies'. *Journal of Contemporary History* 37, no. 1 (2002): 21–43.
Groeneveld, Gerard. *Zo Zong de NSB: Liedcultuur van de NSB 1931–1945*. Nijmegen: Vantilt, 2007.
Groeneveld, Gerard. *Zwaard van de Geest: Het Bruine Boek in Nederland, 1921–1945*. Nijmegen: Vantilt, 2001.
Grunwald, Henning. *Courtroom to Revolutionary Stage: Performance and Ideology in Weimar Political Trials*. Oxford: Oxford University Press, 2012.
Gunnarsson, Lars. *Kyrkan, Nazismen och Demokratin: Åsiktsbildning kring svensk kyrklighet 1919–1945*. Stockholm: Almqvist & Wiksell, 1995.
Gyllenhaal, Lars, and Lennart Westberg. *Svenskar i Krig, 1914–1945*. Stockholm: Historiska Media, 2008.
Haapala, Pertti, and Marko Tikka. 'Revolution, Civil War, and Terror in Finland in 1918'. In *War in Peace: Paramilitary Violence in Europe after the Great War*, edited by Robert Gerwarth and John Horne. Oxford: Oxford University Press, 2013.
Hadenius, Stig. *Svensk politik under 1900-talet: Konflikt och samförstånd*. 4th Edition. Stockholm: Tiden Athena, 1996.
Hadenius, Stig. *Swedish Politics during the 20th Century: Conflict and Consensus*. 5th Edition. Trelleborg: Swedish Institute, 1999.
Hagtvet, Bernt. 'On the Fringe: Swedish Fascism 1920–1945'. In *Who Were the Fascists?*, edited by Stein U. Larsen. Oslo: Universitetsförlaget, 1980.
Halttunen, Karen. 'Cultural History and the Challenge of Narrativity'. In *Beyond the Cultural Turn: New Directions in the Study of Society and Culture*, edited by Victoria E. Bonnell et al. California: University of California Press, 1999.
Halvarson, Arne. *Sveriges Statsskick: En faktasamling*. Stockholm: Norstedts, 1986.
Hamre, Martin Kristoffer. 'Norwegian Fascism in a Transnational Perspective: The Influence of German National Socialism and Italian Fascism on the Nasjonal Samling, 1933–1936'. *Fascism: Journal of Comparative Fascism Studies* 8, (2019): 36–60.
Hansen, Erik. 'Fascism and Nazism in the Netherlands, 1929–39'. *European Studies Review* 3, (1981): 355–85.
Hansen, Erik and Peter A. Jr Prosper. 'Political Economy and Political Action: The Programmatic Response of Dutch Social Democracy to the Depression Crisis, 1929–39'. *Journal of Contemporary History* 29, no. 1 (1994): 129–54.
Have, Wichert Ten. *De Nederlandse Unie: Aanpassing, Vernieuwing en Confrontatie in Bezettingstijd 1940-1941*. Amsterdam: Prometheus, 1999.
Havenaar, Ronald. *Anton Adriaan Mussert: Verrader voor het Vaderland*. Den Haag: Kruseman, 1984.
Havenaar, Ronald. *De NSB tussen Nationalisme en 'Volkse' Solidariteit: De Vooroorlogse Ideologie van de Nationaal-Socialistische Beweging in Nederland*. 's-Gravenhage: Staatsuitgeverij, 1983.

Heijningen, René van. *De Muur van Mussert*. Amsterdam: Boom, 2015.
Hellborn, Thorleif and Peter Gullers. *Stockholm: Om livet på torgen*. Stockholm: Gullersbild, 1996.
Hilson, Mary. 'Scandinavia'. In *Twisted Paths: Europe. 1914–1945*, edited by Robert Gerwarth. Oxford: Oxford University Press, 2007.
Hirschfeld, Gerhard. *Nazi Rule and Dutch Collaboration: The Netherlands under German Occupation 1940–1945*. Oxford: Berg, 1988.
Hollywood, Amy. 'Performativity, Citationality, Ritualization'. *History of Religions* 42, no. 2 (2002): 93–115.
Holmberg, Claes-Göran, Ingemar Oscarsson, and Per Rydén. *En Svensk Presshistoria*. Solna: Esselte studium, 1983.
Huberts, Willem. *In de Ban van een Beter Verleden: Het Nederlandse Fascisme, 1923–1945*. Nijmegen: Vantilt, 2017.
Hübinette, Tobias. *Den Svenska Nationalsocialismen: Medlemmar och sympatisörer*. Stockholm: Carlsson Förlag, 2002.
Iordachi, Constantin, ed. *Comparative Fascist Studies: New Perspectives*. London: Routledge, 2010.
Jarausch, Konrad Hugo. *Out of Ashes: A New History of Europe in the Twentieth Century*. Princeton: Princeton University Press, 2015.
Jong, Gerie de, Kok René and Erik Somers. *Naar Eer en Geweten: Gewone Nederlanders in een Ongewone* Tijd *1940–1945*. Zwolle: Uitgeverij Waanders, 2001.
Jong, Louis de. *Het Koninkrijk der Nederlanden in de Tweede* Wereldoorlog, *1: Voorspel*. 's-Gravenhage: Martinus Nijhoff, 1969.
Jonge, A. A. de. *Crisis en Critiek der Democratie: Anti-Democratische Stromingen en de daarin Levende Denkbeelden over de Staat in Nederland tussen de Wereldoorlogen*. Utrecht: HES, 1982.
Jonge, A. A. de. *Het Nationaal-Socialisme in Nederland: Voorgeschiedenis, Ontstaan en Ontwikkeling*. 2nd Edition. Den Haag: Kruseman, 1979.
Jonsson, Stefan. *Crowds and Democracy: The Idea and Image of the Masses from Revolution to Fascism*. New York: Columbia University Press, 2013.
Joosten, L. M. H. *Katholieken en Fascisme in Nederland 1920–1940*. 2nd Edition. Utrecht: HES, 1982.
Kallis, Aristotle. 'Fascism and the Right in Interwar Europe: Interaction, Entanglement, Hybridity'. In *The Oxford Handbook of European History, 1914–1945*, edited by Nicholas Doumanis. Oxford: Oxford University Press, 2016.
Kallis, Aristotle. 'Fascism, "Charisma" and Charismatisation: Weber's Model of "Charismatic Domination" and Interwar European Fascism'. *Totalitarian Movements and Political Religions* 7, no. 1 (2006): 25–43.
Kallis, Aristotle. 'Fascism, "Licence" and Genocide: From the Chimera of Rebirth to the Authorization of Mass Murder'. In *Rethinking the Nature of Fascism: Comparative Perspectives*, edited by António Costa Pinto, 227–70. Basingstoke: Palgrave Macmillan, 2011.
Kallis, Aristotle. 'The "Fascist Effect": On the Dynamics of Political Hybridization in Inter-War Europe'. In *Rethinking Fascism and Dictatorship in Europe*, edited by Aristotle Kallis and António Costa Pinto, 13–41. Basingstoke: Palgrave Macmillan, 2014.
Kallis, Aristotle. 'When Fascism Became Mainstream: The Challenge of Extremism in Times of Crisis'. *Fascism: Journal of Comparative Fascism Studies* 4, (2015): 1–24.
Kampman, Dick. *De NSB en de NSB'ers: Kennisonrechtvaardigheid en Stereotypering*. Amsterdam: VU University Press, 2015.

Kampman, Dick. *Kritische Beschouwingen over Collaboratie: Stereotypering van de NSB.* Assen: Van Gorcum, 2012.
Karlsson, Ingemar, and Arne Ruth. *Samhället som Teater: Estetik och Politik i Tredje Riket.* Stockholm: Liber, 1983.
Kedward, H.R. *Fascism in Western Europe, 1900–45.* Glasgow: Blackie, 1969.
Kellogg, Michael. *The Russian Roots of Nazism: White Émigrés and the Making of National Socialism, 1917–1945.* Cambridge: Cambridge University Press, 2005.
Kennedy, Dennis. *The Spectator and the Spectacle: Audiences in Modernity and Postmodernity.* Cambridge: Cambridge University Press, 2009.
Kent, Neil. *A Concise History of Sweden.* Cambridge: Cambridge University Press, 2008.
Kershaw, Ian. *Hitler: 1889–1936, Hubris.* vol. 1. London: Norton, 2000.
Kershaw, Ian. *The 'Hitler Myth': Image and Reality in the Third Reich.* Oxford: Clarendon, 1987.
Kershaw, Ian. *To Hell and Back: Europe, 1914–1949.* London: Penguin Random House, 2015.
Kertzer, David I. *Ritual, Politics, and Power.* London: Yale University Press, 1988.
Kooy, G. A. *Het Echec van een 'Volkse' Beweging: Nazificatie en Denazificatie in Nederland 1931–1945.* Utrecht: HES, 1982.
Kramár, Leo. 'Fascism som ideologi och praktik: Några reflektioner med anledning av Henrik Arnstads bok Älskade Fascism'. *Historisk Tidskrift* 134, no. 1 (2014): 64–70.
Kristel, Conny. *De Oorlog van Anderen: Nederlanders en Oorlogsgeweld, 1914–1918.* Amsterdam: De Bezige Bij, 2016.
Kroll, Frank-Lothar. 'Endzeit, Apokalypse, Neuer Mensch - Utopische Potentiale im Nationalsozialismus und im Bolschewismus'. In *Rechtsextreme Ideologien in Geschichte und Gegenwart*, edited by Uwe Backes, 139–57. Köln: Böhlau, 2003.
Kunkeler, Nathaniël. 'Narratives of Decline in the Dutch National Socialist Movement, 1931–1945'. *The Historical Journal* 61, no. 1 (2018): 205–25. https://doi.org/10.1017/S0018246X17000188.
Kunkeler, Nathaniël. 'Sven Olov Lindholm and the Literary Inspirations of Swedish Fascism'. *Scandinavian Journal of History* 44, no. 1 (2019): 77–102.
Kunkeler, Nathaniël. 'The Evolution of Swedish Fascism: Self-Identification and Ideology in Interwar Sweden'. *Patterns of Prejudice* 50, no. 4–5 (2016): 378–97.
Kwiet, Konrad. *Reichskommissariat Niederlande: Versuch und Scheitern Nationalsozialistischer Neuordnung.* Stuttgart: Deutsche Verlags-Anstalt, 1968.
Kwiet, Konrad. 'Zur Geschichte Der Mussert-Bewegung'. *Vierteljahrshefte für Zeitgeschichte* 18, no. 2 (1970): 164–95.
Laqueur, Walter, ed. *Fascism: A Reader's Guide.* Aldershot: Wildwood House, 1976.
Larsen, Stein U. 'Charisma from Below? The Quisling Case in Norway'. *Totalitarian Movements and Political Religions* 7, no. 2 (2006): 235–44.
Larsen, Stein U. 'Conservatives and Fascists in the Nordic Countries: Norway, Sweden, Denmark and Finland, 1918–45'. In *Fascists and Conservatives: The Radical Right and the Establishment in Twentieth-Century Europe*, edited by Martin Blinkhorn. London: Unwin Hyman, 1990.
Larsen, Stein U. 'Introduction: Fascism and National Socialism in the Nordic Countries'. In *Who Were the Fascists?*, edited by Stein U. Larsen et al. Oslo: Universitetsforlaget, 1980.
Larsson, Olle, and Andreas Marklund. *Svensk Historia.* Lund: Historiska Media, 2012.
Larsson, Torbjörn. *Det Svenska Statsskicket.* 2nd Edition. Lund: Studentlitteratur, 1994.
Ledeen, Michael Arthur. *Universal Fascism: The Theory and Practice of the Fascist International, 1928–1936.* New York: Howard Fertig, 1972.

Levy, Carl. 'Fascism, National Socialism and Conservatives in Europe, 1914-1945: Issues for Comparativists'. *Contemporary European History* 8, no. 1 (1999): 97-126.

Lind, Martin. *Kristendom och Nazism: Frågan om kristendom och nazism belyst av olika ställningstaganden i Tyskland och Sverige, 1933-1945*. Lund: H. Ohlsson, 1975.

Lindström, Ulf. *Fascism in Scandinavia, 1920-40*. PhD thesis. University of Umeå, 1982.

Lööw, Heléne. *Hakkorset och Wasakärven: En studie av nationalsocialismen i Sverige 1924-1950*. Gothenburg: Magnus Mölner & Jörgen Weibull, 1990.

Lööw, Heléne. *Nazismen i Sverige, 1924-1979: Pionjärerna, partierna, propagandan*. Stockholm: Ordfront Förlag, 2004.

Lööw, Heléne. *Nazismen i Sverige 1980-1999: Den rasistiska undergroundrörelsen: musiken, myterna, riterna*. 2nd Edition. Stockholm: Ordfront Förlag, 2000.

Loxley, James. *Performativity*. London: Routledge, 2007.

Lundberg, Victor. *En Idé Större än Döden: En fascistisk arbetarrörelse i Sverige, 1933-1945*. Stockholm: Gidlunds Förlag, 2014.

Lundberg, Victor. 'Within the Fascist World of Work: Sven Olov Lindholm, Ernst Jünger and the Pursuit of Proletarian Fascism in Sweden, 1933-1945'. In *New Political Ideas in the Aftermath of the Great War*, edited by Salvador Alessandro and Anders G. Kjøstvedt, 199-217. Basingstoke: Palgrave Macmillan, 2016.

Mak, Geert, Jan Bank, Gijsbert Van Es, Piet de Rooy, and René van Stipriaan. *Verleden van Nederland*. Amsterdam: Olympus, 2015.

Mall, Kurt. *Der Nationalsozialismus in Schweden im Spiegel seiner Kampfpresse*. PhD Thesis. University of Heidelberg, 1936.

Mann, Michael. *Fascists*. Cambridge: Cambridge University Press, 2004.

Mark, Ethan. 'Fascisms Seen and Unseen: The Netherlands, Japan, Indonesia, and the Relationalities of Imperial Crisis'. In *Visualizing Fascism: The Twentieth-Century Rise of the Global Right*, edited by Julia Adeney Thomas and Geoff Eley. Durham, North Carolina: Duke University Press, 2020.

Markwick, Roger D., and Nicholas Doumanis. 'The Nationalization of the Masses'. In *The Oxford Handbook of European History, 1914-1945*, edited by Nicholas Doumanis. Oxford: Oxford University Press, 2016.

Martschukat, Jürgen, and Steffen Patzold. 'Geschichtswissenschaft und "Performative Turn"'. In *Geschichtswissenschaft und 'Performative Turn': Ritual, Inszenierung und Performanz vom Mittelalter bis zur Neuzeit*, edited by Jürgen Martschukat and Steffen Patzold, 1-32. Köln: Böhlau, 2003.

Mason, Tim. 'Whatever Happened to Fascism?'. *Radical History Review* 49, (1991): 89-98.

Matthée, Zonneke. *Voor Volk en Vaderland: Vrouwen in de NSB 1931-1948*. Amsterdam: Balans, 2007.

Mazower, Mark. *Dark Continent: Europe's Twentieth Century*. London: Penguin, 1998.

Mazower, Mark. *Hitler's Empire: Nazi Rule in Occupied Europe*. London: Penguin, 2009.

McDonough, Frank. *Hitler and the Rise of the Nazi Party*. 2nd Edition. Harlow: Pearson, 2012.

McElligott, Anthony. *Contested City: Municipal Politics and the Rise of Nazism in Altona 1917-1937*. Michigan: University of Michigan Press, 1998.

Melin, Jan, Alf W. Johansson, and Susanna Hedenborg. *Sveriges Historia: Koncentrerad Uppslagsbok: Fakta, årtal, kartor, tabeller*. Stockholm: Rabén Prisma (Tiden Athena), 1997.

Meyers, Jan. *Mussert: Een Politiek Leven*. Amsterdam: Uitgeverij De Arbeiderspers, 1984.

Misgeld, Klaus, Karl Molin, and Klas Åmark, eds. *Creating Social Democracy: A Century of the Social Democratic Labor Party in Sweden*. Pennsylvania: Pennsylvania State University Press, 1992.

Moore, Bob. 'The Netherlands'. In *The Oxford Handbook of Fascism*, edited by R.J.B. Bosworth, 453–69. Oxford: Oxford University Press, 2010.
Morgan, Philip. *Fascism in Europe, 1919–1945*. London: Routledge, 2003.
Mosse, George L. *Fallen Soldiers: Reshaping the Memory of the World Wars*. Oxford: Oxford University Press, 1991.
Mosse, George L. 'Fascist Aesthetics and Society: Some Considerations'. *Journal of Contemporary History* 31, no. 2 (1996): 245–52.
Mosse, George L. *Nazi Culture: Intellectual, Cultural and Social Life in the Third Reich*. New York: Schocken Books, 1986.
Mosse, George L. *The Culture of Western Europe*. Chicago: Rand McNally, 1974.
Mosse, George L. *The Fascist Revolution: Toward a General Theory of Fascism*. New York: Howard Fertig, 1999.
Mosse, George L. *The Image of Man: The Creation of Modern Masculinity*. Oxford: Oxford University Press, 1998.
Mosse, George L. *The Nationalization of the Masses: Political Symbolism and Mass Movements in Germany from the Napoleonic Wars through the Third Reich*. New York: Howard Fertig, 1975.
Müssener, Helmut. *Exil in Schweden: Politische und kulturelle Emigration nach 1933*. München: Carl Hanser Verlag, 1974.
Neocleous, Mark. *Fascism*. Buckingham: Open University Press, 1997.
Neocleous, Mark. 'Long Live Death!'. *Journal of Political Ideologies* 10, no. 1 (2015): 31–49.
Nietzsche, Friedrich. *Zur Genealogie der Moral: Ein Streitschrift*. Leipzig: C.G. Naumann Verlag, 1907.
Nilsson, Karl N. Alvar. *Svensk Överklassnazism, 1930–1945*. Stockholm: Carlsson, 1996.
Noakes, Jeremy. *The Nazi Party in Lower Saxony, 1921–1933*. Oxford: Oxford University Press, 1971.
Noakes, J. and G. Pridham. *Nazism, 1919–1945, 1: The Rise to Power, 1919–1934*. Exeter: University of Exeter Press, 1994.
Nolte, Ernst. *Three Faces of Fascism: Action Française, Italian Fascism, National Socialism*. New York: Times Mirror, 1965.
Nordlund, Sven. '"Tyskarna själva gör ju ingen hemlighet av detta." Sverige och ariseringen av tyskägda företag och dotterbolag'. *Historisk Tidskrift* 125, no. 4 (2005): 609–41.
O Broin, Turlach. 'Mail-Order Demagogues: The NSDAP School for Speakers, 1928–34'. *Journal of Contemporary History* 51, no. 4 (1 October 2016): 715–37. https://doi.org/10.1177/0022009415609681.
Ohlsson, Per T. *Svensk Politik*. Lund: Historiska Media, 2014.
Oredsson, Sverker. 'Stormaktsdrömmar och Stridsiver: Ett tema i svensk opinionsbildning och politik 1910–1942'. *Scandia* 59, no. 2 (1993): 257–96.
Orlow, Dietrich. *The History of the Nazi Party, 1919–33*. Vol. 1. 2 vols. Newton Abbot: David & Charles, 1971.
Orlow, Dietrich. *The Lure of Fascism in Western Europe: German Nazis, Dutch and French Fascists, 1933–1939*. Basingstoke: Palgrave Macmillan, 2009.
Östling, Johan. 'Swedish Narratives of the Second World War: A European Perspective'. *Contemporary European History* 17, no. 2 (2008): 197–211.
O'Sullivan, Noël. *Fascism*. London: J.M. Dent & Sons, 1983.
Parker, Andrew, and Eve Kosofsky Sedgwick, eds. *Performativity and Performance*. London: Routledge, 1995.

Passmore, Kevin. 'Fascism as a Social Movement in a Transnational Context'. In *The History of Social Movements in Global Perspective*, edited by S. Berger and H. Nehring, 579–617. Basingstoke: Palgrave Macmillan, 2017.

Patel, Kiran Klaus. 'In Search of a Transnational Historicization: National Socialism and Its Place in History'. In *Conflicted Memories: Europeanizing Contemporary Histories*, edited by Konrad Jarausch and Thomas Lindenberger, with the collaboration of Annelie Ramsbrock. Oxford: Bergahn, 2007.

Paul, Gerhard. *Aufstand der Bilder: Die NS-Propaganda vor 1933*. Bonn: J.H.W. Dietz Nachf., 1990.

Pauw, J.L. van der. *De Actualisten: De Kinderjaren van het Georganiseerde Fascisme in Nederland 1923–1924*. Amsterdam: Sijthoff, 1987.

Paxton, Robert O. *The Anatomy of Fascism*. London: Penguin, 2005.

Paxton, Robert O. 'The Five Stages of Fascism'. *Journal of Modern History* 70, no. 1 (1998): 1–23.

Payne, Stanley G. *A History of Fascism, 1914–1945*. Wisconsin: University of Wisconsin Press, 1995.

Payne, Stanley G. *Fascism: Comparison and Definition*. London: University of Wisconsin Press, 1980.

Peters, Jan. *Exilland Schweden: Deutsche und Schwedische Antifaschisten, 1933–1945*. Berlin: Akademie-Verlag, 1984.

Pinto, António Costa. *The Nature of Fascism Revisited*. New York: Colombia University Press, 2012.

Pinto, António Costa, and Aristotle Kallis, eds. *Rethinking Fascism and Dictatorship in Europe*. Basingstoke: Palgrave Macmillan, 2014.

Pollard, John. 'Skinhead Culture: The Ideologies, Mythologies, Religions and Conspiracy Theories of Racist Skinheads'. *Patterns of Prejudice* 50, no. 4–5 (2016): 398–419.

Pollard, John. *The Fascist Experience in Italy*. London: Routledge, 1998.

Pollard, John. *The Papacy in the Age of Totalitarianism*. Oxford: Oxford University Press, 2014.

Pollmann, Tessell. *Mussert & Co: De NSB-Leider en zijn Vetrouwelingen*. Amsterdam: Boom, 2012.

Rees, Philip. *Biographical Dictionary of the Extreme Right since 1890*. New York: Harvester Wheatsheaf, 1990.

Reich, Wilhelm. *The Mass Psychology of Fascism*. 3rd edition London; Souvenir Press & Academic, 1970.

Reichardt, Sven. *Faschistische Kampfbünde: Gewalt und Gemeinschaft im Italienischen Squadrismus und in der Deutschen SA*. Köln: Böhlau, 2002.

Reichardt, Sven. 'Faschistische Tatgemeinschaften: Anmerkungen zu einer praxeologischen Analyse'. In *Der Faschismus in Europa: Wege der Forschung*, edited by Thomas Schlemmer and Hans Woller, 73–88. München: Oldenbourg Wissenschaftsverlag, 2014.

Reichardt, Sven. 'Fascist Marches in Italy and Germany: Squadre and SA before the Seizure of Power'. In *The Street as Stage: Protest Marches and Public Rallies since the Nineteenth Century*, edited by Matthias Reiss. Oxford: Oxford University Press, 2007.

Reichardt, Sven. 'Gewalt, Körper, Politik. Paradoxien in der deutschen Kulturgeschichte der Zwischenkriegszeit'. *Geschichte und Geselffschaft. Sonderheft* 21, (2005): 205–39.

Reichardt, Sven. 'Klaus Theweleits "Männerphantasien" – ein Erfolgsbuch der 1970er-Jahre'. *Zeithistorische Forschungen/Studies in Contemporary History* 3, (2006): 401–21.

Reichardt, Sven. 'Praxeologie und Faschismus. Gewalt und Gemeinschaft als Elemente eines Praxeologischen Faschismusbegriffs'. In *Doing Culture: Neue Positionen Zum Verhältnis von Kultur Und Sozialer Praxis*, edited by Karl H. Hörning and Julia Reuter, 129–53. Berlin: De Gruyter, 2004.

Reichardt, Sven. 'Violence and Community: A Micro-Study on Nazi Storm Troopers'. *Central European History* 46, (2013): 275–97.

Reiss, Matthias. 'Introduction'. In *The Street as Stage: Protest Marches and Public Rallies since the Nineteenth Century*. Oxford: Oxford University Press, 2007.

Roberts, David D. 'Fascism and the Framework for Interactive Political Innovation during the Era of the Two World Wars'. In *Rethinking Fascism and Dictatorship in Europe*, edited by António Costa Pinto and Aristotle Kallis. Basingstoke: Palgrave Macmillan, 2014.

Roberts, David D. *Fascist Interactions: Proposals for a New Approach to Fascism and Its Era, 1919–1945*. New York: Bergahn, 2016.

Roberts, David D. 'Myth, Style, Substance and the Totalitarian Dynamic in Fascist Italy'. *Contemporary European History* 16, no. 1 (2007): 1–36.

Roberts, David D. '"Political Religion" and the Totalitarian Departures of Inter-war Europe: On the Uses and Disadvantages of a Category'. *Contemporary European History* 18, no. 4 (2009): 381–414.

Roberts, David D. *The Totalitarian Experiment in Twentieth-Century Europe: Understanding the Poverty of Great Politics*. New York: Routledge, 2006.

Roberts, David D., Alexander De Grand, Mark Antliff and Thomas Linehan. 'Comments on Roger Griffin, "The Primacy of Culture"'. *Journal of Contemporary History* 37, no. 2 (2002): 259–74.

Roberts, Kenneth M. 'Populism, Social Movements, and Popular Subjectivity'. In *The Oxford Handbook of Social Movements*, edited by Donatella Della Porta and Mario Dani. Oxford: Oxford University Press, 2015.

Romijn, Peter. *Burgemeesters in Oorlogstijd: Besturen tijdens de Duitse Bezetting*. Amsterdam: Balans, 2006.

Romijn, Peter. 'Politiek Geweld op Straat: Succes en falen van de Weerafdeling van de NSB'. In *Met Alle Geweld: Botsingen en Tegenstellingen in Burgerlijk Nederland*, edited by Conny Kristel et al. Amsterdam: Balans, 2003.

Roon, Ger van. *Zwischen Neutralismus und Solidarität: Die evangelischen Niederlande und der deutsche Kirchenkampf, 1933–1942*. Stuttgart: Deutsche Verlags-Anstalt, 1983.

Rossol, Nadine. 'Performing the Nation: Sports, Spectacles, and Aesthetics in Germany, 1926–1936'. *Central European History* 43, no. 4 (2010): 616–38.

Rulof, Bernard. 'Selling Social Democracy in the Netherlands: Activism and Its Sources of Inspiration during the 1930s'. *Contemporary European History* 18, no. 4 (2009): 478–97.

Sastamoinen, Armas. *Hitlers Svenska Förtrupper*. Stockholm: Federativs, 1947.

Saunders, Thomas J. 'A "New Man": Fascism, Cinema and Image Creation'. *International Journal of Politics, Culture, and Society* 12, no. 2 (1998): 227–46.

Schlemmer, Thomas, and Hans Woller. 'Politischer Deutungskampf und wissenschafliche Deutungsmacht: Konjunkturen der Faschismusforschung'. In *Der Faschismus in Europe: Wege der Forschung*, edited by Thomas Schlemmer and Hans Woller, 7–16. München: Oldenbourg Wissenschaftsverlag, 2014.

Schnapp, Jeffrey T. *Staging Fascism: 18 BL and the Theater of Masses for Masses*. Stanford: Stanford University, 1996.

Schulz, Gerhard. *Faschismus, Nationalsozialismus; Versionen und theoretische Kontroversen, 1922–1972*. Frankfurt: Propyläen, 1974.

Schuursma, R. L. *Het Onaannemelijk Tractaat: Het Verdrag met België van 3 April 1925 in de Nederlandse Publieke Opinie.* Groningen: H. D. Tjeenk Willink, 1975.
Seigel, Jerrold E. *Modernity and Bourgeois Life: Society, Politics and Culture in England, France and Germany since 1750.* Cambridge: Cambridge University Press, 2012.
Sejersted, Francis. *The Age of Social Democracy: Norway and Sweden in the Twentieth Century.* Princeton: Princeton University Press, 2011.
Sewell, William H. 'Historical Events as Transformations of Structures: Inventing Revolution at the Bastille'. *Theory and Society* 25, no. 6 (1996): 841–81.
Sewell, William H. 'Space in Contentious Politics'. In *Silence and Voice in the Study of Contentious Politics*, Ronald R. Aminzade, Jack A. Goldstone, Doug McAdam, Elizabeth J. Perry, William H. Sewell, Sidney G Tarrow, and Charles Tilley, 51–88. Cambridge: Cambridge University Press, 2001.
Sewell, William H. 'The Concept(s) of Culture'. In *Practicing History: New Directions in Historical Writing after the Linguistic Turn*, edited by Gabrielle M. Spiegel, 76–95. London: Routledge, 2005.
Siltala, Juha. 'Dissolution and Reintegration in Finland, 1914–1932: How Did a Disarmed Country Become Absorbed into Brutalization?' *Journal of Baltic Studies* 46, no. 1 (2015): 11–33.
Silvennoinen, Oula. 'Demokratins framgångshistoria? Skogsindustrin, arbetsmarknaden och en fascistisk samhällssyn 1918–1940'. In *Demokratins drivkrafter: Kontext och särdrag i Finlands och Sveriges demokratier 1890–2020*, edited by Henrik Meinander, Petri Karonen, and Kjell Östberg. Stockholm: Appell, 2018.
Slaa, Robin te, and Edwin Klijn. *De NSB: Ontstaan en Opkomst van de Nationaal-Socialistische Beweging, 1931–1935.* Amsterdam: Boom, 2010.
Spencer, Martin E. 'What Is Charisma?' *The British Journal of Sociology* 24, no. 3 (1973): 341–54.
Spiegel, Gabrielle M., ed. 'Introduction'. In *Practicing History: New Directions in Historical Writing after the Linguistic Turn,* 1–32. London: Routledge, 2005.
Spurr, Michael A. '"Living the Blackshirt Life": Culture, Community and the British Union of Fascists, 1932–1940'. *Contemporary European History* 12, no. 3 (2003): 305–22.
Stenfeldt, Johan. *Renegater: Nils Flyg och Sven Olov Lindholm i gränslandet mellan kommunism och nazism.* Lund: Nordic Academic Press, 2019.
Stenfeldt, Johan. 'The Fascist Who Fought for World Peace: Conversions and Core Concepts in the Ideology of the Swedish Nazi Leader Sven Olov Lindholm'. *Fascism: Journal of Comparative Fascism Studies* 8, (2019): 9–35.
Stern, J. P. *Hitler: The Führer and the People.* London: Flamingo, 1984.
Sternhell, Zeev. *The Birth of Fascist Ideology: From Cultural Rebellion to Political Revolution.* Princeton: Princeton University Press, 1994.
Stjernquist, Nils. *Tvåkammartiden: Sveriges Riksdag 1867–1970.* Lund: Sveriges Riksdag, 1996.
Stoop, J. P. *Om het Volvoeren van een Christelijke Staatkunde: De Anti-Revolutionaire Partij in het Interbellum.* Hilversum: Verloren, 2001.
Stoop, Paul. *Niederländische Presse unter Druck: Deutsche Auswärtige Pressepolitik und die Niederlande 1933–1940.* München: Saur, 1987.
Svensson, Per. *Vasakärven och Järnröret: Om den långa bruna skuggan från Lund.* Stockholm: Weyler, 2014.
Sydow, Björn von. *Parlamentarismen i Sverige: Utveckling och utformning till 1945.* Stockholm: Gidlunds Förlag, 1997.
Tames, Ismee. *Besmette Jeugd: De Kinderen van NSB'ers na de Oorlog.* Amsterdam: Balans, 2009.

Tarrow, Sidney. *Strangers at the Gates*. Cambridge: Cambridge University Press, 2012.
Ther, Philipp. 'Beyond the Nation: The Relational Basis of a Comparative History of Germany and Europe'. *Central European History* 36, no. 1 (2003): 45–73.
Theweleit, Klaus. *Male Fantasies, II: Male Bodies: Psychoanalyzing the White Terror*. Cambridge: Polity, 1988.
Thomas, Julia Adeney. 'Introduction; A Portable Concept of Fascism'. In *Visualizing Fascism: The Twentieth-Century Rise of the Global Right*, edited by Julia Adeney Thomas and Geoff Eley, 1–20. Durham, North Carolina: Duke University Press, 2020.
Thurlow, Richard. 'European Fascism'. In *A Companion to Modern European History, 1871-1945*, edited by Martin Pugh, 194–209. Oxford: Blackwell, 1997.
Tijssen, Henk. *De Dominee van de NSB: Boissevain en zijn gang van de Nederlandse Hervormde Kerk naar het Nationaal Socialisme*. Kampen: Omniboek, 2009.
Timm, Annette F. 'Mothers, Whores, or Sentimental Dupes?' In *Beyond the Racial State: Rethinking Nazi Germany*, edited by Devin O. Pendas, Mark Roseman and Richard F. Wetzell. Cambridge: Cambridge University Press, 2017.
Toorn, Maarten Cornelis van den. *Wij Melden U den Nieuwen Tijd: Een Beschouwing van het Woordgebruik van de Nederlandse Nationaal-Socialisten*. 's-Gravenhage: SDU, 1991.
Umbach, Maiken. 'Selfhood, Place, and Ideology in German Photo Albums, 1933–1945'. *Central European History* 48, no. 3 (2015): 335–65.
Verhagen, Frans. *Toen de Katholieken Nederland Veroverden: Charles Ruijs de Beerenbrouck 1873–1936*. Amsterdam: Boom, 2015.
Vermaat, Emerson. *Anton Mussert en zijn conflict met de SS*. Soesterberg: Aspekt, 2011.
Vickers, Adrian. *A History of Modern Indonesia*. Cambridge: Cambridge University Press, 2005.
Vincent, Mary. 'Political Violence and Mass Society: A European Civil War?' In *The Oxford Handbook of European History, 1914–1945*, edited by Nicholas Doumanis, 389–404. Oxford: Oxford University Press, 2016.
Vivarelli, Roberto. 'Interpretations of the Origins of Fascism'. *Journal of Modern History* 63, no. 1 (1991): 29–43.
Vossen, Koen. *Vrij Vissen in het Vondelpark: Kleine Politieke Partijen in Nederland 1918–1940*. Amsterdam: Wereldbibliotheek, 2003.
Vree, Frank van. *De Nederlandse Pers en Duitsland, 1930–1939: Een Studie over de Vorming van de Publieke Opinie*. Groningen: Historische Uitgeverij, 1989.
Vulovic, Jimmy. *Reform eller Revolt: Litterär propaganda i socialdemokratisk, kommunistisk och nationalsocialistisk press*. Halmstad: Ellerströms, 2013.
Wärenstam, Eric. *Fascismen och Nazismen i Sverige 1920–1940: Studier i den Svenska nationalsocialismens, fascismens och antisemitismens organisationer, ideologier och propaganda under mellankrigsåren*. Stockholm: Almqvist & Wiksell, 1970.
Warmbrunn, Werner. *The Dutch under German Occupation, 1940–1945*. Stanford: Stanford University Press, 1963.
Weindling, Paul. 'International Eugenics: Swedish Sterilization in Context'. *Scandinavian Journal of History* 24, no. 2 (1999): 179–97.
Wester, Sivert. *Martin Ekström: Orädd frivillig i fem krig*. Västervik: Militärhistoriska Förlaget, 1995.
Wielenga, Friso. *A History of the Netherlands: From the Sixteenth Century to the Present Day*. London: Bloomsbury, 2015.
Williams, Raymond. *Culture*. Glasgow: Fontana, 1981.
Williams, Raymond. *Keywords: A Vocabulary of Culture and Society*. Revised Edition. Oxford: Oxford University Press, 1983.

Wippermann, Wolfgang. *Faschismus: eine Weltgeschichte vom 19, Jahrhundert bis heute.* Darmstadt: Primus, 2009.
Woller, Hans. 'Machtpolitisches Kalkül Oder Ideologische Affinität? Zur Frage Des Verhältnisses Zwischen Mussolini Und Hitler Vor 1933'. In *Der Nationalsozialismus: Studien zur Ideologie und Herrschaft*, edited by W. Benz and H. Mommsen. Frankfurt am Main: Geschichte Fischer, 1993.
Woltjer, J.J. *Recent Verleden: Nederland in de Twintigste Eeuw.* Amsterdam: Balans, 2005.
Woodley, Daniel. *Fascism and Political Theory: Critical Perspectives on Fascist Ideology.* London: Routledge, 2010.
Yeomans, Rory, ed. *The Utopia of Terror: Life and Death in Wartime Croatia.* Suffolk: University of Rochester Press, 2015.
Zaal, Wim. *De Nederlandse Fascisten.* Amsterdam: Aspekt, 2016.
Zanden, Jan L. van. *The Economic History of the Netherlands, 1914–1995: A Small Open Economy in the 'Long' Twentieth Century.* London: Routledge, 1998.
Zee, Sytze van der. *Voor Führer, Volk en Vaderland Sneuvelde ... : De SS in Nederland, Nederland in de S S.* Den Haag: Kruseman's, 1975.

Index

Alfredsson, Carl A. 134
Algemeen Handelsblad 86, 112, 148
Algemeen Leider (General Leader). *See* Mussert, Anton
Anti-Revolutionaire Partij (ARP, Anti-Revolutionairy Party) 31, 32, 36–8, 89
anti-Semitism 8, 14, 38, 45–7, 143, 170, 171, 174, 175
årsting (NSAP/SSS) 63, 77, 80–2, 108, 114, 117, 133–42
   context and preparation 129–33
   landdag and 126–9, 157–62
   Sveatinget 129, 134–6, 138, 141–2, 145, 148, 157, 159

Beerenbrouck, Charles Ruijs de 36
Belgian Treaty 39, 74, 75, 173
Bilderbeek, Christina Wilhelm van 52
Bilderbeek, Friedrich Wilhelm van 53
Boddé, John 65, 82
Bolsheviks 7, 21, 34, 43, 138
borggårdskrisen (Courtyard Crisis) 43
Brisman, Bertil 52, 86, 109

Calvinism 31, 35–8, 87, 155
Carlberg, Carl-Enfrid 131
Catholicism 6, 30, 31, 33, 35–7, 39, 40, 52, 66, 73, 76, 82, 87
Christelijk-Historische Unie (CHU, Christian-Historical Union) 32, 36, 37, 89
Clementsson, Arne 75, 94, 100, 103, 113, 166, 167
Colijn, Hendricus 37–40, 44, 87, 143
colporteurs 56–7, 113
communism 39, 45, 96, 110, 111, 163, 168
conservatism 42, 66
Cort van der Linden, Pieter Wilhelm Adrianus 32, 33

Dagens Nyheter (DN, The Daily News) 41, 157
Dahlberg, Per 50–1, 75, 133
Dahlin, L. E. 135
Dahlrot, Nils 130, 140
Dahlström, Björn 51, 54
De Haagsche Courant 154
De Maasbode 90, 148, 154
Den Svenske Folksocialisten (DSF, The Swedish People's Socialist) 164
Den Svenske Nationalsocialisten (DSN, The Swedish National Socialist) 55–8, 63, 75–81, 85, 105–7, 110, 112, 114, 117, 126, 128–30, 132–7, 140–2, 146, 159
De Rotterdammer 89, 90
De Standaard (The Standard (of the Word of God)) 35, 148, 154, 155
De Telegraaf 148
De Tijd (Catholic daily) 76, 79, 90, 111, 115, 154–6
De Tribune 111
Diepenhorst, Pieter Arie 16
Dietsland ideology 150, 226–7 n.54
Distriktschefer (NSAP/SSS) 53–4
Documentation Service (NSB) 54

Edén, Nils 33, 41
Ekegren, Karl Erik 136
Ekman, Carl Gustaf 42
Ekström, Martin 47, 129
Eriksson, Elof 6, 7, 45, 46, 123

Fahl, Erik 51, 66
Fascism (Italian) 6, 7, 109, 114, 177
fetishism 120, 166, 167
   and private use 105–9
finances 20, 49, 55, 63, 64, 141
Finnish Civil War 7, 32, 34, 47, 111
First World War 4, 6, 7, 25, 27, 29–35, 41, 44, 74, 177

Flyg, Nils 16, 42, 69
folkgemenskap 130, 170
Freikorps 8, 46, 96
Friheten leve! (Freedom lives) 80, 81, 134, 135
frontavdelningar (FA, Front Department) 57
Führerprinzip (Leader principle) 50, 69, 155
Furugård, Birger 46, 47, 54, 71, 85, 90, 91, 129, 173

Geelkerken, Cornelis van 34, 52, 64, 74, 75, 107, 119, 144, 146, 148–50
Geer, Dirk Jan de 37, 87
gender 5, 22, 24, 172
Gerhardsson, Arvid 142
Gewestelijken Vervoerdienst (Regional Transport Service, NSB) 60
Ginneken, Jacques van 35–6, 123
Goes van Naters, W. van der 64, 83
Göteborgs-Posten 90, 107, 114
Grail movement 35–6, 123
Great Depression 26, 37, 43

Hagespraken 82, 87, 88, 127, 128, 144, 145, 147, 148, 158, 159
Hague, The 53, 99, 128, 143–8, 155, 157–9
Haighton, Alfred 39
Hallgren, Konrad 45, 46
Hammarskjöld, Hjalmar 32–3
Hansson, Per Albin 9, 42–4
Hartman, A. J. 98
Hedengren, Sven 45, 46, 48, 108, 111, 163
Hedin, Sven 42, 43
Hervormd-Gereformeerde Staatspartij (HGS, Reformed-Reformed State Party) 37
Het Nationale Dagblad (The National Daily) 55
Het Volk 35, 90, 112, 114, 115, 147, 152, 154–5
Heutsz, Joannes Benedictus van 39
Hitler, Adolf 2, 8, 10, 40, 41, 45, 69–71, 90, 164, 167, 168
Hogewind, Jan 53, 83, 91, 98, 101, 106, 111, 113, 152, 173, 191 n.18
Höglund, Zeth 33, 44
House of Orange 5, 30, 86, 104

Huizinga, Johan 9, 177
Hultberg, Herbert 51–2, 63

Indonesia 29, 38, 39, 53
Instruktioner for Frontavdelningar (IF, Instructions for Front Departments) 136

Katholieke Staatkunde (Catholic Political Science) 6, 39
Kjellén, Rudolf 45
kohandeln (horse trading) 43
kretschefer (NSAP/SSS) 54
Kuyper, Abraham 31, 32, 35, 37–8

Landahl, Oscar 51
landdag 28, 82, 83, 99, 109, 112, 114, 126–8, 143–57
and *årsting* 126–9, 157–62
ländermän (NSAP/SSS) 54
Lantsorganisationen (LO, Swedish Trade Union Federation) 42
law against
  paramilitaries 46, 111, 115
  political uniforms 66, 67, 98, 110, 114
  revolutionary organizations 74, 86
le Bon, Gustave 10
liberalism 2–4, 29–38, 40, 56, 66, 69, 73–5, 86, 107, 155, 165
Lindholm, Sven Olov 1, 2, 15, 27, 45–8, 50–3, 55, 56, 58–60, 62–5, 67, 69–86, 88, 90–4, 99–102, 104, 108, 110–13, 115–18, 126, 127, 129–42, 153, 157, 161, 163–70, 173, 174
Lindman, Arvid 30–1, 43
Lundborg, Herman 45

Mannerheim, Gustav 34
marches 1, 22, 25, 26, 35, 81, 102, 104, 111, 116–18, 120, 127, 129, 132, 135–7, 139, 147, 152, 164, 166
March on Rome 6, 8, 39
Marchant et d'Ansembourg, Maximlianus 52, 75, 107, 143, 150
Mein Kampf 17, 74, 75
military
  commanders 76
  life 72, 74
  and respectability 100–3

subculture 95, 116–21
Munck Corps 46, 111
music 17, 61, 73, 95, 104, 123, 126, 130, 134, 135, 137, 138, 142, 148, 150–2, 160
Mussert, Anton 2, 27, 28, 39–41, 50, 52, 53, 55–7, 62–6, 69–71, 73–80, 82–4, 86–94, 100, 104, 105, 107–11, 113–19, 127, 143–57, 160, 161, 163–8, 171, 173, 174, 176
Mussolini, Benito 6–8, 10, 12, 38, 39, 69, 70, 74, 95, 100, 143, 167

Nationaal-Socialistische Nederlandsche Arbeiterpartij (NSNAP, National Socialist Dutch Workers' Party) 40, 175
Nationale Jeugdstorm (NJS, National Youth Storm) 52
National Socialist Bloc 47
National Socialist People's Party (NSFP) 46
Nationalsozialistische Deutsche Arbeiterpartei (NSDAP, National Socialist German Workers' Party) 2, 16, 45, 46, 49, 50, 53, 62, 67, 71, 74, 101, 112, 123, 126, 174
Nationen (The Nation) 7, 45
Nazism (German) 7, 11–12, 14, 38, 40, 41, 46, 109, 164, 170
  Third Reich 12, 69
Nederlandsche Nationaal-Socialistische Uitgeverij (Nenasu, Dutch National Socialist Publisher) 55, 87, 152
Nederlandsch Indische Fascisten Organisatie (NIFO, Dutch Indies Fascist Organization) 39
Nieuwe Rotterdamsche Courant (NRC, New Rotterdammer Newspaper) 35, 75, 90, 111, 148
Nordisk Ungdom (NU, Nordic Youth) 58, 65, 75, 83, 94, 100, 102, 103, 108, 134–6, 138, 157, 172, 173
November Revolution (1918, German) 33, 34
Nuremberg rally *(Nürnberg Parteitage)* 12, 123
Ny Dag 112, 113
nyorientering (New Direction) 51, 91, 104, 108, 174

Nysvenska Nationalsocialistiska Partiet, (New-Swedish National Socialist Party) 46

Occupation of the Netherlands 16, 17, 38, 53, 64, 73, 74, 84, 93, 164, 165, 169, 171
Öresundsting (Malmö convention) 127, 157

paramilitaries 2, 4, 7, 8, 28, 34, 40, 45–7, 53, 57, 58, 61, 64, 95, 110–12, 115, 129, 152, 153, 164, 167
Partiledaren (Party Leader). *See* Lindholm, Sven Olov
Partiorganisationen (*Porg*, Party Organisation) 54–5, 58, 60, 99, 105
Pehrsson-Bramstorp, Axel 44
Pferdekämper, Max 46, 126
Pflugk-Harttung, Horst von 46
pillarization *(verzuiling)* 31, 35–7, 40
props 120, 121, 166, 169, 170, 172, 176
  and public space 103–4

race 8, 14, 43, 45, 47, 72, 87, 101, 170–1, 174, 226 n.54
Randstad (conurbation) 53, 128, 145, 192 n.20
revolution 2, 7, 8, 13, 18, 30, 31, 33–6, 40, 44, 45, 66, 67, 74, 75, 85–7, 101, 105, 148, 167, 168
Rhenström, Sven 133
riksdagen (Swedish parliament) 29, 30, 44
Romeins-Katholieke Staatspartij (RKSP, Roman-Catholic State Party) 36–7
Roskam, Evert Jan 52–3, 82, 150, 171
Rost van Tonningen, Martinus Meinoud 53, 55, 165
Russian revolutions 7, 33, 34
Rydberg, Viktor 140–1

Schutzstaffel (SS, Protection Staff) 74, 148, 165, 171, 174
Second World War 16, 31, 42, 52, 69, 164, 174
Sinclair de Rochemont, Hugues Alexandre 39

Sociaal-Democratische Arbeiders Partij (SDAP, Social Democratic Workers' Party) 7, 30, 33, 35, 36, 87, 106, 112, 123, 128, 154, 168

Social-Demokraten (The Social Democrat) 120

socialism 6, 9, 30, 34, 42, 168

Solkorset (The Sun Cross) 92, 94

Speer, Albert 1, 12

squadristi 4, 95, 112

Staaff, Karl 42, 43

Staatkundig Gereformeerde Partij (SGP, State Reformed Party) 36–7

Sterner, Wilhelm 136, 138

Stockholms-Tidningen (The Stockholm Newspaper) 41, 116

stormavdelning (SA, Storm Department/ Section) 4, 57, 59, 67, 76, 80, 92, 95, 97, 98, 102, 106, 108, 109, 111, 112, 118, 143

Svalander, Gunnar 50, 51, 60, 65, 108, 130–3, 135, 141, 142

Sveaborg 164

Svenska Dagbladet (The Swedish Daily) 41, 138

Svenska Nationalsocialistiska Partiet (SNSP, Swedish National Socialist Party) 15, 46, 47, 51, 54, 71, 75, 84, 85, 101, 126, 129, 134, 173, 174, 197 n.128

Svenska Socialdemokratiska Arbetarpartiet (SSAP, Sweden's Social Democratic Worker's Party) 30, 33, 42–4, 168

Svensksocialistisk Samling (SSS, Swedish Socialist Union) 47, 163–4

Sveriges Fascistiska Kamporganisation (SFKO, Sweden's Fascist Combat Organization) 45, 46, 71, 75, 108, 111, 170, 173, 174

Sveriges Nationella Ungdomsforbund (SNU, Sweden's National Youth League) 43

Swartz, Carl 33

Svenska brigaden (Swedish Brigade) 34

Swedish National Socialist Freedom League (SNFF) 45

symbols 9, 10, 12, 28, 76, 92, 95, 100–1, 104, 118–21, 134, 135, 159, 166, 167, 170, 172

Thingspiel 12, 124

Tjänsteföreskrifter (TF, Service Regulations) 54–5

Troelstra, Pieter Jelles 7, 33, 34, 36

uniforms 4, 28, 40, 47, 57, 66, 67, 95–100, 110–12, 114, 116–21, 133, 159, 164
 fetishism 105–9
 militarism 100–3
 props 103–4
 public reactions 109–16

Vaderlandsche Club (VC, Fatherland Club) 39

Van Schaik, Josef 110

Verviers, Emile 6, 7, 39

Vinterpalatset 131

violence 67, 97, 100, 115, 120, 153
 armed 111
 politics of 178
 spectre of 168
 street 96
 uniform and 105, 106, 108

Volk en Vaderland (VoVa, People and Fatherland) 55–8, 76–80, 82, 84, 87, 90, 97, 98, 100, 106, 107, 109, 110, 113, 115, 117, 146–9, 151–4, 156

volks 226 n.54

Vries, Jacob de 144, 146, 147

Weerafdeeling 40, 98

Weerbaarheidsafdeeling (WA, Defence Department/Section) 40, 53, 57, 64, 98, 99, 106, 107, 111, 113, 118, 144–7, 152, 155, 159, 165, 172

Wilhelmina, Queen 32, 36, 86, 117

Zeven Provinciën (Seven Provinces) 38

www.ingramcontent.com/pod-product-compliance
Lightning Source LLC
Chambersburg PA
CBHW062130300426
44115CB00012BA/1879